THE COMPANION GUIDE TO
BURGUNDY

THE COMPANION GUIDES

*It is the aim of these guides to provide a Companion
in the person of the author, who knows intimately
the places and people of whom he writes, and is able to
communicate this knowledge and affection to his readers.
It is hoped that the text and pictures will aid them
in their preparations and in their travels, and will
help them remember on their return.*

THE COUNTRY ROUND PARIS
DEVON · EAST ANGLIA
EDINBURGH AND THE BORDER COUNTRY
GASCONY AND THE DORDOGNE · LONDON
MADRID AND CENTRAL SPAIN
MAINLAND GREECE · NEW YORK
SOUTH OF FRANCE · TURKEY
JUGOSLAVIA

In preparation
SICILY · VENICE · ROME · FLORENCE

THE COMPANION GUIDE TO

BURGUNDY

ROBERT SPEAIGHT

REVISED AND EXPANDED BY
FRANCIS PAGAN

COMPANION GUIDES

First published 1975
First revised edition 1990
Second revised edition 1996
Companion Guides, Woodbridge

ISBN 978-1-900639-17-0

Companion Guides is an imprint of Boydell & Brewer Ltd
PO Box 9, Woodbridge, Suffolk IP12 3DF, UK
and of Boydell & Brewer Inc.
668 Mt Hope Avenue, Rochester, NY 14620, USA
website: www.boydellandbrewer.com

Transferred to digital printing

This publication is printed on acid-free paper

Contents

List of Maps

Illustrations

For Marie-Catherine and Maurice Zuber

and now for
Fitz-le-Cerf

Preface to this edition

The original *Burgundy* by Robert Speaight, first published in 1975, is now entering on its second major revision, with an important further innovation. By including a new chapter on Nevers and the Nivernais I throw off the reluctance of Speaight and the refusal of *Blue Guide France* to recognize that the department of Nièvre is an integral part of the region of Grande Bourgogne, and I hope that readers who travel there will agree that it deserves to take its place in that noble company.

F.P. 1996

Acknowledgements

I wish to thank a number of people whose help and, in many cases, whose hospitality have speeded me in the writing of this book. The Marquis and Marquise de Virieu, Comte Jean de Guitaut, Colonel and Madame Darly, Professor Grivelet, M. François de Seynes-Lalenque, M. and Madame Jacques Chevignard, Mr Kit Cope, Mr H. W. Yoxall, and the librarians at the Institut Français and the Senate House of London University.

R. S. 1975

I wish to thank many people and institutions for their help and encouragement in preparing this extensively revised edition. In particular I repeat my gratitude to the Conseilleur Culturel of the French Embassy in London for opening so many doors in Burgundy; for enlightenment on the complexities of its wine trade to M. Pierre Maufoux, M. Wilmotte of Moillard, M. Bertelot of Doudet-Naudin and Mr Crawford of Louis Latour, as well as for their hospitality, and especially on both counts to M. Jean-Paul Thorin and his wife. To their number I now add M. Berteloot of Doudet-Naudin, and Messrs Berry Bros & Rudd, as well as introducing me to these prestigious firms, have kindly allowed me to draw on the account of Doudet-Naudin in their house magazine, 'Number Three'.

My greatest debt remains to the admirable and patient guides to so many places of interest, and to the owners of several historic properties who have taken the trouble to show a stranger their homes.

F. P. 1995

Introduction

Burgundy defies definition. Nevertheless the reader of this book
will want to know where he or she is going. Between the mediaeval duchy that extended from the Low Countries to the borders
of Provence and the 'province' of today about whose limits not
even Burgundians are agreed, a line must be drawn for the purposes of travel, even though it may beg a few questions of topog-
raphy. In the following pages we have generally confined
ourselves to the four *départements* of Yonne, Côte d'Or, Saône-et-
Loire and Nièvre, only trespassing into Loire for the sake of Charlieu and into Ain to visit the Église de Brou. While Brittany or
Normandy, Périgord or Provence evoke a picture for the mind
acquainted with the map of France, for many people Burgundy is
no more than a generic name for a variety of labels on a bottle. In
fact it has no frontiers today, and the motorist speeding down the
autoroute to the south is hardly aware when he has entered it and
when he has left it.

Distinct in some respects, Burgundy is diverse in others. The
eye trained to the niceties of Romanesque or Gothic architecture
will detect the Burgundian accent in Notre-Dame at Dijon or in
St-Philibert at Tournus. On the other hand you could hardly
imagine two artists more opposed than Rude and Gislebertus,
writers more different than Colette and Lamartine, or landscape
more contrasting than the Puisaye and the Bresse, the Auxois and
the Mâconnais, the Morvan and the Montagne. A country which
produced both St Bernard and Bussy-Rabutin may claim to have
reconciled within its borders the extremes of human nature. From
its neighbours it has absorbed more than it has exported, with the
exception of its wines. In the north – at Sens for example – you
will find the influence of the Île de France or Champagne. In the
south the Lombardic towers of the Brionnais will remind you of
Italy. The work of Claus Sluter and Claus Werve at Dijon is
obviously Flemish in character. For just as Burgundy now stands

on the high road of pleasure to the south, so in earlier times it marked the crossing of trade routes from south to north and from east to west – from the Mediterranean coast to Paris and the Channel ports, over the mountain passes from the Lombard plain to Bordeaux and the Atlantic. As Michelet wrote, the country is 'apte à réconcilier le nord et le midi'.

Prosperity has given to Burgundy a smile which warms the heart. The good temper matches the good cheer, a natural conjunction of the works of nature and of man. This is the 'country of the great dukes and the great abbeys, the country of the good wine and the abundant life, the country of bold and mischievous gaiety, and also the country of great men and great artists'.* The Burgundian – though it would not be hard to find exceptions – is earthy and realistic, well balanced, physically tough, eloquent, argumentative and prone to irreverence. Burgundians may quarrel among themselves, but present a solid front to outsiders.

A word about gastronomy. Burgundians like to eat well, but they also like value for money. Eating is a family pursuit, much enjoyed, but you will not find their families in expensive star-studded restaurants. These will give a special kind of pleasure to visitors who enjoy the best, but few can afford to make a habit of paying for it at that level; even here the trimmings and the mystique often glamorize a cuisine which has become national, even international, rather than regional. The bourgeois Burgundian is after something more real and satisfying; he knows where to find it, and if you follow him you will find it too. But is there a *cuisine bourguignonne*? In a general sense, yes; the produce of its fields, farmyards and *marchés*, backed up by its herbs and its sauces rich with cream, wine, and the mustards of Dijon, has a Burgundian essence. If you are looking more particularly for regional dishes and special recipes, you may find them in homes and restaurants where *grand-mère* still rules, but not on the menus of hard-worked, hard-pressed kitchens. Even in Burgundy a *menu gastronomique* differs from those at a lower price only in having six courses instead of four, with more choice at each stage. The individual dishes are unlikely to be better or more original, and you may fare as well by choosing two dishes from their *à la carte*

* Drouot and Calmette, *Histoire de Bourgogne*, 1928.

specialities, which may include a legacy from *grand-mère*.

A meal in an honest family-run Burgundy restaurant is always a delightful experience. It will be well cooked, properly presented and smilingly served. Even the smallest place will have a generous selection of burgundies at most prices, though the *vins de garde* will be no cheaper than they are in a London restaurant, and a *vin de table* from a *pichet* can be as satisfying, if not as delectable, a choice. The value for money (and that includes entertainment value) cannot be equalled in the Anglo-Saxon world, and is rarely better in other parts of France.

Burgundy can be reached by many routes. Many times a day the TGVs hurtle down from Paris to Dijon in an hour and three-quarters, three of four times to Beaune and Chalon-sur-Saône. You can put your car on a train in Paris and drive it away from the station in Lyon two hours later. You can round Paris and join the *autoroute du sud* to arrive at Beaune without having to look at a map. Or you can take your time getting there by uncrowded departmental roads, sampling other parts of France on the way. Once there, we are assuming that this is the way you will prefer to explore Burgundy. Local trains are no longer an option, and bus services are hard to pin down. The cross-country routes we suggest are arbitrary but practical; they can be varied or reversed without difficulty. In most cases they are intended to give the traveller a distinct idea of the character of the *régions*, another topographical term difficult to define, except possibly from the wine lists. The general drift is from north to south, and most chapters will have as their climax or centrepiece one or other of the great experiences of the province.

The most reliable source for opening times of châteaux and museums is the local Syndicat d'Initiatives. Almost all buildings capable of doing so will close for at least two hours at midday, and on the stroke of twelve. Museums will almost invariably be closed on Tuesdays. The most difficult problem is getting inside the smaller churches. Thefts and vandalism have become so common that they are often kept locked, but if you enquire diligently you will probably be able to locate the guardian of the key nearby. If you succeed, you may discover a gem, and to light a pair of candles to the patron saint is the least you can do in gratitude. You will rarely find yourself locked out on Sundays.

If you are free to take your holiday when you choose, a fine May is the best time of year for visiting Burgundy. The days are long, the roads are relatively uncrowded, the hotels are rarely full and the forests bursting into leaf present a dazzling variety of green. October will give you more certain weather, and for the eye an even richer symphony of colour; but the shorter days will curtail your movement. For cruising on the Yonne, or sailing on the lakes of the Morvan, the summer months are preferable; and the fisherman will know his times and seasons. It has been said that the gods have given three gifts to Burgundy: 'wine, art, and archaeology'. They have given much else besides.

Years of travelling in France have failed to find a better friend than the red *Guide Michelin*. Once you have learnt to interpret all its little symbols you will usually be able to visualize exactly the kind of hotel it is offering, and to choose the one which suits you. In the same way, though maps on a larger scale may give more topographical information, the ordinary *Pneu Michelin* for the area (1cm to 2km) will provide many clues to your enjoyment or otherwise. The most pleasantly remote hotels are marked accurately with a special sign, and the interest or age of a church or ruin is also carefully indicated by symbols, and so is the presence of a factory or power-station you may wish to avoid. The appropriate green Michelin *Guide de Tourisme* (*Bourgogne et Morvan*) gives a lot of useful information, including the conditions of opening for most of your objectives.

Historical Background

You will hear it said that 'happy is the country which has no history'; Burgundy is none the sadder for having had a great deal. Of pre-history too there are ample traces: a Neolithic culture has been unearthed at Solutré in the Mâconnais; there was a Bronze Age settlement at Alésia in the Auxois, where the rough tracks that threaded the primeval forest were known as the high road of amber and tin; most striking of all was a royal establishment of the early Iron Age on Mont Lassois, north of Châtillon-sur-Seine.

In the first century BC, all Gaul was divided not only into three parts but between a network of Celtic tribes, generically known as Gauls but far from being united as a nation. In what is now Burgundy the **Senones** gave their name to Sens, the **Aedui** had their capital at Bibracte, a few miles from Autun, and the **Mandubii** occupied a large *oppidum* on the earlier Bronze Age site of Alésia. These tribes, with the **Sequani** to the east of the Saône (then called the Arar), dominated the land between the upper Loire and the Jura. Their subjugation by Julius Caesar is recorded in his terse Commentaries *de Bello Gallico*. When all the tribes combined for the first and only time in the rising of 52 BC they made their heroic but unavailing last stand at Alésia, where a gigantic bronze statue of their chieftain Vercingetorix was erected in the last century.

They submitted to what in the end was a civilizing intrusion, though when Caesar said that the conquered tribes worshipped the deities of the Roman pantheon it was probably propaganda, as was a good part of the Commentaries. In fact, local cults persisted throughout Gaul just as they did in the Italian countryside, and in Burgundy we can be sure that rural preoccupations prevailed: most were concerned with the produce of nature and the earth-mother goddesses with their cornucopias, water nymphs, and wine-loving field-gods.

The 'Borgondes'

The decline of the Roman empire in the fourth century exposed Gaul to invasion by barbarian peoples from the north and east, and gave Burgundy its name. Why Burgundy? The most attractive derivation of the name was suggested by Professor Karsten of the University of Helsinki. He believes the 'Borgondes', as they were known in the second century AD, came originally from Sweden, and settled for a time on the Danish island of Bornholm, for which the old Danish name was *Borghunderholm*. In historical records they first appear in western Poland, between the Oder and the Vistula, but caught up in the general southerly migration during the third century they established themselves (with the approval of the emperor Probus) in a large area between the Main and the upper waters of the Danube. The fifth-century writer Apollinarius Sidonius says they were of giant stature – some being 'septipedes', as much as seven feet tall – dyed their hair blond and smeared it with rancid butter. There was more to them than such travellers' tales allowed, however. The Romans saw them as a well-organized community who could be relied on as allies against more menacing tribes such as the Alemanni; towards the end of the fourth century Valentinian was content to see them move west to occupy land on both sides of the Rhine-frontier.

At this point history, legend and myth become entangled. Beowulf tells us of one Gebicca, king of the Borgondes of the Rhine, though his name appears also as an attribute of Wotan, ruler of Valhalla. In 411 we know that a king called **Gunthiar** proclaimed the usurper Jovinus as emperor at Mainz. Now this is the Gunther of the Nibelung legends (Gunnar in the *sagas*, and we find that his royal dynasty was indeed known as the Nibelungs, though hardly the dwarfs from whom Alberich stole the gold of the Ring. The *Nibelungenlied* tells how Gunther's army was defeated, and he and his people massacred, by Attila the Hun in 437.

The First Kingdom of Burgundy

Their remnants (still a people to be reckoned with) were settled by the Roman general Aetius in Sapaudia, or Savoy. Their new kingdom was based on Geneva, but extended as far as Grenoble and Die. Gunther was succeeded by his son **Gundioc**, who repaid

Aetius and avenged his father by joining the alliance which defeated Attila near Chalons-sur-Marne in 451. As a reward, his territory was allowed to spread over the large area of Sequania (the old territory of the Sequani), which brought the Burgundians for the first time to the banks of the Saône north of Lyon.

After Gundioc's death in about 470 this extensive kingdom was divided between his sons Gundobad, Chilperic and Godesigel. Gundobad had spent his youth in Rome, and though baptized a Christian he had embraced the Arian heresy, which maintained that the Son of God was inferior to the Father, not only in dignity but in essence. He returned to establish himself at Vienne, while Chilperic resided at Lyon and Godesigel at Geneva. Chilperic will be remembered chiefly as the father of Clothilde, who married the Frankish king Clovis and converted him to Christianity in the true Catholic faith. The story that he and all his family except Clothilde were murdered by Gundobad is generally discounted as a Frankish slander; it seems however that after Chilperic's (natural) death Godesigel conspired with Clovis in an eventually unsuccessful move to oust his brother from Vienne, and was killed for his pains.

This left **Gundobad** in sole control of a very large kingdom. Now for the first time we hear it called Burgundia, the name used in 506 by his powerful Arian neighbour Theodoric, king of the Ostrogoths. He was probably no less ruthless than contemporaryrulers, but he was a good deal more enlightened. The 'loi Gombette', or *lex Gambetta*, which obtained in Burgundy under his rule, was one of the earliest to be codified in Europe, and, though it subscribed to customs such as trial by ordeal, it established murder as a crime against society rather than against an individual which called only for revenge, and it was the first to enshrine the laws of hospitality and the rights of women and children. By the time of his death in 516, after a reign of forty-two years, Burgundy was a kingdom which with its dependencies extended from Basle, Langres and Nevers in the north to Arles, Marseille and Fréjus on the south coast. After his death his feeble successors were unable to resist further attacks by the sons of Clovis; in 534 they captured Autun, and the kingdom of Burgundy was annexed to that of the Merovingian Franks.

Christianity came early to Burgundy, though not as early as it did to Provence. Many of the evangelizing saints made their way up from the south during the fourth century, and it was not long before the cult of the martyrs and their relics became widespread. There is no doubt that the conversion of Clovis to the Catholic faith ensured that the Arian heresy – mostly thereafter confined to north Africa – failed to make ground in eastern France. It was doubly welcome to the Catholic bishops, who won not only a convert but a warlord who would fight their battles. Clothilde outlived her husband by thirty-four years, and was canonized immediately after her death in 545.

The death of Clovis led to a period of fratricidal anarchy which left **Clothaire I** the sole inheritor of the Merovingian kingdom (founded in 447 by a shadowy figure called Merovius) which now included Burgundy. When he died in 562 the kingdom was again split between his sons – Austrasia in the north-east, Neustria in the north-west, Burgundy in the south-east. Another period of ghastly internecine carnage followed. In the words of the historian G. H. Neel (1878-1971), 'it is impossible to feel any respect for these early Merovingian kings. One or two of them had aspirations towards art and letters, but basically they were bloodthirsty ruffians, lustful and treacherous, atrociously cruel and indifferent to human life, only interested in enlarging their dominions by eliminating any rivals or near relations who stood in their way'. We must remember that these were not Burgundians but Franks, among the most bloodthirsty of the barbarian invaders.

The Second Kingdom of Burgundy

One of the exceptions was **Gontran**, to whom the kingdom of Burgundy was assigned. By all accounts he was a civilized man and a good churchman, and he is remembered for many acts of wisdom during his thirty-three years' rule. Not so his brothers. The worst was Chilpéric I of Neustria, whose third wife **Frédégonde** outdid in murders Agrippina the mother of Nero. Between them they were responsible for the deaths of the king's first two wives, and subsequently of his elder brother Sigibert of Austrasia. It so happened that Sigibert's wife **Brunéhaut** was the sister of Chilpéric's murdered second wife – both being daughters of the king of the Visigoths – and the two sisters-in-law became implacable enemies. Chilpéric himself met a violent death, probably at the hands of his own household.

On Sigibert's death Gontran moved quickly to secure Austrasia, and shortly after his death in 593 Brunéhaut became regent of both Burgundy and Austrasia in the name of their grandson Theuderic (or Thierry), and the most powerful woman in France. Frédégonde's murderous career ended in a natural death in 597, but her son **Clothaire II** ended the ferocious vendetta by capturing Brunéhaut and having her body shattered by being tied to an unbroken stallion. Her ashes were preserved in the abbey of St-Martin at Autun, which she had helped to found.

One dwells on this unsavoury period not so much for its sensationalism but with the knowledge that the chief characters appear in the Frankish legends which accompanied the *Nibelungenlied* and the Icelandic *Volsungasaga* to provide the outline story of the Wagnerian *Ring* cycle. This is even more apparent when we find that the name Brunéhaut – a romantic heroine to posterity – is a French version of Brunnhilde, that Sigibert can be identified with Siegfried (Sigurd in the *sagas*) and when we remember Brunnhilde's feud with Gudrun.

Clothaire finally succeeded as king of all the Franks in 613 by murdering his cousin Sigibert II of Austrasia and Burgundy. He was succeeded by his son **Dagobert I**, the most respectable figure since Gontran but the last Merovingian to have any real power. Even he is best remembered in the jingle:

> le bon roi Dagobert
> ne se lavait jamais en hiver.

Later kings became more and more degenerate and incompetent. Effective power passed to the chief ministers of the kingdom, known as Mayors of the Palace, while their masters are dismissed as 'rois fainéants', or do-nothing kings. Among the early Mayors was Pepin I, who was to found a dynasty which included Charles Martel, destroyer of the Saracens at the battle of Poitiers, and Pepin the Short, whose son Charlemagne not only consolidated all the kingdoms of France but in 800 forced Pope Leo III to crown him as Holy Roman Emperor.

The Carolingians

During the reign of **Charlemagne** all power was concentrated in his hands, and he ruled over an empire bounded by lines drawn from the North Sea and the Channel to the Pyrenees, along the Mediterranean coast, and from Rome to the Baltic. When he died in 814 the empire gradually disintegrated. His only surviving son, Louis the Pious, was incapable of holding it together, and in the end the succession was fought over by his three grandsons, Lothaire, Charles and Louis. In the battle of Fontanet (Fontenoy in the Puisaye) Charles and Louis defeated their elder brother, and by the **Treaty of Verdun** in 843 Lothaire was forced to agree to a partition by which Charles the Bald secured what had been the kingdom of Neustria plus the whole of Aquitaine (which had fallen to the lot of a fourth brother who died young), and Louis the German the eastern or Germanic lands from the Adriatic to the Baltic. Lothaire had to be content with a heterogeneous strip of territory between them, from the Netherlands to the borders of Calabria. It was called the Middle Kingdom, or Lotharingia, a name which clung only to a small part of it, modern Lorraine, and it included Burgundy and Provence.

Although Charlemagne had disposed of the immediate threat of the Saracens, the ninth century brought new menaces to the divided kingdoms, and invaders as distinct as the Norsemen (Vikings and Danes) and the Hungarian Magyars created havoc among the cities of France. A legendary name in Burgundian history was **Girard de Roussillon**, count of Lyon and Vienne. He was chief minister to Lothaire and his son Lothaire II, and virtually ruled southern Burgundy from 853 to 870. History owes him much, for in 858 he and his wife Berthe founded the monastery which was to become the shrine of the Madeleine at Vézelay, and five years later another at Pothières near Châtillon-sur-Seine. In 859 he combined with Charles the Bald to drive the Normans out of Provence and into the sea, but once that threat was removed Charles turned on his upstart ally. Girard fought him off once near Vézelay, but three years later he and Berthe were cornered at Vienne and had to surrender. He died at Avallon aged nearly eighty, and they were both buried at Pothières. In the twelfth-century *chansons de geste* Girard appears with Ganelon as a traitor to the crown, but in Burgundy he has always been a national hero – King Alfred and Hereward the Wake rolled into one. The Wagnerian parallels continue, with the devoted Girard and Berthe as possible prototypes for Tristan and Isolde.

The Foundation of the Duchy

Girard was replaced as count of Vienne and Governor of Burgundy by Boso, a brother-in-law of Charles the Bald, who by right of his marriage to the daughter of the emperor Louis II claimed the kingdom itself – though in practice his title was limited to lower Burgundy which in those days meant the kingdom of Arles in Provence. However, he appointed his brother Richard as count of Autun, which was to be a significant move because Richard (the Justiciar, as he was called) was an able administrator and succeeded in establishing an independent **Duchy of Burgundy**, while the kingdom became more and more fragmented. In the early tenth century the Saracens had returned in a terrible combination with the ferocious Magyars. There was widespread devastation until Conrad the Peaceful, who had consolidated the southern kingdom of Boso, joined the emperor Otto I to remove these menaces finally from the shores of Europe.

The story of Burgundy as we know it becomes from this point the story of the duchy, separate from the kingdom of Arles, which again fragmented and was annexed under the imperial crown by Conrad II in 1032. We should also record the creation of an independent *comté* of Burgundy, later to be known as the Franche-Comté and generally held as a fief of the empire. Meanwhile as peace returned to the land the power and achievements of the Church and its monasteries grew greater yearly, until from the abbey of Cluny (not originally within the duchy) their civilizing influence spread throughout Europe. **Richard the Justiciar** was nominally a vassal of the king of France, but was in practice an independent sovereign. He and his successors were closely connected with the French crown, however, and his eldest son Raoul became king in 923 – whereupon he handed the duchy over to his younger brother Hugues 'the Black'. A new French royal dynasty began with the accession of Hugues Capet in 987, and in 1032 his grandson Henri I gave the duchy to his brother Robert Sans-Terre, the first of the Capetian dukes.

The Capetian Dukes

With their close ties of blood and marriage the dukes thereafter were generally found allied with the French kings, though a strong Burgundian personality asserted itself over the three centuries of their rule, during which we read the recurring names of Hugues, Eudes and Robert. Politically they achieved little except in providing stability for a period – between the defeat of the last Saracen invaders and the outbreak of the Hundred Years' War – when there were extraordinary developments in thought and art in Burgundy. The growing wealth of the monastic foundations, supported by the aristocracy, harnessed the inventiveness, the imagination and the technical skill of local builders, masons and sculptors to produce a flood of abbeys and churches of all sizes, something which a naturally proud and pious people relished. The monasteries themselves were the greatest if not the only source of wider education, and the Church produced thinkers as far apart in their convictions as Abélard and St Bernard. Abbots and bishops were chosen from the aristocracy and, though interests sometimes clashed, this cross-fertilization was on the whole beneficial to both worlds. The other factor which released so much creative activity so suddenly was the safe passing of the year 1000, when the end of the world and the Second Coming had long been predicted. Now at last man could build for his future on earth.

The long line of Capetian kings came to an end with the death of Charles IV in 1328, to be succeeded by Philippe VI of Valois, grandson of Philippe III and Isabella of Aragon. (This was the point when Edward III of England decided to press his claim to the French throne through his mother Isabel, herself a granddaughter of Philippe III, which was the basis for the Hundred Years' War.) The duchy soon followed suit when Philippe de Rouvres, the last Capetian descendant of Robert Sans-Terre, died in 1361. Jean II of France promptly presented it to his younger son Philippe 'le Hardi' who married the widow of Philippe de Rouvres, and thus initiated the glorious era of the Valois dukes.

The Valois Dukes

For the next hundred years they hold the stage of Burgundy. Entitled, or entitling themselves, the 'grand ducs de l'Occident' they justified the description of their house as a 'maison de plus en plus princière et envahissante', and of their reign (in the words of a Dutch historian) as a 'memorable story of fine diplomacy, high-handed enterprise and good luck'. Their little empire comprised eventually Belgium and Holland, Picardy and Artois, Luxembourg, lower Lorraine and upper Alsace, the comtés of Thionville and Rethel, Charollais and Nevers, and the Franche-Comté of Burgundy. The events of this period, which corresponds roughly with that of the Hundred Years' War, are covered to a large extent by the narrative of the chapters which follow. The characters of the four dukes are discussed in the chapter on Dijon, and the reader is referred also to the Genealogical Tables at the end of the book, but we can give here an outline of the process by which the Duchy expanded and was finally brought to an end.

Philippe le Hardi (Philip the Bold) was born in Paris in 1332. At the age of thirty-seven he married Marguerite of Flanders, described by a contemporary as 'laide et creuse', who was the childless widow of Philippe de Rouvres, and on her father's death in 1384 he inherited not only the Flemish territories but also Artois, Nevers, Rethel and the Franche-Comté. He transferred his headquarters to Ghent, while Marguerite was installed at Dijon with his four unmarried sisters 'to enjoy better air and nourishment, which they would not have had in Flanders, and to allow our son to get to know the nobles of Burgundy'. He ruled for forty years and remained on good terms with the kings of France; he arranged the marriage between Charles VI and Isabeau de Bavière when Charles was only seventeen. On 7 February he met the king at Châtillon-sur-Seine and escorted him to Dijon, where, we are told, 'le roi fit éclater sa magnificence'. The walls and garden of a monastery were summarily cleared to make room for their fraternal jousting. He built the Chartreuse de Champnol on the outskirts of Dijon to house his tomb, the masterpiece by Claus Sluter and Claus de Werve which may be seen in the Musée des Beaux Arts in Dijon. He died at the Stag Inn at Mal, near Brussels, on 24 April 1404.

His son, **Jean Sans-Peur**, was born at Dijon in 1371. Pope Gregory VII was his godfather. In 1396 he had led the Nicopolis Crusade against the redoubtable Bajazit, for which his father had raised 700,000 gold francs. At Nicopolis he was taken prisoner and ransomed by his father for another million francs. In 1404 he inherited the duchy, attended the Conseil du Roi in Paris, quarrelled with Louis, duke of Orléans, and had him assassinated. This was the duke of Burgundy who after the defeat of the French army at Agincourt negotiated the peace which was sealed by the marriage of Henry V and the princess Katharine. Shakespeare makes him a man of eloquence rather than of war. In 1419 he was murdered by partisans of the Dauphin (Joan of Arc's Dauphin, who became Charles VII) on the bridge at Montereau, north-west of Sens.

Philippe le Bon – born in Dijon in 1396 – was also known as the 'duc soleil', a title which foreshadowed the royal image of Louis XIV. His father's murder threw him into the arms of the English, with whom he must share the responsibility for the burning of Joan of Arc. He was the most cultivated and in many ways the most successful of the Valois dukes. He had the good sense to appoint Nicolas Rolin as his Chancellor, and the good taste to enlist Jan van Eyck as a member of his household. In 1430 he married Isabella of Portugal as his third wife, and instituted the Order of the Golden Fleece. During his reign he acquired by one means or another the duchies of Brabant, Luxembourg and Limburg, and the *comtés* of Namur, Hainault, Mâcon and Auxerre – the last two as a result of the peace treaty he signed at Arras in 1435 with Charles VII.

He died at Bruges in 1467 and was succeeded by his son **Charles le Téméraire** (usually rendered as Charles 'the Bold', though 'the Rash' would be more appropriate). The last and in the end the least successful of the great dukes, he lost his head and in consequence the duchy. He had already antagonized Louis XI and was defeated by him in the field at Monthéry, but on his accession he excited a revolt at Liège and took the king prisoner at Péronne. Louis was soon freed, but Charles persisted in his extravagant ambitions, which centred on a plan to turn his dukedom into a kingdom. He had made a treaty of alliance with Edward IV of England, and sealed it by his marriage with the king's sister, Margaret of York; in 1474 the Treaty of London committed them both to war against Louis. However, overtures to the Emperor Frederick to join them were rejected, Edward made peace with Louis, and he was attacked by the duke of Lorraine and the Swiss confederation. A series of defeats was followed by his death in 1477 before the walls of Nancy, where he was attempting to besiege the duke of Lorraine. The Burgundians were betrayed by an Italian *condottiere*, and Charles's body was found after the battle embedded in the icy mud.

During the fifteenth century the annual revenues of the duchy amounted to 110,000 ducats, almost equal to those of Venice and four times those of Florence. Two-thirds came from the Low Countries, and the dukes were also aided by bankers from northern Italy. One of them, Giovanni Arnolfini, comes to us in a famous portrait by van Eyck. The duchy was not without representative institutions. The grand assembly which had met at Dijon under the Capetian dynasty was attended by a hundred and ten nobles, the representatives of eighteen abbeys and eleven cathedral chapters, and deputies from eleven Burgundian towns. The Three Estates met, but only when required, at Beaune, Dijon or elsewhere in the duchy.

The Fall of the Duchy

Louis XI was only waiting for the ripe plum to fall into his lap, but the marriage of Charles le Téméraire's daughter, **Marie de Bourgogne**, in 1478 to Emperor Maximilian of Austria ensured that his success was only partial. The rich lands of Flanders were secured for the empire, and their son Philippe le Beau was to inherit the Franche-Comté. But Louis lost no time in invading central Burgundy and occupying Dijon. The 'palais des ducs' became the 'logis du roi', and he built a fortress at the gates of the town to make it clear who owned it. 'Burgundy' was now a province of the kingdom under the authority of a Governor.

Marie's marriage to Maximilian was a happy one. Maximilian once declared to the States-General 'There is nothing in the world I desire more than to be in her company, to see her and to please her'. Indeed, few dynastic marriages were so happy, but their joy proved short-lived, for in 1482 she died after falling from her horse. Louis and Maximilian then patched up an alliance by arranging for the emperor's daughter, **Marguerite d'Autriche**, to marry the Dauphin (the future Charles VIII) which would have attached Burgundy formally to the French crown. Matters did not work out so neatly. Marguerite, aged two, was duly brought to France and spent the next nine years at the château of Amboise waiting for the marriage to be consummated. In the meantime Charles had succeeded to the throne, and in pursuit of a different dynastic policy he married Anne de Bretagne instead. (Charles died in 1498 and the widowed Anne eventually married Louis XII.) The rest of the story as it concerned Marguerite is told in the final chapter of the book, when we visit the church of Brou in Bresse which she built as a memorial to her last husband Philibert of Savoy.

It was she who instigated the attack on Dijon by Swiss and German troops in 1513, when Louis XII's Governor extricated himself and the town from a desperate situation by the ruse we describe in Chapter 10. When Maximilian died in 1519 and was succeeded by her nephew Charles, she still hoped to recover all her grandfather's lands. **Charles V** indeed claimed rightly that he had Burgundian blood in his veins, and when he succeeded in defeating François I at Pavia he planned to recover the lost province. Too much occupied in Italy, he had to let the opportunity go, and by the time of her death in 1530 Marguerite had given up the struggle.

The Province

The history of Burgundy is henceforward inseparable from that of France, and is marked mainly by the isolated events and personalities which will appear in subsequent chapters. The remainder of the sixteenth century was occupied largely with the wars of religion, the long struggle between Catholics and Protestants which was as hard fought in Burgundy as anywhere in the kingdom – though at least it had no part in the massacres of St Bartholomew's Day 1572. Prince Louis I of Bourbon, the Protestant head of the Burgundian family of Condé, was killed at the battle of Jarnac in 1569, the climax of a series of Catholic victories, but next year the young Henry of Navarre won his spurs in the remarkable Huguenot victory against odds at Arnay-le-Duc. The Protestant faction, as we shall see, met frequently at the château of Tanlay, though in 1574 the Catholic duc de Mayenne became Governor of the province, and the parliament of the Ligue met in Dijon. At Fontaine-Française stands the monument to the final victory of Henri IV over Mayenne and the Ligue in 1595. He had by then decided that Paris was worth a Mass, and renounced his Protestant faith if not his terrestrial ambitions.

Another generation of Condé, in the person of the more spectacular Prince Louis II, the 'Great Condé', figures in the two Fronde revolts by the people of Paris against Mazarin and Anne of Austria, queen regent for the boy king Louis XIV. At the time of the abortive first Fronde of 1648 he was Governor of Burgundy and commanded the royal army which suppressed it, but he was later arrested and imprisoned for his arrogant pretensions. Rescued by supporters, he instigated a second Fronde, entering Paris with the assistance of the Grande Mademoiselle (whom we shall find later on in her château of St-Fargeau in the Puisaye). There was no real support for such a grandiose character; Mazarin and the queen had to wait only a few months for it to melt away. Condé went off to Spain to pursue other hares, and Louis XIV was able to begin his long and glorious reign without further opposition. Before long he was able to secure the Franche-Comté, then in Spanish hands, and add it to the province – whose institutions he respected, while gradually whittling away its independent powers.

In the eighteenth century Dijon became again a brilliant centre of society and intellectual life. Its **Académie** was founded in 1723, and the Université de Bourgogne in 1750. Though the Revolution was generally welcomed when it came, and it was less bloody in Burgundy than elsewhere, there was a great deal of senseless iconoclasm, and irreparable damage was done to the matchless monuments of the Church. The aristocratic families came off lightly, both because they usually lived on their estates and also because of the sympathy and trust they had inspired around them; a common bond made them all Burgundians. Yet the last shreds of autonomy were lost, and the new artificial system of *départements* took its place under the central authority of the State. It says much for the Burgundian personality that it has resisted this dismembering. The rare talents and rich characters it continued to produce will be noted as we come upon them.

Of Napoleon's generals, Junot came from Bussy-le-Grand, Marmont from Châtillon-sur-Seine, Carnot from Nolay. On 5

October 1815 the emperors of Austria and Russia, Wellington and the king of Prussia reviewed their troops on the plain of Arc-sur-Tille. Vauban was born in the Morvan, Maurice de MacMahon, duc de Magenta, at Sully-en-Auxois. MacMahon was President of the Third Republic after the Franco-Prussian War, in which Burgundy did much to redeem the failures of the French army elsewhere. The defence of Dijon was rewarded by the addition of the Croix de la Légion d'Honneur to its arms. At the battle of Nuits in December 1870, and again in the following January, rare French victories were won. This did not, of course, affect the outcome of the war, and Burgundy remained under German occupation until October 1871.

World War I left Burgundy more or less unscathed, except for the rows of names which appeared on its war memorials, but some indiscriminate bombardments in the last war destroyed more of its precious fabrics. There was prolonged and often heroic resistance by *maquisards* based in the forests of the Châtillonais and the Morvan. As in most parts of France there are few towns or villages without their moving records of 'les fusillés' who died for France, and of vicious reprisals during the German withdrawal of 1944.

Since then Burgundy has largely escaped industrial development and pollution. Her ploughlands, her pastures, her rivers and forests (needless to say her vineyards) remain inviolate. Ancient estates have been rejuvenated, whether by their founding families or by wealthy and enlightened newcomers from the cities. Most encouraging of all, the little Romanesque churches throughout the land are being restored to health and beauty one by one, funded by local enterprise with substantial backing from the State. Burgundy may no longer send out great statesmen, soldiers or artists, but sooner or later most of them come here to enjoy its pleasures, perhaps to be enrolled among the Chevaliers du Tastevin at one of the 'Trois Glorieuses'.

CHAPTER ONE

Sens and the Senonais

Road travellers from Britain have two logical ways of reaching Burgundy; which they take must depend on where they cross the Channel. From the northern ports of Dunkirk, Calais or Boulogne, the shortest way lies north and east of Paris, whether you take the autoroute or the quieter roads through Amiens, Soissons and Château-Thierry. From Le Havre or St Malo it is more sensible to keep south of Paris, and this will give you a chance to visit Chartres and Bourges on the way, as alternatives to Amiens and Reims. In either case you will be entering Burgundy from the north – 'lower Burgundy' they call it, because it takes in the lower reaches of the Yonne and its many tributaries. The rolling countryside between the river valleys rarely rises more than a thousand feet above sea level. This is prosperous farming country – a green and bright yellow patchwork of young corn and rape in spring, golden with ripe corn and sunflower heads in summer and autumn.

You will find no vineyards yet. South of the Aube and the Seine the light chalky soil of the Champagne dies out, and but for the small but important wine-producing areas round Chablis and Auxerre you will have to wait till you reach the Côte d'Or south of Dijon to see the massed rows of vines which illustrate so many books on Burgundy – and even then they cover only a small proportion of its cultivated land. Nor will you find yourself immediately surrounded by romantic mediaeval castles or grand Renaissance châteaux. They will come later, as you reach the old frontier along the line of the Armançon between Burgundy and the western outposts of the Empire.

Here is a different kind of frontier, across which in the late twelfth century new ideas in church architecture began to spread from the north-west, especially from Paris and the Île de France. This was the start of the Gothic revolution, which produced the soaring masterpieces of Amiens and Beauvais, Chartres and

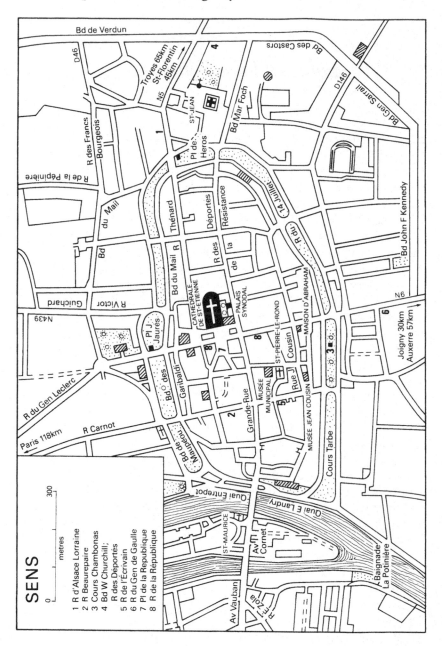

SENS

metres 0 — 300

1 R d'Alsace Lorraine
2 R Beaurepaire
3 Cours Chambonas
4 Bd W Churchill;
   R des Déportés
5 R de l'Ecrivain
6 R du Gen de Gaulle
7 Pl de la Republique
8 R de la République

Bourges, and which quickly took hold throughout western Europe. In Burgundy there was resistance, because of the powerful tradition of Romanesque architecture which had its origins in Lombardy and Provence. Cluny and Paray-le-Monial, Tournus and Vézelay had by 1100 established a distinctive base for large-scale church building throughout Burgundy, however much they differed over its development. When Gothic architects and master masons brought their ideas in from the north, the result was a fusion of styles which has become known as Burgundian Gothic, as distinct from the High Gothic of Amiens and Chartres.

Sens, the first city we shall visit in lower Burgundy, has the first Gothic cathedral to be built in France; yet in it we can recognize many elements derived from the Romanesque tradition – in particular from early Cistercian abbeys such as Fontenay and Pontigny. The cathedral is the natural centre of this easily negotiated town, whose history goes back well beyond the Christian era. The site commands the valley of the Yonne, whose waters join the Seine to flow through Paris to the Channel coast – a natural highway to and from the south-east of France. It takes its name from the Senones, a Gallic tribe who under their chieftain Brennus joined the invading armies which swarmed into northern Italy around 400BC and led the successful attack on Rome itself in 391. After Julius Caesar's conquest of Gaul it became an administrative centre, known as Agedincum.

Christianity was brought to Sens by St Savinien and St Potentien in the third century. Both were martyred here, but not before they had evangelized much of the country to the north-east. The early bishops were men of action, too, and helped to keep at bay marauding bands from the armies of the Merovingian kings. In 732 the fighting archbishop St Ebbon defeated the Saracens at Seignelay. Already by then there were five abbeys within the city walls, and though Sens began slowly to cede political supremacy to Paris it was to remain for nearly a thousand years the religious centre of France. The archbishop was described by Odoranne of Sens, a mediaeval chronicler, as 'a second Pope', and into the early years of the seventeenth century the Chapter of St Etienne could boast the acronymic motto CAMPONT, signifying that the bishoprics of Chartres, Auxerre, Meaux, Paris, Orléans, Nevers and Troyes were subject to its metropolitan authority.

It was here that in 1140 a Council of the Church, spurred on by the polemical zeal of St Bernard, condemned Abélard for refusing to set a limit to the activities of human reason. It was here in 1164 that Pope Alexander III confirmed Becket in the Primacy of England, and here that they met during his exile. It was in the cathedral of Sens that in 1234 St Louis married Marguerite of Provence.

The building of the present **Cathedral of St-Etienne** was begun under Archbishop Sanglier – not unnaturally known as 'the Boar' – between 1130 and 1135, and was almost complete at the death of Archbishop Hugues of Toucy in 1168. Among all the French prelates of the time Henri Sanglier was the most thorough exponent of the reforms of St Bernard, whose austere regime was spreading through the daughter foundations of Cîteaux, the abbey founded by Robert of Molesme in protest at the lax and indulgent practices of Cluny. St Bernard himself was the founder and first abbot of Clairvaux, some fifty miles north of Dijon, having served his novitiate in the cloister of Cîteaux. Before attempting to describe the cathedral and register its magnificence, we should try to understand the ideals which gave it its character.

In the first place it is, as we have seen, the earliest of the great Gothic cathedrals of France; in the second, thanks to the influence of St Bernard, it is a Cistercian cathedral, which means that we must expect a noble simplicity of style, a general adherence to the plans of the Order, and that it will rely to an almost mystical extent on an understanding of mathematical proportions. In common with St Augustine (and with Plato), St Bernard distrusted images and believed in the metaphysical significance of mathematical and musical relationships. Their relevance to architecture was not hard to establish, and we shall be able to see how they were employed in the abbey churches of Pontigny and Fontenay. Yet St Bernard realized that total austerity as prescribed for a closed community of monks was out of place in a cathedral which served a large population; so we shall find the outlines of Sens gentler than those of Pontigny, softened in places by decoration, and an overall plan modified to suit the needs of a great city church.

Parking in Sens is not difficult, and there is usually space to be found outside the western entrance to the Cathedral. Whereas at Chartres the famous west portal is flanked by two disconcertingly dissimilar towers, at Sens two towers were planned to match each

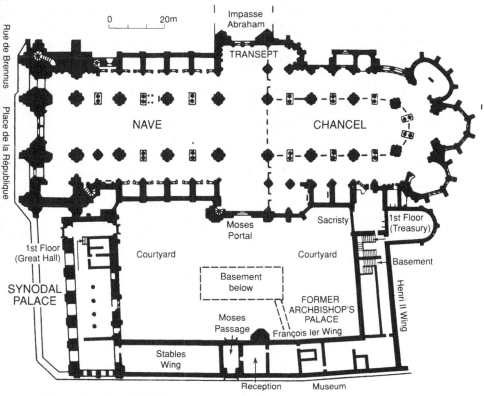

other, but only the southern one, known as the Tour de Pierre, was
finished. This was crowned in 1576 by a Renaissance campanile to
take the big bell with its inscription:

> Les borgois de Sens m'ont fait faire
> l'an M cing cens soixante seize

which gives us its date exactly.

Work on the northern tower, the Tour de Plomb (so called because of the lead sheeting used in its early stages) was halted for
good in 1200. The Tour de Pierre collapsed on the Thursday in
Holy Week 1267, wrecking parts of the façade, the nave and the
Synodal Palace which adjoined it to the south. It was rebuilt in

5

stages up to the end of the fourteenth century, and its balustrades were added in 1532. The little campanile with its semicircular arches may seem a discordant addition to a Gothic building, but in an odd way it compensates for the absence of a balancing tower to the north.

As so often when one pushes one's way blindly through the awkward doors of a cathedral's main entrance, the first glance up the whole length of the church from west to east sets the mood in which one approaches the interior. Sens does not stun you with its height, like Amiens or Beauvais; too early to rely on flying buttresses, its builders knew their limits. In any case St Bernard and his architectural followers were not primarily concerned with height, but with due proportion. Experts in these matters will tell us that the width of the nave is twice that of the side aisles, and that you find the same proportion in their height. The two-to-one ratio is kept in the elevation of both nave and choir, though above the triforium it was broken when the clerestory windows were heightened after a fire in 1184.

There is no striving after effect. The harmony of mass and line is undisturbed, and as in other great buildings it is the shape and dimensions of the space enclosed which impress, rather than the structure of the surrounding walls. Gradually the details sink in. The round intermediate pillars of the nave are crowned by dignified Corinthian capitals; in pairs they alternate with the weight-bearing pillars, which throw up a cluster of half-columns to reach clerestory level without a break, introducing strong vertical lines between a horizontal sequence in a way that may remind us of Canterbury. If so, it is not so surprising when we learn that it was William of Sens who rebuilt the choir at Canterbury. The vaulting owes its smooth and serene effect partly to perspective and proportion, partly to the multitude of small stones which compose its under surface; the use of ribs – the hallmark of the new Gothic style – enhances its elegance.

The side aisles and ambulatory remind us that this is early twelfth-century architecture, with vaulting and blind arcading which is fully semicircular, while the ambulatory capitals are Romanesque in spirit. In spite of St Bernard we can find rustic scenes, legendary and monstrous creatures, griffins, winged lizards and dragons. Most endearing is the little owl, or *chouette*, which looks down from one of the half-columns of the northern ambulatory. The even pattern of the triforium runs the length of the nave, and is repeated in the choir. Not so in the transepts, where in true Gothic spirit light floods in through the huge windows – late fifteenth-century to the south, early sixteenth to the north – above which the glowing sixteenth-century glass points up the flowing tracery of the two central rose windows.

No time need be spent in the chapels to north and south of the nave, which are mostly nineteenth-century accretions. The ambulatory chapels are a different matter, and if we follow them round from the head of the south aisle there is a lot to see – not least the glass in windows so far hidden from us. First we come to the **Chapel of the Virgin**, which like its counterpart to the north is really a modification of the Cistercian tradition of chapels projecting to the east from the transepts. The smiling statue of the Virgin over the altar is of the fourteenth century, contemporary with the chapel as a whole. Next come the two less important chapels of **St Martial** and **St Apolline**, the former with a sixteenth-century *retable* by Nicholas Godinet, with figures of the twelve apostles.

At this point we reach the doorway to the sacristy, whose tympanum carries a twelfth-century sculpture of the Lamb of God. The first chapel of the central three is dedicated to the **Sacred Heart**. The glass in its mullioned windows is by the artist Jean Cousin, who lived in Sens and whose work was prized locally in the sixteenth century. It is a curious composition, representing the Sibyl of Timur pointing upwards for the benefit of the emperor Augustus to the Virgin who is to bring forth the Saviour of the world. This was the prophetic interpretation given in the Renaissance to the fourth *Eclogue* of Virgil, though the wonder child expected there was probably that of Augustus's daughter Julia and her first husband, Marcus Marcellus.

The chapel of the central apse is appropriately dedicated to **St Savinien**, first bishop of Sens. Its effect in this prime position is marred by an eighteenth-century stucco group representing the saint's martyrdom, but there can be no complaint about the five superb windows which fill the apse with the subdued reddish glow of their thirteenth-century glass. In the centre is shown the life of St Savinien, with that of St Paul to the right and St John the Evangelist to the left. Moving round into the northern ambulatory we come to the chapel of **Ste Colombe**. This is an eighteenth-century creation, whose builders converted the vaulting space to accommodate an oval ceiling. Here we find the mausoleum put up by Louis XV to the memory of the Dauphin (father of Louis XVI) and his wife Marie-Joseph of Saxony, who died within two years of each other.

The two windows of the next bay of the ambulatory return us to the middle ages, with their deep colours and intriguing designs. The one on the right ostensibly covers the parable of the Good Samaritan, but the panels which flank the central lozenges are concerned with a sequence of Old and New Testament scenes to illustrate the redemption of the world – from the original sin of Adam to the death and resurrection of Christ. On the left we can follow the adventures of the Prodigal Son, told with impressive mastery in this short compass.

Thomas à Becket, 'Saint Thomas de Cantorbéry' as the French call him, Henry II's one-time friend, archbishop and 'turbulent priest', was a close associate of the archbishop of Sens and spent four years of his exile in the town. He is commemorated here in one of the next pair of windows which light the ambulatory. It takes up the story from the point where Louis VII of France brings Henry and Becket together in an insincere and inconclusive peace; then it shows Becket returning to England, welcomed by the people of Canterbury, preaching and ministering to them, and finally murdered by the four knights. The subject is all but obscured by the jewelled magnificence of the glass, composed in medallions of glowing colour. Some French authorities date it to the twelfth century, and the same date is suggested for the right-hand window of the pair, a marvellous concoction of almond-shaped panels depicting the life of St Eustace, who is connected with the chapel behind. This group of four windows is the finest in Burgundy, though perhaps only the Becket window approaches the brilliance to be seen in Bourges or Chartres. Under it we find the statue of a seated bishop, found in 1897 in the wall of a house near the cathedral which Becket is believed to have occupied during his stay in Sens; the deduction was that it represented the archbishop himself.

Between the fifth and sixth pillars on the north side of the nave is the strange monument raised in the sixteenth century by Archbishop Tristan de Salazar in memory of his parents. Four tall black marble columns hold aloft a heavy slab on which kneels the statue of the archbishop's father, Jean de Salazar. That of his mother, Marguerite de la Trémoille, was destroyed in the Revolution. Both of them would have been facing a black marble altar surmounted by a *retable* of astonishing flamboyant virtuosity. Statues of St Savinien, the Virgin and St Etienne appear under a canopy of stone so carved as to call forth the comment of the French art critic, M. de Montaiglon: 'Jamais le bois, jamais le bronze ou l'argent, n'ont obéi à une gouge et un ciseau plus fermes, plus surs et plus fins.'

To take in the outside of a cathedral in a big city is not easy. The west front is usually the most accessible, and at Sens its three portals can be seen clearly from the Place de la République. The carving on the **Central Portal** was savagely mutilated by the iconoclasts of the Revolution, but for some reason they left intact the lovely statue of St Stephen on the *trumeau* – the pier dividing the doors. The supple drapery, the hair falling in cylindrical curls, the noble expression and posture stamp it as an example of how Gothic sculpture was beginning to free itself from the inheritance of Byzantine formalism. To the left is the **Portal of St John**, dating from the end of the twelfth century, where the vigorous and accomplished carving of the tympanum and archivolts describe scenes from the life of St John the Baptist (some of them bordering on fantasy) and the loss and recovery of his relics. The right-hand entrance is the **Portal of Notre-Dame**, a more delicate work which replaced the earlier one which was ruined when the tower fell, and so is assigned to the early thirteenth century.

The most elaborate of the entrances is through the **Portal of Abraham**, and this takes us a long way from St Bernard. It leads into the north transept, and though the niches over the doorway have been despoiled of their statues you hardly notice this as you take in the flamboyant delights above. A feathery pinnacle rises across a decorated balustrade to meet the bottom of the intricate wave-like tracery of the huge rose window of the transept. The final gable and the balustrade at the top of the side turrets add more flamboyance, while the whole is crowned by a (modern) statue of Abraham. Except for Abraham, all that you see in front of you was designed by the early sixteenth-century architect Martin Cambiges in a final glorious fling of Gothic art. You have a good view of it from a side road leading off the rue Thénard, which runs parallel to the cathedral on the north side. The south transept doorway, the **Portal of Moses**, is a little earlier in date, more restrained but still beautiful.

A word should be said about the cathedral bells. Two of them, called 'Savinienne' and 'Potentienne' after the founding bishops, are of enormous weight and dimensions. They were cast about 1560 by Gaspard Mongin-Viard, a master foundryman from Auxerre. They miraculously survived the Revolution – perhaps they were too heavy to move – when eleven of their bronze companions were carried off to Paris to be melted down for cannon.

Next to the cathedral, and extending south from its western corner, is the **Synodal Palace**, which was built in the middle of the thirteenth century by Archbishop Gauthier Cornu. It provided a meeting place when required for the assembled clergy, not only of the diocese of Sens but of all the constituent members of CAMPONT. Viollet-le-Duc called it a monument unique in France, and the grandeur of its construction underlines the overwhelming authority exercised by the archbishops of Sens. It had been severely damaged when the southern tower collapsed in 1267, and it was Viollet-le-Duc who directed its restoration at Government expense in 1861.

Seen from the west it presents a regular façade of six bays, with pairs of beautifully moulded windows balancing a deep-set rose window between their elegant Gothic noses. The same window design appears at the southern end of the Great Hall, a chamber which triumphantly repeats the proportions of the cathedral itself. It is reached by a stairway from the ground floor, which contained the official secretariat, the tribunal and the prisons. In the Middle Ages it was customary for religious authority to extend into the civil sphere, administering justice and punishment to all under the laws of the land. The pathetic *graffiti* we find on the walls of the prison galleries remind us that both could be severe.

Entrance to the Synodal Palace is at the northern end of the building, from a vaulted passage which leads straight through into a rectangular courtyard extending almost the whole length of the cathedral – the courtyard of the **Archbishop's Palace**. The long range of buildings to the south is divided into two by another vaulted passage, known as the Moses passage from its alignment with the south transept doorway of the same name. Here you will find the entrance to what is now the Cathedral Museum, well planned and equipped in a scheme begun in 1985 to house exhibits which illustrate the long history and rich traditions of the Senonais and its communities, culminating in the unique collection known as the **Trésor de Sens**. The first room on the ground floor is a handsome panelled apartment, the only survivor of the state rooms of the François I wing of the former Archbishop's palace. Beyond it are displays of artefacts and burial sites from pre-history and the Bronze Age. At the end of this section you turn left into the later Henry II wing to find a literally monumental exhibition of Gallo-Roman culture, centred on a big Roman baths complex of the fourth century AD, with bits and pieces from the first century. Some of the most fascinating objects are to be found in the newly opened cellars beneath this section.

Next you come to a fine wide staircase which communicates with the upper floors of the Henri II wing. It ends in the oak-raftered attics, now a picture gallery, but once the servants' quarters. To reach them the servants had to climb the stairs past other rooms, so the brick treads were edged with wood to muffle their comings and goings – a detail you can still see if you look closely. Halfway up there is a new entrance to the Treasury, which should be the culmination of your visit to the museum. There is a great deal to see, and if you have spent most of the morning in the Cathedral it could be wise to come back here in the afternoon; the lunch hour can be well spent in the vicinity.

The Treasure of Sens is not just the gleaming collection of vessels and vestments one expects in such a context. Most of its gold and silver disappeared in the Revolution, but what has survived is probably of greater interest. In these small rooms are preserved in the proverbial nutshell the most diverse examples of the religious art of the Christian world over fifteen centuries. The list of *trésoriers*, among the most important dignitaries of the Chapter, goes back to the fourth century, and according to an inventory of the twelfth century Charlemagne bequeathed to Sens all the relics and jewels from his own chapel.

The principal room, once the Archbishop's private chapel, is dominated by a gorgeous fifteenth-century tapestry *retable* of the Coronation of the Virgin, presented by the Cardinal de Bourbon. Below it to the right is a large ivory casket, or *coffret reliquaire*, said to be Italian work from between the eleventh and thirteenth centuries. On it are figured episodes from the lives of biblical characters, with bands depicting more lively secular hunting scenes. If sculpture in wood or stone attracts you, you will be moved by the thirteenth-century wooden figures here, and by the three seated statues of the Virgin and Child — one each from the twelfth, thirteenth and fifteenth centuries.

One category on display will fascinate the historian, the artist and the craftsman alike. In contrast to the gilded caskets made by later generations to contain holy relics, here are fragments of the original silken material in which the relics were first wrapped for transport from the holy places of the east. Arranged in two glass-topped cabinets are Coptic tissues from Egyptian workshops of the fifth and sixth centuries, Persian fragments of the fifth to the eighth centuries, pieces from Byzantine shrouds of the eighth to the twelfth centuries and Saracen materials from the thirteenth. Unfortunately in the subdued lighting thought necessary to pre-serve them they are not easy to identify, but most of them are more delicate in design, more refined in workmanship than one would have believed possible of their periods.

In a room next door are vestments with an historic as well as an artistic interest, such as the chasuble, stole and maniple of St Thomas à Becket, who has a show case to himself. So does an-other exile, St Edmund of Canterbury, and it even includes his priestly slippers and pendants from his mitre. One of the finest on show is the chasuble given by Blanche of Navarre to the collegial church of St Loup in Brienon; behind and almost concealed by it, look for the so-called 'Tau of St Loup', a pastoral staff of wood topped with a rock crystal in the shape of a 'T' and sheathed in silver. This is a Carolingian example of what was widely carried by bishops before the Cross became more general.

The third room contains a unique collection of ivory objects connected with the church. The earliest is a round sixth-century pyx, or small coffer, whose profane decoration in relief of a hunt-ing scene is as fresh and vivid as on the day it was carved. Another circular coffer is Islamic work of the twelfth century, which carries a long moralizing inscription in Arabic round its upper and lower rims. The most curious item is a 'liturgical comb' said to have belonged to St Loup. It has two sets of ivory teeth, separated by a semicircular heraldic device with a gold filigree border and a row of semi-precious stones; these may be later additions to the comb itself, which is given an eighth-century date.

This whole ambitious project will eventually be completed by bringing into use the block which begins west of the Moses passage, converted to a stable wing in 1760. Other places you can see in the town are the **Maison d'Abraham**, with its intricate carving of the Tree of Jesse, which faces the intersection of the rue de la Republique and the rue Jean Cousin, and the **Church of St-Savinien** (in the suburb of the same name) which is the oldest sanctuary in Sens. It was rebuilt over the saint's tomb in the eleventh century, and saved from the Revolution by one Simon Blanchet, who bought it and presented it to the parish for public worship. The crypt occupies the site of the primitive *martyrium*, and contains a stone altar stained with what is piously believed to be the martyr's blood.

2

Within a semicircle of twenty kilometres' radius north of Sens there are several places which illustrate how varied are the attractions of northern Burgundy. The Yonne, whose department we are in, is one of the loveliest and most gracious of the rivers of France. The busy N6 highway on its way to Paris crosses it at **Pont-sur-Yonne**. Only a single arch of the ancient bridge remains, and the view of this is obscured by the iron construction which has replaced it. But look upstream from the open-air café which has been built over the surviving arch, and the charm of the placid river gliding between its wooded banks will captivate you. The barges pass up and down – there is no need for a canal here – and the old men below you are absorbed in their fishing. The church has a fine position and an array of spires, but the inside is disappointing.

Another seven kilometres up the N6 brings you to the small town of Champigny, where a right-hand turn leads in the direction of **Courlon-sur-Yonne**. You will find a pleasant frontage near the junction of the river and a short stretch of canal, where ducks enjoy a stroll by the water. The church of St-Loup is set farther back in the town, and like others in a region not far from Paris it

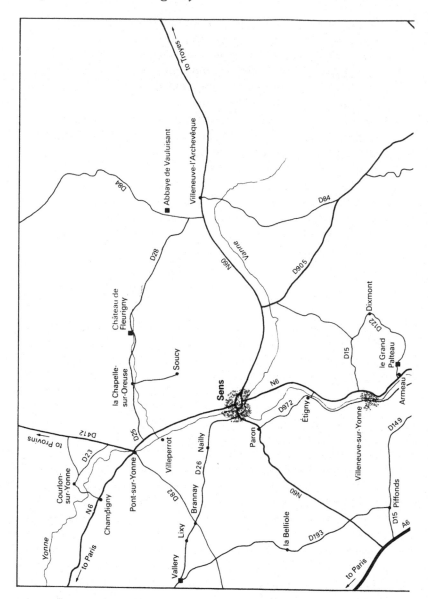

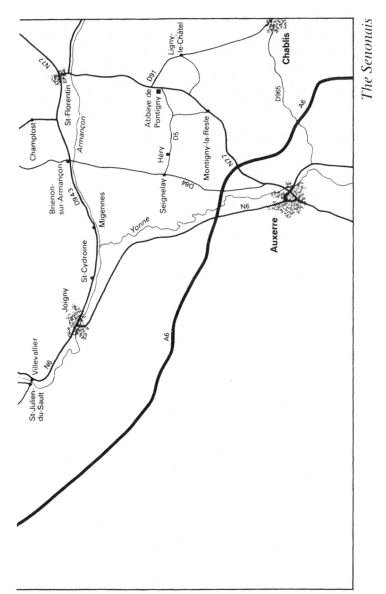

The Senonais

has notable Renaissance features; though the first church on the site (beside the old Roman road) was built by the early Christians to replace a temple of Mercury, Courlon stood for the Catholic Ligue during the wars of religion, and the thirteenth-century church was burnt by the Huguenots under the elder Condé. It was rebuilt in 1631 by order of Richelieu, and the tower was made still higher.

The nave contains some magnificent Renaissance *boiserie* – pulpit, seigneurial pew, and rood screen leading to a fully panelled choir. The screen, with its crucifixion flanked by the Virgin and St John, is beautifully simple for its period, and the eye passes easily through it to the rich culmination of the choir. The seigneurial pew (or *banc d'œuvre*) has the initials S and L – for Saint Loup – elegantly intertwined under its canopy. A great craftsman-artist of his period was at work here. Across the east end of the choir is some more spectacular woodwork of the eighteenth century, a carved altar surmounted by an elaborate baldachino with fluted columns – even the gathered drapery over the altar is realistically carved in wood. The effect is sumptuous but not heavy.

If from Pont-sur-Yonne you turn east along the D25 you come to **la Chapelle-sur-Oreuse**, signalling that you are in the valley of one of the delightful tributaries of the Yonne. The Senonais is good farming country, wide acres of arable interrupted only by woodland, with no outstanding contours to mark the horizons. In the village of la Chapelle you find a typical combination of farm and manor house – turrets on the *manoir*, peacocks in its garden, willows and fruit trees to frame it.

The last stop on this day's expedition could be at **Fleurigny**, where the château – now privately owned and domestic – has been called 'the pearl of the Senonais'. Visiting hours are limited, and should be checked in advance. Owned and lived in by the marquise de Castellane-Esparron, its peace and privacy are naturally valued, and a special effort to reach it will be well rewarded. A secret and lovely place, it reveals itself only at the end of a thickly wooded drive. The two main fronts of the building, north and south, are in strong contrast. The entrance is from the north, across a stone bridge to a conventional fortified gateway between two towers. Two corner towers complete the appearance of a *château-fort* as it stood during the Hundred Years' War. Only the brickwork and the Renaissance windows of the upper rooms reveal that the present building dates mostly from the sixteenth century – though it is none the worse for that.

It is difficult to believe that this peaceful place was contended for bitterly by French and English armies, finally to be dismantled by order of Charles VII. The dispossessed owner, Jeanne de Fleurigny, returned in her old age as a childless widow. She gave the château and its lands to her cousin François le Clerc on condition that he rebuild it, and that his son Charles should take the name and arms of Fleurigny. Le Clerc was the chamberlain of François I, and received his king here after he had rebuilt the château. The present owner, the marquise, is descended from that family, and the place has never been sold.

The contrast when you pass through the gateway into the *cour d'honneur* is a surprise, though you may have had an inkling of it as you walked up the drive. The fourth or south side of the courtyard was pulled down in the last century to allow grassy lawns to spread down to the edge of the moat, which is fresh with spring-fed water, and enlivened by cruising swans and mallards. Behind them is revealed the warm red brick of an essentially Renaissance building so modified that it resembles an English manor house with all its charm and formal insouciance. A closer look will find stylistic variations from several centuries – in particular the delicately carved doorway to the chapel which completes the east wing. It is known as the 'porte de l'escargot de Bourgogne' and the reason is not far to find.

The chapel is one of the main features of the château shown to the public. Its lower floor is ornate and unremarkable except for its window by Jean Cousin, whose work we saw in the cathedral at Sens. Its theme is the same – the Sybil pointing prophetically to the cloud-enthroned Virgin and Child for the benefit of the Roman emperor. The treatment is more lively and detailed here, and on the left we see St Paul preaching to the people of Ephesus. Much of the ornament of the chapel is also by Cousin or his school. He was orphaned in early childhood, and earned his living by keeping pigs until a villager, struck by his designs, took him under his care to study. He became an engraver, sculptor, writer and geometrician, setting out his ideas in a *Traité des Perspectives*; he went to Paris in 1547 and was employed by Henri II. Cousin also designed the huge chimneypiece in the *salle des gardes*, where the mediaeval fireplace is almost hidden beneath a monumental stone structure, five metres high, with a band of hunting scenes below an elaborate gallery and cornice.

A spiral staircase leads to the first floor, and the visitor is shown a small bedroom whose walls are covered with painted panels of local hunting scenes, and sprawling versions of mythological subjects typical of the seventeenth century. A corridor on the same floor leads to the upper part of the chapel wing, which has a carved wooden ceiling; it also contains a Merovingian sarcophagus found in the grounds.

The history of Fleurigny is that of a family determined to preserve or recreate it at times when others might have abandoned it in despair. In the Revolution it was sacked and confiscated when Auguste de Fleurigny was a small boy. He escaped with his mother abroad, but returned at the Restoration as the marquis de Fleurigny to repair the damage to his family home. Finally the marquis and marquise de Castellane arrived here in 1943 as a newly married couple to find that their home had been pillaged and wrecked by the occupying German troops. Its appearance today is the greatest tribute to their devotion and fine taste in once more restoring it to beauty.

At the eastern end of our semicircle is the town of **Villeneuve l'Archevêque**, a matter of sixteen kilometres along the D 28. It was founded in the twelfth century by the archbishop of Sens (hence its name) and it was here that St Louis and Marguerite de Provence received from the Venetians the Crown of Thorns, for which they built the Sainte-Chapelle in Paris. The **Church of Notre-Dame** has a strong, four-square Gothic tower and dates from the thirteenth and sixteenth centuries. The interior has recently been restored, allowing one to admire the spacious proportions of nave and crossing – though one hopes that the old unvarnished pews will stay as they are. Under the war memorial near the west door is a remarkable **Sepulchre**: behind the tomb stand the Virgin, St John, and St Mary Magdalene holding a veil as if she had been wiping her eyes. St Joseph of Arimathea is realistically dressed, with a pouch at his waist, while two other figures stand by with gravecloths and oil jars for embalming. The

Crown of Thorns lies on the ground in front. This is a marvellous work, with clean, clear lines and eloquent expressions on the faces of the mourners.

One reads that it was given to the church by Baron Campi of Vauluisant in 1823, together with some other statuary. On the north wall of the nave St Anne is teaching the Virgin as a small child to read; on the corbels each side of the nave there is a series of lively figures including St Roch with his faithful dog, and almost a caricature of an anonymous fat bishop.

The former **Abbey of Vauluisant** is just off to the right of the D84, three kilometres north of Villeneuve. It is now a large farm, though behind what remains of the monastic buildings stands the late eighteenth-century château of the Baron Campi who rescued the Sepulchre and presented it to the church of Notre-Dame. You enter the farm through the original abbey gateway, and conspicuous to the right is a long, beautifully roofed barn, with buttresses, wooden rafters and three lancet windows. The abbey church was destroyed in the Revolution, but a high-standing chapel survives on the left as you enter, with the farmer's living quarters alongside. The whole is enclosed in extensive parkland, with good trees and a carpet of flowers in spring; through it runs a stream with sluices and weirs, which must have served a mill. A tall octagonal dovecote by the stream completes a comfortable group of mediaeval, monastic, nineteenth-century domestic, and modern farm life.

Another expedition to the south of Sens would begin with a short spell on the N6 leading to **Villeneuve-sur-Yonne**. The main road bypasses the town, but this is no reason for you to do the same. Its long straight central street runs between two stone gateways – the Porte de Sens and the Porte de Joigny. The **Church of Notre-Dame** stands halfway between them. Though its foundation stone was laid by Alexander III in 1163, you will see that its façade is draped in classical ornament. Inside, the vast proportions of the Gothic nave are a reminder that the architects of Champagne and the Île de France, whose influence was as strong in northern Burgundy, achieved the effect of height by raising the roofs of their churches rather than by building high towers above them. When they tried to do both, the towers not infrequently fell down. If you find the western doors shut, the

Presbytery is halfway down a narrow lane to your right, and the curé or his wife will admit you through a small door opposite.

The classical note of the façade is not repeated inside except in the stone screen to the first chapel of the south aisle. The apse, with its three radiating chapels, is elegantly Gothic, only spoilt by the rococo sunburst stuck above the two pillars which frame the altar. There is much to admire in this fine church, and the stained glass — mostly of the sixteenth century — contributes richly to its character. Look particularly at the glass in the first chapel of the south aisle, which records scenes in the life of the Virgin, from the Nativity to the Assumption and Coronation. To the left of the window a figure in a red robe is seated below the Virgin's bed, reading a book with the aid of spectacles; one would have to search hard in the history of stained glass to find a parallel. High above, the Virgin sits enthroned, with suppliants below, amid a gorgeous vista of blue domes and palaces which make up heaven. The lower panels have portraits of the window's donors. Next to this is a chapel dedicated to St Nicholas, patron saint of mariners. Its classical screen carries symbols of the life of boatmen on the Yonne, who formed an important guild in the towns along the river. The country was, and still is, well forested, and for timber the Yonne was the easiest means of transport.

Halfway down the northern ambulatory another fine window cleverly represents the Tree of Jesse by using the stonework of the mullion as the trunk of the tree, and piling up its fruit in bright colours on either side. The final fork, as the tree branches, makes a nest for Virgin and Child. The third chapel of the north aisle contains a curiosity worth some study. *In toto* it is another **Sepulchre**, in which the stone figures surrounding the tomb are attributed to Jean Goujon, a sixteenth-century artist who collaborated in the decoration of the Louvre. The figure of Christ, however, was carved in limewood two centuries earlier, and its provenance is unknown. This tree was in favour with early woodcarvers because it retains its shape in delicate work longer than any other. Here the lower covering of the body is hollowed out round the legs, and the spines of the Crown of Thorns are as sharp as when they were carved. A last look down the nave to the west catches the light outlined by the whirling tracery of its high rose window; like a Catherine wheel, you can almost sense it turning.

A pleasant walk along the mall beside the Yonne brings you to the **Tour de Louis le Gros**, standing in a circle of plane trees. Its proportions suit the nickname associated with it; it was the keep and is now all that remains of the former château of Villeneuve. At the southern end of the street, close to the Porte de Joigny, the old posting inn Le Dauphin is being reconstituted inside to provide more modern bedrooms. A few have already been completed, and the modest restaurant below still serves good food.

Among the low hills to the east of the Yonne, where a chalky plateau is strewn with megaliths, dolmens and menhirs, there is an interesting church at **Dixmont**. The interest begins on a triangle of grass under an oak tree at the east end of the church, where a large stone block is set with protruding surfaces for sharpening flint axes and other tools – a *polissoir*, to give it its proper name. On the base of the tower is carved a Visitation, in which with a knowing smile the Virgin is admiring the swelling womb of her cousin Elizabeth. In the south aisle there is a wooden group of St Anne holding an adult Virgin Mary with her left arm, who in turn balances her Child in her lap. This representation of three spotless generations is unusual but not unique; in Greek iconography you find the three figures stacked up frontally in a sitting position, but here the composition is freer and more natural.

You can rejoin the N6 by a pretty cross-country road which passes the **Château du Grand Palteau**, an attractive building of mixed periods which has been converted to a sensible use as a *station de vacances* for school children, with a riding school attached. You then drop steeply through the trees to the village of Armeau, and shortly afterwards at Villevallier you can cross the Yonne (and the railway) to reach **St-Julien-du-Sault**. The name commemorates a legendary leap by the saint to escape his pursuers. The collegial church of St-Julien is a magnificent building where the beauties of the thirteenth century combine with the splendours of the sixteenth. The Renaissance dominates the outside, with flying buttresses soaring to support an immensely high nave and chevet, but the graceful arched porticos which provide entrances from north and south are of the earlier period. Inside, the nave remains thirteenth-century as far as the lower levels of the choir. It is at clerestory level in the choir that the Renaissance alterations so evident from the outside began. Light pours in through the big Renaissance windows above the ambulatory, but down below it is a surprise to find that the three apsidal chapels are of perfect thirteenth-century form with contemporary glass in their tall lancets.

The glass here is almost as fine as in the corresponding windows of Sens cathedral. Simple, naïve, small-scale pictures are set in panels whose shapes vary for every window. The details are marvellous, and the colours – deep reds and blues, maroon and light green – seem just right in the context. Both design and execution deserve long study. The middle chapel has as its central theme the life of Christ; to the right is that of St Nicholas, to the left the martyrdom of St Blaize, St Peter and St Paul. The right-hand chapel belongs to the Virgin, the left-hand has St John the Baptist in the centre, the Evangelist to the right, the birth and childhood of Jesus to the left. Further round the ambulatory to the north is another window of the same date with the life and martyrdom of St Margaret as its subject. It need be no surprise to learn that the glass in these ten windows is by the same artist who created those of the Sainte-Chapelle. No doubt St Louis and his queen had a hand in this.

If you look south from the small *place* at the west end of the church you will see a distinctive isolated hill, capped by a tall structure which is difficult to make out. This turns out to be – you can drive up to confirm it – the east end of the chapel and all that is left of the mediaeval château of **Vauquillain**. Everything else has disappeared except for the south range of wall and the base of the south-west tower. One can only reflect that if the whole of the château was built as majestically high as this defiant little remnant it must have been something exceptional. The view over the town and the Yonne is that in any case.

You are now on your way to a different part of the Senonais, which will call for a change of base to explore it. Before leaving Sens for good the great Burgundian name of Condé calls for a visit to the family château at **Valléry**, about twenty kilometres west of the town. All that remains of the mediaeval castle is a pair of round towers enclosing a low, farmlike dwelling. A new residential château was begun by the Maréchal de Saint-André, friend of Henri II, but only part of it was finished. At his death it passed to his widow, who gave it to Louis I of Bourbon, Prince of Condé, in the hope that he would marry her; the same hope led her to turn Protestant. Both gestures were in vain – Louis accepted the château but disappointed her hopes. He was killed at the battle of Jarnac in 1569, but his great-grandson Louis II, who has always been called the great Condé – largely on account of his arrogance – was brought up at Valléry. The château stands on the side of a wooded hill, surrounded by a moat, and can be visited from the outside only between 1500 and 1800 at weekends and on public holidays, though good views can be had from both front and rear. The restored brick and stone façade is a rather harsh example of its period, but seen from behind across the moat it looks more inviting and domestic. The family mausoleum is a chapel attached to the village church, and it contains the tomb of Prince Henri II of Condé, whose son the Grand Condé was born in 1621.

3

It is time now to turn east, away from the valley of the Yonne, though we shall have its company as far as **Joigny**, where Renard de Sens built a fortress in the seventh century. We read that the cloth market was attracting trade by 1224, and of the thirteenth-century ramparts the Porte du Bois, which opens on to the Forèt d'Othe, is still standing. In 1530 the town was almost totally destroyed by fire, but there were enough resources to rebuild it quickly. The eighteenth-century bridge over the Yonne has kept six of its original arches, but the long riverside frontage is unworthy of the river it borders, and is thronged at most times by industrial and commercial traffic. Behind it rises the old town, picturesque enough in its steep narrow alleys and bewildering turns, but no place to visit by car. You will do better to leave yours in the *parking* off the Quai Général Leclerc, and walk up first to the **Church of St-Thibault**.

St Thibault is an oddity among Burgundian saints. He was born about 1130 near Provins in Champagne to a wealthy family, but after living the life of a young *grand seigneur* he was converted to a religious life at the age of twenty-four. He left his family home, and in the company of his esquire – who seems to have felt the same call – he set off towards Luxembourg, where they found work as labourers in the diocese of Trèves. Three years later they arrived in Spain on a pilgrimage to St James of Compostela , and from there they went to Italy. In the woods near Vicenza they lived as hermits until the younger man died. Taken up by the abbot of a nearby monastery, and ordained priest by the bishop of Vicenza, Thibault reverted to a hermit's life. He died on 30 June 1066 ; his body was brought to Vicenza and buried in the cathedral; a few years later he was canonized by Alexander II. Then his brother, who had found a more comfortable position as abbot of Sainte-Colombe in Sens, went to Italy to bring back some of his remains to France. On the way home he stopped at Joigny, and the relics were lodged for the night in a modest oratory outside the town walls. The present church was begun on the same site (now incorporated within the walls) about 1450, and was completed in 1528 – only to be badly damaged in the fire of 1530. Over the northern doorway there is a lively carving of the young Thibault on horseback, off to the hunt with his dog. The best thing in the church is a lovely **Vierge-au-Sourire** of the fourteenth century, which was chosen for the Charles V exhibition at the Grand Palais in 1981. The vaulting of the choir comes to a point in a superb stone *corona*; it collapsed early this century and has only just been restored to its place.

The main road to the east continues through dispiriting semi-industrial suburbs as far as Migennes. However, if you watch for a sign on the left of the road about halfway there, it will direct you to the early Romanesque church of **St-Cydroine**, a rarity in these parts which should make up for any tedium you may have suffered. Its importance is recognized by the Ministry of Culture and Communications, which has undertaken its thorough restoration. A substantial octagonal tower is planted firmly over the high crossing, while a long plain nave with lancet windows leads to the Romanesque apse – disfigured only by a neoclassical *retable*. The roof of the nave has been made good with wooden tie-beams, and the cupola replaced by a raftered ceiling – though the octagonal structure and its supporting squinches are still there. There are nightmarish carved capitals to the east of the crossing: strange animals devour or regurgitate human corpses; two birds with human heads have hands issuing from their mouths, while their claws grasp a small head – all apocalyptic conceits difficult to explain.

St Cydroine was among a group of Christians arrested in 274 under Aurelian. He was condemned to death, but managed to escape his guards and took refuge in a village near the confluence of the Yonne and the Armançon – just a mile away from where we are now. He was recognized by a body of Roman soldiers, taken away and executed. His bones were rescued and buried on the site where his church stands. The village now has another martyr: Paul Borsin, who was born here, was carried off by German soldiers in 1944 to their headquarters in Clamecy. There he was shot for his part in the Resistance, and the road which passes the west end of the church is named after him. If you find the church shut, you will find the key at 6 rue Paul Borsin, round the corner to the left.

Once past Migennes you will have left the Yonne to follow the line of the Canal de Bourgogne, which doubles with the winding river Armançon on its way down from **St-Florentin**. This was the Roman Castrodunum, or 'fort on a hill', built above the spot where the Armance flows into the Armançon, which is a favourite place for fishermen. Some excellent cheeses are made in the neighbourhood, in particular the St-Florentin and the Soumaintrain. The church was begun in 1376, and is another good example of how late Gothic and early Renaissance mix in northern Burgundy. It was extensively rebuilt between 1500 and 1614, and even then the nave was never finished. This may have been because of the exigencies of the site, which occupies the highest ground in the town, but as it is the choir is longer by one bay than the nave.

In the late Gothic ambulatory there are five fine windows. The first three are dedicated to St Nicholas, St Florentin and St Martin (a popular saint in Burgundy); the fourth is a unique representation of the Creation of the World. It begins at the top left-hand panel with God, in the attire of a Byzantine bishop, pulling the blazing sun out of a blue void; later we see Adam and Eve looking very bemused at finding themselves together in Paradise; the fifth window celebrates the Immaculate Conception.

You are now only ten kilometres from the Cistercian abbey of Pontigny, but it would be wise to set aside a good part of the day to visit it. For the moment, then, go back along the D905 to Brienon-sur-Armançon and turn left down the D84 to **Seignelay,** the traditional scene of the great victory of Archbishop St Ebbon over the Saracens. The church of St-Martial has a tower whose fortifying buttresses are said to date from the twelfth century, though the nave and choir are two or three hundred years later. Outside the west door a plaque records the passage of St Joan on her way to Reims in 1429, while a baby salamander over the south door suggests a connection with François I. The **Halles** down in the middle of the village are exceptionally fine and well preserved for so small a place.

The D84 leads on to Auxerre, which we shall be visiting in the next chapter, where the reasonably priced Seignelay has comfortable rooms and a good table. On the other hand if you turn east through Hèry and Rouvray you can reach **Montigny-la-Resle**, where the Soleil d'Or would be a useful base from which to visit both Pontigny and Auxerre at your leisure. This is a *restaurant avec chambres*, and its rooms are in a modern and well planned extension away from the main road.

Not only that, but Montigny has a distinguished and mainly twelfth-century church. The nave and choir, of equal height, are both pure late Romanesque; the nave is extended to north and south by later chapels which have the effect of transepts. The chief interest lies in the choir, which begins with a pair of blind double arcades on either side, with 'nailhead' decoration both outside and inside the mouldings. Then comes a slightly raised sanctuary, cut off at the east end with restored windows of Romanesque pattern. Here again there are two wide arcades on the north side, each enclosing a pair of arches, all displaying the nail motif around the moulding. On the south side is a similarly arched doorway to a Sacristy, and an unusual wavy-topped piscina. A well fed *chouette* looks down from the capital of the first pillar south of the choir, where the abacus repeats the nail pattern.

At **Ligny-le-Châtel**, just east of Pontigny, the church of St Peter and St Paul is a curiosity. The interior of the nave is Romanesque, and the crossing vault is an example of the earliest use of ribs in the Yonne, yet from the outside both north and south fronts have an ornate Renaissance elevation, with absurd false chimneys between the gables of the side chapels.

So finally to **Pontigny** and St Bernard, with whom this chapter began. Pontigny is a place with many English associations. In 1113 the land was offered to Stephen Harding, then abbot of Cîteaux; a year later twelve monks with Hugues de Mâcon at their head were sent to found a monastery on the banks of the river Serein, where the soil was fallow but suitable for cultivation. The new abbey, the second daughter of Cîteaux, stood at the meeting-point of three bishoprics, Auxerre, Sens and Langres, and of three *comtés*, Auxerre, Tonnerre and Champagne – so that it used to be said that the abbot, three bishops and three counts could dine on the bridge at Pontigny without leaving their territories. For the growing community a new church was begun about 1145 with funds supplied by Thibault, count of Champagne. The nave was finished a little more than ten years later, and the original *chevet* (where the work had begun) was replaced by the present one before the end of the century.

Three archbishops of Canterbury found refuge at Pontigny. Thomas à Becket, at the height of his quarrel with Henry II, retired here in 1164, and the fasts and vigils did nothing to modify his intransigence. He remained, a troublesome guest, for four years. Stephen Langton, at loggerheads with King John, stayed here from 1208 to 1213; Edmund Rich spent the last year of his life at Pontigny, and was buried behind the high altar. Rich was afterwards canonized as St Edmé, and his relics are still venerated – witness the *ex voto* tablets in his chapel in the ambulatory.

Although forty-five monasteries had been founded from the abbey, it declined in the sixteenth century. When the Protestants took over Auxerre in 1567 it was invaded and pillaged by Huguenot troops. At the Revolution the conventual buildings were put up for sale and the cloister demolished. By this time only twenty-five monks were left, and all but one took refuge with their families in the neighbourhood. The exception stayed behind to act as *curé* for the parish, while the abbot himself retired to St Florentin. The Société Populaire demanded that the candelabra and the wrought-iron gates before the sanctuary should be melted down; the gates were preserved but the candelabra disappeared. The furnishings were appropriated by other churches in Burgundy and Champagne, and it was not till 1843 that Prosper Mérimée persuaded the State to preserve the buildings.

As we approach down an avenue of limes we encounter again the formidable spirit of St Bernard. Two schools of Burgundian Romanesque building must be carefully distinguished: one is the

Cluniac, derived initially from Lombardy and well established by 1100; the other is Cistercian, taking its name from Cîteaux and developing a style of its own in protest against the Cluniac elaboration. We shall discuss the characteristics of Cluniac Romanesque later in our journey; meanwhile listen to St Bernard's rebuke to his Cluniac brethren:

The faithful are more engaged in admiring the beauty of the statues than in honouring the virtues of the saints . . . The church sparkles on every side, but the poor go hungry. The walls of the church are covered in gold, but its children go naked. And in the cloister, what are these monsters doing – these horrible beauties and beautiful horrors, these disgusting apes, ferocious lions and monstrous centaurs? . . . There you have a head on several bodies, there a body with several heads; there is a quadruped with the tail of a snake, and there another that finishes as a fish; here is a beast that begins like a horse and ends up as a goat; and here a horned animal with a horse's rump. In God's name, if you are not ashamed of these idiocies, why at least are you not sorry to put yourselves to such expense?

Fortunately, we may think, the mediaeval imagination survived even the eloquence of St Bernard, and we can still enjoy these riots of fancy and the technical skill which produced them – though nothing like them was allowed to intrude into the austere harmonies of Pontigny.

The intriguingly simple west front gives little idea of the dimensions you will find inside. In fact they are not fully revealed as you enter the nave, for the long view eastward is interrupted by a heavy wooden eighteenth-century organ buffet. However, the lightness and elegance of the nave are apparent at once, a lightness engendered both by the milky-white Champenois stone and by the clerestory windows, then for the first time made possible by the new development of groined vaulting. The true character and proportions of the church are revealed only when you step aside and follow one of the side aisles towards transept and choir.

It is at this point that the heavenly proportions of Cistercian mathematics assert themselves. Details of column and capital, of arch and vaulting, become irrelevant as the shape of the space and its outlines impose themselves on the eye. This was the effect St Bernard intended, where human stature is dwarfed and man's contributions seem puny. Yet this church like all others was built by practical men whose expertise was at least as great as their inspiration. The massive pillars of the crossing fit unobtrusively into a harmonious design; the slighter columns of the sanctuary are beautifully proportioned for their place in it.

The harmony persists if you turn and look westward down the side aisles from the transept. If you walk on round the big semicircle of the ambulatory you will find no lessening of Cistercian austerity, even though it was built some fifty years later than the nave. The eleven radiating chapels are uniform in their plainness and very nearly in their detail. Some have carved altar fronts, some do not; all originally had a double piscina in exactly the same place on the right-hand wall. We have noted the *ex voto* tablets in St Edmé's chapel, but the English visitor may be more surprised to find at the back of the high altar a placard which confirms that it is the burial place of St Edmund of Canterbury, and gives a summary of his life. What French archbishop can claim such recognition in England?

The only stone statuary allowed in the abbey, dedicated as were all Cistercian foundations to Our Lady, was the familiar one in the south transept of the Virgin enclosing her people within the folds of her cloak. The only exceptions to the plain glass rule are the two later rose windows of the transept, and even they are only faintly tinted with *grisaille*. But St Bernard would never have tolerated the unashamedly exuberant organ screen, or the flighty pairs of angels that decorate the choir stalls.

From the outside there are two contrasting views of the abbey. Seen from the open ground to the south and east the lines of the church are uniform and unadorned. The Cistercian rule forbade a tower, so there is nothing to break them but the high roof of the transept. One affectionate simile has compared this view to a squatting mother hen with her wings outspread to protect her brood of chickens. To the cross-Channel traveller it may look more like a celestial hovercraft stranded in fields far from the sea. That is partly the effect of the flying buttresses which link the east end of the choir to the ambulatory chapels below – not, if you look closely, an even semicircle, but a polygonal outline with angles which are almost imperceptibly obtuse.

To the north and west the view is different. The north front reveals the only remaining range of the cloister – the mediaeval one had given way to a Renaissance design, only to have three sides of it destroyed at the Revolution. A door in the north aisle still gives access to the grounds of the conventual buildings, now transformed into a more worldly scene. In front of the abbot's lodging are green lawns shaded by a copper beech and a cedar of Lebanon; beyond them a path leads to an espaliered fruit garden, where one of the huge shallow washbasins from the cloister is in service as a fountain. A stylish new range of building extends to the north, with more green lawns and flower gardens.

We need to explain how this came about. In the last century what remained of the conventual buildings became the headquarters of the *Société des Pères de St Edmé*. They amounted to the entrance porch, two pavilions and a long hall with a loft above. In 1901 the Fathers were dispersed by anticlerical legislation, and the property was eventually acquired by the philosopher Paul Desjardins. During the 1930s – every summer until 1939 – he lent it and his prestige to the *rencontres*, or 'décades', for which Pontigny became famous. For ten days it was transformed into a lay monastery of contemplatives, where figures from the literary world met to discuss contemporary trends and problems – a dialogue of European minds *avant le déluge*. They read aloud from their plays and poetry, and judging from the personalities it must have involved a great airing of egos and jealousies and not much asceticism. There was André Gide, equivocally charming, Charles du Bos, solemn and sympathetic, Enid Starkie, flashing (as Maurice Bowra put it) 'in all the colours of the Rimbaud', François Mauriac with his hoarse voice, Ernst Robert Curtius, T. S. Eliot, Thomas Mann and many others. To play to them in the evenings was the Rumanian pianist Youra Guller, married to Jacques Schiffrin, publisher of the *Bibliothèque de la Pleïade*.

After the war and the death of Desjardins, the Pères de St Edmé returned to found a Franco-American college in the restored and modernized buildings, which later became the seminary of the *Mission de France*. In the 1980s the grounds and buildings were taken over by the State as a *Centre de Réeducation professionale*, so that in surroundings as privileged as those of an aristocratically owned château the unemployed professional classes learn new trades, and the noticeboards alongside the functional lecture rooms display trades union propaganda. What would St Bernard make of it all?

CHAPTER TWO

The Tonnerrois and Auxerre

This slice of country across a widening Burgundy is cut by the three river valleys of Yonne, Serein and Armançon, leaving wooded uplands in between. The Serein and Armançon are tributary to the queenly Yonne, Armançon the senior of the two, Serein the more demure and delightful.

The natural base for exploring the area is **Chablis**, the famous wine centre built on rising ground above the Serein. Unfortunately there is no longer a strong argument for making a base at l'Étoile, for all the hotel's long and distinguished history. It has changed hands in the last few years, and only the old wine list maintains the standards of the Bergerand family. However, local allegiance has moved to the elegant new Hostellerie des Clos (named after the best known of the *grand cru* vineyards) which has already won its Michelin rosette for M. Vignaud's cuisine. Prices are fairly high – especially for breakfast – but the *vignerons* of Chablis consider they get good value, and the rooms are modern.

In a good year the *grands crus* of Chablis hold up their heads against Meursault and Montrachet, and in any year their qualities are distinctive. These vineyards are the northernmost in France, apart from Champagne, and the smallest area to produce wine of the finest quality anywhere in the world. The plateau on which they stand is 1,500 feet above sea level, and exposed to frost in the early spring. The slopes though are mostly steep, and allow the worst of the frost to run off downhill. The vines are trained on wires that follow the slopes, and among them you will notice various heating devices to counter the threat from frost. The total area of the vineyards has now reached 5,000 acres, but of these only 250 produce a wine of top quality. With an output so restricted and vulnerable, even a good year for the Côte d'Or may be bad for Chablis; there is no wine on the market about whose label and provenance you must be more careful.

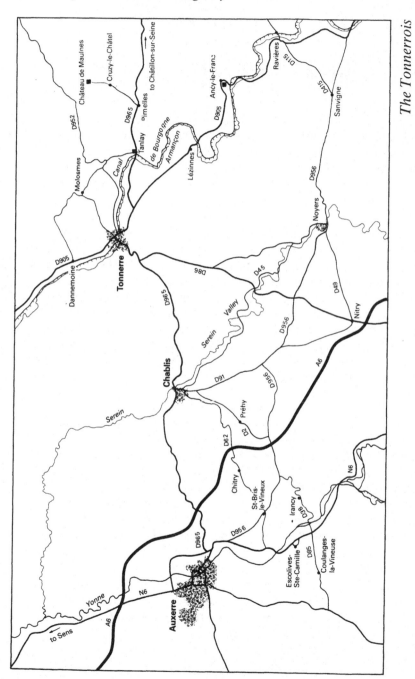

In 1759 the Chanoine Gaudon was writing to Madame d'Espi-
nay: 'My Chablis this year has a fine rich aroma; after it has been
drunk it perfumes and charms the throat and leaves behind it a soft
mushroom fragrance.' Others have compared the taste of the wine
to a *goût de pierre-à-fusil*, though the taste of gunflint must be
imagined rather than experienced. Its qualities derive from soil of
a nature found nowhere else but above Kimmeridge Bay in Dorset. The underlying strata are composed of alternate beds of clay
and marl, with intrusions of greyish marly limestone and grey and
pink shell beds – which contain the fossilized *ostrea virgula* found
also at Kimmeridge. Perhaps only lack of sunshine prevents Dorset winegrowers from rivalling those of Chablis?

In a sense Chablis may claim to be a daughter rather than a
distant cousin of the Côte d'Or, for it was the Cistercians of Pontigny who acquired an extensive vineyard on the terrain and cultivated it with all the experience they brought from their mother
house at Cîteaux. The best vineyards are those immediately surrounding the town; all are planted with the *pinot chardonnay*
grape, known here as the *beaunois*. The wine is classified as
follows: the *grands crus*, producing not more than 2,400 bottles an
acre, with an alcoholic content of 11% or more; the *premier crus*,
producing slightly more with a minimum alcoholic content of
10.5%; then simple chablis with a similar output but a lower
alcoholic content. For *petit chablis*, where it need reach only 9%,
output is not restricted, and any grape may be used so long as it
comes from ungrafted briars. Most chablis requires discreet sugar-
ing, but not enough unduly to soften its dryness. The vineyards are
cooperatively owned and worked by their proprietors.

Chablis is a pleasant town when free from the heavy traffic
moving between Auxerre and Tonnerre. The **Collegial Church of
St-Martin**, begun in 1160, is one of the earliest examples of
Gothic architecture in France, and a replica on a reduced scale of
the cathedral of Sens. The nave has six bays, with clerestory and
side aisles; the ambulatory recalls that of Pontigny without rivalling its proportions. The horseshoes fixed to the Romanesque
south porch are peculiar to churches dedicated to St Martin, the
patron saint of cavaliers; a large bas-relief over the west door
shows him in the familiar gesture of dividing his cloak with the
beggar. There is a legend that Joan of Arc nailed up one of the

horseshoes as she rode through Chablis on her way to Chinon in 1429.

The streets near the church are peaceful to wander in, and in the Place Gambetta you will find a dignified creeper-clad house such as might grace an English provincial town. It seems natural that it should belong to the principal *notaire* of Chablis, though the three brass balls hanging above the door would in England suggest a different *métier*.

Tonnerre, the Roman Tornodurum and chief town of a Gallic *pagus*, lies sixteen kilometres to the east along a well wooded road. Its outstanding monument is the **Hôpital de Notre-Dame-des-Fontenilles**, founded in 1293 by Marguerite de Bourgogne, comtesse de Tonnerre and sister-in-law of Saint Louis. This exceptional woman also carried the title of Queen of Jerusalem, Naples and Sicily, by virtue of her marriage in 1268 to Charles d'Anjou – a marriage which gave her close experience of the extremes of luxury, violence and bloodshed. The kingdom of Jerusalem had been a mere symbolic purchase by the crusading Charles, but his title to the two Sicilies was a dynastic inheritance brought to a violent conclusion. Instigator of the Sicilian Vespers of 1282, when 8,000 of the rebellious population were massacred on Easter Day, he was soon isolated and ousted by the royal house of Aragon, and he died at Foggia in 1285.

His widow had been gently brought up as a girl at the abbey of Fontevraud under the wing of her aunt, Mathilda of Courtenay, who had taken her vows there. Now she returned to her family home near Tonnerre, haunted by the suffering she had seen among ordinary people exposed to war, famine and disease, and she determined to make up for the wrongs she had seen done to the human race. At her own expense this centre for the nursing and treatment of poor invalids was established in Tonnerre, and no sooner was it finished than she built on adjoining land a modest new château for herself so that she could supervise personally everything that went on inside. A passageway connected her private apartments with a raised gallery running all round inside the walls of the hospital.

Not much has changed since the thirteenth century. The huge single chamber, eighty metres long by eighteen and a half wide, is spanned by a magnificent oak *charpente*, tiled above, masked underneath by a barrel-vaulted ceiling made up of thousands of small chestnut slats. It has needed only minor repairs since it was put up. The oak timbers came from the forest of Maulnes; the slats were made of Spanish chestnut because that is the most resistant of all woods to destructive insects, and even spiders keep their distance from it.

It is said that Queen Margaret put more faith in the healthy atmosphere of this light, cool and airy chamber – perhaps even more in the religious comforts provided – than she did in the medical skill of the time. If so, she was probably right. One may be reminded of the Infirmary of the Knights in Rhodes, built with similar dimensions, but that was about two hundred years later, and its aristocratic patients had little in common with the poor creatures who sometimes lay as many as six to a straw pallet in curtained alcoves ranged along the outer walls. The chamber was lit by tall windows in deep embrasures, and freshened by running water carried in a channel down the centre of the floor.

The east end was the chapel, where Mass could be followed or at least heard by all the inhabitants. Above the altar hangs a magnificent fourteenth-century painting of the Virgin and Child, with a tiny figure of Moses below contemplating the 'burning bush'. To the left of the sanctuary is the tombstone of the marquis de Louvois, count of Tonnerre and minister of Louis XIV; he was buried in Paris, but the tombstone was brought there after the Revolution. the seventeenth-century choir stalls are fitted with misericordes, and there is a select row of little box pews on the right for minor dignitaries.

Before the altar was placed the tomb of the patroness when she died in 1308. Her bronze effigy was flanked by two censor-swinging angels; at her feet a lion, to the right the arms of Burgundy, to the left those of Sicily. We speak in the past tense, because the tomb was totally destroyed in the Revolution, to be replaced in 1826 by an unworthy monument. Her biographer Robert Luyt wrote in 1653:

De Reyne de trois royaumes florissants, elle devient servante des pauvres de Jésus-Christ. De ces mêmes mains dont elle avait autrefois maniés les sceptres et les couronnes, elle touche les plaies des pauvres, agence leurs lits, ôte leurs ordures, lave leurs vieux ulcères.

The hospital has survived many dangers. In the winter of 1359-60 Edward III arrived before Tonnerre with an English army and captured it. After drinking 3,000 bottles of Tonnerrois wine, having set fire to the town and church of Notre-Dame, they made off west into the Auxerrois for further plunder. The hospital was spared only because the king had lodged there after the siege. In the fifteenth century the town suffered during the furious war between Burgundians and Armagnacs, and the hospital was reduced to bankruptcy. However, its national importance was underlined when François I received a declaration of war here from the envoy of the emperor Charles V. In 1763 a partition wall was built across the west end to form a raised tribune overlooking the hall, with a separate administrative chamber behind. At the same time the original porch was demolished, leaving the west end as we see it today. The new arrangement suited the new masters of the Revolution, for the local Revolutionary Council met in the back room, while the main hall was the assembly place for the *citoyens* of Tonnerre. Shops were later put up inside to trade in grain and fodder, and it was not until 1812 that the hospital was restored to the foundation. In 1918 it did duty as an arsenal for the American forces, and though it was not directly involved in the last war it suffered badly from ill-directed bombardments which wrecked the church of Notre-Dame a few hundred yards away. Today it is the centrepiece of a busy *Centre Hospitalier* where the auxiliary departments of modern medical care are concentrated in a park-like area adjoining it to the north. Tourist income goes to the *Centre*, and an annual *kermesse* or charity gala is held in the great hall.

The Salle de Conseil, as the revolutionaries called it, is now taken up with an exhibition of relics and manuscripts connected with the Hospital. Among other treasures it has the Papal Bull of 1292 authorizing its building, the Foundation Charter of 1293 and Queen Marguerite's will. A collection of jewellery includes a gold cross said to contain a fragment of the Holy Cross, itself set inside a silver crucifix.

An adjoining room is cleverly and realistically fitted out as the nineteenth-century 'sick room' of the hospital, where the wealthier invalids could be given special care. It has a fine *cheminée*, and kitchen equipment of the period. Other connecting rooms include one which displays rich church plate and vestments and a fourteenth-century stone *pietà*; another reproduces an operating theatre still in use in 1900, and there is a dispensary, where drugs and herbal medicaments are stored in blue and white jars.

Two singularities in the great hall are not to be missed. In a crypt under the sacristy is the earliest and one of the finest examples in France of a **Sepulchre**, or entombment of Christ. It was commissioned in 1454 from Jean-Michiel and Georges de la Sonnette, described in contemporary accounts as 'ymageurs'. Their names appear nowhere else, but they followed Donatello in Italy and Hans Decker at Heidelberg in creating a new art form in the French churches. The clear lines and realism of the carving are like nothing that preceded it, and perhaps they are only matched (in a different medium) at Villeneuve-l'Archevêque.

The other curiosity is a scientific one. In 1785 the hospital administrators were persuaded to allow a Benedictine monk, Dom Camille Férouillat, to construct the mathematical and astronomical device known as a **Gnomon** on the floor of the chamber. This involved cutting narrow grooves in the stone, to be filled with thin iron bars, on the north-south meridian of Tonnerre, so that a spot of sunlight admitted through a small hole in a blind window embrasure still records the daily passage of the sun towards its midday zenith. Local noon arrives when each day the spot of light cuts the meridian line, which it does at different points between the summer and winter solstices. From this an observer could mark the passage of time, months and seasons. Dom Camille's calculations were confirmed by the Academy of Sciences, and on 7 October 1786 the device was inaugurated in the presence of the young Count of Tonnerre. As he was only three at the time, it must have made an impressive beginning to his scientific education. The Gnomon was badly damaged by horses' hooves and cart wheels while the hall was a corn market during the Revolution, and parts of it are still missing.

The **Parish Church of Notre-Dame** is simple, harmonious and dignified, mostly rebuilt after a fire in 1556. It was severely damaged by the bombardment of May 1944, but has now been perfectly restored. The troubled history of the parish comes alive in two tablets on the left-hand wall of the chapel of St Roch in the north aisle. The larger one records the people's gratitude to St Roch for bringing an end to the plagues of 1632-3 in which more than 3,500 died but more than 1,200 were cured – probably thanks to the care they received in Queen Margaret's hospital. A smaller tablet below tells us that the church was 'entièrement brulée' on 8 July 1556, and prescribes an annual procession to remember the disaster. Another tablet in the choir is in memory of the *curé* of the parish who was killed in the early German attacks of 1940.

The imposing collegial **Church of St-Pierre** stands on a rocky terrace above the town. Most of what you see now dates only from the sixteenth and seventeenth centuries, after the same fire which destroyed Notre-Dame in 1556. Survivals from earlier times are the Romanesque south doorway, with St Peter on its *trumeau*, and a restored thirteenth-century apse. The seventeenth century contributed the pulpit and the organ loft. From the terrace outside there is a fine view over the rest of the town, which has other places of intriguing historical interest.

High on the list is the **Hôtel d'Uzés**, a gem of Renaissance architecture, now the Caisse d'Epargne, but in 1728 the birthplace of the eccentric and sexually ambiguous Chevalier d'Éon. Charles Geneviève Louis Auguste César Andrée Timothée d'Éon de Beaumont studied in Paris and was sent to Russia as a secret agent in feminine disguise – to which his physique and certain of his Christian names plausibly lent themselves. His mission to the Empress Elizabeth was so successful that on his return he was appointed secretary to the embassy in London, with the simpler title of the Chevalier d'Éon and a clear declaration that he was a man. Like many another diplomat, he demanded more money for his expenses; when this was refused he resigned from the service, remained in England, and announced that he had now become a woman. He was commonly supposed to be a hermaphrodite, although Versailles remembered him as a keen horseman with beard and moustache. While on a short visit to France he was mockingly dubbed *chevalier* by Marie Antoinette and recommended to try her corsetmaker; the king, hearing that he intended instead to resume his military uniform, imprisoned him for a month in Dijon. This decided him to return to England, where he lodged near Westminster Bridge with an octogenarian friend, Mary Cole. At 65 he was amusing the public by fencing with an old companion in the London squares.

Eventually he returned to France, restored his property on the outskirts of Tonnerre, and -- now apparently a bent old maid --

practised musketry with the neighbours. His appetite was enormous. He was known to have consumed at a single meal an entire chicken, *haricots verts*, *tarte frangipane*, fresh cream and apples, all washed down by the wine of Epineuil. He loved the *bons crus* of the Tonnerrois, and boasted that he had given the diplomatic corps a taste for them. When he died at the age of 82 the doctor declared that he had the perfectly formed body of a man. The Chevalier d'Éon was not a typical Burgundian, but Burgundy can claim him.

Another of the curiosities of Tonnerre is the **Fosse Dionne**, which can be reached by following a steep path down to the houses on the far side of the hill of St-Pierre. This is a huge clasically designed stone basin, fifteen metres in diameter, fed by water from a spring which was the only source of water supply in Gallo-Roman times. Coloured a bluish green by algae, it issues from a hollow in the rock above and falls out through a conduit to the town below.

Just north of Tonnerre on the main road to St Florentin is an interesting church at **Dannemoine**, with a late thirteenth-century statue of St Roch, a saint so popular in Burgundy that his legend is worth recalling. Born in Montpellier about 1356, he gave all his money to the poor and went on a pilgrimage to Rome, where he stayed for three years. Finding the town of Acquapendente in the Apennines ravaged by plague, he comforted the sick and cured many of them by making the sign of the Cross over their diseased limbs. At Piacenza he was warned by an angel that he too would soon be stricken; when this happened he withdrew to the solitude of a forest. An angel applied balm to the ulcer on his groin, a spring was provided to quench his thirst, and every day a dog belonging to a local lord brought him a loaf from his master's table. Rocco, as the Italians knew him, was eventually cured, but was badly disfigured and thrown into prison as a spy. Here, at the age of twenty-seven, he was found dead by his jailer, radiating a supernatural light. It was only in the fifteenth century, when Florence was threatened by an outbreak of plague, that his cult became widespread, though it subsided when the danger was over. He was canonized by Urban VIII in the seventeenth century, and two hundred years later the Burgundians invoked him against the outbreak of phylloxera. You can recognize him in his statues by the pilgrim's cape, staff, gourd and scrip, and by the ulcer decorously placed not in his groin but on his thigh. He is sometimes shown in company with the angel who dressed his sores and the dog who brought him bread.

Following the D965 due east fron Tonnerre you come upon **Tanlay**, one of the most celebrated and beautiful châteaux in Burgundy. In 1533 Louise de Montmorency, mother of Admiral Gaspard de Coligny, the Protestant leader assassinated in 1572, inherited the property from Edmond de Courcelles on behalf of her fourth son, François d'Andelot, who was still a minor. It was then a partly ruined mediaeval fortress, but on coming of age in 1547 François set about restoring it and converting it to a *château de plaisance*. The work was held up by his military career, but by the time of his death in 1569 he had largely restored the Grand Château and made a start on an elaborate gatehouse he called the Petit Château. During the wars of religion it was a favourite rendezvous for the Protestant faction to which his family belonged.

In 1574 Anne de Coligny, daughter of François d'Andelot, married Jacques Chabot, Lieutenant-Governor of Burgundy, who finished the upper part of the Petit Château and built the stables. In 1642 Tanlay was bought by Michel Particelli d'Hémery, superintendent of the royal exchequer and a very rich man. He employed the architect Pierre le Muet to redesign the Grand Château, organized the water supply to the moat, and put in hand a programme of subsidiary building. In 1704 Tanlay was sold to Jehan Thévenin, Royal Counsellor and Governor of Saint-Denis, who was created marquis de Tanlay by Louis XIV. It has remained in the same family ever since.

Approaching from the east you pass through the admission point in the Petit Château into the Cour Verte, so called for its well tended grass. On your right are the stables, an elegant formal quadrilateral enclosing more wide green lawns. You cross the bridge over the moat between a pair of sentry boxes crowned by obelisks, and find yourself in front of the Grand Château. The *cour d'honneur* is another imposing quadrilateral, with the arcaded wings joined to the central part by two domed turrets. Round towers stand at each angle of the *cour*, two of them capped by hemispherical domes.

A tour of the inside is a pleasure. The chief rooms, *salon sur cour*, *salon de compagnie*, *salle à manger*, are pleasantly welcoming, and the guide is intelligently informative. The family care very much for their ancestral home, come often to live here, and are slowly restoring it where necessary, room by room. Décor and furniture suit the rooms admirably, and there is some good painting by minor artists. Several recent royal visits are commemorated by signed photographs in the *salon sur cour*: there is our Queen Elizabeth II, the King and Queen of Sweden, Queen Juliana and Prince Bernhard of the Netherlands, and the Japanese Crown Prince. They must all have enjoyed their visits, and there were special reasons for two of them. The King of Sweden was honouring a Thévenin who had been ambassador in Stockholm, while Queen Juliana came as a descendant of Louise de Coligny, daughter of the Admiral and wife of William of Orange; she was on her way to visit the former principality of Orange-Nassau in Provence.

Among other treasures in the *salon de compagnie* is a piano by Pleyel and a delightful escritoire doubling as a *priedieu* . As in so many French châteaux you are shown a portrait of Madame de Sévigné – here with the nice description 'qui écrit beaucoup de lettres'. A more formal note is struck by the long gallery where statues in niches, trophies in apparent bas-relief and neoclassical conversation pieces on the vaulted ceiling all turn out to be executed in *trompe l'œil* by the Italian artists introduced by Particelli d'Hémery in 1645.

Another remarkable piece of decoration is to be seen in the upper room of the **Tour de la Ligue**, reached by a spiral staircase in the north-west corner tower. This circular neoclassical chamber is crowned by a cupola in which artists of the school of Fontainebleau have painted a ring of figures ostensibly representing the gods and goddesses of Olympus. In fact they are full-length portraits of the sixteenth-century court of Henri II, delineated with a wit which must have delighted contemporary visitors. They are divided into two groups by the figure of Henry of Navarre, the future Henri IV, presented as Janus. Of his two heads one looks right to the Catholics, the other left to the Protestants of the court. Among some brilliant portraits we find Admiral Coligny as Neptune, his brother François as Hercules, and the Cardinal of Lorraine as a dashing Mercury. Of Catherine de'Medici as Juno (with peacock) we are allowed only a backside view, but full justice is done to the beauty of face and body of Diane de Poitiers.

Through the forbiddingly classical **Vestibule des Césars** one emerges in front of le Muet's masterpiece, the north façade. Up to the end of the eighteenth century it overlooked a *parterre* in the

French manner, but then to conform with the fashion of the time the garden was converted to blend with the trees and the distance, as a *parc à l'anglais*. It is pleasant to record that the family is as well regarded today as it was at the time of the Revolution, when no move was made locally to disturb them or their home.

In the heart of the forest land to the north of Cruzy-le-Châtel is one of the strangest buildings in Burgundy. This is the **Château of Maulnes**, built between 1562 and 1570 by the duc d'Uzés as a hunting lodge. You could mistake it for the keep of a mediaeval castle, standing on high ground with a fortified north entrance and lofty machicolated walls – though its four prominent chimneys and Renaissance windows give the lie to that idea. It turns out to be a rare pentagonal domestic château, and its other features are just as unusual. If you study the machicolations carefully you will see that in between are carved the heads of long-eared hounds – basset-hounds, perhaps – making a frieze along the obtusely angled walls to left and right of the entrance.

In the centre of the southern and longest of the five fronts a rectangular pool extends under the building, fed by a hidden spring. A classical conceit, with a niche in the back wall for a statue, it can be reached from inside the château by doors on either side. A few years ago excavations had revealed a second pool further out from the façade, and walls to east and west which enclosed a garden *parterre*. They have now been abandoned, and the ground to the south is overgrown with brambles. The château itself has been uninhabited for many years, and the whole property seems to have been abandoned to its fate.

Even sadder is the present state of the stables and kennels, which once occupied an unusual semi-circular block of tiled outbuildings, connected by a gallery with the château. Their elegant round-arched entrances have mostly fallen in, and wild shrubs and tree roots have undermined the walls. This culpable neglect has all but destroyed one of Burgundy's most unusual architectural designs, but we can still just imagine the life spent here in their leisure retreat by the dukes and their successors. On either side the forests of Maulnes and Cruzy look as if they still harbour plenty of deer – and even perhaps a *sanglier* or two.

The architect of this unusual ensemble is believed to have been Sebastien Serlio, designer of the nearby château of **Ancy-le-Franc**.

You will find this famous place – next to Tanlay perhaps the best-known in northern Burgundy – fifteen kilometres south-east from Tonnerre on the inside of a loop in the D905, where the Armançon runs close beside the Canal de Bourgogne. From the outside you see another handsome foursquare building with Renaissance façades enclosing the *cour d'honneur*; behind the façades it is very different from its neighbour at Tanlay, and the reason lies in the history of its building and interior decoration.

It was built by Antoine de Clermont, count of Tonnerre, brother-in-law of Diane de Poitiers, in 1546-7. The architect was Sebastien Serlio, an Italian who had been summoned to the court of François I, and it was his Italian influence which produced the Corinthian pilasters of the principal façade. The interior decoration was entrusted to another Italian, Francesco Primaticio, known in France as Le Primatice. Painter, sculptor and architect, he was appointed superintendent of royal buildings in 1559. Later work inside is attributed to Nicolo dell'Abate, who arrived in France in 1552. In 1683 the domain was bought by the marquis de Louvois, a minister of the crown, and it remained in his family until the middle of the nineteenth century, when it was bought back by a descendant of the house of Clermont-Tonnerre, whose ancestors had entertained three kings at Ancy-le-Franc – Henri IV in 1592, Louis XIII in 1630 and Louis XIV in 1674. With the last-named had come the marquis de Louvois, who was sufficiently impressed to buy it nine years later. As we have come to expect in Burgundy, there is a room on the first floor where Madame de Sévigné wrote some of her letters. In 1986 Ancy was bought by a distinguished civil servant, M. de Menton, who has plans – already in hand – to present musical and operatic events in the *cour d'honneur*. This will take advantage of the best feature of the château, Serlio's classical façades.

The tone of the interior was set by Primaticio, and it exemplifies some of the extremes to which Italian artists went between the seventeenth and nineteenth centuries. Ostentatious gilded ceilings and pictorial panelling on a monumental scale give the eye little rest. The **Gallery of Sacrifices** displays a variety of animals being slaughtered on classical altars; the **Hall of the Roman Emperors** lives up to its name; the **Room of Judith** tells the unedifying story of Judith and Holofernes, in which Diane de Poitiers is cast as the heroine, François I as Nebuchadnezzar's general. A curious feature in this room is the crow painted above a statue of Anet de Clermont, who like many Frenchmen of the time bought himself a Knighthood of Malta in the seventeenth century. The crow recalls the custom by which the knights offered such a bird to the king of France. The room where Louis XIV slept was converted to a family living room by the last marquis de Louvois in 1824; decorated in blue and gold, it makes play with the family coat of arms and its motto *melius frangi quam flecti*. The walls of the **Chamber of Arts** are covered with fleshy figures in oval medallions who stand for such concepts as Rhetoric, Grammar, Logic, Geometry, Astronomy, Arithmetic and Music.

This overpowering Italian influence is softened by two smaller rooms where French artists were at work. The **Room of the Faithful Shepherd** (*Pastor Fido*) was the favourite of Madame de Sévigné, and you can see why. The eleven charming paintings on a pastoral theme are by Philippe Quantin of Dijon, who died in 1636. A tiny bedroom called the **Room of Flowers** has its bed in an alcove and its panelling covered with posies and individual stems of forty-six varieties of wild and garden flowers; this too is a French contribution. Some dignity is to be found in the **Library**, redecorated in the nineteenth century to house the 1,800 volumes belonging to Anne-Antoine de Clermont, who was Cardinal of Toulouse in 1825.

The kitchens with their nineteenth-century equipment, and one or two other rooms on the ground floor of no great interest, can be seen without a guide before the official visit begins. The stables are being used as an automobile museum.

A quiet route back to Auxerre passes through **Noyers**, another pleasant place to stay when exploring the neighbourhood. Cradled in a bend of the Serein, with a gateway at either end and half-timbered houses overhanging the cobbled streets, the little mediaeval town has a charm which attracts many tourists. On the corner of the Place de la Petite Étape aux Vins an extravagantly mediaeval building is still the formal meeting place for the *marchands des vins*. Other street names breathe of the past: off the Place du Marché au Blé is the rue de Jeu-de-Paume, and there was indeed a royal tennis court there in the sixteenth century.

The handsome **Church of Notre-Dame** dates from the early years of that century. Founded in 1491, it was dedicated in 1515, and both the strongly turreted tower and the double west entrance have flamboyant elements. The nave is tall, and the choir matches it with its high lancet windows. The polished pews are nicely topped with little balusters, and the atmosphere is one of a well loved parish church.

You can return to Chablis by a quiet winding road, the D45, which follows the course of the delicious river Serein all the way. If you are bound for Auxerre you can follow a more southerly route which takes in a little-known but important wine-growing area. After crossing the A6 autoroute your D956 forks right to **St-Bris-le-Vineux**. This is lovely country, especially in spring, with cowslips and wild orchids flowering at the roadside, and the little town of St-Bris is set among cherry orchards. The name is a corruption of St Prix, who was martyred in the Puisaye in the third century. A fellow Christian called St Cot survived the massacre and buried St Prix's head in an adjoining village. St Germain of Auxerre found it beside the body of St Cot, and built a church at St Bris dedicated to them both. The affix 'le Vineux' was earned by the local vineyards. The best wine here is a gentle fruity white made from the Sauvignon grape – quite a contrast if you have been sampling the Chardonnay wines of Chablis.

The church has come a long way from the days of St Germain. It stands high, with arched flying buttresses, false chimneys and Renaissance windows, and there is an elaborate Lady Chapel. The originally Romanesque west doorway was altered to accommodate flamboyant designs of the fifteenth century. Inside, the sixteenth-century pulpit has seven facets, each with two panels, on which birds, grapes, snails, ears of corn, a fence, a stream, a wild boar and a dog catching a rabbit are fluently represented. The glass in the windows is all of the later sixteenth century.

A richly carved Renaissance archway leads down a slope to the open space in front of the former Hôtel-de-Ville, now the school . This is an unusually fine building for such a use, and could have been a private château before the Revolution. Across the road outside the east end of the church are the offices and cellars of M. Louis Bersan *et fils*, the leading wine merchants of St-Bris. The cellars are extraordinary. The two principal ones run side by side, with barrel-vaulted ceilings; beyond them are seemingly endless ramifications of smaller chambers with mouldering fungus-infested walls and racks of unidentifiable cobwebbed bottles. The proprietors – who are glad to show them to visitors – say they were in use in the twelfth century. Indeed you would hardly quarrel with a theory that they began as early Christian catacombs.

Just south of St-Bris is **Irancy**, noted in the district for its red wine. You will rarely find it on a list outside the region, but like other regional wines it maintains a high standard, and in a good year it reaches even higher. Irancy also has a fine thirteenth-century church, of which the nave has been well restored. It is normally kept shut, as so many French churches are nowadays in the face of widespread theft and vandalism, but the key can be found at a house nearby.

The vineyards of lower Burgundy (the epithet refers to the flow of the rivers rather than to a north-south aspect) form an enclave of unusual character. Decimated by phylloxera in 1875-85, they lacked the resources to replant on the scale possible in the Côte d'Or. However, the area under vines has gradually increased again, and the traditional skill of the *vignerons* makes good use of the same compact clay and calciferous soil. The wines produced are best described as *petit bourgogne*, and though not as long-lasting they share many characteristics with their famous cousins of the Côte d'Or. Their modest prices make them doubly attractive.

Across the Yonne from Irancy is **Coulanges-la-Vineuse**, whose name announces more vineyards with an increasing reputation. In the nineteenth century a local *vigneron* was accused of fortifying the rich local wine with alcohol when he tried to sell it in Paris, and was only believed when he added to it a third quantity of water. He returned with an order for two barrels. From Coulanges you can regain the N6 leading north into Auxerre either directly on the D85 or by minor roads which pass through or near to the village of **Escolives-Ste-Camille**. In either case nobody interested in the history, architecture or wines of Burgundy should fail to visit it. The twelfth-century church was built to house the relics of St Camille, one of the three saintly women who escorted the body of StGermain home from Ravenna in 448. The exterior is striking, with a tall octagonal tower capped by a slender brick-tiled steeple, and a wide arcaded Romanesque porch across the western entrance. A door on the right at the end of the nave leads down to a crypt (light switch on the left at the head of the steps) where the saint's relics are preserved behind a locked wooden door. The crypt itself has been authentically restored, with its six pillars and its lancet windows in the apse. On a marble slab below the altar is carved the early Christian *chi-rho* symbol, with an alpha and an omega to left and right. At the foot of the steps you will see a large stone slab fitted with ring bolts; this gives access to a lower crypt, where in times of trouble the church's treasures – and probably the holy relics – were concealed.

The key to the church is kept by M. Gérard Borgnat, a *vigneron* whose offices and cellars occupy what is left of a mediaeval château about a hundred yards down the road beyond the church. He knows the history of the neighbourhood well, and is proud of belonging to the third generation to carry on the wine business from the château formerly owned by the seigneurs of Coulanges. Like M. Bersan at St-Bris he has a twelfth-century cellar, and with justification he believes it to be the longest in Burgundy. The steps down to it are grooved in the middle to hold the rope with which the barrels were brought up or down. Cellar and premises are beautifully kept, and the wine he sells from his small vineyard is an authentic *petit bourgogne* similar to that of Coulanges-la-Vineuse.

Between the village and the church, on the way to join the N6, is the rue Raymond Kapps, named after the man who in 1955 discovered the site of a Gallo-Roman temple of the second century, with some decorative carving of vines which shows how ancient the viniculture of the region is. Kapps died in 1984, but left behind an illustrated book on the subject published in Dijon. The site lies behind a green fence – no. 9 in the rue Raymond Kapps.

2

Auxerre – pronounced Ausserre by Burgundians – was the Roman Antissiodurum, where the suffix *durum* indicates a fortified town. A bishopric from the late third century, by 561 it had seven chapels or churches within its walls. The most celebrated of its early bishops was St Germain. Probably a native of Auxerre, he was born in 378, and after education locally and in Rome he became the fifth historically identified occupant of the see. During his eighteen years of office he evangelized much of Roman Gaul and prepared St Patrick for his mission to Ireland (432-461).

In 448 St Germain visited Ravenna, where he was taken ill and died on 30 July. The Empress Galla Placidia saw to it that his last wish was observed, by sending his body back to rest in Auxerre. On the journey it was escorted by three women of the Roman church, Saints Camille, Magnance and Pallaye, all of whom are commemorated in churches of lower Burgundy. On 1 October he was laid to rest in a small oratory he had built himself, and thereafter Auxerre was an important and prosperous centre of pilgrimage. As Pierre Grognet wrote in the sixteenth century:

> Tu as bon vin, bonne eau, bon pain,
> Aussi tu as le corps de Saint Germain.

Auxerre became a *comté* under Charlemagne, and quickly grew in size and importance. The twelfth-century fortifications were destroyed in the eighteenth and nineteenth centuries, and replaced by boulevards. Under the *ancien régime* the Corporation of Mariners had their headquarters at Auxerre, and a statue of St Nicholas stands at the foot of the hill overlooking the river whose traffic he is expected to protect.

In 1793 the city witnessed a bizarre ceremony when Robespierre commanded that the Feast of Reason should be celebrated in the cathedral. The statues of St Stephen and other saints were removed, and the Fathers of the Church over the doorways were decapitated. The Goddess of Liberty, a certain Marie-Marguerite Duthé, was enthroned and led into the Jardins de l'Arquebuse, where three mannequins representing Despotism, Fanaticism and Federalism were propelled towards her and set on fire. She pushed them back into a brazier – they were only made of willow – while the cannon proclaimed her triumph. Mlle Duthé later married and became the concierge of the local prison.

Viewed from across the river to the east the **Cathedral of St-Etienne** rises imperiously clear of the surrounding buildings, with its high Gothic chevet and ring of rose windows in the clerestory. There was a sanctuary built on this site about 400 by St Amâtre, and embellished during the following centuries, but it was entirely destroyed in 1023. Hugues of Chalon then undertook the construction of a Romanesque church, of which only the crypt remains. In 1215 Bishop Guillaume de Seignelay, captivated by the Gothic fashion spreading south from the Île de France, began to rebuild it from top to bottom. He gave nearly a thousand *livres* of his own money for the work, and his successor Henri de Ville-neuve left an equal sum and donated the glass for the windows. In 1217 the south tower collapsed on the Sunday before Advent, in spite of warnings from a mason's apprentice, and was never re-built. By 1234 the apse was completed, though parts of it had to be rebuilt or restored at the end of the century. By 1400 the choir, nave, aisles and side chapels were finished, and by 1520 the cathe-dral stood as it does today.

Over the central doorway of the flamboyant west façade Christ is enthroned between the Virgin and St John, and on either side of the doorway the wise and foolish virgins are seen, with their lamps held respectively upright or upside down. The rest of the sculpture here lacks originality, and it has been badly mutilated – especially at the time of the Revolution.

The interior is important in the early development of the Gothic style in Burgundy. The influence of Chartres and the Île de France is marked, particularly in the use of piers flanked by four half-columns, in the rosette windows of the clerestory, and in the struts between the upper and lower flying buttresses. Contemporar-ies described the church as *structura clarior*, in contrast to the older buildings of the region. Since then its architecture has been rightly described as diaphanous, an outstanding example of the *rayonnant* style which was developed in Burgundy from the middle of the thirteenth century. One aspect of this is that where a support is apparently essential to the part supported the true function of the support is not always what it seems. An example of this illusion is provided by the slender isolated columns in front of the apsidal chapel. Each column supports four ribs, but the vaulting only seems to depart from the impost; in fact the thrust of the component arches meets well above it, so that, as one authority has it: 'The balancing, as it were, of the four different arches on the small summit of a slender column is striking evidence of the architect's inventiveness and of his ability to maintain the illusion of weightlessness.' Similarly the tall thin columns of the triforium are reinforced on the rear side by longitudinal arches, cleverly concealed from view.

These are subtleties which may not be immediately obvious. Among the features which will strike the visitor at first entry are the multiple shafts of the crossing pillars, which rise without a break from floor to vaulting. The impression of lightness given by the rows of slender half columns on each face reminds one of the fluting on classical pillars, designed to give the same effect. The glass in the windows round the ambulatory, predominantly in reds and blues, is all of the thirteenth century; it has a jewelled brilliance that you meet nowhere else in Burgundy but at Sens. The two shallow transepts mark a change to the flamboyant idiom, and there are rose windows to north and south. As you look back, the huge rose window at the west end seems to radiate tongues of fire from its centre.

The first chapel on the south side of the nave is dedicated to St Germain. It contains a reliquary for bones, and a modern statue in wood of excellent workmanship. A plaque on the wall records the thanks of the townspeople to St Germain for protecting Auxerre on 24 August 1944 – and indeed they were luckier than some.

If you prefer the severity of the Romanesque to the subtleties of Gothic architecture, the **Crypt of St Etienne** will satisfy you. There is nothing finer of its kind in the province. What you see is a complete underground church, with a nave and two side aisles. The sturdy pillars support the groined vaulting in a display of the strength necessary when you consider the weight of the church above. Between nave and apse is a curious central pillar, ringed by three collarets below the capital. Through the arch you reach the barrel-vaulted apse, with frescos on both the vaulting and the half dome. On the vaulting a blond Christ attended by four mounted angels is riding a white horse towards the east; there in the half dome we see him seated in majesty, with seven stars, seven candelabra and the symbols of the four evangelists. These remarkable paintings are all that remain of the set commissioned by Bishop Humbaud (1087-1114) to cover the entire cathedral and crypt. The scene on the vaulting is said to be unique.

The most important things in the **Treasury** (to see it, ring the bell by the door at the head of the south aisle and wait hopefully) are the manuscripts and early printed books. Here you find a thirteenth-century illuminated Bible on parchment, rebound in the fifteenth century; a thirteenth-century missal of Etienne Becquard;

the earliest printed Book of Hours (1488) executed for Geoffroy de Manref, and another printed in Paris in 1520; notable too are the first and second books of the *Sentences* of Peter Lombard. Entry tickets to the Treasury will also admit you to the Crypt, which it is possible to visit without a guide.

After leaving the cathedral of St-Etienne it is a walk of only a hundred yards or so along the rue Cochois to the **Abbey of St-Germain**. In the sixth century Queen Clothilde, who had converted her husband Clovis to Christianity, replaced St Germain's oratory with a larger basilica and founded a community of monks to watch over his tomb and organize the increasing number of pilgrims. In the ninth century some important additions were made by count Conrad, an uncle of Charles le Chauve who had become lay abbot of St-Germain. These included a narthex at the west end of the church, but more significant was a complex and ingenious extension below ground of the sixth-century oratory, or *confessio*, of St Clothilde.

Above ground the abbatial church was to have a disturbed life. An enlarged Romanesque building of the eleventh and twelfth centuries had to be completely rebuilt, the work beginning in 1277 under the abbot Jean de Joceval; it was completed in the second half of the fourteenth century with the encouragement of Pope Urban V. This church lasted until 1811, when the three western bays of the nave were pulled down by Napoleon, to be replaced by a neo-Gothic façade in 1817. Since then the western tower has stood on its own, sole survivor of the Romanesque period.

The Gothic choir and apse remain, high, cool and elegant, another example of the *rayonnant* techniques widespread by the end of the thirteenth century. However, the chief interest for the visitor is again below ground level, in the **Carolingian crypt**. Only guided visits can be made, at half-hourly intervals during the summer months, hourly at other times. Guides are informative, but not always easy to follow, so it may help to trace the route they usually follow through this ancient, complicated and numinous place.

Entrance from the church above is by a stairway in the south ambulatory. You descend into a chamber whose vaulting springs from a single Carolingian pillar; off this opens the chapel of St Laurent, with the remains of an early fresco of the Adoration of the

Magi. Following the ambulatory round to the east you see first the ninth-century fresco portraits of two contemporary bishops, then the sarcophagus of Bishop Betton, who died in 918; at this point one enters the Carolingian passage which leads eastward to the axial chapel, or rotunda, built like the church above in the thirteenth century. Ten radial ribs support the vaulting, and the design is mirrored in another chapel immediately below – crypt upon crypt.

Returning to the main ambulatory we see a grille in the stone floor over a vault seemingly littered with sarcophagi. This was the chosen burial place for a number of fifth and sixth-century bishops of Auxerre whose last wish was to be buried close to their patron saint. Finally at the west end of the northern ambulatory we come to the three oldest religious wall-paintings in France. They portray vividly the martyrdom of St Stephen – his arrest, trial before the Sanhedrin, and on the right-hand wall the scene of his stoning. In a dramatic intervention the hand of God parts the clouds to give courage and hope to the dying man. We know that the whole of the ninth-century wall space was covered with contemporary frescos; the few surviving examples may give a faint idea of their effect – lit as they would have been only by the flickering of candles or torches.

A few steps on the left lead down into the most ancient and hallowed part of this extraordinary place. The tomb chamber made for St Germain in the sixth century was surrounded in the ninth by the thick walls of this tiny underground vaulted church. The low barrel vaulting of its nave and side aisles is supported by two pairs of Gallo-Roman pillars with Carolingian capitals. Heavy oak beams supply an architrave on either side, and if we reflect that they have never been moved or replaced for over a thousand years we may find our ideas of time and age expanding. This tiny church, or *confessio*, has been closed to the public to preserve it from damage. Make sure your guide allows you to look through an opening at the top of the steps, from which you can see this extraordinary and moving survival. The tomb itself (temporarily emptied during the Norman invasions so that the saint's bones could be hidden in the vault below) was afterwards moved to the west end, where it stands today behind a grille. Eastward from here there is a unique sequence of building from the ninth to the thirteenth century, concentrated in a remarkably small compass. Some of what you have seen may be hard to believe in retrospect.

Important restoration work has been done, and is still continuing, on what remains of other parts of the abbey. You can now enjoy the fine Romanesque arches leading to the Chapter House, and the whole of the Renaissance cloister can be seen again. The monks' cellar and work room have been revealed, and the *dortoir* has been adapted as a museum. In it you can see what may have been the oldest object of all to come to light in the crypt. This is a stone slab hollowed out to leave in relief the Christian *chi-rho* symbol; it is believed to have formed the frontal of the fifth-century altar beneath which St Germain's body was first entombed.

In a city of such importance and character there is inevitably more to be seen than can be accomplished in a day. One of the busiest central streets runs through a wide archway which forms part of the **Tour d'Horloge**, a striking feature on the site of the principal gateway to the Gallo-Roman town, and once part of the mediaeval walls. The tower itself stands to one side, and it takes its name from the elaborate gilded clock-faces added in the seventeenth century on either side of the arch. One face registers the position of the sun and moon during the day, the other the hours.

As at Tonnerre it would be rash to explore further by car, especially as there are ample car parks on either side of the rue d'Horloge, as well as at the west end of the cathedral. But Auxerre is fortunate in its churches, and it would be a pity not to make your way through the narrow streets as far as the collegial (now the parish) **Church of St-Eusèbe**. Its remarkable twelfth-century tower rises in three storeys, the first square, the second and third octagonal, and is capped by a spire with flamboyant dormer openings. The wooden figures of St Eusèbe and St Laurent on the west door are dated 1633. Inside, one is struck by the height of the vaulting over the choir. It rises higher than the earlier nave, where the sturdy well-proportioned elevation of the triforium reminds one of Sens. The sixteenth-century Lady Chapel has a central pillar to support the gracefully radiating ribs of the vaulting, and the richly coloured glass there and in the windows on either side of the ambulatory are of the same period.

The greatest treasure in the church is the reputed *suaire*, or shroud, of St Germain. This is a piece of silk cloth, woven in a Byzantine workshop in the ninth century, a lovely design of eagles and roses in blue and gold. It was said to have been presented by the Emperor to Charles the Bald to enwrap the relics of St Germain when they were translated to the abbey crypt in 859. The piece which survives measures only 1.60 metres by 1.20, but a good deal of it must have been snipped away by relic-hungry pilgrims. This precious piece of cloth is kept in a locked cupboard in the chapel of St Germain off the south aisle. A photograph is displayed outside, but though it shows the delicacy of the design it gives no idea of the colouring. The key of the cupboard is kept at the Presbytery close by, but you may not be lucky enough to find anyone there to open it. Failing that, some of the Byzantine silks we saw in the Treasury at Sens may give the best idea of its quality.

A short walk north-west from St Eusèbe brings you to the **Musée-Leblanc-Duvernoy**, just beyond the Place Louis Bart and at the end of a garden fronting on to the rue d'Egléry. This is a privately owned eighteenth-century mansion on several floors, and the museum's speciality is a unique collection of faience and other glazed pottery of the region; one roomful commemorates the first Montgolfier balloon ascent of 1783. Other tastes may prefer the room specially designed to display a superb sequence of Beauvais tapestries depicting the travels of a Chinese emperor through a fairy-tale countryside – a style and technique which remind one of the Don Quixote panels in the Musée des Tapisseries at Aix-en-Provence. The present owner takes a pride in the house and its contents, and she invites you to write your name in the visitors' book.

The nearby bridge, the **Pont Paul Bert**, is named after a citizen of the town who lived from 1833 to 1886. To add to a career in local and national politics he became Professor of Zoology at the universities of Bordeaux and the Sorbonne. He made a study of viruses and the effects of opium, and debated hotly with Victor Hugo on the subject of vivisection, a practice which the practical professor favoured. Dubbed a scoundrel by Hugo, Bert replied 'If I am a scoundrel, it is because I am too good. How would you have discovered a cure for whooping cough, if you had not practised vivisection?' However, he opposed capital punishment for humans, and towards the end of his life went to Indo-China on a mission of peace, and died at Hanoi.

Auxerre is an excellent starting-point for a holiday on the rivers and canals of Burgundy, with access not only to the parent river

Yonne but to the navigable canals which cross some of its peaceful countryside. From Auxerre you can sail north down the Yonne to Joigny and Sens, or turn eastward near Migennes to join the Canal de Bourgogne on its cross-country journey past St Florentin, Tonnerre and Montbard to St-Jean-de-Losne. There it meets the river Saône not far from its junction with the Canal du Centre. Alternatively you can go south along the Canal du Nivernais to Decize, and join the Canal Lateral à la Loire and the Canal de Briare. Small Broads-style motor cruisers are available in large numbers, or there are more comfortable converted barges which take parties of up to twelve on charter, or just for day trips.

We shall meet the Yonne again higher up on its course, but we can already appreciate what Marie Nol (1883-1969) wrote of it (as she might have written of most rivers):

> La rivière qui n'est jamais finie,
> Qui passe et ne reviendra jamais.

CHAPTER THREE

The Puisaye

Striking westward from Auxerre you soon notice a change in the landscape. Instead of the wide river valleys, rolling arable land and wooded hills of the Auxerrois, you find yourself at first among clusters of small villages and pastures bounded by hedges – farm land on a domestic scale which might recall Somerset. Beyond Toucy the horizon widens, the woodland thickens, and the land gradually falls away to a network of little rivers and lakes which announce the nearness of the Loire valley to the western frontier of Burgundy. Rivers abound – Loing, Vrin, Ouanne, Branlin, Orcière, Agriou and Bourdon are just a few – though none of them has the charm or the importance of the Yonne.

This is the **Puisaye**, a word probably of Celtic origin said to be a corruption of *poël* (lake, swamp or pool) and *say* (forest). Colette, who was born at St-Sauveur-en-Puisaye, described it as a poor district 'principally exploited by the charcoal-burners, expert at constructing the fine ricks where a vertical thread of blue smoke went up from each dome, secretly lit, in the damp mornings'. Today it is still one of the most secret countrysides in France.

Although several expeditions would be needed to cover the region properly, one might begin towards the north-west, where the D89 leads from Auxerre to Aillant-sur-Tholon. Just beyond Aillant is **Villiers-sur-Tholon**, where the dignified church of St John has a flamboyant south porch (shamefully mutilated) which sports a turret and a low arcaded gallery with fluted pilasters. Inside are some good modern choir stalls, and in the chapel south of the nave is a charmingly framed classical tablet to the 'vivante femme' of Abel Cormon, Avocat in Parliament, who died on 28 May 1665, aged 48. Somehow this brief inscription brings both characters to life.

Eight kilometres further west is **la Ferté-Loupière**, which has a church with some exceptional features, difficult to date as a whole. The nave vaulting is concealed by a *berceau* ceiling made up of wooden slats and strengthened by tie beams. Wide low arches separate the nave from the side aisles, which must have been added a good deal later, for they incorporate buttresses to support the nave walls. There are timber frames for the crossing roof, and a curious spiral stairway leads to a tower above the north transept.

The unique feature of the church is a fifteenth-century wall painting of a *danse macabre* on the north wall of the nave. A fantastic procession of children, citizens, an emperor, a king, a cardinal, a papal legate, an archbishop, a hermit, a constable, a lady of fashion and a baby snatched from its cradle are all marshalled to whatever awaits them in eternity by walking skeletons of the dead. To help them on their way the skeletons are playing musical instruments.

Taking the main road south to Toucy, you may like to turn aside for two utterly contrasting views of Burgundy life. In the valley of the Ouanne the village of **Grandchamp** has an immaculately kept *château de plaisance* built with brick and stucco in a strange mixture of neo-Renaissance and nineteenth-century mediaeval styles. There is an imitation portcullis, and the pepper-pot turrets of the gateway have had circular brick-framed windows disconcertingly inserted in their spires. There are long rows of stable buildings on each side of the drive, and the château is surrounded by a moat fed from the waters of the Ouanne. I am sure they live well there.

This is one way to live in the country. Another can be found down a nearby lane off the road to Toucy – the little seventeenth-century *manoir* of **le Bréau**. Adjoining pleasant red-brick farm buildings, it has an eighteenth-century west front, but no trimmings; the Ouanne itself runs quietly under its old brick walls. Although owned by the farmer it is unoccupied at present; its seclusion and intimate charm call for someone to live in and love it. Most of the building in this part of the Puisaye is in brick, for there is little if any stone available for quarrying.

So to **Toucy**, the principal town of the Puisaye, but one which has never had much character since church and town were sacked and burnt by Anglo-Burgundian troops in the Hundred Years' War. The first wooden church was burnt in 1060 during a private war between the baron of Toucy and the count of Champagne, and a Romanesque barrel-vaulted church was begun in 1080, inside the town walls which Baron Narjot built to protect his château from

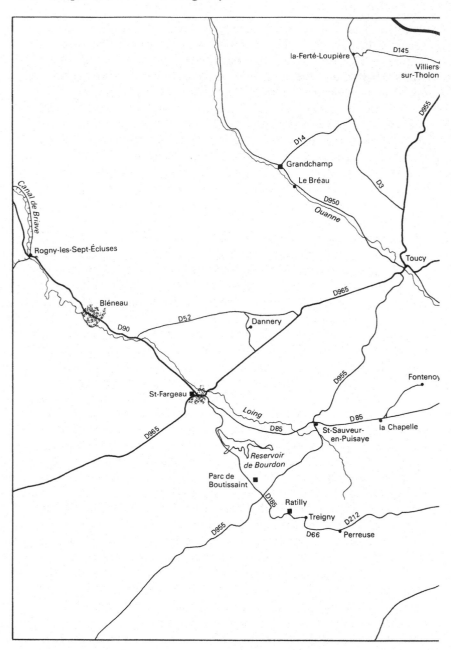

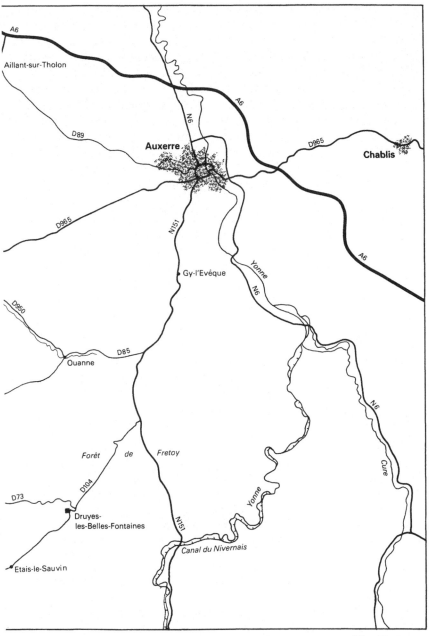

further attacks. After the destruction of 1423, work began on a new church in 1536, incorporating at its west end the forbidding rampart wall and its two eleventh-century towers. This work was interrupted by the wars of religion and never finished, while the seventeenth- century steeple was replaced in 1891 after being struck by lightning.

All this has resulted, it must be said, in an indigestible 'fortified' church of considerable ugliness. The interrupted rebuilding pro-gramme left it with two naves: one is the big Renaissance affair which has had its altar at the *west* end since 1689 – orientation was unimpor-tant during the 'age of reason'; the lower Romanesque nave and apse are only a projection to the east beyond the organ loft.

A nineteenth-century inheritor of the age of reason was born here in 1817 – Pierre Larousse, to whom any serious student of French is indebted. He was the first director of the *École Primaire* founded in the town by Guizot; in 1849 he published his *Grammaire, Cours de Style* and *Traité d'Analyse*; in 1852 he inaugurated a classical li-brary and began his famous *Dictionaire Universel*. At the same time he began to edit his educational journal, *l'École Normale*. Larousse worked fifteen or sixteen hours a day, 'my brain and my heart swelling with Burgundian sap'; if advised to lay off a little he replied that eternity would be enough for that. In Paris as a young man he lived in a garret on a pot of butter sent weekly by his mother, onions and bread. Sometimes in collaboration with another Burgundian, Augustin Boyer, he published twenty works in as many years.

Sixteen kilometres to the south, along the pleasant D955, is **St-Sauveur-en-Puisaye**, birthplace of the much-loved novelist Colette who lived here from 1873 to 1954. She describes the family home as:

a dark, double-fronted house, with large windows and small grace, the middle-class house of an old village, but the steep slope of the street jostled its gravity a little, and the steps up to the door went limping, four on one side, six on the other. A big, serious, peevish house, where you rang the bell as you would to an orphanage, and where the thick bolts on the door reminded you of a gaol; a house that smiled on only one side of its face.

There it stands, halfway down a side road off the rue de la Roche; you can park in the *place* and walk there in a few minutes. The present occupant of the **Maison Colette** is a doctor, and the only thing which would recall Colette's childhood is the little walled orchard opposite. Mauriac compared her to a 'fat bee', and perhaps you can imagine her buzzing round the fruit trees in spring. She was not the less a Burgundian for dying in the Palais Royal, for just as Chambertin and Clos Vougeot had strengthened her as a child, so on her eightieth birthday a hundred bottles of Meursault arrived to celebrate the occasion.

Commercial interest in Colette today has shifted to the higher ground, where the dark bulk of a ruinous twelfth-century tower looms over an eighteenth-century château. Neither had any connection with the writer, but the château is being restored to form the basis of a Museum devoted to her work and character. The stable block has been beautifully restored to provide more rooms for the exhibition. The restoration began in March 1994, and visits are possible from 1995 onwards.

For a change from town life and church architecture you may like to visit the **Parc Naturel St Hubert**, which is attached to the little domestic château of **Boutissaint**. You will find it to the south-west of St-Sauveur, right on the boundary line between the departments of Yonne and Nièvre, and you can reach it by following the D955 to the south and after eight kilometres turning right on to the D185. The owners of the property have turned their extensive woodland (and one or two shallow lakes) into a wildlife park for game animals. There are roe deer, fallow deer, European bison, Corsican wild sheep, or *moufflons*, and a generous enclosure by the biggest lake for wild boar and their offspring.

You can wander as you like along the tracks which pass the various enclosures or strike deep into the woods, but it is as well to acquire a map of it all from the gatehouse where you buy your entry ticket. There are informative notice-boards at several points: one of the most interesting explains the life-cycle of the *sanglier*, or wild boar. Up to six months the young animal is attractively striped and known as a *marcassin*; between six and twelve months the coat changes and the male is called a *bête rousse*; from one to two years old he is a *bête de campagne*, between two and three a *ragot*, from four to five a *quartannier*. At five he is fully grown and a *grand sanglier*. At six he is a *grand vieux sanglier*, while after the age of seven he separates from the main herd and continues as a *solitaire* – maybe for another twenty years. The males rut from November to January; the females produce four to eight *marcassins* in a *nid*, or litter, and the gestation period is four and a half months. They are all great mud-lovers.

One could spend a long day here, picnicking and enjoying a variety of walks, and there are hides for bird or wild animal watchers. In the entrance car park fantail pigeons display, and you may return to find a peacock decorating the bonnet of your car.

The D185 runs on past the huge **Reservoir de Bourdon**, which provides a marvellous setting for all kind of aquatic diversions, especially dinghy sailing, and there is well organized 'camping' nearby. As you can imagine, these are not visits to hurry through at the end of a day, and you may sensibly decide to turn back towards your base from St-Sauveur, leaving Boutissaint for another day.

If so, and you still have time, turn aside just after the village of la Chapelle on the D1 to **Fontenoy**, a name which may stir historical memories, though not perhaps the right ones. This was not the scene of the English defeat by Maurice de Saxe during the war of the Austrian Succession, for that was in the Netherlands. According to local authorities it was where the grandsons of Charlemagne met on the field of battle in 841 to settle their territorial inheritance. The outcome, in favour of an alliance of the two younger brothers, Charles 'the Bald' and Louis 'the German', meant that at the subsequent Treaty of Verdun Charles succeeded to almost the whole of what is now France, and Louis to the eastern domains beyond the Rhine (later to become the 'Empire'). Their elder brother Lothaire had to be content with a heterogeneous territory narrowly sandwiched between them, which ran from Friesia in the north, through Lorraine (Lotharingia), Burgundy and Provence as far as the Alpes Maritimes, then through Lombardy to Rome and the borders of Calabria. This unwieldy 'kingdom' did however form the mediaeval power of Burgundy.

The earlier place name was *Fontanet*, which may explain why some historians say the battle was fought at Fontenay. We can only refer them to the obelisk set up to commemorate it here in the nineteenth century, which stands on the right of the D3 just outside the village to the south. There is no doubt that the battle affected the political history of Europe for centuries.

On the way back to Auxerre you will pass through **Ouanne**, where there is a fifteenth-century church of cathedral-like proportions which has preserved an earlier and very beautiful east end. At the west end, south of the entrance, appears the horizontal effigy of a man in a recess of the wall – not a *gisant*, as it would appear at first sight, but an anonymous corpse whose flesh is being realistically eaten by worms. Under this grisly *memento mori* are carved the words of St Paul: 'Avec mes yeux je verrai mon Sauveur'.

The most notable building in the Puisaye is the **Château of St-Fargeau**, and it would be the natural first objective of any *sortie* further west in the region. It can be reached rapidly down the D965, with no need to stop halfway at Toucy, if you have already been there. The château will always be connected with the *Grande Mademoiselle*, Anne-Marie-Louise de Montpensier (1627-93), who was the stormy, strong-minded and somewhat masculine daughter of Gaston d'Orléans, brother of Louis XIII. She was therefore a first cousin of Louis XIV, whom she would have liked to marry – in default of the King of Spain, the Emperor of Austria and Charles II of England. She joined Condé during the Fronde and fired the cannon from the Bastille to save him – which provoked Mazarin's comment: 'Mademoiselle vient de perdre son mari'. She presided over the Council of War at Bléneau, and rode into Orléans at the head of Condé's troops, but when he and the king were reconciled in 1652 she retired by royal command to her abandoned château at St-Fargeau.

Arriving at two o'clock in the morning with her lady-in-waiting, *maître d'hôtel* and six servants, she found the bridge broken down and was forced to scramble knee-deep through the grass of the moat. Faced with the six massive round towers, she could see 'only an old house with neither doors nor windows, which filled me with dismay. They led me into a dreadful room, with an upright beam in the middle of it. Fear, horror and grief so took possession of me that I began to cry. I considered myself most unhappy, exiled from the Court as I was, having no better residence, and realizing that *this* was the finest of all my châteaux.' Accordingly she rode off to her *manoir* at Dannery, nine kilometres away, and returned two days later. She brought in an architect from Paris, François le Vau, brother of Louis le Vau who had worked at Versailles. When the place had been altered to her liking she set up a handpress and wrote her *Memoirs*. 'St-Fargeau', she wrote, 'was a wild place when I came there; one could not find a herb to put in the pot.' To put this right she planted a mall, cut away the brambles and brought in fresh soil.

From the terrace she could see the woods where she loved to ride, or to walk her two greyhounds, La Reine and Madame Souris. There was good hunting with a pack of harriers brought from England, and she delighted in a team of cream-coloured ponies with black manes from Germany. She played battledore and shuttlecock for two hours in the morning and again after luncheon; there were picnics to the accompaniment of violins, and in the evening a troupe of actors from Lyon – known as the 'comédiens de Mademoiselle' – played in the private theatre. Altogether she spent another four years at St-Fargeau, but in 1752 a fire destroyed, with much else, the rooms where she had received the Grand Condé, Turenne and of course Madame de Sévigné.

The original *château-fort* was built about 900 by Hérébert, bishop of Auxerre and the natural half-brother of Hugues Capet, founder of the Capet dynasty of kings of France. Hérébert's successor at Auxerre, Hugues de Chalon, presented his lands to a southern grandee, Ilthier de Narbonne, who added the local title of 'de Toucy' to his name. Four generations died crusading in the Holy Land; the last of the line, Jeanne, married Thibaud, Comte de Bar, in 1260. These two names, Toucy and Bar, were given to the twin towers on either side of the main entrance, while the more substantial **Tour Jacques-Cœur** remembers the brief ownership (1450-51) of the financier who underwrote Charles VII's campaign against the English. In fact he had no time for any building, and after his disgrace the property passed to one of the king's favourites, Antoine de Chabannes. It was he who gave the old fortified hunting lodge the external appearance it has today, using brick as being the main building material available in Puisaye.

Complex family, legal and political moves brought St-Fargeau in 1566 into the possession of François de Bourbon, duke of Montpensier, from whom it passed to his great-granddaughter, the *Grande Mademoiselle*. In spite of being the richest heiress of the kingdom it was only at the age of 54, after (it is said) thirty-two unsuccessful approaches, that she married in secret Antonin Nompar, count and later duke of Lauzun. Her five years at the château, though longer than she had expected her exile to last, were soon

over. After her death the duke sold it, and it came into the possession of the well-known eighteenth-century family of Lepeletier
des Forts, whose parliamentary connections preserved it from
revolutionary damage. Indeed, Louis Michel Lepeletier was President of the National Assembly in 1790 and voted for the death of
Louis XVI – only to be promptly assassinated by a royalist sympa-
thizer. His tomb is in the chapel.

During the Lepeletier period there was the disastrous fire of
1752, an undistinguished west wing was added to replace the
seventeenth-century terrace overlooking the town, and in 1809 le
Vau's French garden was transformed into the fashionable *parc à
l'anglais* which the visitor enjoys today. Another fire in 1853 destroyed yet more of the interior, and though repairs were made in
the 1860's it has taken another hundred years for a complete
programme of restoration to be put in hand. The present owners
are Michel and Jacques Guyot, who bought the château in 1979
from a Belgian company. They immediately admitted visitors to
the few rooms that could quickly be made good, and began a
ten-year plan to restore as far as possible the seventeenth-century
home of the *Grande Mademoiselle*, as well as later features of the
eighteenth and nineteenth centuries.

In the early days the Guyot brothers employed local artisans
and friends who gave their services free. Work was financed not
only by gradually increasing charges for admission, but by indoor
theatrical shows and outdoor spectacles. The programme is still
going on under the direction of members of the same family, who
recognize it as the work of a lifetime.

Once inside the five-sided *cour d'honneur* we are surrounded
mainly by the work of le Vau, a magnificent Renaissance achievement, whose centrepiece is the flight of twenty concentric semicircular steps leading up to the entrance to the Chapel. Although
the range of rooms to the left here were the first part of the
interior to be opened to the public, they were neither the principal
rooms nor the private apartments of Mlle de Montpensier. They
and the huge mediaeval *salle des gardes* to the right can be visited
without a guide. Much use has been made of life-size (and
life-like) model figures dressed in eighteenth-century costume. In
one room on the ground floor you see the master of the house,
Michel Lepeletier, being waited on by servants and maids of

honour in colourful dresses; another reproduces the scene in the kitchen, where preparations are under way to receive him and a hundred retainers on their return to Paris; there is Nicolas Latour, *régisseur* of the château after the Revolution, at work in his study; there is a little courtyard with a gallery where servants are hanging washing out to dry, and other glimpses of contemporary life (and even death). The figures are so naturally posed as to be unexpectedly eerie when met suddenly round a corner. On the first floor are more formal apartments with dark panelling, silk fabrics and parquet floors.

More impressive are the recently opened state rooms on the far side of the *cour d'honneur*. On the ground floor is an antechamber with trappings from the hunting field, including a marble-topped *table de chasse* where game was laid out by returning guns – the marble protected the wooden surface from the blood. Next is a billiards room hung with *toile de Flandre*. The panelled dining room on the first floor, looking out over the lake, has a seven-teenth-century marble fireplace and a portrait of Gaston d'Orléans; the *salon*, which has windows on both sides, has an eclectic selec-tion of furniture, a medallion-framed portrait of *la Grande Made-moiselle*, and also one of Louis XIV's mistress, Mme de Maintenon; the library is fitted with bookshelves of Renaissance design, for which a specially light and lustrous kind of oak was imported from Hungary..

Work is still in hand to restore the private apartments, while repairs to the whole range of roofs were rightly considered more urgent. Now that they are complete, a tour of the *charpente* which runs all the way round is the highlight of the visit. Little of the mediaeval timber has had to be replaced, and you can follow exactly the original structure. It is fascinating to pass from range to range, round the intervening towers, through a maze of criss-cross beams and rafters secured only with wooden pins.

In the stable courtyard one side has been given over to a fasci-nating exhibition of all manner of nineteenth-century horse-drawn vehicles and harness. On the opposite side are stalls distinguished by their past or present inmates' names, one or two being still inhabited. Through the southern gateway one passes over the moat into the green parkland, with its long sickle-shaped lake fringed by woods. During July and August seating is set up to face the south front, where Friday and Saturday evening performances of *son et lumière* in the French manner are staged. Yet it will be the memory of the midday sunshine on warm brick walls, and the glistening slate roofs of the angle towers with their jaunty *lanternons* which you are more likely to take away with you – and perhaps something of the spirit of the remarkable woman who brought it to life but lived there herself for only five years.

From St-Fargeau the D90 runs north-west to **Bléneau**, a small town which not only received the leaders of the Fronde, including Mlle de Montpensier, but saw the eventual defeat of Condé by Turenne in 1652 – a victory for the royal party which saved the fourteen-year-old Louis XIV, who escaped to the Loire at Gien. The twelfth-century church of St-Loup-de-Troyes is one of the earliest in Yonne to have ribbed vaulting. This can be seen in the restored main apse and in the south transept; elsewhere there are slightly pointed barrel vaults. The nave is later, lit by circular windows.

It is well worth continuing your journey to the limits of western Burgundy at **Rogny-les-Sept-Écluses**, for not only is it a *centre nautique* for holiday boats to take advantage of the junction of the Canal de Briare and the river Loing, but as its name declares it boasts one of the great feats of commercial engineering in France – comparable with the work of Isambard Brunel in west-country England, but accomplished more than 200 years earlier. In 1604 Henri IV ordered his engineer Hugues Cosnier to build a ladder of locks which would enable the barge trade to negotiate the sharp falls in level of this important canal linking the Seine with the Loire. After six years the work was abandoned when Henri died, but it was restarted in 1638 by Guyon, seigneur de Chesnoy, and the seven locks, with a total rise and fall of thirty-four metres, were ready for traffic in 1642. For 245 years barges climbed and descended the ladder, but before the end of the nineteenth century it was found too cumbersome to negotiate. In 1887 a bypass canal was built, but even today it takes four or five locks at longer intervals to adjust the levels.

Although weed-grown and enclosing only a little stagnant water, each of the seven locks is surrounded by undamaged stonework, presenting an astonishing perspective in either direction. Boats can be hired here for this attractive stretch of the wide Briare canal, criss-crossing with its parent river between Rogny and Montargis – though only for a few kilometres in either direction is it strictly in Burgundy.

There remains an interesting drive which would skirt the southern border of the Puisaye between the departments of Yonne and Nièvre. The route to take would be south from Auxerre through Gy l'Evêque and Courson-les-Carrières, where the D104 branches off through the Forêt de Frétoy to **Druyes-les-Belles-Fontaines**. The springs which give rise to the name feed a little tributary of the Yonne, and the pleasant little town – barely more than a village – has two great attractions. Perhaps one should first take in the huge ruined château which stands on a bluff above it. It dates from the twelfth century, and was the fortress home of the Courtenay family, who were counts of Auxerre. Here in 1216 Pierre de Courtenay received the emissaries who had come to offer him the imperial crown of Constantinople – a Latin empire since the dishonourable capture of Byzantium by the leaders of the Fourth Crusade. The Courtenays had been as much involved in the Holy Land as the Toucys, and at a higher level, for Joscelin de Courtenay (though a penniless younger son) proved a valuable lieutenant to his cousin Baldwin II of Jerusalem.

You pass first under a heavily machicolated gateway into a wide grass-edged approach road lined by cottages, as in a mediaeval village; then you come up short in front of the formidable *porche d'entrée* of the castle itself, which is the northern entrance to what is now an empty space surrounded by the high walls of the *enceinte*. It opens for visits only between July and September, but there is little to see inside, and at any time you are free to walk round outside to admire the nine Romanesque bays of the gallery in the south wall, and the view over the village below.

Prominent in the view is the important Romanesque church of **St-Romain**. This dates from the eleventh and twelfth centuries, and has the familiar pattern of a nave and two side aisles ending in a central apse and two absidioles. The nave is high and unlit by windows, its slightly pointed barrel vault supported by the ribbed groin vaulting of the side aisles. The gables of the transept, which does not project to either side, were pierced to receive Gothic windows, but the apse remains pure Romanesque, with three lancet windows. There should be three of them, but the middle one has been blocked by a square sacristy which disfigures the

Sens: the cathedral from the south

Château de Tanlay

chevet when seen from the outside. The western façade is alive with decorative motifs – nail pattern, *entrelacs* and short pillars with delicate foliated capitals. A defensive tower was added to the south-west corner, probably in the fifteenth century. The key is most obligingly held at a house in the village beyond the bridge, though its release may have to be authorized by the *curé* , who lives in the Maison de Retraite at Étais-la-Sauvin.

A cross-country journey by little roads, for which no apology is needed in the Puisaye, will bring you to **Treigny**, which like Ouanne has a church built on the lines of a cathedral. Flamboyant Gothic of the fifteenth century gives a rousing presence to its western façade. There are two portals, major and minor, both carved in the ebullient manner of the age. Inside there is a noble nave of four bays, rising uninterrupted by capitals to support the Gothic arches. The ribbed vaulting becomes more elaborate as you move east; crossing and choir have been converted to a heavier Renaissance style. A note at the west end tells you that the church was consecrated by the bishop of Auxerre in 1492, and enlarged sixty years later to provide a choir and ambulatory.

Propped against the wall at the east end of the south aisle the writer found a wooden figure of the crucified Christ, lacking a cross but fixed to a temporary board. This Christ, like at least one other in Burgundy, has all fingers and toes missing, and therefore is said to have been carved by a leper. Its history is well documented: it came from a lepers' chapel between Treigny and le Chaîneau, and it was buried when the chapel was destroyed in the Revolution. It was rediscovered early this century by a workman, and for a time graced the private chapel of Canon Grossier of Chaîneau. It came to the church after his death in 1968, and will surely find a worthier setting before long.

The parish of Treigny was noted for its adherence to Jansenism, a seventeenth-century offshoot of the Roman church which believed in predestination and the natural perverseness of the human soul. The figure of Christ crucified over the inside of the main entrance is 'du genre Janseniste', with head and shoulders below the horizontal beam, the arms stretched high to meet it. The crucifix is surrounded by pictures of the fathers of the Latin Church, while inside the smaller portal is hung a 'résumé du catéchisme Janseniste'.

Close to Treigny, and approached by a straight avenue to the right off the D185, is the **Château de Ratilly**. The *Grande Mademoiselle* is said to have spent a week here, and shortly afterwards it harboured a colony of Jansenists who printed a clandestine broadsheet while hiding from the royal investigators. For once the present is more interesting than the historical or legendary past. The château itself is fascinatingly unusual, built in the thirteenth century of a reddish sandstone, now attractively weathered, with a deep moat (now dry). Two round towers, welcoming rather than forbidding, flank the gateway, and the view through the formal iron gates at the head of the drive is disarming.

Even more friendly is the interior courtyard. Hardly now a *cour d'honneur*, it has grass lawns underfoot, shaded by a wide-spreading tree, and the range of buildings on two sides is almost purely domestic. The third side, to the left as you enter, is taken up by a long barn-like building which is both a display area for the pottery made by and under the direction of Norbert and Jeanne Pierlot, and a museum of the art which has flourished in the neighbourhood since the seventeenth century.

The earliest pottery is recorded at le Boissenet, just across the road from Ratilly, in 1650; between then and 1813 sixteen others were founded nearby. Why so many just here? In general the Puisaye has little stone available or suitable for building, but in this particular area its ochreous flinty soil provides a clay easily worked to produce the stoneware called *grès*, which is the foundation of the local industry. Pottery was always a family business here, and skills were passed down from one generation to another. Its centre today is at St-Amand-en-Puisaye, where in 1888 the sculptor Carrier came from Paris to 'travailler les grès'.

Ratilly was bought in 1951 by Norbert Pierlot, an actor of distinction who had been taught pottery by his wife. Together with their daughter Natalie they run a school of pottery here during the summer. In the great barn alongside the courtyard (originally a wooden structure, but rebuilt in stone after being burnt out in 1972) thousands of samples are set out for exhibition and sale, as well as showcases containing prime examples of work by contemporary and earlier potters. They include the Japanese artist Shoji Hamada, who came to work with M. Pierlot in 1963. In the workshops which adjoin the barn the wheel can be seen constantly at work.

More conventional features of a Burgundian château are the *pigeonnier* in the southwest corner, and a few rooms with sixteenth-century *cheminées*. Ratilly and its pottery can be visited at most times, provided one of the family is at home. You are invited to ring the bell just inside the gatehouse.

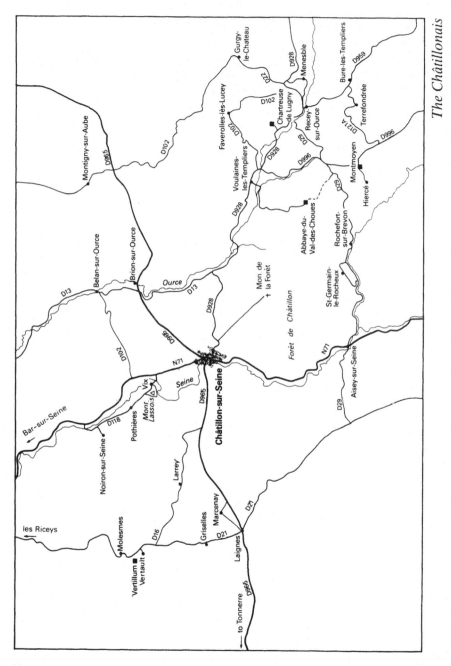

CHAPTER FOUR

The Châtillonais

Away on the north-eastern frontier of Burgundy, on much the same latitude as Auxerre, the route covers a little-known area of which the principal town is Châtillon-sur-Seine. This is the northern approach to the Côte d'Or, or if you are aiming for the vineyards of the Côte itself you may find yourself driving down the N71 from Troyes, rather than heading eastward from the Yonne. If you make Châtillon your base, you can stay in comfort still at the Hôtel Côte d'Or, though its restaurant has lost the cachet of a Michelin rosette. Bar-sur-Seine to the north and Aisey-sur-Seine to the south have good simple hotels, while at Voulaines-les-Templiers to the east the idiosyncratic La Forestière has ten charming rooms but no restaurant.

An alternative approach to Châtillon is to fork right off the N71 just after Bar-sur-Seine and follow the valley of the Laignes through les Riceys. This will bring you to **Molesmes**, just over the border between Aube and Côte d'Or. Here was founded one of the seminal Benedictine abbeys of Burgundy, for it was Robert of Molesme who left it in 1098 to found Cîteaux. Nothing is left of the eleventh-century abbey, whose heyday was in the sixteenth century when the abbot presided over a community of 150 monks. It was mostly destroyed in the Revolution, though the fine Renaissance façade of the abbot's lodging survives. Henri Riche, the owner, has over the years and with a talent near to genius, transformed all that is left, including the monastic garden and vineyard. His family bought the whole site after the Revolution, built a small domestic chateau in the grounds, and has lived there ever since. A handsome Renaissance gateway is the main entrance from the east, and beyond it is the parish church. Though Romanesque in origin, this is of no great interest, apart from a number of popular Burgundian statues of the fifteenth century.

In the surviving southern facade of the abbey there is now a sequence of fine rooms lit by tall windows, beginning with the refectory, now used to display a collection of chasubles arranged according to the different festivals in the calendar. The prior's dining room has been reconstituted, and next to it is a *salon* with wall mirrors and windows giving on to green lawns. Both these rooms have a curiously elegant system of vaulting best described as '*en parapluie*'. Further along there is a smaller room, an *atelier* which illustrates M. Riche's quite extraordinary talents as inventor and craftsman, and finally a display of early carriages and other domestic vehicles.

The cellars extend most of the way under the wing, dating from the thirteenth to the fifteenth centuries. They have holes in the roof at intervals, through which the wine could be poured into barrels, and slits in the walls to keep the air at an even temperature. All the work on the property has been financed by M. Riche, and most of it carried out with his own hands.

A side road at this point leading to the hamlet of Vertault passes the site of the Gallo-Roman city of **Vertillum**, now a pleasant hill-top of flowery scrubland and small copses. Before its destruction in the fifth century it had 5,000 inhabitants, and the ramparts enclosed an area comparable with Alésia or Bibracte. Discovered in 1850, it has been fitfully excavated to reveal a length of the southern ramparts, the ground plan of a temple and baths, and a large underground chamber, probably the cellar of an important house. There are easy walks around the site, and signposts point to the principal excavations.

Five kilometres further on is the pretty village of **Griselles**; the river there is alive with ducks. Soon after that comes **Laignes** (named after the river) with its reputation for 'beau clocher, belles filles, belles fontaines'. The church of St Didier is handsome enough, though it and its *clocher* have been harshly restored. The *belles fontaines* feed a large rectangular pool which graces the centre of the small town, and a pair of swans completes the picture. As for the *belles filles*, you may or may not be lucky – Burgundy has plenty.

If you are now turning east for Châtillon, do take a loop off the main road which takes you through **Marcenay**, which has a church about which the authorities are strangely silent. Dedicated to its first *curé*, St Vorles, who was born in the village about 530, it was the resting place for his bones until they were transferred for safety in 868 to the big church in Châtillon which now bears his name. His fame in the neighbourhood is explained first of all by his parentage – he is said to have been a son of Gontran, king of Burgundy – and then by a miraculous event during a Mass he was celebrating in the original church. King Gontran was a severe and sometimes brutal ruler, but his son (who, we must suppose, was called Vorelius) 'tempered his cruelty, converted him to Christianity and baptized the whole court'. One Sunday while celebrating Mass before his father, the young *curé* suddenly fell silent and grew rigid, as though turned to stone. His trance continued for a whole hour, during which the congregation dared not stir. Later it emerged that during this time a young boy had been rescued from a burning house in a village some fifteen miles away by a mysterious figure in church vestments who appeared from nowhere and then immediately vanished. A miracle was declared, and the story is told pictorially in a sixteenth-century window at the east end of the church.

St Vorles died in 591, and was buried in a stone coffin in the sixth-century crypt before the high altar. The coffin is still visible through a grille. Pilgrims were attracted in large numbers, but during the Norman onslaughts of the ninth century it was thought wise to remove the relics to greater safety in Châtillon. A piece of bone was returned here in 1737 by Mgr de Montmorin, bishop of Langres, and you can see it set in a gilded *chasse* below an eighteenth-century bust of the saint, at the head of the south aisle. The nave, with its groined vaulting, is of the eleventh century, and the north and south aisles both end in fully semicircular arches. Beyond two more lofty Romanesque arches at the west end are the later foundations of a square tower, rebuilt in 1773 but still Romanesque in character. The other attraction of Marcenay is a large *étang* to the north of the village, with various sporting facilities, seating for picnics under trees on the south bank, and an interesting population of wildfowl.

By the time the Seine reaches **Châtillon-sur-Seine** it has travelled a bare fifty kilometres from its source. Though its constricted course in two channels through the town is not impressive, it receives impetus from the copious waters of the Drouix, which emerge from an underground source in the eastern quarter. It was probably in the pool formed here that St Bernard plunged 'to extinguish the fire kindled in his veins by one of those faces which it is impossible to hate'. The increased flow of water meant that from here on the river became navigable for small craft on their way to north-western France, while south-flowing rivers like the Saône began their journey to the Mediterranean not far away. This sets Châtillon in a key trading position, and helps to explain an astonishing archaeological find.

The neighbourhood of Mont Lassois, an Iron Age hill fort in the commune of **Vix** (Latin *vicus*, a village) a mile or two up the main road to the north, had been systematically explored since 1929. Traces were found of occupation in the Neolithic and Bronze Ages, but it became clear that from the sixth century BC it was a rich and important centre of trade and culture. On the hilltop itself, finds between 1929 and 1947 produced amber from the Baltic, coral from the Mediterranean, Attic black-figure pottery, arms, jewels and brooches, together with worked Neolithic flints and a comprehensive collection of tools and household implements from the Gallo-Roman period. Then in 1953 a landowner noticed that in one of his fields below the hill the plough had thrown up pieces of stone which were foreign to the terrain. This put archaeologists on the scent, and the remains of a tumulus were discovered, forty metres in diameter and probably five or six metres high at its summit. Beneath the tumulus was a burial chamber, whose wooden roof had collapsed without seriously damaging the contents – indeed, the collapse had probably saved them from being plundered.

The chamber was about three metres square, and in the north-west corner stood an immense bronze vase – the **Vase de Vix** – the largest yet known from antiquity. It is properly a *krater*, or Greek mixing vessel, cast in a single piece, and could have held 1,100 litres of liquid. The two voluted handles enclose Gorgons' heads, and the monsters' hands rest upon two snakes which part like legs beneath the body in the erotic pose which became familiar in mediaeval Burgundian sculpture. A beautifully executed frieze runs round the neck of the vessel, in which eight chariots, each followed by an armed hoplite, are drawn by teams of four horses. The lid is a work of art in itself. Its base was pierced with holes in a pattern of flower petals, and an umbilical cone in the centre supported the statuette of a woman, 19 centimetres high, wearing the simple drapery and the stylized 'archaic smile' of the period. It is thought to have been made about 530 BC by an artist working in one of the Greek colonies of southern Italy.

A silver cup was found resting on the lid, with two Attic pottery bowls. On the floor beside the *krater* was an Etruscan wine pitcher, and three Etruscan bowls were found stacked against the western wall. Remarkable as these finds were, the most historically interesting were connected with the royal occupant of the tomb. In the middle of it was the metal framework of a funeral car — a kind of litter on wheels — from which most of the wood and leather fittings had perished, though the sides were still decorated with plaques of perforated bronze. After being drawn by hand into the tomb its wheels had been dismantled and ranged along the eastern wall, leaving the litter to stand on its wooden feet.

Inside was a skeleton, with the skull of a woman aged about thirty. She was lying on her back, adorned with all her jewels. She had anklets of bronze, a bronze torque resting on her abdomen, three bronze and shale bracelets on each wrist, a necklace of ten amber and stone beads, and seven brooches. A heavy diadem of gold, with a lion's paw and a little winged horse at its extremities, had tilted the skull backwards with its weight. Queen or princess, her royal status and the wealth and position of her family were obvious.

How do we account for such wealth and importance in a Celtic community as far north as the borders of Burgundy and Champagne? The French archaeologist René Joffroy has suggested that the vase was part of a commercial tribute levied by the Celtic princes of Mont Lassois on Etruscan merchants after they had crossed the Swiss alps and reached the plateau of Langres. This sounds fanciful, and it seems more likely that such a rare object was a gift from some powerful prince of the south, or even brought back by a member of the ruling family after a visit to Italy. Even the suggested route is an odd one, for the great river valleys of the Rhône and Saône would have been much easier to travel than the alpine passes. There was undoubtedly trade passing this way from Mediterranean countries into north-western Europe, carried by natural waterways such as the Seine and Marne.

The whole of the Trésor de Vix has been housed since the 1950s in the **Maison Philandrier**, a Renaissance town house of dignity and character which escaped destruction when the town centre was destroyed under German attack in 1940. It was built by an unknown architect (not, as was once believed, by the native-born Philandrier) for one Antoine Thomelin, a *nouveau riche* citizen who was made bankrupt by the expense involved. It has a richly decorated street façade on the rue du Bourg, and a distinctive turret with a spiral stairway opening on to the garden courtyard.

The royal treasures from Vix are what most people come to see, but this museum contains in all one of the best regional collections of artefacts in France, from Neolithic to Renaissance times. You could linger for hours over the jewellery and objects of domestic use from Mont Lassois and Vertillum: rings, brooches, beads, pins and needles, knives and forks, candle-holders and even ophthalmic instruments. All these are to be seen on the first floor of the museum, with a collection of Gallo-Roman tools which show how little the design of essential things has changed in two thousand years.

On the steeply rising hill to the south-east of the town, known as le Bourg, a community of fourth-century Christians built an underground oratory, over which a hundred years later a larger church was built and dedicated to St Martin – always a favourite Burgundian saint. In 980 it was replaced by the present **Church of St-Vorles**, built by Bruno de Roucy, bishop of Langres. Much altered and restored in the following centuries, it is still an important example of primitive Romanesque. One feature is even Carolingian, where the interior porch has two lateral chapels, in effect a western transept. Seen from the outside the east end makes a notable architectural group, in which the transept proper combines with the central apse and the short tower over the crossing, and blind Lombardic arcading decorates the walls below the roof lines. Unfortunately the two outer apses have been replaced by incongruous later additions, and the western tower was added in 1619 as a belfry and watch-tower.

Inside the church a programme of restoration has been going on for several years. It has revealed the quality of the original groined vaulting in the nave, which is unusually narrow for its height; of the transepts, which have retained their narrow lancet windows; and of the simple high crossing with its octagon-based cupola and squinches. Of great interest too is the restored chapel of St Bernard, on a lower level off the north aisle, not only because its apse could have belonged to the original crypt, but because it now contains the church's greatest artistic treasure, a dramatically grouped sixteenth-century **Sepulchre**. There is a tradition that when St-Bernard was praying here once he saw the statue of the Virgin move, and she revealed to him the mystery of the Incarnation.

It may be a surprise to find that the cemetery beyond the east end is sandwiched between a large section of mediaeval wall and a tower – the **Tour de Gissey** – with embrasures and arrow-slits. This is all that is left of the *château-fort* built for mutual advantage by the dukes of Burgundy in a compact with the bishops of Langres, who until then had been lords of the rival cities of Chaumont (or Mont Chauve) and le Bourg, which faced each other across the lower ground where the modern town grew up. The castle gave the dukes a foothold on le Bourg, while it protected the church and its sacred relics from external assault. The cemetery contains the tomb of Napoleon's Marshal Marmont, a native of Châtillon who is also commemorated in the Parc Marmont to the north of the town. In the park is the château where another great soldier of France, General Joffre, set up his headquarters in September 1914 and rallied the French armies with his Order of the Day: 'Au moment où s'engage une bataille dont dépend le salut du pays, il importe à rappeler à tous que le moment n'est plus de regarder en arrière.'

Châtillon was never far from a war zone. In 1870 Garibaldi's *francs-tireurs* clashed with the occupying German troops; in 1944 Generals Leclerc and de Lattre de Tassigny joined forces with the local *maquisards* to expel the enemy from France. The Croix de Guerre awarded to the city in 1945 was well deserved.

The **Abbey Church of Notre-Dame** stands on the right of what is now the rue de la Libération, the main artery leading out of the town to the north. Entered from the street through an eighteenth-century façade, it is all that remains of the Abbaye Ste-Marie, founded in 1135 by the canons of St-Vorles with the encouragement of St Bernard. The two eastern bays of the nave and the choir beyond have been walled off for the purposes of the Hospice St-Pierre, of which it is now a part. Inmates and visitors can enjoy a spacious courtyard to the north of the church, with grass plots and fruit trees. From it you have a good view of the long line of tiled roof and the regular sequence of Romanesque windows along the side of the building.

In spite of its Cistercian origins, the history of the Abbey was not always restrained or even respectable. One licentious abbess, Rose le Bourgeois, is said to have kept a whipped and branded prostitute as her personal maid, while lovers were admitted through a trapdoor, and balls were held in the convent. Another colourful character was François de Bois-Robert, canon of Rouen and prior of la Ferté. As the titular abbot of Notre-Dame he was conspicuous for his absences and for activities not relevant to his office, though this was not unusual for seventeenth-century abbots. One of the first members of the *Académie française*, he was encouraged by Richelieu to contribute light entertainment for the cardinal's household. He seldom resided in the Abbey, and on the rare occasions when he said Mass there it was claimed that his chasuble was woven out of a dress worn by the notorious Ninon d'Enclos. He gambled and lost the Abbey revenues, and resigned the benefice two years before he died. He could still write of his 'joli Chastillon':

> J'y suis aimé, j'y passe pour habile,
> J'y suis enfin le premier de la ville.

The parish **Church of St-Nicholas** has more interest today, being a model of orderly development from the pure Romanesque of the twelfth-century façade to the restrained flamboyant choir with its intricate ogival vaulting. The glass in the fine Gothic windows of the apse is modern, but elsewhere you can see examples of sixteenth-century *verrières* at their best. In the chapel to the right of the apse the east-facing window has a lively sequence of subjects connected with the Compostela pilgrimages; at the head of the north aisle, facing north, is a beautifully conceived Tree of Jesse with a lovely range of colours. Unfortunately the two paintings once associated with the church, a Massacre of the Innocents and a most delicate Virgin and Child with a *corbeille de fruits*, have had to be removed for security. They will no doubt find a home in the Maison Philandrier.

The early sixteenth-century **Church of St-Jean** is of little interest except for a very small Christ de Pitié to the left of the apse, and a polychrome St Anne whose serene face is alight with understanding and responsibility as she regards her daughter. Outside there is architectural interest in the flying buttresses which span a cobbled alleyway, but they are curious rather than beautiful. The tower was rebuilt in 1820.

Before we leave Châtillon, the memory of the treasures we have seen should prompt a visit to the Mont Lassois. Nothing can now be seen of the excavations, but on the hilltop overlooking the village of Vix is the little Romanesque **Church of St-Marcel**. Restoration by the 'amis de St-Marcel' has cleaned up its harmonious exterior and the original short tower. The nave and single south aisle are revealed as purely Romanesque, though the transept and choir are obviously later. To the south-east the Forêt de Châtillon opens out before you, a huge natural area which has some right to call itself the Bois des Cerfs – and genuine hunters could probably find a few *sangliers* as well. It is not, as so many French woodlands are, divided up by a grid of forest rides where Sunday 'chasseurs' park their cars and bang away at whatever moves. Occasionally in winter the colourful if artificial performances of the 'Piqu'Avant Bourgogne' disturb or enliven the scene with horn and hounds, but for most of the year it remains a wild and secret place. As such it was good cover for the *maquisards* who resisted the German troops in the last war. Almost at its centre, where two roads meet, is the **Monument de la Forêt**, which remembers thirty-seven of their number who were either killed or taken prisoner and shot in June 1944.

Eastward from Châtillon the D928 skirts the northern edge of the Forêt, and at **Voulaines-les-Templiers** you will find a useful base for exploring further, with its peaceful hotel on the far side of the Ource and a good meal to be had at the Hostellerie des Templiers in the village. The little market centre was once the seat of the Grand Prieuré of the Knights of St John in the Champagne, but of their fourteenth-century *château-fort* only one tower remains. As the name implies, the Knights Templar were there before them, but their Order was suppressed by Philip the Fair in 1307 when they began to exert too much secular and financial influence in Paris.

From here there is a chance of another expedition into the heart of the forest. A turning off the D928 to the south, across the river Ource from Voulaines, leads through thick woods to the isolated and superbly romantic **Abbaye du Val-des-Choues**. We must insist that this is the valley not of the cabbages but of the owls, for the word *chou* covers the larger varieties of owl and has its plural properly in *-es* rather than *-x*, as it is sometimes printed locally. There are plenty of them around. The abbey was founded in 1193 by Eudes III of Burgundy, and was for a time the mother house of the Cistercian order. A large monastic entity, with a lofty basilica church, it was reformed at the beginning of the seventeenth century, when first Louis XIII and then Louis XIV came here to enjoy *retraite* from the tiring splendours of the French court.

The church was totally destroyed in the Revolution, but the monastic buildings were adapted to secular use and have mostly survived. The gateway is in the high northern wall, and beside it stand two stone basins where pilgrims washed their feet before entry. It leads into a big courtyard with the former stables on either side. Before you enter this you are directed to a range of buildings on your left, where the first room is a spectacular *salle de chasse*, crammed with sporting trophies. There is hardly a foot of wall space not occupied by mounted antlers, each recording the date the animal was shot, and there are cases full of hunting horns and riding helmets. Beyond it there is a handsome square room which the monks used as a confessional; by a trick of acoustic the priest was able to hear two confessions without either being audible to the other. It has a lovely view over the nearby fields, grazed by the horses which the owners breed as one of their chief interests, and beyond them the woodlands stretch for ever.

In case you are put off by the early emphasis on the chase, a more interesting room on the next floor is entirely devoted to photographs of wild life taken by M. and Mme Beaufort, friends of the Monod family who have taken over and developed the whole property. There are superb colour photographs of deer and even wild boar surprised in their natural habitat. You then enter the *grand cour*, where the range of buildings on the right has been used for a brilliantly executed display of wild life of every imaginable European species, grouped in recreated natural surroundings. At the far end you pass through an archway in the southern range, known in its heyday as the *Maison des Princes*, where the royal visitors would have lodged.

The vista now opens out into a wide formal garden of green lawns and topiary. To the right are the ruins of an old mill, whose upper storey has been converted to an aviary, and beyond it are enclosures for wild varieties of familiar animals, including a charming family of Tibetan goats. In similar enclosures opposite there are Shetland and other miniature ponies grazing happily. Beyond the lawn area is a big rectangular bassin with assorted wildfowl, and beyond it again an area laid out as a childrens' playground, its equipment all beautifully built of local wood.

At the north-east corner of the lawns is a roped-off path leading to a little spinney where Père Viard, the founder of the abbey, once lived as a hermit. The history of this fascinating place is told in a brochure available at the reception point to the right of the entry gate. You will also be given details of the three *chambres d'hôte* available in the old stable block next door, which would be a wonderful base for a holiday among these secret woodlands. The left-hand range of stables is still used by the family – in particular by the young M. Monod, who has so brilliantly taken over from his father the direction of this unique property.

If you leave Voulaines by the D928 you will first pass the ancient **Chartreuse de Lugny**, and if you take the short approach road to the left you can investigate from the outside the priory buildings of the twelfth to seventeenth centuries, which have been converted to a private *château de plaisance*. The chapel has been rebuilt in the neoclassical style and is not beautiful. Down the road at **Recey-sur-Ource** you are in the birthplace of Henri Lacordaire, of Dijon and Flavigny-sur-Ozerain, where we shall find him later. He was baptized in the Romanesque church of St-Rémy, and his statue stands at the west end of the north aisle. The three western bays of the nave date from the twelfth century, the choir and south aisle from the thirteenth, but alterations went on into the nineteenth century. The high altar was rescued in 1792 from the Chartreuse de Lugny by Henri's father.

Surrounding Recey are the villages of the **Haut-Châtillonais**, some of the remotest and least frequented places in Burgundy. This is Templars' country, for in the twelfth and thirteenth centuries their *commanderies* kept open and secure the borders of Burgundy and Champagne, while the knights regarded themselves as the seigneurs of a land where no great nobleman had thought it worthwhile to live or build. As well as keeping the peace and guarding the pilgrim routes they built sturdy little churches for themselves and the local populations. Whether they stuck by choice to the Romanesque tradition and examples of the south, or whether it was a lack of material or skilled craftsmen, their churches owed nothing to the Gothic innovations which by the thirteenth century were sweeping through northern Burgundy from the west. The villages have changed little since their days. Tractors have replaced horses, but the tumbledown barns support an un-varying way of life for the farmers and their families. You can visit them in any order, as the roads meander up and down hill with no great distances between them – though it may help to follow the local signposting of the 'Circuit des Templiers'.

You will soon recognize the common features of the village churches. Of no great size in the first place, they are still humble but dignified places of worship, and essentially as the knights left them. The typical though not universal example will have two naves, major and minor, alongside each other. The higher and larger was intended for the knights and their company, the smaller for the soldiery and the parish community. When they took over an existing single-naved church they sometimes built the second nave later, sometimes never got round to it. The small rose window, or *oculus*, is a constant feature, usually placed above a group of two or three round-headed lancet windows at the east end – which was invariably flat. The tower was short, square and defensible, usually offset to the north or south of the principal nave, having no tran-sept crossing to support it.

The best example is to be found at **Bure-les-Templiers**. Not only is its church the epitome of Templar work in these parts, but the village was the regional headquarters of the Order from 1133 to its suppression in 1307. By 1350 the *commanderie* had been taken over by the Knights Hospitaller of St John, who maintained it till they moved to Voulaines in 1421. The headquarters itself was a small fortified building known as the **Cour Carrée**, whose over-grown remains can be seen beyond the west end of the church. The church is older than the *commanderie*. Its choir and the eastern-most bay of the principal nave date from the eleventh century – all pure Romanesque except for the Templars' *oculus* at the east end. The north aisle was added in the thirteenth century, according to the Templars' practice, but the whole western end fell into ruins and was rebuilt in 1771.

Other Templar churches, each with a special character, can be picked almost at random. One of the oldest and most attractive is at **Menesble**, where the village name is said to derive from that of the goddess Minerva. The smallest village is **Terrefondrée**, with only seventy-three inhabitants at the last count; the church there has an arcaded fourteenth-century porch with a roof of heavy stone tiles. At **Faverolles-lès-Lucey** there is an unusual western entrance to the church, where the porch is divided in two by a central column, with matching half-columns to either side. The church of St-Michel at **Gurgy-le-Château** is an exception. Once the chapel of a vanished castle, it was extensively renewed in the eighteenth century and given a striking tower with pinnacles and a six-sided steeple. Standing high over the west end, it is reckoned one of the sights of the neighbourhood.

There are few places in France with the unworldly appeal of the Haut-Châtillonais. Its little churches in their different village settings speak of a time when their building must have brought new life, social as well as religious, to humble communities. The communities are still humble, and no doubt religious after their fashion, but the Templar knights and their ladies disappeared centuries ago.

Before leaving the district there may be time to pause on the way back to Châtillon or Voulaines to glance at the seventeenth-century château in **Montmoyen**, which has a faded charm about it. Then go on to the next-door hamlet of **Hiercé**, where there is a tiny sixteenth-century chapel. Finally, at a crossroads on the higher ground just beyond Hiercé, you will come with surprise upon a noble **Christ de Pitié**, sitting upright and tragic in a sentry-box shrine among the wild flowers of the roadside.

CHAPTER FIVE

From Châtillon to Vézelay

This journey involves a long south-westerly diagonal. Take the D980 southwards out of Châtillon, then turn right through Savoisy for **Asnières-en-Montagne**. The 'montagne' is a plateau of open agricultural land between the Forêt de Rochefort, the Bois de Ravières and the Bois d'Arrans, and in the courtyard of M. Abriet's farm in the village you will find a fascinating agricultural museum. There are hoes and axes, types of plough and yoke, bark slicers, sheaf binders, kitchen implements, spades and scythes of all kinds.

The simple Gothic church of St-Pierre, perhaps of the mid-thirteenth century, was restored in 1832 by the then Mayor, and again a hundred years later by the Abbé Bonnard, *curé* of Asnières, 'helped by the generosity of the inhabitants and friends of the parish'. The later enterprise was a job well done, preserving the church's early Gothic lines and stonework. The varied statuary inside includes a rather grim-faced Virgin enfolding her people, and a fine St Barbe with her tower beside her; her face is full of defiant character. A vigorous young St Roch has crossed keys on his broad hat to show he is on a pilgrimage to Rome, and St Sebastian in his agony has a sympathetic squirrel peeping out of the tree to which he is bound. One ancient short column survives among the four which support the stone altar.

The road from Asnières to Cry-sur-Armançon drops quickly through the woods to the river valley. Halfway down, the ruins of the château of **Rochefort** stand up dramatically among the trees high on your left – even more so if you look back as you approach Cry. An overgrown path leads up from the road, but when you emerge on to the bluff it turns out to be a sad rather than a romantic ruin. This is a shame, because there was a fortress here as early as the eleventh century, and although it was dismantled by Duke Jean-sans-Peur in 1411 the family of Rochefort built a superb replacement for it at the end of the fifteenth century. It was abandoned in the nineteenth, and much of the stone was robbed for other building, but enough remains to make it an exciting discovery – should the owner relent and allow one to get in.

When you reach the valley you will find the D905 dodging back and forth across the Armançon on its way south to Montbard. One of its sharpest changes of course is at Aisy-sur-Armançon, where it suddenly darts across the river and runs close under the village of **Rougemont**, which has a church of great interest. An *abbatiale* of the thirteenth century, it served a convent of Benedictine nuns under an abbess until Louis XIV had them removed to Dijon. The east end was destroyed in the Revolution, and has given place to farm buildings, but the four remaining bays of the nave suggest a master architect who took many of his ideas from the abbey church of Notre-Dame at Semur-en-Auxois, especially in the height given to the clerestory. Among the treasures inside is a thirteenth-century group of Virgin and Child – she holds out a bunch of grapes, and the Child stretches out to touch them; high on the end wall of the north aisle is a delightful Annunciation of the same date. The last abbess is buried in the nave.

The exciting part is the western façade, where there is a wide narthex with a low chamber above it. On either side of the doorway are statues of St Peter and St Paul, with a Virgin and Child over the central pillar and a powerfully carved tympanum in three registers. On the lowest level is a Nativity, where the Virgin's hand rocks the cradle under the approving attention of ox and ass. In the middle band Herod's soldiers (in Crusader armour) are seen slaughtering the Innocents, while to the right two armed horsemen pursue the Holy Family on their way to Egypt. Above are scenes from the Passion – the scourging, the entombment and the appearance of the risen Christ in the garden. The stonework is battered, and no one has tried to restore it yet, but the proud figure of the Virgin stands out clearly – a joyful creation. The tower was originally higher (it collapsed in a storm) and both it and the porch were fortified during the Hundred Years' War. There are plans to restore it all, but in the meantime it is usually kept locked. A notice by the western entrance tells you most helpfully where you can apply for admission.

Crossing the river again to Aisy, your westward journey takes you once more to Noyers, which is always worth a second visit,

87

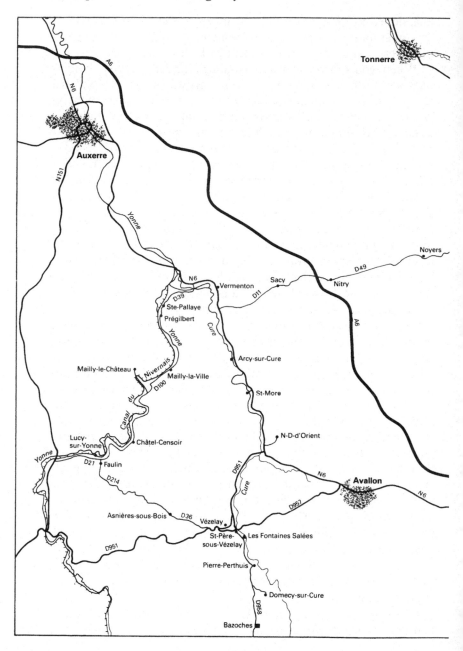

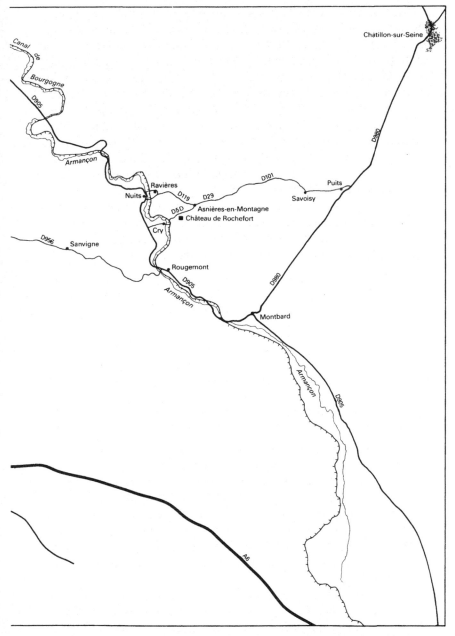

Châtillon to Vézelay

and then on across the A6 autoroute – which has as little to do with its surroundings as a railway line – to **Sacy**. This town was the birthplace of Nicolas Restif de la Bretonne (1734-1806). The author of fifty novels, friend of Beaumarchais and Mme de Staël, he was a well known womanizer who kept a calendar of his mistresses – one for each day of the year, it was said. With this penchant went some higher ideals, and like Rousseau he dreamed of a new society which would revive the golden age and the 'noble savage'. He remembered Sacy as he had known it when a boy: 'I was born in a village where life was never worried by a master, where hunting was free for any man with a gun, where wood was common property, and where people met to elect their syndics, their tax collectors, their shepherds and their schoolmasters.'

In Restif's house at Sacy there is a large room where a historian of the Yonne describes a scene which must have been matched often in the eighteenth-century countryside of Burgundy:

It was there that they supped, with Restif's father seated like a patriarch in the middle of twenty-two guests. Children, ploughboys, drovers, shepherds and a couple of servants all sat at the same table . . . Everyone ate the same bread, for the odious distinction – so Restif tells us – between white and brown was unknown in the house. The children drank nothing but water – that was the rule; and it was only when they were past the age of forty that the women actually had a little wine mixed with it. After supper the father read aloud from the Scriptures, and was respectfully listened to. During Advent he liked to sing the Noëls – the old Burgundian Noëls merrily sung by the fireside, familiar, happy and naive, with their Jesus a Jesus that simple decent folk could recognize.

The twelfth-century church at Sacy has a stumpy octagonal tower, with the very high nave and transept one sees often in this part of the Auxerrois. The mayor has charge of the key, but like many of his kind today (and perhaps of Restif's day too) he is a working man and can be contacted only during the 'heures de repas'. If you are lucky, you will find a two-storeyed Romanesque nave, with Gothic choir and transept. The height of the transept allows for tall windows to the south, while to the north a little Gothic turret has been added.

At **Vermenton**, a small town on the N6 which overlooks the river Cure, the church of Notre-Dame has interested many writers on Burgundian architecture. It was founded about 1170 by

Mathilda, wife of the count of Nevers, and there are several features which link it with early Gothic churches further north in the neighbourhood of Sens and Provins, and through them with new practices in the Île-de-France. The ribbed vaulting, which originally covered only the nave, is an early example, and so are the capitals at the east end. Most unusual in Burgundy, though found occasionally further north, is the zig-zag moulding of the soffit, or under-surface, of one of the principal arches of the nave.

It seems no accident that Vermenton is on the main road from Paris which passes through Sens on the way to Chalon-sur-Saône and the south. Along this road travelled the high-ranking clergy and noblemen who were the chief patrons of church building. The actual builders and masons were often members of travelling companies who set up shops close to where buildings were projected; they would use the same high roads and carry technical and decorative ideas with them from site to site. The high and ornate north-west tower, with colonnaded tabernacles at the corners below the spire, also derives from the Île-de-France.

From here you can cross over to the charming valley of the Yonne and follow it upstream to **Mailly-le-Château**, built above a sudden loop in the river and its attendant Canal du Nivernais. Here lived the 'three sisters of Mailly', all of them mistresses of Louis XV – the youngest became duchess of Châteauroux. On the way you pass the simple twelfth-century Romanesque church of **Sainte-Pallaye**, dedicated to another of the three saintly women who brought St Germain's relics home from Ravenna to Auxerre; at **Prégilbert**, tightly bunched between road and canal, you will see a later Gothic one with a short but immensely high nave. The church seems little used, but the cemetery is well populated.

At Mailly the château is still privately owned and occupied, but the town is a pleasant place to spend an hour, or even a night or two. Its centre is the Place de l'Église, graced by tall chestnut trees and spreading limes. Nearby are several seventeenth-century houses and the peaceful two-star hotel Le Castel; the garden of the Presbytery has a magnificent view over the Yonne valley. The *curés* of Mailly have served their church well in recent years, commissioning some respectable sculpture for the Stations of the Cross and some excellent stained glass for a window which tells the story of St Adrian, its dedicatee.

The church is again thirteenth-century Gothic, with a high nave supported by flying buttresses, though the plain triforium has semicircular arcades. The western façade is unique. Instead of biblical figures or saintly statues over the doorway, we see at clerestory level a full-length portrait in stone of the Comtesse Mahaut de Courtenay, flanked on either side by two unhappy-looking labourers who carry on their heads the weight of the four short columns which support the arches above them all. The scene is said to express the gratitude of the people to the Comtesse for alleviating their lot, though to look at it you would hardly think so. Across the river, on the far bank of the canal, **Mailly-la-Ville** has an attractive waterside frontage, popular with hired boats cruising between Auxerre and Clamecy – a scene which may remind some of the Norfolk rivers.

If you follow the D100 south from Mailly-la-Ville, or join it from Mailly-le-Chateau, it will be keeping company with a familiar combination of the Yonne and the Canal du Nivernais, which join and separate in a more than usually flirtatious way. Almost at once a succession of fantastic chalky cliffs rise on the left of the road, culminating in the **Rochers du Saussois**, just upstream of a point where river and canal combine to form a wide basin, which is ideal for a busy *centre nautique*.

This picturesque road continues to **Châtel-Censoir**, a walled mediaeval town with a gateway and the ruins of a small *château-fort*. The collegial church of St-Potentien has suffered all kinds of disaster in its time, leaving only the choir and apse from the early Romanesque period; nave, side aisles and the two entry portals are all Renaissance work. The contrast of styles, with no intervening Gothic, is remarkable, and came about because the nave which in 1460 replaced its Romanesque predecessor was burnt down almost as soon as it was built. The eleventh-century choir, however, is built over a possible fifth-century crypt, which was accidentally discovered in 1898 when the *curé* found a tunnel leading into it from outside. At that time there was a flight of steps between the nave and the choir which blocked access from inside the church.

The crypt is obviously very early, with a wide semi-circular vault over the east end, where the saint's relics were displayed on the altar. They are now enclosed in the high altar of the choir above. The canons whose 'college' maintained the sixteenth-century establishment had their twelve wooden stalls behind the altar, and their picturesque houses surround the church as in a cathedral close. In the choir we have a unique glimpse of how exactly the mediaeval sculptor went to work. On the north side only two capitals are complete; the others have been divided into three zones ready for carving, and to varying extents they have been brought into relief without ever being completed. In some cases only a rough beginning was made.

The Renaissance embellishment of the nave was done by Italian artists under orders from the Italian-born Gonzague, duc de Nevers, and they extended their work into the choir and its side aisles by using fluted half-columns to match those in the nave. On the north side a spirited artist has produced a polychrome carving of a Last Supper, with a defiant Peter and a secretive Judas clutching his bag of silver. The table is laid more invitingly than usual, with a large lidded wine jar prominent, and the row of apostolic feet below the cloth is very natural.

The next village up river is Lucy-sur-Yonne, and if you turn sharply back left here on the D214 you will pass close to the **Chateau de Faulin**. A few years ago it was deserted and almost ruinous; restoration work is still going on, but already it promises to be one of the finest chateaux in Burgundy. It parades its history proudly: mediaeval gateway and portcullis, *donjon*, solid curtain walls with flanking towers, comfortable-looking Renauissance living quarters behind. Privately owned and occupied, it may yet open to the public, which would be an experience not to miss.

Your road leads on through Lichères-sur-Yonne to Vézelay, but first we might consider an alternative way of getting there from Vermenton. This would be by the N6 highway, which by now is following the right bank of the river Cure on its way to join the Yonne at Gravant. It will take you to the grottos of **Arcy-sur-Cure**, deep in the limestone cliffs which form the eastern edge of the watershed between Yonne and Cure. The grottoes might have been carved by a stage designer for a production of *The Tempest*; Prospero's cave could not give a clearer intimation of magic. Discovered in 1666 but closed to the public till 1903, they extend for 876 metres in a succession of halls and galleries, with a lake of emerald green. They were frequented for twenty years by a singular priest, Père Lebeu, who had found a secondary vocation in the hunting of snakes (following the example of St Honoratus in the Îles-de-Lerins off the Riviera coast). The caves were known to the naturalist and engineer Buffon in the eighteenth century, who noted 'the representation of various kinds of animals, fruits, plants, furniture and implements, parts of buildings and draperies'. You will be shown the Hall of a Thousand Columns and the Hall of the Waves; the Wash-house of the Fairies; the outlines of mammoths, and the Salle du Cheval where a horse seems to have been carved out of the rock. Open during the usual hours except between October and Easter, it will take you three-quarters of an hour to explore the caves from end to end. Near at hand are the grotto and fountain of St-More, a favourite quarry for sarcophagi in the Middle Ages, and – no doubt thanks to a stretch of Roman road which crosses the watershed – the Gallo-Roman ruins of the 'Camp de Cora'.

A mile before the junction of the N6 (leading to Avallon) and the D951 to Vézelay, a series of sandy lanes leads up through the woods to the highly romantic site of the chapel of **Notre-Dame-d'Orient** and its look-out tower. A striking modern chapel stands on an ancient base, once important enough to be approached by a broad hexagonal flight of steps. Designed by Marc Hénard, the decorative architect who built the entrance to the Cistercian abbey of la Pierre-qui-Vire in the heart of the Morvan forest, it is still a goal for pilgrims. Cleverly adapted to ground levels, it is entered low from the east and rises in height to the west, where a massive altar of rough stone, polished on top, is lit by four tall windows of modern glass. The unusual scene is completed by a nineteenth-century octagonal tower and by a statue of the Virgin who looks out high above the valley of the Cure. The approach is drivable most of the way, but it could be an opportunity for a country walk and a picnic among wild strawberries and Solomon's Seal.

2

'**Vézelay** rises from its luminous hilltop, solid and authoritarian, like the country's act of faith.' So said Gaston Roupnel, and the sanctuary of St Mary Magdalene ('la Madeleine' as her adoptive countrymen universally call it) is more than a monument or a

Capitals in the right aisle

1. A duel
2. Lust and despair
3. Legend of St Hubert
4. Sign of the zodiac: the scales
5. The mystic mill: (Moses and St Paul)
6. The death of Lazarus
7. Lamech kills Cain
8. The four winds
9. Samson astride a lion
10. St Martin
11. Daniel unhurt by the lions
12. Jacob wrestles with an angel
13. Isaac blessed with Jacob

Capitals in the left aisle

14. St Peter freed from prison
15. Adam and Eve
16. The legend of St Anthony
17. The execution of Agag
18. Legend of St Eugenie
19. Death of St Paul the Hermit
20. Moses and the Golden Calf
21. The death of Absalom
22. David and Goliath
23. Moses kills the Egyptian
24. Judith and Holofernes
25. Slander and avarice
26. Entry to the crypt

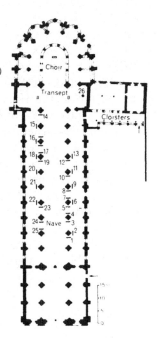

THE BASILICA OF
LA MADELEINE, VÉZELAY

shrine. Visible for miles around, it stands like a sentinel guarding the hills and forests of the Morvan. Its interior is one of the most lovely and uplifting sights in the world.

The winding approach to its hill-top is as crowded now with coaches, cars and service vehicles as it would have been with pilgrims on foot or on horseback in the early Middle Ages. As you round the north side you might pass without noticing it a cross which commemorates the spot where St Bernard stood to make the fiery speech which launched the Second Crusade. You rarely lose sight of the **Madeleine** on the way up, and its south-west tower appears at the head of the long straight street which climbs to it. Tourist traffic is advised (though not compelled) to park below, and the walk is not arduous. Buildings on either side have been kept tidy, tourism has been restrained, and there are well preserved mediaeval houses to be seen as you emerge into the *place* before the west end of the church.

A monastery for women was founded in 858 by Girard de Roussillon (whose exploits as count of Lyon and Vienne are recorded in the *chansons de geste*) in the valley where the village of Saint-Père now stands. In 863 a Bull of Pope Nicholas I put it under the protection of the Holy See. Fifteen years later monks had replaced the nuns at Saint-Père, and in 887 the Normans sacked and burnt the monastery. The monks took refuge on the top of the hill, where there were already the remains of a Celtic *oppidum*, and early in the tenth century they began to build a new monastery; in 1050 it was dedicated to St Mary Magdalene.

It was reported widely that the saint's remains had been brought to Vézelay from Provence to save them from Saracen raiders, and pilgrims crowded to see them. In 1104 the abbot Artaud conse-crated the new abbey church he had built to house the relics, but two years later the abbot was killed in an anti-clerical riot, and his church lasted only another fourteen years before being destroyed by fire. After rapid rebuilding the present basilica was consecrated – though not by then necessarily complete – by Pope Innocent III in 1132. In 1279 came a disastrous declaration by Boniface III that the Magdalene relics were bogus, and that none of her bones had ever left the crypt of St-Maximin in Provence.

In Vézelay both trade and piety suffered. Here St Bernard had preached the Second Crusade; St Thomas of Canterbury had prayed here during his seven years' exile; the roads to Jerusalem and Compostela crossed at Vézelay; both Philippe Auguste and Richard Cœur-de-Lion had assembled their crusading armies here; three years before his death St Louis came for the last time to implore the intercession of St Mary. But these memories grew dim, and Vézelay passed into eclipse. In 1537 secular canons replaced the monks, and in 1569 it was the scene of a revolting massacre by the Huguenots. In the seventeenth century the abbey was put under the authority of the bishop of Autun, and in 1796 the monastic buildings were sold as national property and completely destroyed. Gradually the church fell into decay, and on 22 October 1819 a thunderbolt struck the west tower – the only one to have been completed from the original plan. When Viollet-le-Duc saw it in 1840 the great basilica was no more than a rotting corpse, and that it stands today in the radiance of its resurrection is due to him, and to him alone. Some critics have declared that he spoilt it; it should not be forgotten that he saved it.

The basilica itself was extended westward about 1140 by a solid-walled vestibule, or **Narthex**, and the present main door-way is on its south side. When you enter it you will be sharing the experience of the early pilgrims, of people awaiting baptism or confirmation, and of all the throngs of clergy and laity who assembled here before a ceremonial entry to the main church beyond. The chamber above the narthex was originally a chapel to St Michael; it now contains a display of sculptural antiquities. Though not always open to the public, its eastern gallery, or tribune, can be seen from the nave below – an interesting composition which is covered by another very early Gothic ribbed vault.

To understand the purpose of the narthex, a feature of many cathedrals and abbey churches, it helps to remember that in the twelfth century it was commonly known as a 'Galilee', the name by which its equivalent in Durham Cathedral is still known. It was to Mary Magdalene that the angel who met the women at the tomb on the morning of Christs resurrection said: 'He goeth before you unto Galilee ; there shall ye see him, as he said unto you.' 'Galilee' therefore became a place of assembly before witnessing some great event – in this case the Ascension – and symbolized a passing from darkness into light.

No symbolic meaning could be more appropriate as you prepare to pass into the nave of the Magdalene's church at Vézelay. Central to the great archway which is its real entrance is the short pillar on which stands John the Baptist, presenting on the dish he holds before him the Lamb of God. The Latin inscription below reads in translation: 'Let all know that this is John, who gathers the people and shows them Christ.' Above St John the half circle of the archway is filled by a **Tympanum** which is the grandest, the most accomplished and the most moving statuary of its time to be seen in Burgundy, or perhaps anywhere in France. The immense elongated figure of Christ seems almost to sway on his throne, for the multiple folds of drapery are an expression of movement as well as of majesty. He is sending out his apostles on either side with a gesture of his outstretched hands; they too seem mobile, and maybe a little bewildered as they clutch their scriptures and turn to each other as if in doubt how best to set about their task. Below is the fabulous world of which Othello told Desdemona — cynocephalous Indians, pig-snouted Ethiopians, giants and pygmies, Panotians with enormous ears – all derived from Herodotus. Around the central figure are the signs of the Zodiac and the labours of the months, and young men dancing in maytime. Beyond all this animation the eyes of Christ look out with a kind of tragic prescience on the human drama which His coming has unloosed on mankind.

Difficult though it is to turn aside, the portals to right and left deserve a long look, especially the lintel and tympanum over the south entrance. With great charm, and showing all his skill, the Burgundian sculptor tells the story of the Nativity – even the star of Bethlehem is visible over the manger. The north entrance follows the events of the Resurrection, more esoteric perhaps for the layman, but culminating in the tympanum where Christ appears to his disciples at the moment of Ascension.

'Out of darkness into light.' As you pass under the low lintel into the nave your eyes rise unrestrained to take in its more than earthly beauties. Nowhere else in the world has an architect produced such an effect of lightness – weightlessness, almost. As at Sens and Pontigny, the more than human proportions grow on you as you walk up the nave, but here there is joy in them, not gravity or severity. It will, and it should be, some time before you are ready to analyse what you see – a perspective of soaring, rounded arches picked out in alternate blocks of dark and light stone (not so much black and white as cream and soft khaki) which focus attention on the distant vision of choir and apse, all flooded with light from clerestory windows. Such lightness in a Romanesque nave is only possible with groin vaulting, which allows large windows to be inserted between the salient angles of the groins without weakening the structure – though what was here a bold experiment had eventually to be compensated for by flying buttresses.

Now for the analysis. Built on the simplest of lines, the nave has ten bays with fully rounded transverse arches, which support the vault throughout its length. The same configuration is repeated in the side aisles. The arches underline the unambiguous Romanesque character of the church, which the Gothic choir lightens still more but does not disturb. The two-storey elevation of the nave – main arcades and clerestory only – makes a distinct break with the style associated with Cluny. From the shallow transept (not so much a transept as an introduction to the ambulatory) you pass into the delicate Gothic choir. The transept is early, the choir and apse late twelfth-century and probably due to the influence of Abbot Girard d'Arcy (1171-1198). In the choir the triforium interposes another storey between arcading and clerestory.

A truly Burgundian contribution to the Romanesque plan is the carving of the capitals of the nave. We shall see the beginnings of this form of the sculptor's art in the more primitive churches of the Brionnais; we shall see it developed by a genius to the limits of technique and expressiveness in Saint-Lazare at Autun. Here an anonymous school of artist-masons (under the overall charge of Pierre de Montboissier, later abbot of Cluny) has achieved *chapiteaux historiés*, 'stories in stone', just as rich in invention and in some cases as brilliant in execution.

They comprise a hundred in all, various in quality, illogical in sequence and happily capricious in subject. There are classical subjects – the education of Achilles and the rape of Ganymede, which remind us that classical antiquity had been rediscovered in the last years of the eleventh century. Of the many biblical themes – the fall of Adam, the death of Cain, Daniel in the lions' den, David and Goliath, Judith and Holofernes – none is directly related to the life of Christ, and none to St Mary Magdalene. It seems remarkable that there is no graphic reference to the patron saint anywhere in the church, but perhaps it was felt that her relics were enough to convince the pilgrims of her presence there.

An exception to the biblical themes is the capital known as the *Moulin Mystique*, which is both more subtle and more complicated in its symbolism; it is also the most perfect in its execution. A man is pouring grain into a mill while another collects the flour in his hands. The wheel, which is marked with a cross, may be taken to represent Christ, who grinds the grain of the Mosaic law into the nourishing flour of the gospel. The first man can be identified with Moses and the second with St Paul. At the same time it is a human and natural scene, and the intense concentration of the two figures is a masterpiece of delicate imagination and sure technique. Elsewhere there are the four rivers of Paradise, symbolized by naked figures wearing crowns; Noah's ark, with Mrs Noah looking out of the window and wondering how seaworthy is the craft on which she is expected to keep house and home for all its passengers and crew. The deaths of Lazarus and Dives are contrasted in the south aisle: the soul of Lazarus is borne aloft by angels and welcomed by Abraham under the trees of Paradise; Dives, surrounded by prostitutes, has his riches devoured by serpents and his soul wrenched out of him by demons armed with pincers. The contrast between the peace of one death and the violence of the other is naïvely but dramatically made. Repairs to a few of the pillars have revealed patches of mosaic and fresco painting, which indicate unexpectedly what they may have once looked like.

Symbolism takes on a different form in the apse. The altar stands for Christ, and the eleven columns surrounding it for the eleven remaining apostles. On the upper storey twelve columns are grouped round the central pillar of the triforium – Judas here is represented by a square column (the second on the right) said to be a sign of 'imperfection'. The twenty-four aged persons described in the Apocalypse as prostrated before the throne of God in adoration appear as eight groups of three pillars that rise from the columns around the altar; the hundred and forty-four pillars that decorate the chapels of the choir may be compared to the multitude of the saints – twelve times the number of the tribes of Israel. The basilica of the Madeleine at Vézelay is like an illuminated mediaeval manuscript – once you have found the key to it.

Two stairways from the transept lead down into the **Crypt**, which occupies the whole space immediately beneath the choir, and into a different world and time. The floor is solid rock, polished by the feet of millions, the vaulting dark and sombre. In a small recess enclosed by a grating are the supposed relics of St Mary Magdalene, probably undisturbed here since the ninth century. The original roof, as in the crypt of St-Germain at Auxerre, was a plain barrel vault borne on wooden beams; it was replaced by ribbed vaulting in 1165, after a fire. A door at the head of the south aisle leads to the eastern and only remaining range of the cloister, which in turn gives access to the restored chapter house.

A tour of the outside will show that the western façade (thanks to time and the work of Viollet-le-Duc) is a pale echo of the glories facing you inside the narthex. The long walls of the side aisles are

Semur-en-Auxois

Saulieu owl

Bridge over R. Cure

regularly buttressed, while the flying buttresses which spring from there to the walls of the nave were also rebuilt by Viollet-le-Duc — in this case of necessity. The best exterior feature is the *chevet*, a harmony of levels and angles less uncompromising than at Pontigny.

Before leaving Vézelay we should give a thought to two men of different times and character who belong to its history. Théodore de Bèze (1519-1605) was born in Vézelay, but was converted to Protestantism and joined Calvin in Geneva as professor of theology. Perhaps his early acquaintance with the Madeleine helped to soften the tone of his Calvinism, and he did his best to cool the destructive antagonism between the two branches of the Christian faith. Never personally rebuffed by Catholic leaders, and spoken to kindly by Catherine de'Medici and the Cardinal of Lorraine, he may have helped to persuade Henri IV that Paris might after all be worth a Mass. In death he returned to Vézelay for burial; you can see the house where he was born, and a street bears his name.

Romain Rolland, born in 1866 fifteen miles away at Clamecy, was a humanist whose childhood in Burgundy influenced him throughout his life:

I spent my childhood in a lovable and harmonious countryside, and I still know of none that satisfies all my senses so completely . . . the perfect harmony of its supple contours: hills, rivers, woods and meadows; the pink [*rosé*] and white earth and its pure reflection in the water, like a beautiful naked bosom under its scarf of flowering bushes; my grandfather's property at Montboulon where we used to go in the summer, with bees flying over our heads, and the organ pipes of the pines; the taste and smell of the resin, of the honey and the acacias and the warm earth. They have entered into my flesh and bones for ever.

His humanism showed clearly in his biographies of Beethoven and Michelangelo, and in the ten-volume novel which won him the Nobel Prize. It turned to a pacifism which he sustained during and between two world wars, and among his friends were Gandhi and Rabindranath Tagore. Vézelay and the Madeleine reclaimed him too, and he is buried in the cemetery. Perhaps his long correspondence with his fellow novelist Paul Claudel reconciled him a little to Catholicism, but Burgundy was in any case his natural resting place.

From the wide terrace beyond the east end of the church the view extends far to the south-east over the Morvan landscape. Down there in the foreground rises the Gothic tower and spire of St-Père-sous-Vézelay.

CHAPTER SIX

The Avallonais and the Morvan

An unexpected bonus of coming to Vézelay is to find in the village below such a gem of Gothic architecture in its various moods as the church of **St-Père-sous-Vézelay**. The first sight of the shameless flamboyance of its tower makes you catch your breath. Pinnacle caps pinnacle, and at each of the four upper corners an angel sounds a challenging trumpet to the world. Yet neither tower nor the elaborate porch below it fall into the strictly 'flamboyant' period. Both date, surprisingly, from different parts of the thirteenth century, though some of the more ornate parts of the porch came later – and on top of that it was largely restored by Viollet-le-Duc.

Once inside the church you will find as pure an example of thirteenth-century Gothic as anywhere in Burgundy, and all on an appealingly small scale. The intimate proportions of the two-storeyed nave allow you to see at closer quarters than usual the device of the upper wall passage running right round the church, and the whole building is lit by the soaring windows above it. In the choir the delicacy of the finely pointed arches is enhanced by the light creamy stone. Perfection in a small compass is St-Père's answer to the unfettered glories of the Madeleine.

Nevertheless Burgundian sculptors have been allowed their say, from the fine statuary in the porch to curiosities in the nave and choir: one capital in the nave carries an obviously negroid head, another in the choir has a strange scene in which two monsters devour a pair of ears which are deaf to the prayers of the poor. Above a *gisant* tomb in the north aisle the patron of a deceased knight presents his soul to Christ in the shape of a little child. At the west end there is a Carolingian font, and two massive fourteenth-century holy water stoups in the form of upturned iron bells.

Opening times for the church tend to be uncertain, but it would be wise to avoid the two and a half hours after midday to be sure of getting into the **Archaeological Museum** next to it, which occupies the former presbytery. Most of the exhibits come from

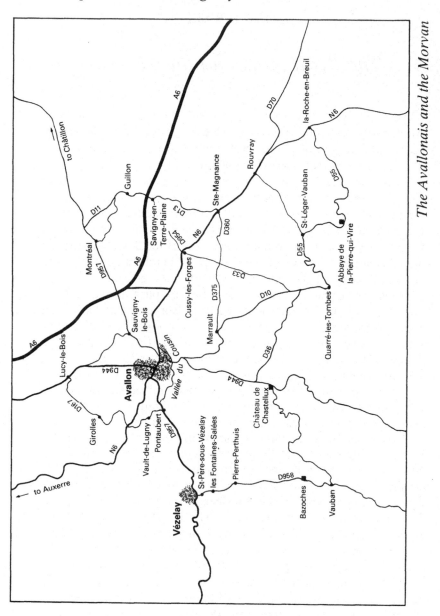

The Avallonais and the Morvan

the Gallo-Roman site known as Les Fontaines Salées, a mile or so down the road to the south, though there are items from the Carolingian and later Christian periods. Most usefully there is a model of the excavations, and an example of the hollowed-out oak vessels which were sunk in the ground to collect water from the mineral springs which give the site its name.

If luxury attracts you, and you can afford it, it is to hand in the hotel-restaurant L'Espérance, where Marc Meneau dispenses a cuisine awarded three rosettes by Michelin in a beautifully converted *manoir* set back from the main road through the village. Alternatively a farm up a lane behind the village has a selection of mature goat cheeses to grace your picnics – and a fifteenth-century cruck barn to store them in.

To reach **Les Fontaines Salées** take the D958 south to Pierre-Perthuis and look for a well marked approach lane to the left. This is a model of a well laid out archaeological site, but its discovery was fortuitous. Clues from local archives mentioning a 'Vau Bouton' between Pierre-Perthuis and Vézelay suggested this could be where Girard de Roussillon fought the battle of Vaubeton described in the twelfth-century *chanson de geste*. A neighbouring field was known as La Gotte Sang – 'the pool of blood' – and there was an old saying that 'en la Vau le sang a coulé'. A thick block of sandstone could have been the 'block of marble from the steps of an ancient temple' beside which the poet had imagined Girard planting his standard. In 1934 these clues were followed up, but instead of ninth-century ruins the archaeologists found a thermal establishment of the second century AD. The circular baths had at first been mistaken for the bases of mediaeval towers.

The site is now a gentle grassy slope beside the river Cure, and it had been inhabited, or at least used, since the Neolithic Age. Numbers of funerary urns from between 1200 and 800 BC were also discovered, but the most remarkable early finds were these wooden catchment wells which date from the first (Hallstadt) Iron Age. Nineteen of them were found, made in a single piece from the trunk of an oak, which had been scooped out after burning the core. They were nearly four metres deep and more than a metre across, sunk in the alluvial sand where salt water was known to emerge. Channels of oak wood, covered with stones, clay and moss, directed the liquid towards the scattered well-heads.

These springs were quickly invested with a sacred character. The Gauls believed that the divinities which inhabited them had curative powers, and in the first century BC they built a circular open-air sanctuary in their honour. The essential element of a Celtic sanctuary was not the temple but the wall enclosing the sacred space, and separating it from unhallowed ground. In the centre of this area was a square pool into which the water sprang perpetually, while a dyke five metres away protected it from impurities. The pool was originally roofed, with four pillars in support, and the whole sanctuary was shaped like a huge wheel. The temple, probably dedicated to the sun god Taranis, was destroyed in the second century AD, and upon its remains the Romans built their thermal station. A certain divinity clung to it, however, since as many as five hundred coins of the fourth century had been showered into the pool by pious hands.

Roman bathrooms took the place of the druidical enclosures – one of the most complete establishments discovered in France. There were separate pools and dressing rooms for men and women, and all the stages of heat allowed for -- the *frigidarium, tepidarium, caldarium* and *laconicum* (this was for steam baths first used by the Spartans in the manner of a *sauna*). The women's side was particularly well preserved, and here were found all the requirements for personal adornment and beauty treatment – brooches, needles, combs and hairpins, make-up pots and vanity cases. One delightful item, now in the museum, was an enamelled bronze clasp in the shape of a wild duck. It is to Petronius Arbiter that we owe the cynical couplet:

> Balnea, vina, Venus corrumpunt corpora nostra.
> Et vitam faciunt balnea, vina, Venus.

Travelling a little further to the south from Pierre-Perthuis on the D958 you will come to the village of **Bazoches**, overlooked from a sloping hill to the east by an illustrious château. In 1675 it was bought and largely rebuilt by the marquis de Vauban, the military architect and engineer whose work in the service of Louis XIV can be appreciated all over France. As Sebastien le Prêtre he was born in 1633 in the village of St-Leger-de-Forcheret, now known as St-Leger-Vauban, near the north-eastern limits of the Morvan. At the age of seventeen he enrolled in the army of the Fronde under

Condé, as it passed through the Morvan, but eventually entered the service of Louis XIV, who appointed him *Commissaire Général des Fortifications* in 1678. As a military architect he had no rivals, covering the frontiers with a chain of fortresses from Lille in the north to Montlouis in the south. Such leisure as he found from these defensive measures he devoted to civic works. He built the canal at St Omer, improved the harbours at Dunkirk and Antibes, constructed the aqueduct at Maintenon and the jetty at Harfleur, and laid plans for joining the Saône and the Loire. In 1703 he was created a Marshal of France.

Although constantly occupied professionally and on active service he spent as much of his time as he could at Bazoches with his wife, sister and two daughters. He was a true son of the Morvan, knew its landscape and its traditions intimately, and in spite of a rough, even coarse appearance he was a kindly and humane man. Another great Burgundian soldier, Carnot, praised him before the *Académie de Dijon* :

Vauban's principal care was always the preservation of his men. This kindness of heart, so characteristic of him, impregnated all his maxims and ideas. He could not bear buildings to be destroyed, or the houses of a besieged town to be fired upon. He liked to speak of the fortresses he designed because they helped, more than anything else, to spare his troops in concealing them from the view of the enemy.

The château is approached by a private road leading up from the village, but unfortunately we can only imagine now the scenes where he worked, for it has recently been closed to the public. We can however think of him working in the square tower which contained his study, with offices for his assistants all along the south front. Horsemen were ready in the stables to take his plans to the four corners of the kingdom. There is a bust of Vauban outside the village church, and he is buried in the transept chapel under the simple inscription: 'Ici repose le Maréchal de Vauban'. In 1805 Napoleon had his heart transferred to the chapel of Les Invalides, where his monument faces that of Turenne.

Having now set foot in the Morvan you will be in no hurry to leave it. For further exploration a base near Avallon is needed, as there is little hotel accommodation to be had in this beautiful, wild and secret region. Avallon itself is an attractive town with a lovely name, but busy and subject to traffic seizures. In the wooded valley of the Cousin, which encircles the granite cliffs which are the southern limits of the town, there are two hotels, the Moulin des Ruats and the Moulin des Templiers, whose names declare their original role beside the fast-flowing little river. The former is renowned and expensive, the latter more modest and charming, though it has fewer rooms.

Simpler, and in its own idiom no less charming, is the Soleil d'Or at **Pontaubert**. This is where the knowledgeable local people come with their families to eat well at prices they can afford. Moreover the village has both history and interest. The road from Vézelay passes the church of la-Sainte-Vierge on the left, but before it sweeps up the hill towards Avallon it crosses a bridge over the Cousin which was first built in the twelfth century by the Knights Hospitaller of St John. Chiefly responsible for building bridge and church was Aubert, brother of Robert le Fort, count of Avallon, so the name of the village includes both the bridge and its builder.

The church, built of the local granite, is a harmonious example of Burgundian Romanesque; most of it dates from 1160, somewhat earlier than the choir at Vézelay. The thirteenth-century tower is built over the first bay of the nave, whose groined vaulting, as at Vézelay, allows light to stream in through its high windows. Special things to look for are the early polychrome wooden figures of the Virgin and St John the Evangelist on each side of the crucifix behind the high altar, and a delightful blue-gowned Ste Syre with her satchel at the head of the north aisle.

If you are now based in or near Pontaubert you will find close by, at **Vault-de-Lugny**, a fifteenth-century church with several features not to be missed. The most striking is a series of frescos painted in the sixteenth century which occupy the diaphragms above every nave bay and continue round the choir above the windows. The subject is the Passion of Christ, and thirteen scenes are presented with artistic feeling and technical skill. Another huge fresco once covered the whole of the west wall of the nave, in which all the figures are black people; the legend which should describe its message is indecipherable. This is a 'collegial' church, run administratively by the canons of the diocese, and it must be the widest for its height ever built: it measures nearly thirty metres from wall to wall, while the nave itself is fourteen metres wide.

The canons profited from these dimensions, for room was found beneath the floor to bury a large number of them under suitably inscribed tombstones which firmly declare 'cette tombe appartient à ... ' Most of them have a date in the seventeen hundreds, but there are also wall plaques for more recently departed canons. Here too is surely the most flamboyant stone pulpit ever carved, though there is more delicate work of the same period in the doorway near the head of the north aisle.

Halfway between Pontaubert and Vault-de-Lugny you pass the gates of a very fine moated château with an L-shaped façade, a mediaeval square donjon and a pair of towers flanking the gateway. This has been converted to a luxury hotel, whose appearance (if not the price of its nine rooms) might tempt you away from Le Soleil d'Or. There are fourteenth-century bridges over the fast-flowing Cousin both at Vault-de-Lugny and at Valloux on the far side of the N6. The former is particularly fine, with its four arches buttressed on the upstream side to break the flow of water, and there is a captivating view of the church and village houses against a green wooded hillside.

At Avallon, as at Vézelay, you are on the very edge of the Morvan, much of which lies within the department of Nièvre, though we shall be skirting it continually as we go south, and shall re-enter it briefly west of Autun. To reach the château of **Chastellux** – which is about ten kilometres along the D944 and directly south of Avallon – it is not necessary to leave Yonne. Pause for a moment on the bridge which crosses the upper and now turbulent waters of the Cure, and there on a peak of granite rock you will see the façade of the château standing up before you. With its walled terrace and its roofs and towers in profile against the sky, it appears almost exactly as a horseman riding over the bridge might have seen it in the fifteenth century. The oldest of the four towers, called St-Jean, dates from the end of the eleventh century. From a distance – and this is all that is permitted – you can make out the square crenellated clock tower from the fifteenth century, and the round Tour d'Amboise, built in 1592. The château was the feudal home of the Maréchal de Chastellux, whose family tomb is in the cathedral of St-Etienne at Auxerre, but it now belongs to the duc de Duras. No matter how distant, the view of the exterior is not to be missed.

The family of Chastellux has not ceased to deserve well of Church and State. In 1850 they gave to Père Muard the property on which now stands the Benedictine abbey of la Pierre-qui-Vire, which takes its name from a huge block of granite on a spur of rock over looking the steep wooded banks of the Triquelin, about twenty kilometres east of Chastellux. The rock does actually turn at a fairly light touch without falling on the inquisitive tourist or into the river below. The abbey is best approached by way of **Quarré-les-Tombes**, a pleasantly relaxed market centre for the region. It has a wide *place*, with useful shops and one good hotel, and it has become popular with both Morvan residents and the tourist. The church of St-Georges is known chiefly for its collection of hundreds of sarcophagi ranged round the graveyard. Probably Merovingian, and all found empty (most of them are only lids) they are now thought to be the products of a 'tomb factory' which made use of the easily quarried local granite, a combination which explains the name of the town. The inside of the church is not unpleasing, though late in date, and it contains a well preserved St George on horseback spearing an indignant dragon.

At the far end of the *place* a striking modern war memorial has a sculptured tableau which commemorates the dead of several units of the Resistance who concentrated here, two thousand strong, on 24 July 1944 to launch a drive to link up with Allied troops and other units of the Free French. Like their comrades in the Châtillonais they suffered heavily, but will not easily be forgotten in Quarré-les-Tombes.

The abbey of **la Pierre-qui-Vire** is buried deep in the Morvan woods to the south of St-Leger-Vauban. Its buildings are modern, except for the nineteenth-century chapel where Mass on Sunday mornings attracts a big congregation. The monks employ a lay architect, Marc Hénard, whose work we saw at Notre-Dame-d'Orient; his characteristic woodcarving can be seen on the wide doorway leading to the *clôture*. The fame of the abbey has spread even beyond the frontiers of France, for here are designed the superb illustrated volumes of the series known as *La Nuit des Temps*, a detailed study of Romanesque architecture and sculpture throughout Europe. Forty-four volumes are currently listed in the series, which seems a natural successor to the illuminated manuscripts produced by monks in the Middle Ages.

Being so remote, the abbey became a natural place of refuge during the German occupation for Resistance or Jewish fugitives, but the monks kept out of trouble. Once a party of soldiers burst into the Refectory during the midday meal, brandishing guns, but the coolness and dignity of their reception seems to have over-awed them, and they left without searching the premises. This detached and business-like Benedictine demeanour is evident to-day, and it contrasts with the cheerful and outgoing spirit you usually find among their Cistercian brethren when off duty. There is a contrast too between their sophisticated erudition and the ancient superstitions which linger in the Morvan. Perhaps even today *bouillon* is sprinkled on village houses on Shrove Tuesday to charm away the snakes, with the old jingle:

Sarpent, sarpent, vai-t'en,
Vouechi [voici] le bouillon de Carmentran.

Here as you look out from Pierre-qui-Vire is 'l'horizon qui toujours finit et recommence', and it extends deep into the department of Saône-et-Loire. The greater part of the Morvan is a regional *parc*, and this protects its wild and varied beauty. It is ideal walking country, where the hills never exceed a height of 3,000ft; the rivers are suitable for canoeing and the lakes ideal for sailing. A heavy annual rainfall (reinforced by snow in winter) collects to form a high water table above an impermeable granite base. The Lac de St-Agnan (190 hectares) just south of Pierre-qui-Vire receives the upper waters of the Cousin, and the Lac du Crescent (138 hectares) stretches for six kilometres south of Chastellux.

Generally the pasture is poor, and farming is on a small scale. The wealth of the Morvan today comes from its forests, where it is good to see broad-leaved plantations of birch, beech, and above all oak, holding their own against intrusive conifers. It would be a lesson for British woodland managers to see how carefully the woods beside the roads are being thinned and cleared of scrub and saplings to allow the best specimens to develop straight and free. There will be no lack of prime oaks in Burgundy in a hundred years' time. Yet conifers are not neglected either, and Christmas trees find a market down in Saulieu as well as in Avallon.

The villages and farms may not look prosperous, but their people live well in country fashion. You will not go far without being offered *jambon de Morvan, soupe aux choux*, or *canard aux châtaignes*, and the trout are abundant. For the geologist, fossils have been found in the crystalline rock; amethyst, malachite, azurite and chalcopyrite have been discovered; the iron at Prabis was exploited by the Aedui, and in our own day manganese has been mined near St Prix, coal in the Gorges de la Canche. Quantities of flint tools are proof of human occupation and industry from the end of the Neolithic Age onwards. The most casually observant visitor will delight in the broom and the bracken, the bilberries, pink heather, purple foxgloves and wild orchids.

The D10 which returns you to Avallon from Quarré-les-Tombes passes through the village of **Marrault**, and before leaving this part of the Morvan there is a chance to see an apt example of countryside development in Burgundy today. At the head of the long étang du Moulin stands a large château, entirely refurbished in recent years in neo-Renaissance style; to it belongs this pair of connecting lakes, and a good deal of land around. Its owner is a French industrialist who has preserved it, uses it as his country retreat, and grows all the necessary produce for his family in the grounds. What he does not own is a neo-Romanesque chapel on the slope below the château, built in 1921 on top of an old cowshed, and presented in perpetuity to the archbishop of Sens, for the use of the parish, by none other than Professor Louis-Pasteur-Valléry-Radot of the *Académie française* and his wife. Both buildings are striking and attractive – they just illustrate different approaches to the twentieth-century environment of Burgundy.

There is still time to complete our circuit of the Avallonais by crossing east to **Ste-Magnance**, some twelve kilometres down the N6 on its way to Saulieu. The name belongs to the third of the three devoted women (with Saints Camille and Pallaye) who in the year 448 escorted the body of St Germain back to Auxerre from Ravenna where he died. St Magnance died in the village when not far from their goal, and some years later a knight passing through dreamed that a snake was putting its head into his mouth, and that Magnance with one of her friends was warning him of the danger. Waking, he found the snake was doing just what he had dreamed, and he afterwards found the head of the saint buried in the village. She is now interred in an elaborate tomb in the church, where the sculptures show the knight asleep with the head of his horse for a pillow, the apparition of the two women, and the snake clearly visible.

You have now exchanged the heights of the Morvan for the wide agricultural plain east of Avallon, and after seven kilometres to the north by the D13 you come to **Savigny-en-Terre-Plaine**. The church here is built of red sandstone, and apart from the perfection of its appointments and upkeep it has a lot of charm. Its tall spire beckons from quite a distance over the flat terrain, and you enter through a tiled and beamed porch with stone pillars which shelters a double Romanesque doorway. Inside is late Burgundian Romanesque at its simple best – slightly pointed arches in the nave and transept, ribbed vaulting in the choir. In the south aisle two more than life-size figures in Elizabethan dress are kneeling at their *prie-Dieu* – the church's sixteenth-century patrons.

You have now almost reached the A6 autoroute, so it is time to turn back along the N6 to **Avallon** itself, perched on its granite promontory between two ravines, and accessible in a few minutes from the valley of the Cousin. The town has had a long and stormy history. The discovery of a Celtic coin with the inscription ABALLO proves that there was a mint here, and the portrait on the reverse side suggests there were Druids too. Under the Roman empire it was an important post on the strategic north-south highway built by Marcus Agrippa for Augustus, and before long Christianity had spread far enough north to replace its pagan temples with churches. However, in 731 the Saracens went through Avallon with fire and sword, followed by the Normans a hundred years later. After this the inhabitants decided to build the first fortifications, and in the ninth century it was important enough for Charlemagne to present the comté first to Louis le Debonnaire and then to his son Pepin, king of Italy.

Its troubles returned when Robert Capet besieged Avallon during his attack on Burgundy, took it after a three months' siege and put the inhabitants to the sword, leaving only three hundred in a state of complete misery. Peace and prosperity returned under the early Burgundian dukes, when in 1200 Eudes III granted the town a charter of freedom, but subsequently it was attacked and occupied by the English during the Hundred Years' War, recaptured by Philip the Good after a six weeks' siege, and pillaged during the wars of religion. Apart from all this there were outbreaks of plague in 1347, 1531, 1585 and 1596.

The surprising thing is that there is still so much of interest to see in the town, and this may be put down to the resilience of its inhabitants, who after every disaster set about immediately restoring its fortifications and public buildings. When its military importance declined, Louis XIV sold the ramparts to the municipality, which has preserved them as a promenade. What was lost irreparably to the iconoclasts of the Revolution was the greater part of some glorious sculpture over the principal doorway of the **Church of St-Lazare**,which stands beside the cobbled rue Bocquillot beyond the southern gateway.

A church was built here in the fourth century, of which only the crypt remains under the present choir. In the year 1000 Henri le Grand, duke of Burgundy, presented the church with a relic of St Lazarus supposed to protect the population against leprosy; by the end of the eleventh century pilgrims were flocking in such large numbers that it was decided, after consulting the architects of Cluny, to enlarge the Carolingian church to include the apse and the choir as you see them today. The new church of St-Lazare was consecrated by Pope Paschal II in 1106, but even then it proved too small, and a further twenty metres were added to the nave – which was finally restored in 1860.

The façade is most unusually placed at an oblique angle to the line of the nave. Originally it had two towers and three doorways, but the north tower collapsed in 1633, destroying the left-hand doorway. The existing tower was raised shortly afterwards to replace it. Had all three doorways survived with their sculpture they would have constituted perhaps the finest group of its kind in France. The smaller right-hand one, with its tympanum, *voussure* and archivolt almost intact, is as rich, varied and inventive a work of Romanesque sculpture as you will find in Burgundy, to say the least of it. On the larger (originally the central) doorway you can still make out the signs of the zodiac and the labours of the months, but the central figure of Christ has gone from the tympanum. St Lazarus has also gone, but there remains an enigmatic statue of an unknown prophet which has finally found a place, after much disturbance, in a corner niche.

Six steps lead down into the nave, which you will see is built on the Vézelay plan, with no triforium, though the principal arches are slightly pointed and the capitals are foliated rather than *historiés.*The nave itself is not high, and the apse even lower, approached down more steps as the body of the church follows the slope of the ground. The chapel of the Sacré-Cœur in the left-hand absidiole has a curious eighteenth-century *trompe l'œil* painting, while in the central apse behind the altar St Theresa is the centre of a formidable trio, the others being St Bernard and St Ignatius Loyola. In the first bay to the right of the nave is a charmingly natural group of the Virgin being taught to read by St Anne.

St-Lazare was a collegial church run by canons controlled by the bishop of Auxerre. Immediately next to it was the parish church of **St-Pierre**, but this has long been disused and closed to the public. A tour of the ramparts can still be made, thanks to the gift of Louis XIV. Starting from the bastion of the Petite Porte at the southern end of the town, you pass the east end of St-Lazare immediately on your left, and the Tour de l'Escharguet a little further on. Turn left at the Tour Beurdelaine, cross the Terreaux Vauban with its statue of the Maréchal at the east end; then turn left again at the bastion of the Porte Auxerroise and continue down the line of wall past the Tour des Vaudois and the Tour du Chapitre, till you reach the Tour Gaujard, opposite your starting point at the Petite Porte. In the middle of the town, on the way down to St-Lazare, you will have passed under the magnificent Tour de l'Horloge, built in the fifteenth century, with its turret and campanile.

Close to the Tour de l'Horloge is the former **Collège**, rebuilt in 1653 by Pierre Odebert, Counsellor in the Burgundian parliament, which now houses (together with the municipal library) one of those excellent small museums which are a feature of French provincial towns. It includes a whole range of discoveries from the long history of the neighbourhood, together with an annexe for research and a laboratory of ethno-zoology – the study of animal bone structures from excavated sites.

The French are proud of the places through which Joan of Arc had passed, very much as the English are proud of the beds in which Queen Elizabeth I slept. The Maid passed through Avallon on her way to Chinon, and again on the journey to Reims. On 16 March 1815 Napoleon found a recalcitrant royalist municipal council, but an enthusiastic populace.

CHAPTER SEVEN

From Avallon to Fontenay

This is another longish cross-country journey, with its principal goal slightly to the north of east. The Morvan is behind you, and for the most part it will take you through typical rolling Burgundian farmland, rising to little more than a thousand feet in places as you cross the plateau between the rivers Serein and Armançon, and pass from the department of Yonne into that of Côte d'Or. Your route avoids great forests; instead man has built widely and comfortably in a pleasant open landscape. In these affluent surroundings Burgundian artists too have flourished.

An obligatory first stop will be at **Montréal**, a convenient twelve kilometres along the D957 on its way east, and a prize for the historically minded traveller. It owes its name (in Latin *Mons Regalis*) to a visit by Queen Brunéhaut, widow of King Sigibert of Austrasia, with her grandson Thierry (Theuderic II) early in the seventh century. She became regent of Burgundy after the deaths of her brother-in-law King Gontran and her son Childebert, whom Gontran had adopted as his heir. The Revolution, which tried to change everything, made a vain attempt to change Montréal's name to Mont Serein, but royalty persisted here if nowhere else. The town is mediaeval to its marrow, and fine houses of many different centuries appear as you round the corners of its narrow, high-walled lanes.

For more than two centuries (1000 to 1225) it was a feudal domain of the Anséric-Beauvoir dynasty, lords also of Chastellux-sur-Cure, but of their fortress on the Serein only the upper and lower gateways, a watch-tower and a few stretches of wall remain. In 1255 a decree of St Louis incorporated Montréal into the duchy of Burgundy, and Henri IV raised what was then a barony to a marquisate. François I came here twice, and gratefully allowed the town to incorporate his salamander into its armorial bearings.

On your left, before entering the principal street through the lower gateway, you will find the twelfth-century Augustinian

Priory of St Bernard (now the hospital of St-Joux) where Vauban received his first lessons in mathematics. It is now a home for old people, but the Romanesque chapel is open and Mass is celebrated there every morning. Do not delay too long, though, before climbing the steep narrow road to the crest of the hill where the castle once stood, and where now the collegial **Church of Notre-Dame** will demand all your attention.

It was founded by Anséric de Montréal in fulfilment of a vow made when he left to join the crusade of 1147, so that building began about 1160 – just at the time of the transition in Burgundy from late Romanesque to early Gothic. Thus it is that we find broken arches and ribbed vaulting in the nave and side aisles, while in the square-ended sanctuary there are three handsome Romanesque lancets above blind semi-circular arcading. The four rose windows – one in the sanctuary, one in each of the two transepts and one over the west door – are among the earliest examples of their kind. The glass in all but the eastern one is plain, which shows up the varied tracery and floods the church with light. Viollet-le-Duc, whose work in restoring it (at a cost of 100,000 francs) can only be admired, was especially struck by these windows, and compared the eastern one to the rose that blossoms over the façade of Notre-Dame in Paris. Unfortunately the coloured glass in it is unworthy of the design.

Over the western entrance a massive stone tribune was built for the use of the Anséric household, supported by pairs of corbelled buttresses with one slender column below. In the furnishings of the church there are several competitors for the first prize. Once it would have been claimed by the fifteenth-century alabaster *retable*, carved by an English artist of the Nottingham school (was he perhaps a serving soldier in the Hundred Years' War seduced to stay behind in France?), but a particularly damaging and malicious theft in 1971 has left only three of the original seven bas-relief panels. Of the other four, which have never been heard of since, it was fortunate that a M. Kill of Avallon had in his personal collection the photographic reproductions which now complete the number – mounted on the left-hand wall of the sanctuary.

The base of the hexagonal wooden pulpit is carved with such vivid scenes of bare-breasted and Bacchanalian revelry that the apparent attention of the congregation must often have flattered

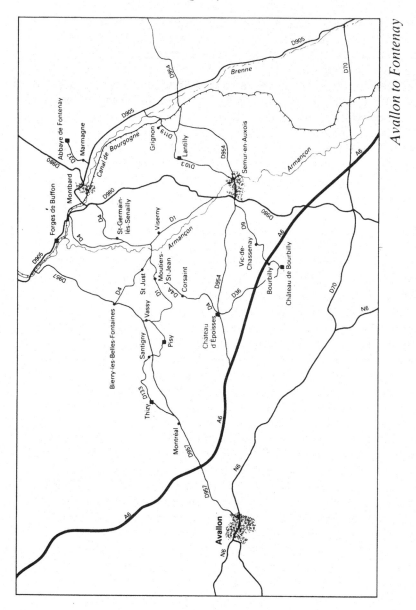

the preacher. On a higher plane, look for a fourteenth-century stone calvary with the sun and moon on one side and the Virgin and Child on the other; then (continuing the church's theme of Our Lady) there is a seventeenth-century Virgin in wood, who is holding her gown over her arm as if preparing to dance. More wonderful still is a fifteenth-century triptych with the figure of Christ in the centre, on one side St Peter, on the other one of the most delightful of all Virgin and Child cameos – the lively little boy grips the strings of his mother's cloak, trying to reach the pear she holds in her right hand. She is young, beautiful and loving, and he is quite prepared to be naughty.

Even in a region where wood-carving reached its highest excellence, the choir stalls stand out unique in technical mastery and brilliance of conception. There are twenty-six carvings in all. Among them you will find Adam and Eve, Samson at grips with his lion, a Visitation (with a background of mountain, château and windmill), the shepherds of the Nativity with tiny, perfectly delineated sheep, the homage of the Magi and a Baptism. Best of all is the scene in Joseph's workshop, where the carpenter is working at a bench, the walls hung with miniature tools of the trade, all exactly carved, while a certain small boy is learning to walk for the first time. Overlooking the scene from the back row of the stalls are the two master carpenters of the sixteenth century, the brothers Rigolley, seated at either end of a trestle table in the act of pouring themselves wine from an outsize *pichet*. These men are known to have been born at Nuits-sous-Ravières near Montbard, and their work here is dated 1522.

On 14 January each year, Montréal used to celebrate the Fête des Buffenis, when the inhabitants walked through the town threatening naughty children. If you come to Burgundy in spring you may also notice the bundles of long branches leaning up against door-frames. These are known as the *mais*, and they are put up by the boys of a village whenever a girl living there is thought to be ripe for marriage.

From the terrace outside you look north across the valley of the Serein towards the hilltop of **Thizy**, where a formidable castle once shared the defence of the valley with Montréal. More striking at a distance than close to, the ruins comprise a thirteenth-century *donjon*, a square corner tower, and a later round one on the south-

ern angle of the *enceinte*. Now only the annexe of a farm, it shares
the fate of so many mediaeval châteaux in Burgundy – not bought
by the wealthy to live in, or grand enough to attract national or
regional interest in preserving them. The church alongside is still
in use and has some good modern glass; in the village below, the
restaurant L'Atelier has a few comfortable rooms and an exhibition of *brocante* and local crafts.

A few miles further up the D957 is **Pisy**, where the château has
suffered the same indignity, and only the walls remain of what was
one of the strongest fortresses in Burgundy. It was begun in 1235
and entirely rebuilt about 1480; huge buttresses support the outer
walls, solidly rooted in the hillside. The church is a different matter, and shows what can be done when good taste is allied to local
enthusiasm in bringing life to an ancient fabric. The Romanesque
east end has been beautifully restored, and the original structure of
the choir and transepts left clear. A curious late feature has been
preserved – a wooden stairway with turned balusters was at some
time (probably in the seventeenth century) introduced between
nave and north transept to reach the short bell tower above; as a
result a small flamboyant doorway in the west wall of the transept
was and remains partially blocked.

Beyond Pisy is **Bierry-les-Belles-Fontaines** (not to be confused with Druyes-les-Belles-Fontaines in the Puisaye) where the
château of **Anstrude** was once an important presence in the neighbourhood. It was built in 1710 by André-François Anstruther, who
no doubt owed his names to some fulfilment of the auld alliance.
The approach still looks important – avenue, bridges over a double
moat, wrought-iron gates leading to a courtyard – but now its
future seems in doubt. Again the church next door has fared better,
if only occasionally used. The upper part of the façade looks
baroque, but the tympanum below, set in a trefoil, is a cleanly
executed fifteenth-century Baptism, where an avuncular St John
(whose church it is) is assisting a cheerful Christ to disrobe, while
an obliging young angel holds the upper garments he has discarded. Above there is a plain, stumpy tower with an incongruous
spire, but the east end is entangled with the inevitable farm buildings. It must be a long time since the owners of the château walked
across the elevated passageway which took them directly into the
west end of the church.

You are now on the borders of the department of Côte d'Or, but rather than the direct route down the valley of the Bornant to Fontenay there remains a worthwhile diversion to the south. **Moutiers-St-Jean** (*moutier* is the old word for *monastère*) claims what was the oldest monastery in Burgundy, founded early in the fifth century, rebuilt in the twelfth and thirteenth, but destroyed in the Revolution. A door of the church may be seen in the Cloisters Museum in New York, and there are some capitals in the Fogg Museum at Harvard University whose style links them with the work of Gislebertus at Autun. St-Vincent-de-Paul founded a hospital on the site, but this has now been sold privately.

The main objective of this detour will be **Époisses**, one of the most individual châteaux in all Burgundy. Unfortunately times for visiting are restricted: in 1995, you could walk round it at a respectful distance between Easter and September but the inside was open only at fixed hours in July and August for guided tours.

If you were tracing the footsteps of St Columba you would not expect to find him here; nevertheless tradition ascribes him a role in the history of Époisses. Queen Brunéhaut, anxious to get her grandson Thierry out of the way during the last years of his minority, brought him here from Montréal and surrounded him in the château with dissolute women to distract him from too much concern with affairs of state. Columba, who was then evangelizing Gaul, arrived at Époisses intending to reproach the young king for his scandalous behaviour. Refusing, however, to enter the château and baptize the king's illegitimate children, or attend a banquet in his own honour, he departed leaving only curses behind him.

Époisses became a ducal residence, but in 1189 Hugues III exchanged it for Montbard. From the counts of Montbard it passed through various hands to Jacques de Savoie, duc de Nemours, a fervent Catholic and as successful in love as he was in war; a century later Mme de Lafayette took him as the hero of *La Princesse de Clèves*. His extravagance was such that in 1561 he was obliged to sell the castle to the Maréchal de Bourdillon, and this was the only time when Époisses has been bought and sold. Bourdillon gave his name to one of the towers, and the château was left to his niece Françoise, the wife of Louis d'Anssienville, baron de Revillon.

From 1589 to 1593 it was pillaged from floor to ceiling by the forces of the Ligue. In 1602 the elected representatives of Burgundy asked for royal permission to demolish it, but Henri IV decided it should be spared. In 1613 Louis XIII raised the barony to a marquisate as a reward for Louis d'Anssienville's services to the crown; his granddaughter Madeleine married Guillaume de Guitaut, and this is how the château came into the possession of the family which has held it ever since. A neighbour was Madame de Sévigné, and Bourbilly, where she spent so much of her childhood with her grandmother, Jeanne de Chantal, was a fief of Époisses. She loved the country and the air – 'which you have only to breathe to get fat' – and she was a frequent guest at Époisses.

At the Revolution the family papers were saved by the devotion of the servants and villagers, for relations were easy between the château and the *bourg*, and the *bourgeois* were allowed to store their wine and grain in the feudal cellars. But in 1793 more than half of the adjacent property was sold by order of the Committee of Public Safety, and it was decided that the château should be destroyed – although M. de Guitaut was eventually allowed to keep whichever half of it he preferred. He chose the more habitable part, but even the towers of this section were ordered to be razed to the level of the living quarters. Fortunately the money to pay the workmen hired to do this ran out. The comte and comtesse were at first imprisoned, but released under Robespierre; they found the courtyard and moats of the château choked with débris and their living quarters half destroyed. They set about restoring them, and throughout the nineteenth century the château gave its hospitality to many illustrious visitors.

If you looked down from the air you would see a double *enceinte* of fortifications with the space between them filled by greensward and the remains of plantations designed by Le Nôtre. The château originally formed a complete oval surrounded by a deep moat, but all the buildings of the southern range were demolished in the Revolution, including three towers. This left the *cour d'honneur* exposed to the south, and in the last century a two-arched balustraded bridge was built over the moat to connect it with the outer walks.

The entrance to the property as a whole is by a gateway and bridge to the east, which brings you into the *avant-cour* ; this is a miniature village in itself, with a row of mediaeval houses backing on to the moat, a round dovecote with 3,000 pigeon-holes, and a small church. Entry to the *cour d'honneur* and the main buildings is through the clock tower, one of the four remaining towers of the château, whose outer walls drop sheer into the moat. Of the other three the **Tour de Condé** is the most prominent, seen to the right as you cross the forecourt, and named after the 'grand Condé' who once owned the château and enjoyed the view from his windows. Its square bulk is softened by alternate bands of pink and grey stone. Central to the present living quarters, though not visible from the inner court, is the little **Tour des Archives**, built in rustic stone and abutting on to the moat. The whole range ends in the solid and ancient **Tour de Bourdillon**, built in the tenth century (and sometimes misleadingly called the Tour de Brunéhaut) but restored by Marshal Bourdillon in the sixteenth century.

The inner façade as you see it from across the *cour d'honneur* has been modified several times in different styles, but the mellow stonework and long curving line of red-tiled roofs blend well today. Compared with grand and assertive places like Tanlay and Ancy-le-Franc, Époisses has an unassumingly domestic look and a rare kind of charm.

In the vestibule the walls are covered with portraits of personalities of their time, and in the adjoining room are those of the comte and comtesse de Guitaut, who rebuilt the château after the Revolution. In the room where Henri IV had slept – the *chambre du roi* – the portraits of Condé and of François de Guitaut are of particular interest. The latter was an experienced diplomat, never more successful than when he brought about a reconciliation between Louis XIII and Anne of Austria. Seizing the opportunity of a rainy evening he persuaded the king to take shelter with his wife in the Louvre – and nine months later Louis XIV was born.

The room which Mme de Sévigné is said to have occupied at Époisses speaks of her personality, resilient and gay. 'The beauty and grandeur of this house are astonishing', she wrote to her daughter in 1673. Her portrait hangs beside the elegant four-poster bed. The famous Époisses cheese is for sale in the village and justifies its reputation – delicious, but difficult to handle when ripe.

If you cross the A6 autoroute by way of the D36 you come to **Bourbilly**, a lesser château in size and reputation, but a delightful family home in a wooded valley of the upper Serein. The short distance from Époisses meant that Mme de Sévigné could equally well spend her time here, and in a way she had more reason to do so. 'I have just arrived', she wrote, 'in the old château of my forebears... here are my beautiful meadows, my little river and my magnificent woods, and my lovely windmill, just where I had left them'. Her family connections went back to Jeanne de Chantal, the Burgundian saint who was as much a character in the early sixteenth century as her granddaughter was to become later on. Born at Dijon, the daughter of a councillor at the *cour de consignés*, she first met St François de Sales, bishop of Geneva, when he was preaching a course of Lenten sermons in the city. Deeply impressed, she moved her seat in the church to see and hear him better, and they soon became close friends.

He was then thirty-six years old, she considerably younger. She subsequently married the baron de Chantal, by whom she had several children – one of them was the father of Mme de Sévigné – and they lived in great happiness at Bourbilly until, after eight years, her husband was killed in a hunting accident. For a long time she was unable to forgive the man who had been the involuntary cause of his death, and François de Sales understood her feelings. 'I know how the blood boils in your veins; nevertheless you must forgive.' In 1607 they founded together the Order of the Visitation at Annecy, where they are buried side by side. Their last meeting was at Lyon: 'Je m'en irai,' said St François, 'sans trompettes.'

This remarkable woman founded seventy-eight small religious houses all over Europe, travelling everywhere on horseback. Her relics are preserved in the chapel of the château of Bourbilly, and every year on her feast day, 21 August, Mass is celebrated there by the abbot of la Pierre-qui-Vire.

The château began as a *maison forte* of the fourteenth century, though a large part of its fortifications was removed in the Revolution. Even so it was still handsome enough not to deserve the pepperpot towers which were put up in the last century, as the present châtelaine is quick to point out. It was her late husband's grandfather, an admirer of Queen Victoria and the British way of life, who was responsible for them, as he was for the Gothick library (some of his books were exhibited at the Crystal Palace) and for putting in the sensible big windows which look out on the parkland behind. His severe portrait keeps odd company in the library with one of the spirited Jeanne.

The *salon* was also rebuilt and elegantly refurnished after the Revolution. In it there is a portrait (by a pupil of David) of the Italian *maestro* Spontini, seated at the first pianoforte ever made in France. It was made in 1777 not by Pleyel but by Sebastian Érard, in imitation of instruments he saw being made in London about the same time, and it was his trade in musical instruments which has helped to support his descendants at Bourbilly ever since. Civil engineering has also contributed, for a member of the present owner's family was involved in building the Canal de Bourgogne, and in first bringing piped water to Dijon.

You will be lucky if Madame Darcy herself is able to show you round. She will take you through *salon*, library and dining room, all of which can be matched in many a domestic Burgundy château, but the **Chapel** at Bourbilly is unique. It was entirely rebuilt between 1952 and 1975 after a fire had gutted its fifteenth-century original, and it owes almost everything in it to the work of the family and their friends, who undertook to restore it in a spirit of love and dedication. The wooden altar was made by the head gardener. Of its eleven legs (for the eleven true apostles) ten are made of different woods; the odd one out is in stone, for St Peter. It was Madame Darcy who modelled the portrait heads of her children on the corbels which support the roof beams, her son-in-law designed the roof itself and the floor paved with multicoloured bricks, and another member of the family painted the wall above the gallery (part of the mediaeval *chemin-de-ronde* with a *danse macabre* sequence derived from the one at la Ferté-Loupière. One of the fathers from la Pierre-qui-Vive painted a fresco of the Visitation, using mediaeval techniques, which recalls the Order founded by Jeanne de Chantal.

Perhaps the most remarkable thing in the chapel is the exquisitely fine wrought-iron grille across the entrance, the work of an unregarded local blacksmith who had sent it up to Paris for an exhibition. It was refused on the grounds that it included symbols connected with freemasonry, and in disgust he left it in the field outside his workshop. After his death his family gave it to the Bourbilly chapel, and you will marvel at the delicacy – in this medium – of a swallow in flight, a cross in the form of a rose, and a beautifully worked Tree of Jesse. Finally the stained glass windows were commissioned from a major artist by a group of friends to celebrate the conclusion of the work in 1975 – which Monsieur Darcy happily lived to see.

Dodging back under the autoroute on the D9 through Vic de Chassenay you can rejoin the D980 as it passes **Semur-en-Auxois,** where you may be looking for a night's rest. There is not a lot of choice in the town, though the Côte dOr is comfortable and has a good bourgeois restaurant. An alternative is the Hôtel du Lac which stands beside the Lac de Pont three kilometres to the south – near but not uncomfortably near the airfield. This is an established family concern and would make a good base for exploring the Auxois.

Before investigating Semur itself I suggest completing the journey which began in Avallon and is due to end at Fontenay. This will give us the chance of visiting **Lantilly** on the way north from Semur, where there is another château with an even closer connection with England than Bourbilly. Built in 1709 by Charles de Chaugy on its ancient foundations, it was sold for the last and only time in 1775 to the vicomte de Virieu, ancestor of the present owner. Unusually, therefore, for Burgundy it presents a homogeneous front of the early eighteenth century, with only the extreme northern end of its range suggesting a mediaeval origin. The few windows there contrast with the abundance elsewhere which has earned its title of 'le château aux cent fenêtres'.

The turbans which are a feature of the Virieu arms celebrate the triumphs of a crusading marquis who decapitated a large number of Turks. It is a play too on the word *vire*, meaning a twist of material, but such rough memories have no place in the elegant rooms now shown to visitors. The key to much of what we see lies in the family's more recent descent on the maternal side, in particular the taste and personality of the grandmother of the present marquis. Born Eugénie de Mun, she married a M. de Blacas, descendant of a French ducal family who had settled in England at the turn of the century. There is an enchanting portrait of her in the library at the age of twelve, and in the same room a silk embroidery panel of the Annunciation, set against a familiar French landscape, which occupied her for fifteen years during her widowhood at Lantilly.

The English influence is most obvious in the dining room, where the *style Empire* of its décor is married to the *style anglais* of its furniture; it also contains a unique service of porcelain from the Paris workshops of Nast. The view, however, from the dining room windows is not of a *parc à l'anglais* — the ground falls away too steeply to the east for that — but of a glorious prospect across the deep valley of the Brenne to Mont Auxois and the Gallic fortress of Alésia. The salon Louis XVI is appropriately furnished, and has on its walls both a portrait of Louis XVIII at the age of sixteen, when he was comte de Provence, and a large contemporary painting by Frédoul of the then vicomte de Virieu presenting the colours of his regiment (the Royal Provence) to the same young man. When he succeeded to the throne in 1814 he presented the picture to the family. Also to be seen here is a lovely fifteenth-century ikon by the Italian Nenni, a fine drum table, and some eighteenth-century Japanese silk hangings which were rolled up and successfully hidden from the German occupiers in the last war.

Not the least of the surprises at Lantilly is the complete surviving installation of the earliest central heating system known since the Roman Empire — a German design of formidable ingenuity. Yet the memory Lantilly leaves is that of a comfortable, elegant and much loved family home.

Barely three kilometres further on is **Grignon**, where a feudal fortress built in the eleventh and twelfth centuries has recently been restored after complete neglect since the beginning of the eighteenth century. There are many reminders within of a romantic past, including the cell where the local martyr Ste Reine is said to have been imprisoned in the third century, but its restoration has brought new owners, and visitors are no longer admitted even within the gates.

There is compensation to be found in the parish church of Grignon. This is not remarkable in itself, though it has a thirteenth-century nave, but in the chapel of the Twelve Apostles in the south transept, dated 1443, there is a curious triangular-headed *retable* carved in stone with scenes from the life of Christ. On the wall opposite is another stone group: Christ is seated with his feet on the world, giving it his blessing, angels fly above his head, and the Apostles stand in two rows beneath. Both these unusual works come from the chapel of Ste Reine in the château, as did probably a stone panel of St Hubert's vision on the right of the *retable*.

You are now close to the D905, which follows the line of the Brenne and the Canal de Bourgogne into **Montbard**. Modern industry crowds the bank of the canal, but between there and the bridge over the Brenne a more mediaeval spirit prevails. It was here in 1423 that Prince John of Lancaster, duke of Bedford, married Anne de Bourgogne to cement the Anglo-Burgundian alliance of the day. Yet of the ducal château only two isolated towers remain, and the memory of the dukes of Burgundy has been eclipsed by the fame of one man – Georges-Louis Leclerc, comte de Buffon, who lived from 1707 to 1788.

As a young man he travelled widely in Europe collecting material for a study of the natural sciences, and in 1739 he was appointed Intendant of the Royal Garden by Louis XV. On easy terms with the king, he responded to a royal request for a roebuck from Montbard by sending him half a carcase, and Louis retaliated by sending him half a pâté. The Emperor of Austria treated him as an equal, 'as one power to another, for here I am on your imperial territory'. However, he spent only four months of the year in Paris, which he hated, and was glad to get back to the study which he had built in the Tour St Louis – having pulled down most of the rest of the château when he bought it in 1744. Here he concentrated on his life's great work, an *Histoire Naturelle* in many volumes (including ones on physics and astronomy), attended by his housekeeper Mlle Blessau, his gardener Dauché, and Père Ignace, a veteran soldier turned Capuchin monk.

In 1752 Buffon was elected to the *Académie française* and delivered his famous oration on style – *le style c'est l'homme* – and he practised what he preached. A dijonnais called Estaunié, standing before the bust by Houdon in the Louvre, noted 'the voluptuous mouth and the wrinkles in the cheeks, so eloquent of bonhomie and the love of well-being. Look particularly at the profile, where the habit of pleasure and a sly mockery are written unforgettably on the features. There you have a key to the man; if you didn't know it already, this bust would have revealed it to you. M. de Buffon is a Burgundian.'

In 1767 Buffon embarked on another astonishingly inventive career, that of ironmaster. He signed an agreement with the comte de Rochefort which allowed him to prospect for and to mine iron in the neighbourhood. The following year, armed with letters patent from Louis XV, he began building a model forge at a spot six kilometres downstream from Montbard, using for all its mechanical processes the water power from a mill-race diverted from the Brenne. This elaborate, practical yet stylishly designed complex, known as the **Forges de Buffon**, took four years to complete, and by 1772 it was in full production. Work was seasonal, though, and the forges closed down during the summer months – which must have helped Buffon with all his other commitments.

The mining of the ore, timberwork and transport were undertaken by the neighbouring villages, the charcoal for the furnaces was provided by communities living in the forests, while the specialist artisans – foundrymen, smiths and furnacemen – were lodged on the site with communal services provided. At the height of its activity (1772-1780) about 300 first rank artisans were employed at the Great Forge, with a backup of 30 to 50 casual labourers.

A project by local student organizations has restored much of the mechanism to working order, beginning with the giant water wheel which transmits the driving power of the mill-race. Visitors are shown the furnaces with their gigantic hydraulic bellows, and working models made by the students. They can also see the *affinerie* where the pig-iron was converted to iron bars, the huge mechanical hammers, and the *fenderie* where the iron bars were chopped into manageable lengths for transport and sale. All these processes went on in architecturally designed stone buildings, with a monumental stairway leading down to the hall where the great furnace sent the stream of molten metal on its way. Set back from the operational buildings is a pleasant courtyard surrounded by what were the workers' lodgings, the overseer's offices, stables and coachhouse, and – conveniently opposite the main working entrance – the little two-storeyed house which Buffon always occupied when he visited the forge.

Buffon remained a bachelor for many years, for he held that a grand passion took four years out of a man's life: 'two months to consummate it, four months to enjoy it, two years to be deceived, and a year to lose weight, travel and pull oneself together'. He confined himself to brief adventures which 'occupied only the two minutes when the angels, as they say, hide their faces with their wings so as not to be jealous of our pleasures'. When he married at the age of 43 he was faithful to his wife, whom he had met in the parlour of an Ursuline convent, and they had five children.

A visit to the Forges de Buffon may surprise those who imagined that the Industrial Revolution began only after the French one, and it does seem incongruous to imagine the great man in his wig, red coat, breeches, silk stockings and buckled shoes walking across to stand in the gallery above the furnace to watch the first stages in a carefully planned production line. A man of true genius, he died in Montbard in 1788, where he is remembered in the Parc Buffon (which he laid out) in the north-west corner of the town; he is buried in the chapel attached to the church of St-Urse. Though work went on at the forge intermittently after his death, production of iron ceased finally in 1866.

So in the end we come to Fontenay, that is to say the **Abbey of Fontenay**, which is best approached from Marmagne, two kilometres east of Montbard on the main road. It is the oldest surviving Cistercian abbey in France, and none demonstrates more clearly the Cistercian genius for choosing a site. It was built in the true spirit of the Order, beside a stream deep in the forest of Fontenay and, though convoys of coaches and sightseers' cars crowd the road up to it, once there you can enjoy the peace and seclusion it still affords.

Fontenay was the second foundation by St Bernard from Clairvaux. In 1118 he despatched a party of twelve monks under his cousin Godefroy de la Roche-Vanneau to found a monastery on the site of a small hermitage near Montbard beside a tributary of the Armançon. Godefroy returned to Clairvaux in 1126, but the community flourished and grew so big that a new site had to be found. In 1130 they established themselves further down the valley, on land given them by St Bernard's uncle, Rainard de Montbard, so that it was a family foundation from its beginnings. Work on the present abbey began in 1139, after a great deal of labour had been spent in diverting the *fontaines* and draining the site.

The force behind the building was an English bishop, Everard of Norwich, who had found sanctuary here from persecution in the reign of Henry I. He brought with him substantial means, and devoted them to building a church worthy of its origins and its needs. It was consecrated in 1147 by the Italian Pope Eugène III, himself a disciple of St Bernard. By the sixteenth century the community comprised more than 300 monks and lay brothers, but decadence set in when abbots came to be appointed by royal favour. The wars of religion hastened its decline, and at the Revolution it was sold and turned into a paper mill.

Entry is still through the **Porter's Lodge**, surmounted by the armorial bearings of the abbey, and as you pass under the vault you will notice a small niche below the staircase. This allowed a watchdog to keep an eye on the entrance, and bark to alert the porter. Turning to the left after entry you will pass a low thirteenth-century building with dormer windows, part of which served as a chapel for lay visitors; the far end was the bakery, where the great oven survives with its flue projecting from the wall above. The small building beyond the bakery was used during the lax years of the seventeenth century as kennels for the hounds belonging to the dukes of Burgundy, but looked after by abbey servants. Another monastic convenience, the dovecote, stands to the right of the approach to the west front of the **Abbey Church of Notre-Dame**.

Here frivolity has no place. It is the most severely satisfying of all the great Cistercian churches – more so than Pontigny and even Senanque. Planned as it may have been by St Bernard himself, it keeps to the mathematical proportions which we have registered in the cathedral of Sens. Such considerations will not be your first as you stand looking eastward up a starkly plain nave, unlit by any windows other than those to east and west, set in groups of round-headed embrasures – seven in the façade behind you, five beautifully spaced in the diaphragm over the archway to the choir, and six in the straight-ended sanctuary wall. There is no clerestory, no triforium, only the noble sequence of pointed arches which sustain the dark tunnel vault, a perspective ever narrowing to the east. From there the light flows in through plain glass, for the rule of St Bernard forbade the use of coloured glass or other ornamentation in windows. The only concession to the artist, which came after the founder's death, is the presence in the sanctuary of a thirteenth-century altar front, and at the entrance to the north transept a most lovely Virgin and Child of the same date. Both are of the Champenois school, carved in a light stone which matches the ethereal grace of their design.

The plan of the church and monastic buildings follows the Cistercian rule. The bays of the side aisles are of equal length and width, and the façade describes a square, if one includes the buttresses and upper string-course. The perfect consonances, so dear to the Christian Platonists, are maintained in the 1:1 ratio of the transept crossing; the 2:3 ratio which regulates the width of the crossing to its length, including the choir, and the relation between the width of the crossing and the total width of the nave with side aisles; and the 3:4 ratio which determines the relation between the total width of the nave plus side aisles and the length of the transept including chapels. If truth lies in proportion, Fontenay illustrates as well as any other sacred building of its time the identity of beauty and truth.

Two rectangular chapels extend eastward from each of the two transepts, and from the south transept a flight of steps leads to the **Monks' Dormitory**. This is a superb room, fifty-three metres long and twelve wide, crowned by a fifteenth-century roof which lies like a great half-barrel on its side, spanned by curving oak beams and cross-ties hewn from single trunks. Along both sides there are windows, but no glass was allowed to shelter the rows of straw palliasses on which the monks slept – to be woken in the earliest hours for the first offices of the day in the church below.

The **Cloister**, where much of the day was spent in work and meditation, is entered by a door at the head of the south aisle. Of the same date as the church and the body of the dormitory, its design is purely Romanesque, with wide arches each enfolding two beautifully proportioned smaller ones, except where access was allowed to the garth. The chapter house, built as usual on the east side of the cloister, lies under the dormitory and has two annexes. The larger of the two was the *scriptorium*, placed conveniently next to the *chauffoir*, which was the only room apart from the kitchens where a fire was allowed. It was this arrangement alone which kept the fingers of the copyists warm enough in winter to work on manuscripts. The heat would not have been allowed to penetrate across a corridor into the prison – which was not intended for erring monks but for those committed under the secular rule which the abbot administered throughout his domains. The **Infirmary** stood at a safe distance from the other buildings to avoid infection, and beside a garden of mediaeval herbs.

Vézelay: nave and choir of la Madeleine

Overleaf: Vézelay: central tympanum of la Madeleine

Saulieu: St-Andoche
(*Balaam and the Ass*)

Vézelay: la Madeleine
(*Noah's Ark*)

Autun: St-Lazare (*the Sleeping Magi*)

Across what is now an open grassy space is a fine long building where some of the most important work of the abbey went on. It may have surprised us to find at the Forges de Buffon an industrial complex of the eighteenth century, but here there was a **Forge** operating several hundred years earlier on something like the same principles. Here too power was derived from a mill-race alongside to drive the drop-hammers and bellows, and the blackening of the lower courses of the stonework betrays the presence of the furnaces. In the nineteenth century the building was converted to a paper mill, bought in 1820 by Élie de Montgolfier (of the balloon family), which turned out paper until 1906 when it was acquired by Edouard Aynard, Montgolfier's son-in-law. He dismantled the modern accretions with the help of his son René, who is the present owner, and left it as we see it today.

Just beyond the west end of the forge is the water tower which overlooks the famous trout pond. There are said to be as many as 10,000 fish in it, and they were formerly reserved for the kings of France and the dukes of Burgundy — though Buffon managed to enjoy them too.

The missing piece of the monastic jigsaw is the **Refectory**, which was pulled down in the eighteenth century before the Revolution. It projected from the south range of the cloister towards the forge, and must have been a magnificent building, with a double nave and a dozen sections of ribbed vaulting. It was replaced in 1856 by a building of similar proportions on an east-west axis, which is today the home of M. René Aynard, to whose family we owe the preservation and impeccable upkeep of the abbey of Fontenay, its appurtenances and its grounds. Nowhere else can you so easily reconstruct the Cistercian way of life. With some of the best guides in the business available, you can have an absorbing visit any day at all times of the year, with only the usual two-hour break at midday to allow for.

CHAPTER EIGHT

Semur and the Auxois

As with most of the regional subdivisions of France, the limits of the Auxois are vague, but its north-eastern corner corresponds roughly with the *pagus alisiensis* of Roman times, which was in the tribal territory of the Mandubii. Here on the flattened crest of Mont Auxois was built the fortified Gallic town, or *oppidum*, of Alésia. The name Auxois is appended to villages almost as far south as Saulieu, where it meets the borders of the Morvan, so this chapter will be concerned both to explore the land lying around Mont Auxois and later to take a wide sweep to the south as far as Saulieu – where there are good reasons for spending some time.

First, though, there is **Semur-en-Auxois** itself, which is a striking sight whether you approach it across a deep ravine from the north-west, or from lower ground to the east and south. The Armançon, joined here by the Soussiotte, winds around its mediaeval walls; the four round fourteenth-century towers, with their pointed red-tiled roofs, stand up boldly on a cliff of pink granite with the twin towers of Notre-Dame in the background. As you cross the ravine by the Pont Joly, the view of the formidable **Tour de l'Orle d'Or**, split from top to bottom by an alarming crack in the masonry, is one of the most familiar in Burgundy. It owes its name to the copper-tinted revetment (*ourlet*) of its original crenellations, which must have glowed like gold in the evening sunshine. The only remaining ramparts are those encircling the granite spur to the west – the *quartier du château* – and you can walk round them in the shade of chestnuts and limes, or below them in the shadow of the rock itself.

The **Church of Notre-Dame** was part of a priory dependent on the Benedictine abbey of St-Pierre at Flavigny-sur-Ozerain; the cloister and monastic quarters are still there, but are now incorporated within the Hôtel-de-Ville. The priory was secularized in

1739, and gave place to a chapter of twelve canons; its church reverted to the parish of Semur in 1812.

The church we see was begun soon after 1218 and probably completed before the end of the century. Building began at the east end, where the architect chose a three-storey Gothic elevation reminiscent of the cathedral of St-Etienne in Auxerre. Indeed the Semur master seems to have compiled for us a list of the buildings he had studied elsewhere. The triplet window in the ambulatory is typical of Picardy and Flanders, the jutting corbels come from Normandy, and the clerestory windows in the choir and transept remind us of Chartres – though not the glass in them, which is modern. The clerestory is exceptionally high, almost equal to the triforium and main arcades combined, and when a later architect produced final plans for the nave he increased the height of the main arcading and suppressed the triforium altogether. The distinctive interior passage, however, continues all round the clerestory.

Not surprisingly, this amalgam of styles and shifting of purpose within a Gothic framework cannot be called harmonious. The nave is narrow, which emphasizes the height of the vaulting without lifting the spirit as other great Gothic cathedrals do. There are no Cistercian beauties of proportion here, and the oversolid pillars of the ambulatory, with their stiff foliated capitals, spoil the effect of the double triforium arches and their slender columns. Perhaps we have Viollet-le-Duc to blame, though as usual it was he who saved Notre-Dame from ruin in the 1840s.

Nor, from close to, is the outside view more harmonious or inspiring. The disproportionate height of the clerestory shows up in the *chevet*, the octagonal tower over the crossing is a clumsy reconstruction, and the western façade is obscured by a large fifteenth-century porch with flamboyant pinnacles and balustrades. Yet it was revolutionary zeal, not an architect's whim, which ruined the tympanum over the west door; fortunately the very fine one over the northern portal is still there to remind us what the thirteenth century could do for sculpture. The chief theme is the little-known legend of St Thomas: his display of incredulity before Christ and the disciples; his voyage (by a remarkably small open boat) to visit Gondoforus, King of the Indians, with a commission to build him a royal palace. We see him presenting his

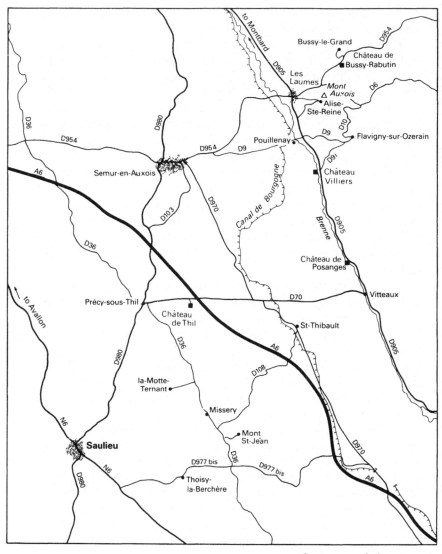

Semur and the Auxois

plans at the dinner table; he distributes his fee to the poor and is put in prison for his pains; finally he shows the king the way to a heavenly palace – conversion to Christianity. The archivolt above has the familiar sequence of the labours of the months, including methods of viniculture still practised in the Auxois. The pair of snails on one of the side columns acknowledge another Burgundian addiction.

Inside the church is some interesting statuary, the most remarkable being a dramatic fifteenth-century **Sepulchre** in polychrome stone, to be found in the second chapel of the north aisle. However, the most unusual feature is the stained glass in the windows of two other chapels off the north aisle, which illustrate work going on in the shops of butchers and drapers in the fifteenth century. Only two lively panels of butchers' work survive in the chapel of St Claude, while of the eight which so clearly picture the stages of cloth manufacture only four are original, the rest being replacements by Viollet-le-Duc. These entertaining views of contemporary life were given to Notre-Dame by the guilds concerned.

The **Museum** is to be found in a former Jacobin convent just before the car park on the rue J-J. Collenot, east of the church . It is mainly concerned with a collection of minerals and fossils, but the Library which shares the building is more interesting and important. It displays a number of precious manuscripts which include one of the tenth century, a missal which belonged to Anne de Bretagne, and one of the earliest of the *incunabula* to come from the Gutenberg press.

On 31 May each year, Semur celebrates the *Fête de la Bague*, during which the oldest horse race in France is run over a two-and-a-half-kilometre course to the south of the town. It was inaugurated in 1639, and the first prize is a gold ring engraved with the arms of the town; the second prize is a white scarf with a gold fringe, the third a pair of gloves. It seems a pity that in the modern world such delightful trophies have to be supplemented by cash.

To reach Mont Auxois from Semur is simple. Follow the rue de la Liberté out of town to the east on the D954, and after thirteen kilometres you will cross the D905 and the railway to find the village of **Alise-Ste-Reine** down a minor road to your right. Built on a shelf below the summit of the 1200ft hill, it takes the first part of its name from Alésia, the Celtic *oppidum* which crowned the hill, and the second from the saint who, they say, was imprisoned during the third century in the château of Grignon – or in whatever building stood there at the time! Ste Reine was a girl of good family who was converted to Christianity by her peasant nurse. Turned out of the house by her parents, she lived rough as a shepherdess, but was unlucky enough to attract the attention of the Roman *praefectus*. For refusing to renounce Christianity and marry him she was beheaded under the walls of Alésia.

The church here was in fact the early Christian basilica of St-Leger, and only changed its dedication to Ste-Reine later on – she is buried not here but in nearby Flavigny. It gets scant attention in guidebooks, which is strange considering that its faithful restoration in 1965 has left us with the best example of a Carolingian church to be found in Burgundy. The south wall of the nave is actually of Merovingian construction; that church was burnt by the Normans, to be partly rebuilt in the late ninth or early tenth century.

The apse has a simple *cul-de-four* in rough stone, and on the face of a side altar you can see a symbol resembling a swastika, which is really a Byzantine cross of about 250 AD known as a fylfot. To the right of the apse a doorway leads into a baptistery of at least Carolingian date; at the west end is an authentic Carolingian holy water stoup. Other treasures of later date are preserved here, and the highly educated principal *gardienne* (who is responsible for its faultless upkeep) will tell you all you wish to know. Most of the glass in the ancient window embrasures is modern, made in the workshops of the Taizé international community near Cluny.

The church's greatest treasure was a fourth-century paten inscribed with the Christian symbol of a fish, but this has been removed for safety to the museum in the village. The fish became a secret symbol of early Christianity by way of an acrostic code incorporating the Greek word for it – *ichthus* – thus:

> Iesus
> CHristos
> THeou
> Uios
> Soter

or Jesus Christ, the Son of God, the Saviour.

The **Museum** has been housed for some time in an endearing building at the far end of the village. As well as the paten, which is cleverly displayed with a mirror to reflect the inscription, there are vessels fashioned in a kind of silver lustre which was made in the workshops of Alésia. The finest is the **Vase Argenté**, with reliefs of Bacchus, Pan, Silenus and their crew. There are a great many other finds from the Gallo-Roman site on Mont Auxois, as well as plans and sectional photographs of its defences. These show the double line of fortifications described by Julius Caesar in his account of the famous siege of Alésia in 52 BC, and they pretty well settle the controversy about the location of the battle he is describing in his *Commentaries*.

In the spring of that year Caesar had been defeated for the first time in Gaul by Vercingetorix, leader of a mass tribal uprising, in a battle near Clermont-Ferrand. He retreated northwards to join his second-in-command, Titus Labienus, in the neighbourhood of Sens, and after reorganizing the cavalry (depleted by the defection of the hitherto loyal tribe of the Aedui) they marched south together. Near Dijon they were met by Vercingetorix, who had the worst of an indecisive engagement. Vercingetorix made the mistake of retreating with his troops into the *oppidum* of Alésia, and the siege began. It lasted for six weeks.

Caesar assembled an army of about 40,000 men, made up of legionary infantry and a now largely German force of cavalry. They surrounded the place with a double line of field works – trenches planted with sharpened stakes, palisades, walls and towers. The inner line, facing the hill, was meant to seal the exit from the town; the second blocked the way of a relieving army which Caesar knew was already on the way. When it arrived, about 250,000 strong, it was unable to penetrate the Roman defences; its cavalry was neutralized by the fresh German squadrons which Caesar had remounted on his spare horses, and which operated outside the defences. The crisis came when Vercingetorix led his troops out of the town in a last throw for victory; like Waterloo it was 'a damned close-run thing', with many changes of fortune.

It was the discipline of the Roman army and the tactical skill of its commanders which prevailed. The attackers faltered, the Romans counter-attacked successfully, and Vercingetorix surrendered to save his people from the threat of starvation and massacre.

Caesar paraded him in triumph through the streets of Rome, kept him in prison for six years, and finally had him put to death – the first and only leader of a united Gaul. It is interesting to read that among Caesar's senior officers in this engagement were Marcus Antonius (Shakespeare's Mark Antony) and the young Marcus Brutus, his eventual assassin.

The capture of Alésia was the end of organized Celtic resistance throughout Gaul, and the hilltop *oppidum* became a centre of the new Gallo-Roman civilization which was to give birth to modern France. The skills in metal-working which had always marked the Celtic peoples were allied to the solid building technique and the highly developed civic organization of the Romans. Large thriving towns grew up round many of the old Gallic sites; here at Alésia we have an open site which was never again built over. There may be still more to be revealed, but already it has given us one of the best pictures of European town life in the early centuries of our era.

A steep track (up which you can drive) leads to a car park outside the excavations. An enormous area was built over for occupation after the defeat of the Gauls, taking advantage of the wide flat ridge which is the summit of Mont Auxois. For the visitor the *Société des Sciences Historiques* of Semur has provided an excellent information sheet which follows the recommended route; its numbered descriptions correspond with the numbers displayed at each part of the site. The sheet is available at the ticket office on entry, your ticket is valid for both the site and the museum, in whichever order you prefer, and the site is open all day and every day from Easter to the end of October.

Alésia is particularly important to the archaeologist because it reveals so many details of town life from as early as the first century AD; whereas in Roman Britain, for example, later buildings of the third and fourth centuries have obscured much of the earlier evidence. The area chiefly connected with religious observance includes more traces of purely Gallic cults, such as that of the fertility goddess Epona, than of orthodox Roman theology. Private houses, shops, sewers and latrines are as prominent as the civic buildings round the Forum. Alésia was famous for its metal-workers in bronze, iron and silver, and in the quarter where these crafts were pursued you can trace furnaces, foundries, and workshops of all sorts. It was here that the technique of putting a silver glaze on pottery was developed.

The latest building on this huge site is the little rectangular basilica of Ste-Reine, whose ground plan has been cleared immediately on the right as you enter, though its allotted site number puts it at the end of your tour. It was a seventh-century church built to house the saint's remains, but eucharistic vessels dating from the fourth century, found under the car park, provide some of the oldest evidence of Christianity in France. Ste Reine's relics were removed to the abbey of St-Pierre in Flavigny in 865, probably after the final destruction of Alésia by the Normans.

In 1865 a giant statue of Vercingetorix by Millet was erected on the hillside immediately above Alise-Ste-Reine, looking westward towards Avallon; near it in 1945 the Théâtre des Roches was built on the classical model for performances of the Mystère de Ste Reine which takes place on the weekend nearest to 7 September as the climax of an annual pilgrimage and festival in her honour. Both she and Vercingetorix will probably live longer in the memories of Burgundy than their Roman conquerors.

If you now regain the D954 and follow the side valley of the Rabutin, a tributary of the Brenne, you will arrive (by way of a short approach road to the right) at a château which has been said to encapsulate the history of France in the seventeenth century . It earned this distinction through its most notorious owner, Roger de Rabutin, Comte de Bussy, and since his time it has always been known as the **Château de Bussy-Rabutin**.

His first reputation was won as a soldier. Born in 1618, he went with his father on campaigns before he was twelve. At sixteen he commanded a regiment, if only by proxy, and during the next six years he saw active service on several fronts in the Thirty Years' War. However, by the time of the Peace of Westphalia in 1648 he was already better known for his *amours*. One such affair landed him in the Bastille for five months on information laid by the husband he had wronged. Married for the first time in 1643 and widowed after four years, he turned his attention to a rich widow called Mme de Miramion, whom he kidnapped as she was returning from a pilgrimage. Forced to return her to her family – with a sweetener of 6,000 livres – he contracted a respectable second marriage with his cousin, Louise de Rouville, though he spent little time in her company.

He had already begun to repair the fabric of the château he had inherited at the time of his first marriage, and the date of 1649 inscribed on a medallion on the main façade must mean that the exterior work was mostly finished by then. However, he was now involved again in national events. Withdrawing from the camp of the Grand Condé, one of whose chief lieutenants he had been, he supported the royal family (Anne of Austria and the young Louis XIV) during the Fronde risings, and he fought in Flanders under Turenne.

It was now that Bussy's mischievous and sometimes scurrilous wit began to get him into trouble. First he made an enemy of Turenne by lampooning him in verse, then, finding himself on holiday outside Paris with a like-minded aristocratic company, he joined in a symposium which began with blasphemous parodies of the liturgy (*alleluias obscènes*) and culminated in Bussy reciting improvised verses on the *amours* of Louis XIV and Marie Mancini, while le Camus (a future cardinal) read the service of baptism over a toad – or as some said over a sucking pig. The scandal was reported and the king packed him off to exile in Burgundy.

To amuse himself during his absence from court he composed a series of malicious pen portraits of women with whom he had been, or would like to have been, involved, enlivened further by a good deal of the court gossip of the time. This work he felicitously entitled *L'Histoire amoureuse des Gaules*, having thinly disguised his characters in a historical context. Nemesis came in 1660 when he was recalled to court, but could not resist taking with him the *Histoire amoureuse* to show to his principal *inamorata* at the time, the marquise de Montglat. (He had also in the meantime paid court to his cousin, Marie de Sévigné; she, sensible woman, would have none of it, though they remained on good terms.) Copies of the work circulated at court, and Mme de Montglat passed hers on to a friend, Mme de la Baume. She, owing no loyalty to Bussy, allowed it to be printed in Liège, where it appeared just after he had been elected to the *Académie française* in 1661.

Louis had at first been more amused than angry, as he recognized the portraits of his courtiers, but the story goes that Condé, in revenge for what had been written about him, produced a fake sequel called *France galante* which concentrated on the affair between the king and Louise de la Vallière. It was the Bastille again for Bussy, and this time he spent thirteen months there before being released (through the efforts of his long-suffering wife) and banished once more to Burgundy.

This account of his life so far – and he was only forty-eight – is needed to explain why he spent the next twenty years in decorating the interior of his house in the extraordinary vein which intrigues the modern visitor. First, though, it is right to take time to admire from the outside one of the most architecturally satisfying of French domestic châteaux. The pathway from the gatehouse takes you to a point where you can appreciate its quality to the full. Framed in a gentle woodland setting, the perfect Renaissance façade is joined at right angles to simple arcaded wings which end in equally simple round towers. The stone is weathered and mellow, and you cross the moat by a balustraded stone bridge into the gracious *cour d'honneur*. The garden front is just as appealing, and the garden itself, though formal, has the lawns, flowerbeds and low clipped hedges you would associate with an English country house.

It is good to record that the official tour of the château, which has belonged to the State since 1929, is now more courteous and enlightening than it was some years ago. The sequence of rooms we are shown is virtually an autobiography of its seventeenth-century owner. We begin on the ground floor with the **Salle des Devises**, which is dominated by a portrait by Lefèvre of Bussy Rabutin wearing the uniform of a lieutenant-general. Round him are panels of allegorical scenes, various emblems, and illustrated riddles bearing on incidents in his life. The **Salon des Grands Hommes de Guerre** naturally includes him prominently among the sixty-five great captains of France – Turenne is banished to a corner, with a contemptuous subscription. The wooden panels are decorated with the interlaced monograms of Bussy and Montglat, which can hardly have pleased his wife Louise, though she seldom visited the château after 1669. In the master bedroom (the **Chambre du Comte**) a gorgeously furnished bed is placed where its occupant could admire the portraits of some of the most famous court beauties of the time, Mme de Maintenon, *la Grande Mademoiselle*, Mme de la Sablière and Gabrielle d'Estés among them. Not so beautiful, but in an interesting triptych by Mignard, we can see the likenesses of Mme de Sévigné, her daughter the comtesse de Grignan, and – prettiest of the three – the disregarded comtesse de Bussy.

The most spectacular decoration is in the **Tour Dorée**, where the oval principal room has a cupola painted with scenes of historic lovers who each hold a shield bearing the Bussy arms, varied with fleurs-de-lys, coronets and the Bussy-Montglat monograms. The walls are divided into three tiers of decoration: uppermost are portraits of the greatest figures of the age, Louis XIII and XIV, Richelieu, Anne of Austria, Mazarin, Gaston d'Orléans and the two Condés. In the central band we are not surprised to find Bussy himself in the character of a Roman emperor, surrounded by the ladies with whom he has been chiefly associated. Beneath each of these we can read the characters he has given them: 'La plus aimable et la plus infidèle', 'Moins fameuse par sa beauté que par l'usage quelle en fit' are two examples of their flavour. Mme de Montglat gets away with 'Plus légère que le vent'. Round the base of the walls are mythological scenes and decorative panels, reinforced by some of Bussy's own mediocre verses:

> Tout le monde en amour est tous les jours dupé,
> Les femmes nous en font accroire.
> Si vous voulez aimer et n'être point trompé,
> Aimez une femme d'ivoire.

A gallery leading from here to the chapel is hung with portraits of the kings of France since Hugues Capet, of the dukes and duchesses of Burgundy, and members of the Bourbon and Bussy-Rabutin families – an arrangement which allowed Bussy to put his own portrait facing that of Louis XIV. What you will not find anywhere in the château is the uncomplimentary device which elsewhere explains the name Rabutin as a combination of *rat* and *butin* (booty or plunder). The chapel itself is in the south tower – to the left as you enter the *cour d'honneur*. The contents are a mixed lot, but they include an Italian stone *retable* of the raising of Lazarus, a Virgin and Child from the school of Andrea del Sarto, and a Burning Bush attributed to Poussin.

Although he returned to court for brief spells in the 1670s, he spent most of his time now in Burgundy. With him lived his favourite daughter Louise, already widowed after a brief marriage to the then marquis de Coligny, and destined to cause her father a great deal of trouble in his later years. She fell under the spell of an adventurer who had introduced himself as Henri François de la Rivière, and she became his mistress. Bussy discovered that the man was really the illegitimate son of a peasant, but he was too late to prevent a secret marriage taking place in his own chapel while he was away from home. Louise, already pregnant, took refuge in the Ursuline convent of Montbard, but her father carried her off to Paris and began proceedings to annul the marriage. He lost his case, but la Rivière calmly agreed to renounce his rights in return for the gift of Bussy's other château at Lanty. The king had pity on his humiliated subject, pardoned him for his impertinences, and in 1691 awarded him a small pension. He died two years later at Autun, where he is buried.

On the high ground across the road is the village of **Bussy-le-Grand**, birthplace of Andoche Junot, one of the most famous of Napoleon's marshals, popularly known as la Tempête on account of his larger-than-life personality. He was involved in both the Peninsular and the Russian campaigns, conquered Portugal, was created the duc d'Abrantes, and was badly wounded in Russia. After the retreat he governed the Illyrian province for a time, fell ill in Italy and returned to Montbard, where he committed suicide by jumping out of a window. He was spared the humiliation of Waterloo, but he remains one of the more pathetic casualties of the Grande Armée.

The twelfth-century **Church of St-Antonin** in Bussy-le-Grand is unusual even for Burgundian Romanesque, with features suggesting both Cluniac and Cistercian influence. The lofty barrel vault of the nave has been strengthened by wooden tie-beams set in the window embrasures, and the transverse ribs are supported on engaged columns which taper to a point some three feet above the ground – said to be a Cistercian device. The octagonal cupola over the crossing is supported by squinches, while the crossing itself is defined by four low arches. The capitals are carved with something of the inventiveness to be found at Saulieu, though a good deal more restrained. The elaborate *ciborium* in the chapel north of the choir was recovered from the garden of the château, where it had been incongruously set up by a nineteenth-century owner. The octagonal apse, with its panelled stalls, abbot's chair and medallions carved in relief, goes back only to the eighteenth century, though the *boiserie* is attractive.

2

The richness of the Auxois in scenery, history and early architecture strikes one again on turning south to **Flavigny-sur-Ozerain** . The tree-lined approach from Alésia and Bussy-Rabutin soon joins the valley of the Ozerain, then climbs to a town where vigorous modern life goes on in an engrossing mediaeval setting. Its practical residents might balk at Chateaubriand's exalted comparison:

I shall be indebted to the valley of Flavigny for one of my most vivid and moving memories. It looks like the valley of Jerusalem. There is Cedron bathing the feet of the Holy City; and those ancient fortifications remind you of the ruined ramparts of the Temple.

but the visitor will soon be searching for words of his own to do it justice.

Flavigny had its moment of importance when in 1589 it was captured from the Catholic Ligue by Guillaume de Travannes, who made it the capital of Burgundy and the seat of the royalist parliament, and there is still an air of dignity within its mediaeval walls. You enter the town through the machicolated **Porte du Bourg**, with its homely statue of the Virgin over the archway, and the main street takes you straight up to the parish **Church of St-Genest**. Purists may decry its architecture as a mismatch of styles, but there are details within which give it an unexpected interest and charm.

The nave and side aisles belong to the late thirteenth century, but the choir and apse, like the vaulting of the nave, were all rebuilt in 1434 by order of the bishop of Auxerre. The side aisles have in effect two storeys, with galleries overlooking the body of the nave – a unique arrangement for a building of this date. In the early sixteenth century the two wooden-fronted galleries were joined by a stone screen which spans the nave just before the crossing. From this vantage you look down on the choir with its intriguingly carved stalls.

These stalls were the object of a tragic act of criminal vandalism in 1978. Two or three men locked themselves in the church overnight, and by the morning they had sawn off the heads of almost all the figures of the stall ends, making off in the early hours no doubt to sell their booty to Parisian antique dealers. So in a few hours we lost nearly all these little gems of the woodcarver's art – one remembers in particular a figure playing bagpipes and another digging out a stone from the sole of his shoe. The most curious one was spared – an enigmatic character holding his nose while inspecting a book – and so, mercifully, was the most beautiful thing in the church. In the third chapel to the right of the nave there stands the sweetly smiling figure in stone of the Angel of the Annunciation. The head is slightly damaged, but the eager poise of the body and the supple lines of the drapery will repay many visits. This is no popular Burgundian work, but another example from the Champenois school such as we admired at Fontenay.

Sadly we shall find it more difficult now to see inside St-Genest. The parish of Flavigny is determined not to lose any more of its treasures, and the visitor is more than likely to find it locked and the guardian of the key unwilling to open it without notice. Sunday is the best chance, but the *curé* (who lives in les Laumes) might be persuaded to authorize a visit at other times.

The **Abbey of St-Pierre** stood in the south-west corner of the town, and what is left of it can be visited by courtesy of the long-established firm which manufactures anise *bon-bons*, which owns the abbey and whose factory (redolent of their product) stands opposite. The firm may be justified in claiming this right, for it is said that their enterprise was begun by the monks of the early Benedictine foundation, built above the crypt where Ste Reine was finally laid to rest in the ninth century. Like those at St-Germain in Auxerre and St-Benigne at Dijon, the crypt was part of a Carolingian structure on two levels, though its extension eastward into a hexagonal chapel (not here a rotunda) was discovered only in 1956. The crypt itself is a vaulted chamber supported by four Gallo-Roman pillars, probably taken from Alésia – perhaps even from the basilica of Ste Reine.

147

Not much remains of the abbey church and monastic buildings above all this – only a few broken arches can be readily seen, while the ruined chapter house contains some dispiriting sculptural fragments. For entry, if no guide is apparent, ring the bell at the factory office on the far side of what would have been the cloister. You will be offered an audio cassette to help you find your way, but it will probably be more illuminating to study a plan of the original buildings just inside what was the south aisle of the church.

From the abbey ruins it is worth while taking a walk under the western walls of the town as far as the picturesque **Porte du Val** with its plump round guardian towers. Beside it is the nineteenth-century **Maison Lacordaire**, which was for some time a *maison de retraite* for women, and has now reverted to being a small Dominican seminary, presided over by a young English priest. He follows in the steps of Henri Lacordaire (1802-1861) whose birthplace we visited at Recey-sur-Ouche in the Haut-Châtillonais. This ambiguous character was in turn agnostic lawyer, ordained priest, compulsive preacher, liberal politician, and friend of advanced thinkers like Lamennais and Montalembert. In 1837 he joined the Dominican order, and twelve years later came to Flavigny to organize a *petite seminaire* in the building which bears his name. He taught just seven novices, allowing them a few beds, a couple of tables, and one chair each which they took with them from room to room. How his presence and his message were received by the people of Flavigny then we do not know; today the community is regarded as vaguely anti-Christian – though no doubt it makes itself more comfortable.

If you have re-entered the town through the Porte du Val and still have time to wander round inside the walls, you will find many mediaeval corners, turreted houses, Renaissance façades, and some unexpected carving on stone lintels. Close to the Porte du Bourg you may sight a covey of black-habited monks who constitute yet another religious entity in Flavigny. This is a Benedictine group who have restored and re-established themselves in an ancient refectory and chapel, with living quarters close by.

Burgundy has never tempted the modern artist as Provence has done, but Flavigny was a favourite place for Augustus John and

William Rothenstein in the early days of the New English Art Club. In *Men and Memories* Rothenstein describes a visit to a Benedictine monastery here, but his description of the beauty of the interior and the sense of peace and security it induced hardly fits the ruined and abandoned state of St-Pierre at the turn of the century. Perhaps it was in the little enclave near the Porte du Bourg that a monk almost persuaded him to stay and take up the peaceful reality of the contemplative life. It was the thought of Alice Kingsley with her bright gold hair waiting outside which clinched the matter. They married soon afterwards, and nobody looking at Rothenstein's portraits of her would be surprised at his decision. Flavigny itself could well tempt the visitor to stay and settle within its walls, but there would be no need to be celibate.

On leaving Flavigny, if you take the D9j rather than the D9 which leads to Semur, it will bring you out on to the D905 immediately opposite an unpretentious – indeed engagingly dilapidated – château standing in decidedly informal surroundings. The **Château de Villiers** (not marked on the Michelin map, for some reason) was bought several years ago by an Englishman, Arnold Fawcus, who divided his time between restoring it, collecting antiquities, breeding rabbits, cultivating delphiniums and managing the Trianon Press in Paris. His ambition to return his home to something like its sixteenth-century state was thwarted sadly by his death, though with the encouragement of Sir Geoffrey Keynes he did rebuild a convincingly Romanesque chapel in the grounds. More to the point for a writer on Burgundy he initiated and published the superb illustrated volume on the sculpture of Gislebertus at Autun which anyone who visits the church of St Lazare should beg, borrow or steal if they cannot find a copy to buy.

The D905 will take you swiftly on south to Vitteaux, following the low swampy ground of the valley of the Brenne. Three kilometres short of the town it passes at **Posanges** a château which has already been impressively restored. In the early 1980s you would have seen a desolate and deserted ruin with weed-enveloped walls, crumbling battlements and a notice *à vendre* on its battered wooden doorway. It was then bought by a wine merchant in Beaune, and in a few years he transformed it into a near perfect example of a mediaeval fortress – a magnificent foursquare building with towers at each corner, a fully restored *pont levis* and machicolated entrance gateway. The moat now runs unsullied all the way round, and is crossed by a firm stone bridge.

The work seems to have been done without a flaw in taste or authenticity (though its interior remains private) and it must be little changed outwardly since it was built in the fifteenth century by Guillaume Dubois, an influential Counsellor at the court of Philip the Good. This could have been the man whose oppressive regime in the neighbourhood inspired the old rhyme:

> Dieu nous garde du feu, de l'eau
> Et du baron de Vitteau

In **Vitteaux**, the church of St-Germain was founded in the ninth century by the Benedictines from Flavigny. Wrecked as so many Carolingian foundations were by the Normans, it was rebuilt in 1160 – but notice the two whole and four engaged octagonal columns at the west end under the tower, with an unusual V-pattern motif in place of capitals. The east end was altered in 1250 and the nave rebuilt in the following century. The rededication at that time is recorded by a tablet to the left of the choir: 'Cette église fut dédiée le tiers du mois de juing 1399 – B. Collardot, prêtre.'

The interior furnishings include fifteenth-century choir stalls with human heads which can only have been local caricatures, and an intricately carved tribune of the same date. In the third chapel on the right of the south aisle (with a crypt below) are buried two sixteenth-century members of the Languet family – Hubert, Minister to the Prince of Orange, and Jean-Jacques, archbishop of Sens. In 1640 Claude Languet opened up the vault and gave it a macabre wall decoration of flames, skulls and crossbones, with which he provided one sarcophagus for himself and another to be shared by his two wives. A large triptych by Nicholas de Hoey, dated 1592, is disappointingly lifeless. On the whole the inside of the church is sombre, though the fifteenth-century wooden doors are more enlivening.

There is nothing sombre about the collegial church of St **Thibault**, just south of the D70 from Vitteaux to Précy-sous-Til. We know little of the earlier twelfth-century church, which was dedicated to St Blaise. It was a dependency of the priory of St-Rigaud-en-Mâconnais, and in 1240 it acquired two ribs of the aristocratic young St Thibault, whose story we told when writing of his church at Joigny. To cope with the immediate influx of pilgrims the whole church was rebuilt and rededicated during the second half of the thirteenth century. It was begun on a modest scale, but about 1270 another architect took over, to whom we owe the highly decorative north transept chapel of St Gilles and probably the magnificent choir and apse. There is nothing like this in Burgundy, and even in the Gothic cathedrals of the north you will not find its equal for lightness and grace.

The exhilarating effect is achieved partly by vertical lines, the main pillars rising without a break for nearly thirty metres to take the vaulting of the five-sided apse. Four storeys contribute to the soaring elevation: first a group of blind arcades; above that the wall is divided into an inner and an outer skin, so that tall sections of lace-like tracery form an open screen in front of the actual windows; next comes the triforium, simple and elegant, with four arches matching those of the ground storey; finally the five great clerestory windows, simple in design but stunningly beautiful in effect. All this is worked in a light creamy stone and celestially lit from the east.

The story of St Thibault can be read in pictures on the wooden *retable* of the high altar, over which hangs a *columbarium* with a system of pulleys and chains to elevate or reserve the Host. The north portal has survived from the early fourteenth century. Its tympanum portrays the death, assumption and coronation of the Virgin, and on either side of the doorway below are statues of those who endowed the church at that time: they are Robert II, duke of Burgundy, his son Hugues V, the duchess Agnes and Hugues d Arcy, bishop of Autun. As at Vitteaux the fifteenth-century wooden doors are remarkably fine, with folding panels carved with figures under Gothic canopies.

From St Thibault you can rejoin the long straight stretch of the D70 which crosses the autoroute on the way to **Précy-sous-Thil**. For the last few kilometres you will have in view to your left a wooded ridge from which rise the ruins of two large buildings. This is the eminence known as **Thil**, under which lie both Précy and the village known, from its Hospice, as Maison-Dieu. To explore the ridge you have to go on into Précy (there is no access from the main road) out towards Maison-Dieu on the D10, and up a straight track to your left before you reach the village. What you will find is worth the trouble.

First you come to the ruins of a huge Gothic church, founded in 1340 as a *collègiale* by Jean II de Thil, Constable of Burgundy. Round this you can only wander and stare, but the tree-lined path leads away from it to something more remarkable. In the tenth century a formidable castle was built here, and you can still trace the oval *enceinte* which once enclosed a Gallo-Roman *oppidum*. The ramparts, battlements and central keep were put up in the thirteenth and fourteenth centuries, but within a hundred years the whole site had been abandoned – perhaps sacked by rampaging English soldiers. Two arches survive of the southern gateway, and to the east of this a tall square tower rises from the walls. From it, had the spiral stairway turret survived, you could see fifty kilometres in any direction. No wonder it was called the 'espionne de l'Auxois'. The keep has been restored as a private dwelling, and there are hopeful signs of work going on elsewhere to wake this giant from its four hundred years' sleep.

Instead of passing on direct to Saulieu, there is a chance to look at a few more places in this beguiling countryside. The D36 south from Précy is the road you want, and the first stop could be at **la Motte-Ternant**, where there is a very early Romanesque church being restored by local enterprise. The short transept still has its barrel vaulting intact, but it must have collapsed in the nave, to be replaced by a flat wooden roof. The three apses all have half-domes and deep window embrasures; in the central one are the remains of a fresco – Christ in majesty, with orb and sceptre – and a two-tiered piscina. Outside, the little tower has a low-pitched roof with gables north and south, and the apses are covered by heavy stone tiles. This very ancient place – perhaps of Carolingian origin – has so far escaped publicity.

Mont-St-Jean is another high wooded hill, on which ancient houses surround a fine twelfth-century château (restored and lived in), foursquare, with round corner towers and a central courtyard. The church alongside has a tall three-storeyed Romanesque tower with a curious cluster of twisting pillars to support double arches high up on two of its faces.

South of Mont-St-Jean the D36 joins the D977 bis, which crosses two arms of the river Serein. If you turn left on it you reach

Thoisy-la-Berchère. The disappointment is to find that when the handsome fifteenth-century château changed hands in 1978 its new owners closed it to the public. Its history may be of interest, though, for it was built between 1430 and 1483 by Cardinal Rolin, bishop of Autun and son of the great Nicolas Rolin, Chancellor to the duke of Burgundy. From outside you can glimpse the original twelfth-century keep, restored in the last century, but that is all. It must be a wonderful place to live, overlooking from quite a height the Auxois valleys to the east; to the west is the Forêt de Thoisy, outrider of the Morvan.

CHAPTER NINE

From Saulieu to Dijon

Saulieu was the Roman Sidolocus, which stood astride the main trade route to the south, now the Route Nationale N6. Geographically it crowns a high windswept ridge between the Auxois and the Morvan; historically it has been a prosperous commercial centre with as many as twelve annual fairs. In the nineteenth century it had a factory where a hundred workmen produced 200,000 pairs of sabots a year for the peasants of the Morvan, but as ways of life changed the importance of Saulieu to the locality declined. Not so, however, its gastronomic reputation. It was a natural halt for motorists needing their *déjeuner* after an early start from Paris, and now it is only a few kilometres from the autoroute.

In our own times a succession of famous chefs – Victor Burtin, Alexandre Dumaine, and now M. Loiseau – have won for the Côte d'Or restaurant a reputation among the highest in France. M. Dumaine described himself as 'simply an artisan with a deep love of my profession, and to exercise it is my *raison d'être*'. He served his apprenticeship under Raymond Baudoin, nicknamed 'le mal necessaire', for he was not the easiest of masters any more than his pupil was the most tolerant of chefs. When Léon Daudet, having ordered a *daube de bœuf,* poured over it a whole pot of mustard, Dumaine went alternately pale and red with anger and took the plate away to the kitchen again. When General de Lattre de Tassigny gave orders that he should be served without a moment's delay, it took all Mme Dumaine's diplomacy to prevent his immediate expulsion. King Alfonso XIII was a faithful client of the Côte d'Or, with a preference for cold saddle of hare and redcurrant jelly, and when Salvador Dali arrived one day he said simply 'Je veux manger comme un roi.' August 21, 1944 was a sad day for M. Dumaine, whatever his political sympathies. Marshal Pétain, under German escort, stopped in Saulieu on his way to Sigmaringen, never again to entei France as a free agent. The menu befitted the occasion - *potage, omelette, salade, fromage à la crème, fruits –*

but we may be sure that each course was impeccably presented. Today your purse needs to be long to eat with M. Loiseau, and even longer if you wish to stay in one of his *appartements*, but other more modest restaurants in the town centre have rooms, and the four-star Hôtel de la Poste is reasonable on both counts.

Good food and Romanesque architecture are among the chief pleasures of travel in France, and at Saulieu you will be wise to give preference to the latter. In other words you should visit the **Church of St-Andoche** before you enter the restaurant of M. Loiseau, for there you will need all your wits about you. Three Christian missionaries from Autun were martyred in Saulieu: Andocius and Thyrsus from Greece, and Felix, who was a merchant in the town. In the fifth century a tomb was raised over their bodies. The monastic community which guarded it drew many pilgrims, among them King Clovis and Queen Clothilde, King Gontran and his sister-in-law Queen Brunéhaut, St Columba and St Germain, and the emperor Charlemagne himself. In 722 the abbot Widradus, or Waré, who had founded St-Pierre at Flavigny, left all his money to the basilica church – which had to be rebuilt by Charlemagne after the Saracen invasions.

Of that church nothing remains above ground. The crypt, which as at St-Germain in Auxerre was extended eastward into a rotunda, was buried during the restorations of the last century. It is hoped that the excavations of 1966-7 will be renewed, and that before long another Carolingian crypt will be revealed for the visitor. The Romanesque church, as it can still be called in spite of later disasters and restorations, dates from the twelfth century. The exact date of its completion is difficult to establish, for it appears that when Pope Calixtus II stopped in Saulieu on his way back from Rome in 1119, he was only called upon to solemnize the occasion when the bones of St Andoche were transferred from the crypt to the new monastery. More reliable evidence suggests that the building of St-Andoche took place slightly later than that of St-Lazare at Autun, which was not begun till 1122, and was consecrated in 1132. Etienne de Bagé, who as bishop of Autun had initiated the work on St-Lazare, was also responsible for the new church at Saulieu.

Early in 1360, just before the Treaty of Brétigny brought a brief respite in the Hundred Years' War, St-Andoche was another victim of the savagery of English marauders, who set fire to it and

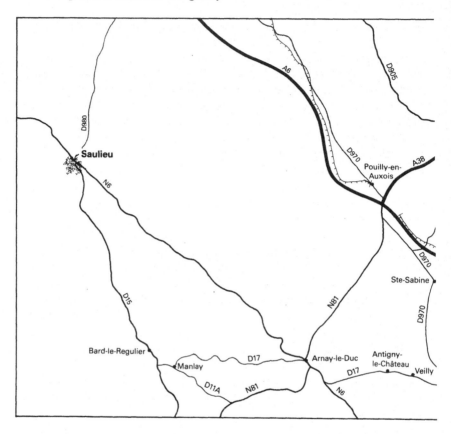

completely destroyed the choir. This had been built more on the Cistercian than on the Cluniac plan, with a single apse, no ambulatory and no projecting transept. In the fifteenth century the bishops of Autun added chapels to the north and south of the side aisles, but the by then ruinous remains of the choir were pulled down in 1702, and a new one was built in the eighteenth-century fashion – the one we see today. Then in 1760 the north-west tower was struck by lightning, rebuilt and capped by an incongruous Italianate dome. The western façade did not survive the Revolution, and its tympanum is a mediocre invention of the last century.

With some relief one steps inside to find a pure Romanesque nave of Cluniac design. Cluniac, that is, in its barrel vault and its

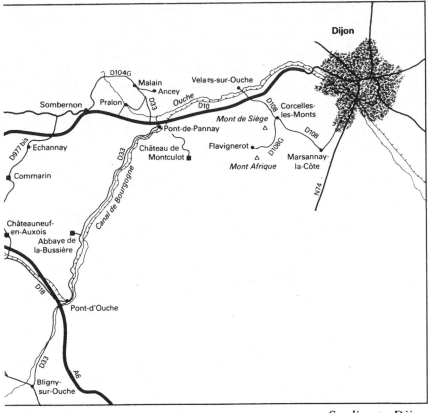

Saulieu to Dijon

three-storey elevation – arcades, blind triforium and high single windows (the last a bold experiment in conjunction with a barrel vault). The hard grey local stone may have precluded some of the rich effects to be seen at Cluny and Autun, but there is an air of calculated sobriety here. A more graceful decorative feature is the little doorway in the south aisle which used to give access to the cloister, before the church was secularized in the later twelfth century and handed over to a college of canons. The thick billet mouldings and inner arch of diamond-pointed stones are unusual, and the tympanum is simply carved with a trefoil design.

A lighter stone brought from the Yonne valley was used for the **Capitals** which adorn the pillars in St-Andoche, and they yield in

157

fame and accomplishment only to those carved by Gislebertus at Autun. For a long time it was disputed whether Gislebertus learned his craft from a master at Saulieu, or *vice versa*, so similar are many of the subjects and their treatment. In the end the experts have convinced themselves that, just as St-Andoche was built a little later than St-Lazare, so many of the capitals we see here were derived from the masterpieces of Gislebertus already in place, and perhaps executed by his pupils. Not only that, it seems that whereas Gislebertus was alone responsible for almost every bit of carving in St-Lazare, there is evidence here of work by at least two hands, and probably more. If anything, the imagination behind the capitals of Saulieu is more startling, while the authority and control of the medium are less sure. A difference noticeable throughout is the decorative use of foliage, whether as a background to the vivid biblical scenes or on its own in the most serene and delicate compositions.

Visitors will find their own favourites – the writer has a soft spot for the two *chouettes* surveying all from their perch among the acanthus leaves – but there are five masterpieces they must not miss: they are *Balaam and his Ass*, the *Flight into Egypt*, the *Temptation of Christ*, the *Meeting with Mary Magdalene* after the Resurrection, and the *Suicide of Judas*. All these must be by the same hand, and each is extraordinary for its emotional and dramatic concentration. Balaam, hammer in hand, rides against a rich background of foliage, feet firmly in the stirrups; the angel, from the left of the ass's head, grasps a branch of the tree and so is integrated in the total design. Another angel supports Christ in the Temptation, where Christ holds the trunk of a tree in his right hand while the Devil proffers a stone with the challenge to turn it into bread. The manic ferocity of the one is contrasted with the enquiring expression of the other, as if Christ was looking beyond the Devil and trying to understand what this trial means.

Even more profound in religious feeling is Christ's appearance to the Magdalene, where the feeling of *noli me tangere* is conveyed by the stylized folds in his robes and by his uplifted, outspread hands. In the Flight into Egypt a rather plain Mother, with pointed nose and receding chin, clasps a worried-looking Infant and rides in profile among oak trees that dangle their heavy acorns. In the Suicide of Judas, implacable in its realism, the tree is obviously functional, and the weight that tightens the noose is a bag of money held by a devil – grinning, as it seems, more in anguish than in mirth. In these astonishing works of art the intensity of feeling breathes through the mastery of form. Certain motifs – the fall of the drapery or the interlacing of a branch – are common to all of them, and are repeated in other capitals which have no human or divine content.

For a gentler rendering of New Testament themes, look further east to where the apse of the eighteenth-century choir is ennobled by a set of superb wooden stalls made in the late fourteenth century. On either side of the centre of the half circle, where in an abbatial church one would expect to find the steps leading to the *cathedra*, are panels of the *Annunciation* and the *Flight into Egypt*, works whose quiet Gothic grace seem to reprove the excesses of the Romanesque masters.

For the collector of curiosities there are two more things to look for. In the chapel at the head of the south aisle is a strange marble sarcophagus said to have been made in the sixth century to hold the relics of St Andoche. Shaped almost like a Victorian travelling trunk, it is marked irregularly with a variety of symbols, not all of them Christian. Among them is a *chi-rho*, or *chrisma*, a Greek cross, and a design of vineleaves. Nothing seems to fit together, and this is because it was reassembled in the nineteenth century from the pieces it had been broken into long before. In a low-arched chapel off the last bay but one of the north aisle there are now displayed two ivory plaques showing Christ between St Peter and St Paul, and the Virgin between the archangels Michael and Gabriel. These are beautiful replicas of very precious sixth-century ivories, which are naturally kept in a safer place.

Next door to the church is a small **Museum**. As well as a mixed collection of local antiquities, it has a complete Morvan kitchen with its utensils, showing how the country people cooked and ate up to 1914. Of more artistic interest are examples of the sculpture of François Pompon (1855-1933) who was born in Saulieu and specialized in studies of animals in motion. Apprenticed to a marble-cutter in Paris, he frequented the Jardin des Plantes to look for models. One of his best known works, *Le Taureau*, can be seen in the triangular *place* Charles de Gaulle in the north of the town.

After church and museum you will have excuses for feeling dazed as you emerge again into the pleasant Place Docteur Roclore, with its fountain and old houses, and you could easily be led astray into the restaurant of M. Loiseau – unless you settle for a woodland picnic in the Morvan, watched keenly by pairs of wheeling buzzards high overhead. In spring I have seen as many as four pairs at a time of these majestic birds swirling over the treetops and fields in flight patterns which must be an exhilarating form of courtship rather than a reconnaissance for their luncheon.

2

To continue your journey, which will take you through the heart of Burgundy, you should follow the D15 south from Saulieu, which leads eventually to Autun. After some twenty kilometres it passes the village of **Bard-le-Regulier**, where there is a notable church dedicated to St John the Evangelist. There was a priory here founded by Augustinian regular canons, which explains part of its name, while close by is the *signal*, or hilltop, of Bard. Only the church remains of the priory buildings, but most of it dates from the late twelfth century, including the rare octagonal tower. It has a Romanesque first storey, but is Gothic above; the barrel vault of choir and transept is pure Romanesque.

Your attention will immediately be caught by the woodwork of the late fourteenth-century stalls, which occupy the last bays of the nave before the choir proper. They are at least a century older than those at Montréal, and if they lack the technical mastery of the Rigolley brothers they make up for it in vigour and invention. Their preoccupation is with animals: tortoise and hare, St Hubert (now headless) with the stag, Samson blinding his lion, a centaur and other strange creatures, and a Nativity where the cattle steal the show, breathing amiably over the crib. The most intriguing carving forms the end piece of one row of stalls, where a woman bends her supple body backwards to support a tall Corinthian pillar on her breasts, while a monk leans nonchalantly on the capital above – symbolizing what, one wonders?

A surprise of a different nature waits at **Manlay**, just to the south of the *signal* of Bard, where there is a very remarkable fortified church. At first sight you would think it was part of a *château-fort*, and that the nave had been built to fill the space between two round gate towers to the west and a massive square *donjon* to the east; it would follow that the ground floor of the latter had been adapted to form the choir and sanctuary. Until recently this was believed to be the case, as it was known that such a fortress existed in Manlay in the thirteenth century, and it is still possible that the two western towers formed part of it. However, a study by M. Albert Colombert of the *Société française d'Archéologie* has established that, while both tradition and the church's Romanesque features argue that there was already one there in the twelfth century, the *donjon* itself cannot be earlier than the fourteenth. *Ergo*, says M. Colombert, the wise villagers decided to use material from the demolished castle to build themselves an impregnable last defence to cover the east end of their church.

Accepting this, we can relax and look at the marvellous work of restoration, completed in 1962, by a group of French, German and British architects as a symbol of reconciliation. For the Germans it was an act of reparation, for in 1944 the retreating German army deliberately destroyed practically the whole village and seriously damaged the church – which had been extensively restored as recently as 1937. The nave is revealed now as wide, plain and uncluttered, lit by Romanesque windows to north and south. The only ecclesiastic furnishings are a fine modern stone altar with a striking bronze cross suspended above it, and a modern font in the base of the south-west tower. (The north-west tower contains the central heating plant!) The great square eastern tower has three more storeys above the choir, each planned as a room of refuge for the people in time of siege. The elaborate wooden *charpente* above it all was adapted in the eighteenth century to take three bells, which were rehung in 1962; when rung from below as a triple they make a lovely noise.

As an *envoi* to our visit, here is an account by an eighteenth-century *curé* of what happened on 25 June 1570:

At the time of the battle which took place near Arnay-le-Duc between the Marshal of Cosse-Brisac and Admiral Coligny, a large contingent of Huguenots descended on the place. The Baron de Chantaut, who had long served the King, put up a valiant defence in the tower of the church of Manlay, and as the assaults became more murderous the Huguenot commander suggested that they should settle the matter in single combat, and that the victor should have the final say. This was accepted by the lord of Chantaut, who killed his man, and the Huguenots melted away.

To reach **Arnay-le-Duc** you can take a minor road which crosses the Forêt de Buan and follows upstream the infant waters of the Arroux. Its position on the highway now known as the N6 brought it what might be called an anecdotal importance. The battle here in 1570, whose aftermath we read about at Manlay, was a resounding victory against the odds for the Huguenots under Coligny, and in it Henry of Navarre won his spurs as a lad of sixteen. Coligny, with the young Henry and Louis I, Prince of Condé, had marched south on what has been called the *voyage des Princes*. Two centuries later a less dignified *voyage des Princesses* was halted here when Adelaide and Victoria, two of the younger daughters of Louis XV (and therefore aunts of Louis XVI) were arrested on their way to safety in Italy and held in the presbytery by the constitutional priest. They had to go to bed immediately after their arrival, having washed their only sets of underwear and hung them out to dry till morning. They were then allowed to proceed, and made their way in safety to Trieste.

The late Gothic church, with its eighteenth-century domed vestibule, lacks interest inside, but immediately behind the apse are the thick walls of the **Tour de la Motte Forte**, with a machicolated upper gallery – all that remains of the fifteenth-century Château d'Arnay, which changed hands several times during the wars of religion and was finally destroyed by the Catholics. Arnay is a sizeable and attractive town, and you can stay and eat in style at the Hotel Chez Camille; alternatively you can stay more modestly at the Poste, and as it has no restaurant you can still treat yourself to a meal Chez Camille.

Striking north from Arnay on the N494 you come to **Pouilly-en-Auxois**, just beyond the spur autoroute which connects Dijon with the A6. There are two good reasons to stop here. The first is a remarkable piece of engineering which enables the Canal de Bourgogne to pass through a tunnel underneath a large part of the town. The north end of the tunnel is to be found beside the main street not far from the parish church – there are directions to it in the town –

and several flights of steps bring you down to a level with the water. You can appreciate the builders' skill from here, in an enterprise which dates from the time of Napoleon and predates the work of the Brunels in England. Furnished with a number of ventilation chimneys, the canal emerges three kilometres away between the autoroute and the village of Créancy. It is interesting to note that the elder Brunel was born in Normandy and served in the French navy before emigrating to America in 1793; he was himself in charge of the first tunnel under the Thames, begun in 1825.

The other attraction in Pouilly is not so easily found, but if you take a side street to the right when going south from the town centre you will find the curious little church of **Notre-Dame-Trouvée**, so called on account of its miraculously discovered statue of the Virgin – which was carried off by thieves again in 1981 and awaits another miracle. Originally a chapel of the vanished ducal château of Pouilly, it has no tower, but a double nave dating from the thirteenth century which is still basically Romanesque. Some authorities put it later, but its only Gothic feature is a window at the west end of the smaller nave. The dramatic sixteenth-century Sepulchre has been overpraised; the best thing in the church is a little wooden Christ, shown in a glass case on the north wall of the principal nave. It comes from the chapel of the Château de Frétois on the Aisne, destroyed by the Germans in 1915, and it was given to this church by the owner at the time. The church is normally kept shut, which is understandable, but the key is readily obtained from a house a little lower down the hill to the east.

Once it has resurfaced, the Canal de Bourgogne follows the line of the autoroute to pass close under the mighty fortress of **Châteauneuf-en-Auxois**, about ten kilometres south of Pouilly. This is one of the great sights of Burgundy, lording it over a clutch of mediaeval houses, some of which clearly belonged to rich Burgundian merchants, and have been well preserved. A striking example of military architecture put later to sophisticated domestic use, it commands the plain to north, south and west with its five towers and high enclosing walls. In a history involving several of the great names of Burgundy we hear of a new castle built in the middle of the twelfth century by Jean de Chaudenay as a present for his son; from this time only the square keep to the north remains. The line of the de Chaudenay lasted at Châteauneuf until it was brought to a sensational end in 1455 when the sole heiress Catherine plotted with her husband's steward to kill his master. She baked him a poisoned cake, but when an unfortunate maidservant also died after eating it the plot was uncovered and both Catherine and her lover were publicly executed in the village.

The castle then reverted to Duke Philip the Good, who gave it to one of his most valued subjects, Philippe Pot, Grand Seneschal of Burgundy and already the owner of the château of Rochepot near Nolay. It was he who rebuilt Châteauneuf as we see it now, all but the *donjon* of Jean de Chaudenay. After his death in 1494 it passed by marriage to the de Montmorency family, which was much involved in the wars of religion in the sixteenth century. Charles de Montmorency, Admiral of France, held it for the Ligue against an attack by the marquis de Mirebeau in 1594. From then on the succession of great family names is bewildering, even for Burgundy. Charles's niece Madeleine married Prince Henry of Luxembourg, and he sold it in 1606 to Charles de Vienne, count of nearby Commarin. The de Vienne kept it until 1766, after which a series of sales and inheritances by marriage left it in the hands of the comtes de Vogüé. In 1936 the comte Georges de Vogüé presented the château and its lands to the State.

There were originally two entrances, both with a *pont-levis* across the moat (now dry). The one to the south-east, now disused, gave access to the church below and was also convenient for the range of guest apartments which stands at that end of the *cour d'honneur*. The other, framed by two round towers, was the main entrance from the village, and is used by visitors today. The courtyard is long, narrow and irregularly shaped, with the principal rooms facing the entrance. You enter first the *salle des gardes*, with a magnificent pillared fireplace (defaced in the Revolution because it carried the arms of Philippe Pot) and a floor laid with painted and glazed terracotta tiles. To the left is the chapel, built in 1481, with a wall painted in the Pot colours of red and black, and a fresco of the Twelve Apostles.

A much later generation designed the little panelled dining room opposite the entrance, with a set of blue-seated Louis XV chairs and a lovely window looking out into the far distance beyond the canal. The same domestic character persists on the first floor, where the rooms, each with its own personality, are divided by oak beams and lath-and-plaster walls. The most impressive is an early seventeenth-century bedroom hung with red damask; it has a four-poster bed in a recess, and portraits of Charles de Vienne and Marguerite his wife. Further along are three later and more sophisticated rooms, one a panelled state bedroom with a little window looking down into the chapel, so that the occupant could attend Mass in a dressing-gown. These rooms have beautiful wooden floors, and they still have an air of civilized domestic occupation over several centuries. As you leave the main building, notice the deep well beside the entrance, with its pulley-wheel sheltered by a neat tiled and timbered roof – the basic water supply of the castle. It can be visited daily (except on Tuesdays) at the usual hours all the year round.

Leave yourself time to wander round the village – which is surprisingly small considering the obvious importance of many of its houses and the resounding names of its streets. If you walk up the Grande Rue to the Place aux Bœufs and out by the north gate , you will find yourself in the Allée de la Chaume, which leads into deep and well timbered woodland. An avenue of ancient oaks brings you after a ten minutes' walk to the chapel of **Notre-Dame-du-Chêne**, an eighteenth-century conceit which consists only of a sanctuary and apse. Lost in the same woods you may come upon in one direction the ruins of the **Hermitage of St-Julien**, with a miraculous fountain; in another the deserted thirteenth-century **Chapel of St-Clement**.

3

There are two places of great interest within easy reach of Châteauneuf, and both have family connections with the families who lived there. First you should make for **la Bussière-sur-Ouche**, and if the forest road which is the shortest way there looks daunting, there is an easier approach by crossing and recrossing the autoroute and canal on the D18, and following it through Crugey to Pont d'Ouche. There the canal joins company with the

Ouche and turns north in the direction of Dijon. The Ouche, which we now meet for the first time, is one of the most delightful of Burgundy's small rivers. From **Bligny-sur-Ouche**, which is also the starting point for an enterprising light tourist railway during the summer, it runs in a pastoral setting of trees and meadows through Pont d'Ouche to Pont de Panay. If you come this way look out for a lovely fourteenth-century bridge which spans the river just before Ste-Marie-sur-Ouche. The road which follows the valley here is the D33, and just after it crosses to the left bank of river and canal it passes by the **Abbey of la Bussière**.

Here we are on holy and historic ground. In 1130 Garnier II, lord of nearby Sombernon, called on Stephen Harding, the English abbot of Cîteaux, to assist in founding a monastery in what was then remote forest land to the south of his family seat. Twelve monks were sent out from the mother abbey, and they chose a site on high ground near the hamlet of Loiserolles, but after a few years their monastery was burnt to the ground and they decided to rebuild it in a more accessible place down by the river. The name Bussière refers to its immediate surroundings, for it goes back through Buissière to the Latin *buxeria*, meaning a plantation of box trees. The site had already known religious life, for we read that in 696 Anobert, bishop of Autun, bequeathed – to the cathedral the country residence he had enjoyed here – probably once a Roman villa.

Between its consecration in 1172 and the English invasions of the Hundred Years' War this was one of the most prosperous and influential foundations in Burgundy, and one of its fourteenth-century abbots was Guy de Châteauneuf. War brought ruin, and the monks drifted away to the security of Dijon. Although there was some rebuilding in the sixteenth and seventeenth centuries the monastery never recovered its status. In 1791 it was forcibly closed, and two years later its estates were sold for 1,600 *livres*.

Its revival has been remarkable. In 1925 the marquis de Ségur, who had married the daughter of a previous owner, decided to restore the abbey to its original function, and he offered the whole estate to the bishop of Dijon as a *maison de retraite*. After the last war an association of Friends of the Abbey was formed to take in hand both its physical reconstruction and its spiritual renewal. A gradual programme of restoration has given the buildings and grounds a mellow beauty, and every year they receive hundreds of groups and individuals who come for peace, reflection, discussion and renewal.

Naturally it is not a place for tourists in quantity, but the five or six sisters who supervise its spiritual life have lay helpers who will show what is permitted to the serious visitor. The main building, in particular the Refectory, suffered by being first restored at the turn of the century, when neo-Gothic was in fashion, but everywhere else a true sense of style has been combined with modern comforts to a remarkable degree. The twelfth-century outbuildings have been treated with great care and respect. There are two dovecotes (only the square one is ancient), a granary, a *pressoir* with an underground cellar, and a delectable mill-house where young people – including parties from the *lycée* in Dijon – are housed during the various courses which the abbey offers them. The grounds are a joy, with green lawns leading to a big oval lake on which rare wildfowl disport themselves. The flower gardens are kept up by student labour, and in 1987 their overseer was a young Pole who had come on a visit a few years before and had stayed there ever since.

The church was severed from the abbey at the Revolution and handed over to the parish. In 1820 the first two bays of the nave were cut off, being in bad repair and not thought worth restoring. Yet the rest of the church is now well maintained, and is notable for a magnificent set of *pierres tombales* ranged against the walls of the south aisle and north transept. They record the deaths of various members of the Sombernon and Montagu families, and there is one for Jehan de Drée, *chevalier*, who died in 1319. Most ancient of all, and an original part of the twelfth-century church, is the **Crypte des Fondateurs**, which is used as a place for private prayers. Now approached only from outside the north-west corner, it is furnished for kneeling rather than sitting, and it is a still hallowed place.

At a roughly equal distance from Châteauneuf, but standing due north of it on the D977 bis, is the **Château de Commarin**, the nearest to Dijon of a line of historic châteaux strung between the Tonnerois and the Auxois, all of them at some time fiefs of the duchy of Burgundy. If we have already visited Tanlay, Ancy-le-Franc, Bussy-Rabutin, Époisses and Châteauneuf we shall have a good idea of their quality and variety. Though all these have remained in the same family for long periods, Commarin is unique in never having been abandoned and never sold. The succession of its owners, whether by direct descent or by marriage alliance, has been unbroken since the thirteenth century. We know of a Seigneur de Commarin of 1241 whose descendant Jacques de Cortiamble built its present chapel in about 1400. During the next century the first full-scale *château-fort* was built by his great-grandson Jacques de Dinteville, Counsellor of Louis XI, and in 1521 he was host here to François I. By his marriage in 1478 to Alix de Pontailler he united two great families, and a third when he married his daughter Bénigne to Girard de Vienne.

The de Vienne held Commarin for two hundred years. In about 1630 Charles de Vienne (who, as we have seen, bought Châteauneuf from Prince Henry of Luxembourg in 1606) took the first step in modernizing the château by building a new west wing, which is named after Louis XIII. Then in 1698 his son Charles II married Anne de Chastellux, a union splendid in itself, and one which was to establish Commarin as the most splendid Burgundian château of the eighteenth century.

The old castle was falling apart. In 1701 one of its towers collapsed 'à l'heure de midi, pendant notre dîner', as Anne wrote in her daybook. Knowing that it adjoined the room where her two-year-old daughter Marie-Judith was, she rushed out into the courtyard to see with relief the nurse holding up the child at the window. The only problem was how to get them down, as the stairway had fallen with the tower. This decided the parents to rebuild Commarin, and in a three-year campaign from 1702 to 1705 they renewed entirely the central block and the west wing, and added a section to connect the eastern tower with the stables. That tower and its fellow in the opposite wing are the only remains of the fifteenth-century castle. With the reconstruction of the stables in 1748 we have a classic example of early eighteenth-century architecture with a harmony of style, if not a strict unity, which manages to be both impressive and endearing. The wrought-iron grilles which formally admit the visitor to the *cour d'honneur*, the three classical façades reflected in the moat, the trim lawns, even the carefully placed clumps of trees – all are outwardly formal, but at the same time serene and friendly.

That the same feelings are aroused when we go inside is to the credit of four *châtelaines* who ever since the arrival of Anne de Chastellux have loved, furnished and preserved their family home. Greatest of them was Marie-Judith de Vienne. Left a widow at thirty-seven with two children and plenty of debts inherited from her husband, the marquis de Damas d'Antigny, she set about rebuilding the family finances by careful management, and her first objective was to find a satisfactory husband for her daughter Alexandrine. When she achieved this by marrying her to the comte Charles-Daniel de Talleyrand she could not have foreseen that her grandson would become not only bishop of Autun, but also the statesman who disposed of kingdoms and governments in the Napoleonic era. When her son married Zephirine de Rochechouart, and into another great (though not Burgundian) family, the future of Commarin was secured, and she set about equipping it with all that her practical good taste suggested. The result is what we see today, virtually unaltered.

You will be well and informatively guided – provided you can cope with some rapid French – so while it seems unnecessary to follow the tour in detail it may be useful to pick out one or two features you might otherwise miss. The chapel of Jacques de Cortiamble was incorporated into the ground floor of the Louis XIII wing, and its fourteenth-century woodwork was brought from the chapel at Châteauneuf by Charles de Vienne. The main stairway, next to the chapel, may recall the Italian Renaissance with its stucco decoration, but to identify the strange animal at its foot you need to know something of the family heraldry. The eagle belonged to de Vienne, and you will find it in several rooms, but the unicorn arrived with Anne de Chastellux. In an unrecorded accident this one lost his horn, and was given in exchange – a poor one – two wooden replacements, which make him look more like a demented antelope.

The stairway leads to the *grande salle*, where the raised dais at the far end gives it the air of a theatre or concert room. Recent generations may have used it as such, but it was really a practical adjustment by Marie-Judith to match the floor level of the adjoining room. The portrait of Louis XIII is a replica of a Van Loo painting in the Dijon museum; that of Charles X is an original by Baron Gérard. The family portraits are much more interesting: there is Anne de Chastellux with her small daughter, and Marie-Judith herself in her prime; then there is the pastel of the beautiful Diane Pastré, widow of Charles de Vogüé. She lost her husband in 1914 and her son and heir in 1940, both killed at the very beginning of their wars, but before she died in 1971 at the age of eighty-three she had done as much for Commarin in the twentieth century as Marie-Judith had done in the eighteenth.

Of the three rooms directly associated with Marie-Judith, the antechamber displays the greatest treasures of Commarin, a set of gorgeous tapestries of the fifteenth and sixteenth centuries composed of panels woven with the arms of Dinteville, Pontailler and de Vogüé. Here too is the portrait of Guillaume de Vienne, the first man to be honoured with the Order of the Golden Fleece, founded in 1430 by Philip the Good, duke of Burgundy. Your guide will point out the anachronism whereby the sixteenth-century artist has painted his subject in the modern dress of his own period.

From here we enter the apartments which Marie-Judith made for herself in one of the old round towers. The choice was typical of this imaginative yet practical woman, for in a round tower she could let in a lot more light to a comparatively small room, which was also easier to heat. The light coming in from both sides is reflected by the splendid mirror she put over the fireplace; a smaller mirror set in a window overlooking the courtyard was taken from her mother's carriage in 1759! The furnishings are just as she left them at her death in 1780, including her bed, which was declared a *monument historique* in 1949. Next door is the charming panelled room occupied by Alexandrine before her marriage, and this too has never been altered.

Marie-Judith was spared the Revolution, and the Revolution spared Commarin, thanks to repeated interventions by the villagers on behalf of her son and successor, Jacques-François de Damas. Even her grandson Charles, who had organized the royal family's flight to Varennes came back unscathed to inherit the property. He died in 1828 without a direct male heir, and this brought in by marriage the first de Vogüé. In 1888 Arthur de Vogüé married Marie de Contades, another woman of charm and character, to whom the family owes much for her research into their archives; they included the *livre de raison* kept by Marie-Judith to record all she did to beautify Commarin. In spite of those tragic deaths in two world wars, the name and title of the de Vogüé survives in a nephew of the comtesse Diane.

The château is open (except on Tuesdays) for guided visits at the usual hours from April to October. A last view of the outside may take in the *grande écurie* which Marie-Judith rebuilt in its original state in 1622. It has the traditional stallion carved in high relief over the main doorway, and an inclined stone ramp allowed the real horses to come down and drink in comfort from the moat.

Your road now runs eastward towards Dijon, and if you want to avoid the new spur autoroute between Pouilly and Dijon you can cross it just after Échannay and carry on through Sombernon. If you have time, it is worth turning off the D16 to the village of **Malain**, though you will look in vain for the ruins of an early Christian basilica marked on the map. Instead, continue towards Ancey, and to the right of the road you will find the excavated site of the Gallo-Roman town known as Mediolanum – which suggests that Malain shares its derivation with Milan in Italy. It was a flourishing market town from the first century BC to the third century AD, and like Alésia it yielded valuable domestic and industrial evidence for those times, though on a much smaller scale.

From Malain you can return quickly towards the autoroute, cross it and the canal at the Pont de Panay, and follow the D35 as it climbs steeply from the river valley into the heart of the Montagne. This is where the hills, divided by narrow wooded valleys, or *combes*, rise to over 600 metres until they fall away abruptly to the Côte. You have left behind the fertile pastures of the Auxois, and ahead are the slopes of gold where Burgundy's richest currency lies.

In the meantime the **Château of Montculot**, isolated on a bend in the road, will introduce us for the first time to a notable Burgundian romantic who really belongs to the Mâconnais. More of him when we get there, but the young Alphonse de Lamartine (1790-1869) spent many holidays here with his uncle the abbé, and inherited the château at his death. Although he had to sell it in 1832 when short of money, he was always happy at Montculot, where he found matter for many of his nature-inspired poems. *La Source dans les bois* was written about a stream which runs through the park, and the romantic seclusion was probably the unconscious background to his *Meditations*. 'This château', he wrote elsewhere, 'was built by the stars, for only they see it'.

171

In its day this was a distinguished eighteenth-century building, its formality underlined by its sombre setting. Today its unassuming outlines are decayed and blurred, for, as so often happens to a château not big, historic or convenient enough to attract a rich buyer, it belongs to a farmer who has use only for its out-buildings. One hopes a rescuer may arrive, but the message 'il ne se visite pas' is enforced by a *chien* not just *méchant* but *furieux*.

From Montculot the road south leads only over the Montagne to join the Côte at Nuits-St-Georges, so for Dijon you must go back again to the autoroute – though you can pass under it at Pont de Panay and take the parallel little D905 as far as Velars-sur-Ouche. To make a really dramatic entry to the capital of the Duchy, cross the main road here again, and climb by way of the D108 to Corcelles-les-Monts, and then by the D108G to **Flavignerot**, beyond which you can go no further. Immediately to the north is the crater – a narrow platform two kilometres long – of Mont Afrique; to the south is the Mont de Siège, and another peak just as high faces you to the west. Away to the east you can see the blue ridges of the Jura; even, on a fine day, Mont Blanc.

So much the motorist can achieve, but the walker should know that the Grande Randonnée 7 climbs from the south side of the N 5 opposite Velars, past the chapel of Notre-Dame-d'Étang, over the two mountain ridges and down to Fixin and the Côte – a route which will give you incomparable views on every side. The Romans built a camp at the south-eastern end of the crater, and a number of tombs have been found there.

The mere motorist, bound for Dijon, must prepare for a sharp contrast in landscape. Continuing along the road from Corcelles-les-Monts, you will come out on to what seems a broad plateau, where the trees have given way to thin pasture and brushwood, then to tentative patches of vines. Suddenly you are at the summit of a *combe*: there below you is the village of **Marsannay-la-Côte**, whose delicious rosé you may presently be drinking; beyond, featureless and indistinct, is the Pays-Bas; everywhere to your right and left, and almost under your feet, are the vineyards which in Belloc's mock-heroic vein 'swell the rich slope, or load the empurpled plain'. There are other ways of approaching Dijon, but none so rewarding as this. A ten minute drive from Marsannay will bring you into the heart of the city.

CHAPTER TEN

Dijon

Dijon has been called the cradle and springboard of the ducal dynasties of Burgundy. Today, with its nearly 150,000 inhabitants, it is the largest city of the province and the capital of the Côte d'Or. It is readily accessible from north or south, since the fastest trains stop there, and a spur autoroute links it with the autoroute du Sud. It can be reached from Switzerland by way of the Jura, or from Italy by Chambéry or Grenoble. If Burgundy itself is a *pays de transition*, as it always had been, Dijon is unmistakably a crossroads. This means that it is naturally busy and inevitably noisy.

The visitor's first problem is where to stay. There are three first-class hotels within the city centre, of which the most prestigious is the Chapeau Rouge, which has the advantage of being very close to the cathedral of St-Bénigne. The Sofitel La Cloche is also handily sited near the place d'Arcy, but the Mercure Château Bourgogne is a good way away near the place de la République to the north. If only for the difficulty or near impossibility of daytime parking (there is one underground car park, but on the streets it is meters only and those apparently in permanent occupation) it is less convenient to stay in one of the surrounding villages – though for other reasons those along the Route des Grands Crus have their attractions.

It would be unreasonable to expect a city which has never admitted to being behind the times to avoid the consequences of industrialism, and ungracious to begrudge it the resulting prosperity. Yet if you choose your moment, when the pavements are less crowded and the noise of the traffic has died down a little, it is a pleasant place to stroll in – at least through the streets of the old city. In the nineteenth century Sainte-Beuve tells us:

> Nous allons admirer clochers, portails et tours,
> Et les vieilles maisons dans les arrièrecours.

In Roman times Dijon (known as Divio, or *castrum Divionense*

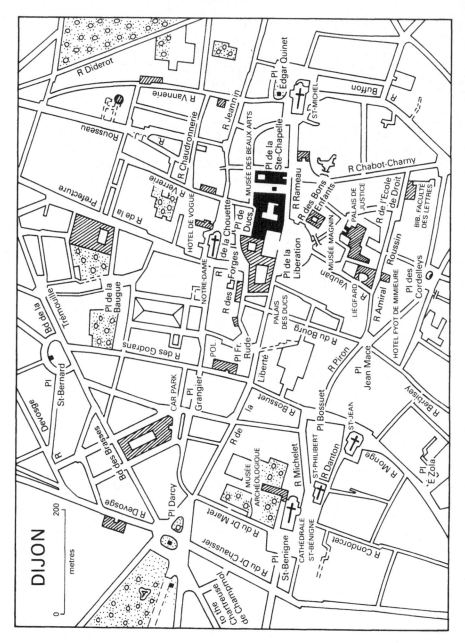

was important as both a military and a trading post, accessible as it is today through the valleys of the Rhône and the Saône, and close to the head waters of the Seine. As a city it was first fortified by the emperor Aurelian in 273AD, and it was the capital of the fifth-century kingdom of Burgundy. Absorbed into the empire of Charlemagne, Burgundy emerged as a separate duchy in the tenth century, and its early dukes were allied with the Capetian royal family of France, their capital being again at Dijon.

The arrival of the Valois kings in Paris brought a change of dynasty in Dijon, and from the accession of Philippe le Hardi in 1363 to the death of Charles le Téméraire in 1476 the Valois dukes maintained a court here every bit as splendid as their nominal overlords did in Paris. Yet conditions for the ordinary citizen of Dijon in the Middle Ages were by modern standards as frightening as they were unsavoury. It was not a pleasant place to stroll in after dark then, and there was no system for disposing of sewage except into the two little tributaries of the Ouche, the Suzon and the Renne, which flowed through the centre. When the curfew rang from the tower of St-Jean the night-watchman began his rounds, a steel bonnet under his hat to protect him against criminal violence. This could come from many sources – hooligans, drunks or professional thieves. One gang was known as *les coquillards* from the pilgrim's scallop shell they wore to deceive their victims. It is said that François Villon was one of them for a time.

Life is more seemly now, even after dark, which is just as well for expeditions on foot, for that is the only sensible way to explore mediaeval Dijon. There are two main areas to concentrate on, and we ought to take as first in seniority the environs of the **Cathedral of St-Bénigne**, for here we go back to a time when Church was more important than State – not its servant, as it became under the proud Valois dukes.

Although the existence of any such saint is unconfirmed in history, the early legends make St Bénigne a disciple of St Polycarp, bishop of Smyrna and himself a disciple of St John the Evangelist. In the second century he came to evangelize Roman Gaul and was martyred under Marcus Aurelius. Together with several other contemporary saints he was buried in a cemetery to the west of the Roman camp site of Divio, where later a particularly grand sarcophagus was found and presumed to be his –

though not before his spirit had appeared to Bishop Gregory of Langres to convince him that it was so. The usual process followed – a *confessio* put up to shelter the tomb, and a community of monks to guard it and control the pilgrims who came to see it. It is likely that the earliest church, built to enclose the tomb which was the centrepiece of the monastery, was a round one built on the model of the Church of the Holy Sepulchre in Jerusalem. Gontran, king of Burgundy in the sixth century, is known to have given generously to the monastery, but it was not until 869 that it was brought under the rule of St Benedict, and a larger church was built which incorporated the rotunda at its east end.

After the troubles and invasions of the ninth and tenth centuries more needed to be done if the shrine were to be worthy of its purpose and able to cope with the growing number of pilgrims. At this point we meet a man who did more than any other to establish a Burgundian style of Romanesque architecture. William of Volpiano, as his name suggests, was a native of Italy. Though nobly born he had become a monk at S. Michele de Locedia near Vercelli, where Abbot Mayeul of Cluny found him, recognized his unusual qualities and brought him back to Burgundy with him in 987. As not only the Carolingian church of St-Bénigne but also the conduct of the abbey community needed attention, William was given the task of refurbishing both on strict Benedictine principles – though the church he built at Dijon was completed some seventy years before St Hugh laid the foundations of the great *abbatiale* at Cluny.

There is no doubt that William of Volpiano was a man of tremendous energy and vision, and that he alone was responsible for the scope and character of the enterprise which occupied the first decade of the new millennium, and was sealed by dedication in 1018. Free now from the prospect of the Second Coming and the Last Judgment, William could build to last, and he called in architects, draughtsmen and masons from both Burgundy and his native Italy. Hence we find that two sources of creative art meet here – the Italianate formality of design and the individual craftsmanship and inventiveness of the Burgundians. The finished church was described by the contemporary monk and historian, Raoul Glaber, as 'the most marvellous basilica in the whole of France'. Yet after all its life was short. It had to be substantially restored after a fire in 1137, only for a large part of the main structure to collapse in 1272. The Gothic church we see today is the work of Abbot Hugues d'Arc, who immediately began to rebuild it in the manner of his time, retaining only the twelfth-century narthex and the extraordinary three-storeyed rotunda from the Romanesque church.

What had it been like, this group of buildings (for Abbot William included the whole range of the Benedictine monastery in his design) which was certainly the most spectacular achievement of Romanesque architecture of the time? Modern research, supported by the eleventh-century *Chronicle of St Bénigne* and by a minute description of the rotunda, illustrated by engravings, given by Dom Urbain Plancher in 1739, has made it possible to reconstruct on paper both the plan and the elevation, and your answer is at hand in a small booklet on sale in the church.

Nothing was spared in the building of it. 'We read with an indescribable pang of envy', writes Violet Markham in her *Romanesque France*, 'of its columns of marble and granite, of its 371 capitals richly decorated with various ornaments and biblical scenes, of its altars of rare stones, its reliquaries of gold and silver'. The essential plan was a nave with double side aisles, leading to a crossing and transept of equal width. Beyond that came the choir and sanctuary, where the design allowed for a central apse with three altars, surrounded by an elaborate pillared ambulatory and flanked by two side aisles ending in absidioles. Beyond that again came this amazing rotunda, with its concentric rings of eight, sixteen and twenty-two columns – the outer ring being in fact engaged half-columns. Nor was this the end of the church. East of the rotunda there was a rectangular projection – what would later be called a Lady Chapel. Built in the same style as the rest of the church, it comprised two vaulted chambers, the easternmost of which contained an altar to Our Lady. Only the underground part of this survived the Revolution, and a study of it has revealed that its foundation was probably a sixth-century mortuary chapel, part of the cemetery where St Bénigne and his fellow saints were first buried. The total length of the church, including the narthex added in the twelfth century, was just on 100 metres.

You now have to take in that from the crossing eastward there was superimposed a second storey which duplicated the design of choir and rotunda, while the central core of the latter rose by a further storey into the cupola, which let in light through a circular opening at the very top. Two flanking towers with spiral stairways connected the three levels, and below it all was a crypt beginning half way along the nave and extended to form the lowest of the three storeys of the rotunda.

It was the inherent strength of the rotunda which enabled Hugues d'Arc to include it in his new Gothic design without alteration. It survived more or less intact for nearly eight hundred years, a living example of Romanesque architecture at its grandest and most original. Tragically it was not proof against the furious and bigoted stupidity of the Revolution, which laid low the two upper storeys, allowing the débris to choke and cover what lay beneath. Only when work began on a new sacristy in 1843 did anyone realize that the lowest storey had survived, and it seemed like a miracle when during the saint's feast days at the end of November that year the lower half of St Bénigne's supposed sarcophagus was disinterred from the rubble.

There is an entrance to what is now called the crypt from outside the east end of the south aisle, so that while we have its history in mind it may repay us to go there first rather than enter the Gothic nave from the west. A flight of steps leads down into the head of the south aisle of the subterranean church, where a few columns of its south transept survive. Accessible from here is the space corresponding with the central apse above, where you find a rectangular pit which holds what is left of the sarcophagus. To right and left are repeated the side aisles of the sanctuary, ending in roughly finished absidioles. From the ambulatory which connects them you enter the basement of the rotunda.

Its proportions are exactly as Abbot William planned it, and much of its material is the same, however refashioned. It was not easy to decide, among the débris of walls and pillars, which stone should go back in what place. Mistakes were made in its reconstruction, but no sensible person would quarrel with the overall result. This forest of pillars, stout as the oaks of the Morvan, was planted to take the weight of the two storeys above it which repeated the same plan, and we can almost visualize what they were like from what we see here. Not quite, because the reconstructed vaulting now blocks access to the central core of the whole building, which rose like a light-well to the crowning cupola and the sky above. The names given to the three storeys were all part of the plan: the lowest was dedicated to St John the Baptist, the forerunner, the next and principal level belonged to the Virgin Mary, and above them all presided the Holy Trinity.

Down here the reconstructed pillars may be convincing, but there is a doubt about their capitals. Some recent opinion has suggested that they are later, perhaps twelfth-century carvings on a par with a mutilated tympanum of Christ in Glory which can be seen in the museum next door. On the other hand these human, semi-human and monstrous figures are so primitive in treatment that (like Violet Markham) we must be tempted to find in them the seeds rather than the flowering of Burgundian sculpture. They have more in common with a child's figure drawings than with the art of Gislebertus and his followers – perhaps recalling the enigmatic figures in the upper narthex of St-Philibert in Tournus. Whatever the truth, no one should be able to dispute the judgment that the rotunda of St-Bénigne anticipated by a thousand years the most startling experiments of Le Corbusier.

A mistake often made in writing about St-Bénigne is to belittle the Gothic church of Abbot Hugh in comparing it with William of Volpiano's basilica and rotunda. The truth is that in it we have one of the purest, if admittedly one of the simplest, examples of advanced Cluniac design. It has never been altered structurally since it was built, and the sober regularity of the nave with its plain pillars and dark four-arched triforium is cleverly relieved by the treatment of the clerestory, so often the focus of attention in Burgundian Gothic. The windows in the nave and choir are very tall, with delicate tracery; in the nave they are set not in the full thickness of the walls but in the outer skin, above and behind a passage which cuts through openings in the main shafts which support the vault. The transverse arches, in a sequence from choir to apse, gradually flatten out from pointed to fully semicircular, a subtle touch which brings the apse forward as an integral part of the church. The absence of a transept contributes to the same effect.

The only additions to the Gothic church have been the wooden choir stalls and panelling, brought in the eighteenth century from the abbey of la Charité-lès-Vesoul, and the splendid rococo tribune at the west end which accommodates an organ built by the Riepp brothers from Germany, considered by Albert Schweitzer as one of the finest instruments in France. The marble high altar (Louis Seize) was rescued and brought here when Dijon's Sainte Chapelle was destroyed in the Revolution.

We must be grateful that the Revolution spared at least some of the monastic buildings, in particular the unusually large **Dortoir** which was part of Abbot Hugh's thirteenth-century plan. A light and perhaps uncomfortably airy chamber, it is 70 metres long and its ribbed vaulting is supported by two rows of slender columns. All down the eastern side are *oculus* windows which let in the morning light to waken the sleepers – the rectangular windows below were put in later. It is here that we find the tympanum of Christ in Glory from the cathedral, and another of the Last Supper; between them is the head and shoulder bust of Christ from Claus Sluter's calvary at the Chartreuse de Champnol on the outskirts of Dijon. Beneath the *dortoir* is the eleventh-century *salle des moines* of Abbot William, an extended crypt with short massive pillars and rough masonry. Some Gallo-Roman statuary has been assembled here, including an intriguing bas-relief of a wine merchant's premises, a bronze goddess from the Source de la Seine, and an exquisite bronze votive offering of a ship with a swan at the prow.

These two buildings form the ground floor and basement of the **Musée Archéologique**, where the upper floor is a more conventional museum with exhibits from the Neolithic and Bronze Ages, and from Gallo-Roman times. One ingenious reconstruction shows a Gallo-Roman settlement with a typical house interior, and there are characteristic finds from all over Burgundy. It is open at the usual hours all the year round, except of course on Tuesdays.

Just across the road from St-Bénigne is the **Church of St-Philibert**. Its presence so close to the *abbatiale* suggests that it had a connected if subservient function. Some have maintained that it was built for the use of novices attached to the monastery, but later it was clearly the parish church of the quarter – one distinguished by its population of wine merchants and vineyard workers. The visitor will be attracted at once by its elegant thirteenth-century porch, where the ceremony of electing the mayor of Dijon used to take place, and by the distinctive stone spire above the west end. Inside (if you succeed in getting in) you will find the only complete surviving example of a Romanesque church in Dijon, for it was built immediately after the fire of 1137 which led to the destruction of William of Volpiano's basilica, and before Hugues d'Arc began its Gothic replacement. Extremely plain and simple, with clear-cut groin vaulting, square unadorned pilasters, and single lancet windows at triforium level, its almost Cistercian austerity is illuminated by a clerestory and well placed *oculi*. St-Philibert is no longer in use as a church, though it seems that restoration is on the cards. Until then you may need special dispensation to see inside.

From here the rue Danton leads into the Place Bossuet, which is distinguished by another disaffected church. The huge dilapidated pile of **St-Jean**, from whose tower the mediaeval curfew bell rang out, has found a new and successful *métier* as a theatre under the direction of the Centre Dramatique Nationale de Bourgogne. The *place* is named after Jacques-Bénigne Bossuet (1627-1704) who was the son of a magistrate living in what was then the Place St-Jean, and was baptized in the church. Educated by the Jesuits at the Hôtel des Godran, he was ordained to the priesthood in Paris in 1652, and became successively bishop of Condom and Meaux, and chaplain to the duchess of Burgundy. He was the friend of the exiled Queen Henrietta Maria, widow of Charles I of England, who gave him on her deathbed an emerald which he wore as a ring on his little finger. He preached her funeral oration – a role which justified Michelet's description of Burgundy as 'the country of orators, of stately and solemn eloquence'. At the corner of the rue Monge, beneath the church-theatre's towering bulk, you will find the tables of a café-restaurant set out in the open air, and in fine weather there is no better place in Dijon to eat a simple *déjeuner* – or indeed to dine modestly on a warm summer evening.

2

Another day should be kept for visiting the **Palais des Ducs et des États de Bourgogne** and its surroundings. A few minutes walk from the Place Bossuet or the Square Darcy will bring you to the Place de la Libération, formerly the Place Royale, which opens out in a graceful semicircle in front of the Palais. An equestrian statue of Louis XIV once stood in the middle of it, but this was broken up by the revolutionaries in 1792 and sent to the foundries at le Creusot as raw material for cannon. Nevertheless the Place Royale reminds us that Louis was fond of Dijon, where, as he said, 'the company is good, and where one lives with the greatest pleasure and in the greatest security under the protection of a careful and constantly active police'. Such even then were the requirements of autocratic rulers.

Opposite the centre of the semicircle is the gateway into the *cour d'honneur* of the Palais des États, built in the seventeenth century to accommodate the Three Estates of Burgundy, which assembled here every three years from 1688 until the Revolution. It also housed their permanent executive, who discharged the duties of a civil service under the Governor, who was himself responsible to the King. Until then the Estates had met in various Burgundian cities, and from the beginning of the seventeenth century they had made use of the Couvent des Cordeliers in Dijon. Eventually they felt the need for a permanent meeting place, and won the permission of Louis XIV to install themselves in the Logis du Roi, formerly a part of the ducal palace.

On your left as you enter the courtyard are the modern offices of the Hôtel-de-Ville; to the right a passage leads into the Cour de Bar, dominated by the four-square mass of the **Tour de Bar**. This was built in the 1360s by Philippe le Hardi, first of the Valois dukes, but its name commemorates a very distinguished prisoner who was lodged there for a time. René of Anjou, duc de Bar and heir to the crown of Sicily, is better known under his later affectionate title of 'le bon roi René' of Provence. He had been captured in a minor engagement by Duke Philippe le Bon and was awaiting ransom – no doubt in comfort, considering his rank. Another vaulted passage leads from the Cour de Bar out into the pleasant little Place des Ducs, from where you have a good view of the royal quarters, and of the fifteenth-century tower of Philippe le Bon.

Returning by the Cour de Bar into the main courtyard, you will find on the far side the entrance to the Cour de Flore, surrounded by buildings of three different periods. Those on the east side were put up under Louis XV, and those on the north and west under Louis XVI. Behind most of the façades are the teeming offices of the Hôtel-de-Ville, but if you enter the passage on the south side which leads back into the rue de la Liberté you will find yourself at the foot of the **Grand Staircase**, with its wrought-iron balustrade, which gives access to the **Salle des États**, a reminder of the grandeur which survived the extinction of the dukes. On the way up you pass the statues of Liberty and Justice, and going forward you enter the hall under a semicircular gallery supported by four pillars. From here you can easily imagine the Three Estates in session, clergy on one side, nobles on the other, the commonalty in the middle, and the Governor on a dais at the farther end. A rather different scene can be imagined when you read on a plaque behind the daïs these words: *En cette salle le 29 février 1944 les patriotes de l'Auxois furent condamnés à mort.*

Beyond the Salle des États you enter the **Chapelle des Élus**, where Mass was celebrated while the états were in session. This is a fine example of seventeenth-century decorative architecture, whose general plan should probably be attributed to Jacques Gabriel, who employed the Italian Spingola to design the marble ornaments and the Fleming Verberckt for the woodwork. The style of both these elements is similar to work done under Gabriel's direction at Versailles.

The Palais des États was still the focus of eighteenth-century Dijon, when it had more than a hundred streets, fifteen squares, two thousand houses, and was one of the best-paved cities in Europe. In it was concentrated the essence of what the Goncourt brothers wrote of the province as a whole:

You then found in that happy Burgundy a cordial good humour; a healthy-mindedness, strong and full; a warm and generous gaiety; a bravura that spoke in a local idiom; fraternity, youth, and the genius of good wine.

Of post-Revolutionary Dijon, Stendhal has a more particular account:

The artists of Dijon are fortunate if they happen to please the Parliamentary society, for this is the class which here forms the aristocracy, and it is generally agreed to have a lively mind. The men that I meet in the streets of Dijon are small, astringent, lively and choleric; you can see that their temperaments are all governed by good wine. For you need more than a logical brain to make a superior man; you need a certain temperamental fire.

The whole of the rest of the palace is now occupied by the Musée des Beaux Arts, the largest and most important museum in France outside Paris. To reach it you will have to regain the rue de la Liberté and follow it past the Place de la Libération until it becomes the rue Rameau. Rounding the corner to the left you will find yourself in the long narrow Place de la Sainte-Chapelle, and there in its exact centre is the statue of Jean-Philippe Rameau, who was born in Dijon in 1683. This is the man (though his statue only hints at it) who was said to have flutes in place of legs and to be more like a ghost than a man. A fellow Dijonnais, meeting him in the garden of the Tuileries, described him as 'nothing more than a long organ pipe without the bellows' – and indeed both he, his father and his brother were all organists, Jean-Philippe taking his father's place at Notre-Dame in Dijon between 1709 and 1714. Better known as a musical theorist and composer of many operas and ballets, he could play the harpsichord at seven, was composing fugues at fourteen; his schoolmaster complained that though he could read any music at sight that was all he could or would read. His later career was spent mainly in Paris, where he married a young singer, the daughter of a royal physician, but he was elected to the *Académie de Dijon* three years before his death.

The building on the far side of the Place, now a theatre, occupies the site of the **Sainte-Chapelle**. This was founded in 1172 by one of the early Capetian dukes, Hugues III, to fulfil a vow taken during a storm at sea on his way to the Holy Land, and dedicated to the Virgin and St John the Evangelist. Its construction was unusual, in that the *chevet* faced north, and the nave had only one bay which embraced a central and two double side aisles. Nevertheless it was one of the glories of early Gothic architecture, and although not completed until the end of the fifteenth century it served as the ducal chapel throughout the rule of the Valois dukes. When Philippe le Bon founded the Toison d'Or he made it the chapel of the Order and provided for a daily Mass to be said there. As in the chapels of the Garter at Windsor and the Bath in Westminster Abbey, the knights of the Golden Fleece had each his own seat in the choir, with his coat of arms emblazoned on the panel above.

In 1433 Pope Eugène IV gave Philip a miraculous relic, known as the Sainte-Hostie, for which Philip's third wife, Isabella of

Portugal, had made a silver-gilt monstrance, and it was kept in one of the chapels of the church. While still a prisoner in the Tour de Bar, René d'Anjou presented to the chapel a window he is said to have designed himself.

This wonderful building with all its treasures stood intact at the Revolution, but then it was at once despoiled of all its rich and precious contents. Spared at the time from actual destruction, it stood only until 1802, when it was decided to demolish it as having no further practical use. Explosives were used to bring it down, and to quote Pierre Quarré, a museum director, 'by the next year there remained only a pile of rubble of what had been the finest Gothic building in Dijon, bearing witness to the splendour of the achievements of the dukes of Burgundy and of the monarchy, the seat of one of the most famous orders of knighthood'.

Opposite the Rameau statue is the entrance to the **Musée des Beaux Arts**, and few entry fees that you will pay in France are better value. The visit normally begins by turning left to the **Kitchens**, built by Philippe le Bon in the mid-fifteenth century. The pairs of huge fireplaces on three sides of the main chamber have their lintels grandly supported by classical columns. Eight ogival arches converge on the central vault, and a round stone indicates the hole through which fumes could escape. The proportions suggest that gargantuan feasts originated here – everything the dukes did was on a huge scale. Also on the ground floor, and to the right of the entrance, is the **Chapter House** – all that remains of the Sainte-Chapelle complex – with a collection of religious statuary and other treasures from the eleventh to the sixteenth centuries.

A stairway leads to the first storey, where more than twenty rooms and galleries display a rich selection of painting and sculpture of many periods and widely varying *provenance*. However much you may be tempted to dally at different points, when you reach the **Salle des Gardes** you feel yourself to be at the heart of the duchy, and that the heart has not ceased to beat. The room was built and sumptuously decorated by Philippe le Bon, the most artistically minded of the dukes, and it saw the state entry to Dijon in 1474 of Charles le Téméraire. However, of the great dukes only Philippe le Hardi and Jean-sans-Peur (with his wife, Marguerite de Bavière) came to rest here after their bodies had been transferred from the Chartreuse de Champnol. Yet as you contemplate these superb effigies it seems as if the dynasty has recovered in death everything it had gained and lost in life. Other tombs may move you more than these; few can equal them in magnificence. Meanwhile it seems natural to consider briefly the life and character not only of these two dukes, but of all four members of the Valois dynasty who ruled here as virtual kings of Burgundy.

Jean de Marville, Claus Sluter and his nephew Claus de Werve worked on the memorial to **Philippe le Hardi** from 1385 to 1411. The recumbent figure, watched over by two angels, rests on a black marble sarcophagus, surrounded by an alabaster arcade in which forty-one *pleurants* – clergy, relatives and officers of state, all hooded – circulate in a doleful procession, each with a different gesture or attitude of grief. Philippe was a genial but authoritative ruler. He had fought against the English as a boy, calling out to his father in the middle of a battle 'Look after your right flank!' On 26 November 1364 he entered Dijon as duke of Burgundy, and made the city his capital.

Although he was inclined to neglect the duchy in favour of his other possessions, the circumstances of his funeral give one a notion not only of what the duchy thought of its duke, but of what it thought about itself. The expenses of the ceremony, set out in a parchment roll eight feet long, are preserved in the archives at Dijon. The duke's body (he had died in Flanders) was clothed in the habit of a Carthusian monk; the entrails were buried on the spot, and his heart was consigned to the abbey of St-Denis. The embalmed corpse was wrapped in thirty-two ells of waxed cloth and three cowhides, and placed in a leaded coffin weighing seven hundred pounds. Plate and jewellery worth six thousand gold crowns were pawned to pay the cost of these magnificent obsequies. The hearse was draped in cloth of gold, embroidered with a crimson cross, and suitable draperies were sent to the twelve churches where the coffin was to rest on its way to Dijon, a blue banner at each of its four corners. It rested for nearly three weeks at St-Seine-l'Abbaye, where the sixty mourners who had accompanied it from Brussels were joined by boys who now led the procession. It was met by the mayor and aldermen of Dijon, a hundred burgesses and a hundred poor men dressed in black. The body was interred at Champnol in the middle of the choir on 16 June, nearly three months after life had left it.

The tomb of **Jean-sans-Peur** and his wife was begun by Jean de la Huerta in 1443 and completed by Antoine le Moiturier in 1470 ; it is similar in design to that of Philippe le Hardi. In 1412 Jean had made a spectacular peace with his uncle the duc de Berri, on a big platform in the courtyard of the abbey of St-Germain in Auxerre. They both left astride the same horse after great feasting, the kind of magnificent gesture which characterized his reign and made him popular in the province. He founded the Order of the Grands Ducs d'Occident to work for Burgundy, its art and its tradition; the members were entitled to wear the ribbon of the order *en cravate* with the gold seal of the duke attached to it. Before his own ordination he took a bath, said a prayer, and then – arrayed in brown boots, white tunic and red surcoat – leaped on to his horse without touching the stirrups, and unhooked an *écu* from a post with the end of his lance as he rode off at a gallop. He would seem to have lived up to his motto, 'Valeur du corps et bonté de l'âme'. We are told how at a ducal banquet the clinking of the knives and forks would replace the clash of arms.

The duc de Brabant has given us this picture of Jean-sans-Peur:

Although there was something haughty and uncontrolled in his character, he was easy for those who worked for him. He listened to their advice, and once you had gained his confidence he trusted you completely. He liked to reward you for your services, and he knew the right way to do it. He had also the qualities appreciated by men of war: untiring, never sparing himself, and enduring patiently hunger and thirst, cold and rain. He was short but robust, with clear blue eyes and a firm expression in them; full in the face, giving you the impression of health and strength.

Other descriptions are less openly flattering. They suggest a suspicious character – he always carried a weapon under his robe – and that he was of a more amorous and wanton disposition than his father.

The shades of the other two great dukes seem to hover over the tombs of their predecessors, as if in protest against their exclusion from this magnificent mausoleum. Both the luxury and the humanism of the Burgundian court were seen at their height under the rule of **Philippe le Bon**. He had a vast library and employed 176 artists to adorn his palaces and châteaux; it was not for nothing that he had watched Van Eyck at work, and he called him into his service from Flanders. He was at once pious and immoral; fond of music, but shocked by licentious plays. On the occasion of his marriage to Isabella of Portugal he founded the Order of the Golden Fleece, or *Toison d'Or*, in emulation of the English Order of the Garter. The members wore a woollen dress at the beginning of their investiture, and then assumed a red velvet tunic lined with white satin and embroidered with gold. At Vespers on St Andrew's Day they paraded on horseback, two by two, accompanied by two hundred gentlemen, twelve trumpeters, heralds and clergy. The protocol at court was exacting and precise; three genuflections were required when you approached the ducal presence. Yet under the good Philip the townsfolk too prospered. In 1436 the population of Dijon was about 6,000; when he died in 1467 it had doubled. In 1443 there were 4,000 people employed in the cloth trade – weavers, cutters, dyers and bleachers. Copious markets for meat, fish, wine, vegetables, eggs and fruit supplied the needs of the town.

The ducal feasts were described by the historian Jules Michelet as *'fougueuses kermesses'*, and this was putting it mildly. When the news came in 1453 that Byzantium had finally fallen to the Turks, the duke decreed a series of jousts and extravagant banquets to enlist support among the chivalry for a new crusade. The climax was the Banquet du Faisan, held not in Dijon but at Lille, which was still an integral part of the duchy. Apart from the feasting, which was prodigious, musical and dramatic entertainment was provided between courses. The twenty-eight musicians and their instruments came into the hall hidden in an enormous pie. On the duke's table was a model of a church, big enough to contain four singers and a bell, which rang at intervals. The committee of three which organized the occasion included Olivier de la Marche, to whose chronicles we owe a description of the proceedings. It was he who was responsible for the *dénouement*, in which he appeared dressed as a nun, riding in a castle on the back of an elephant. Representing Our Mother the Holy Church, he made a speech in verse calling on the company to take an oath to aid her against the infidel.

A fulsome account of Philippe le Bon is given by another chronicler, Georges Chastellain. Physically he is described as of medium height and straight as a reed, bony rather than fleshy, with a broad and full forehead, thick and highly coloured lips, prominent veins and grey eyes. His mere appearance 'proclaimed him an emperor'. As for his character: 'Never, I believe, did a lie pass his lips; his mouth was a seal and his words were as a document'. There is a portrait of Philippe by Rogier van der Weyden in the Salle des Gardes.

Charles le Téméraire, whose undignified death at the siege of Nancy in 1477 brought the line to an end, justified his *soubriquet*, whether you translate it as 'bold' or 'rash', though he was more than the adventurer it suggests. He was muscular and bow-legged, with thick dark curly hair, an olive complexion, round face and slightly prominent lower lip. His shoulders sloped, and he walked with his head thrust forward and his eyes on the ground. When he raised them, the sycophantic Chastellain describes them as 'grey, laughing, and angelically clear'. He was faithful to his wife and concerned for the poor, noted for his cleanliness and austerity, fond of archery and chess. Although his own voice was unmusical, he had musical tastes. His piety was both sombre and bellicose, for he believed that a sovereign was obliged to make war to expiate his sins and those of his subjects. He hated France and Louis XI, or rather, as he put it, loved her so well that he wished her to be governed by six kings instead of one.

Married at seven and widowed at twelve, he had a difficult childhood. Distressed by the presence and importunity of his father's mistresses and bastards, he found consolation in books – the stories of Lancelot and Gawain, and the voyages of Marco Polo, which may have fed the romantic miscalculations of his policy. He married as his second wife Margaret of York, sister of England's Edward IV, but they had no male issue and the doom of the duchy was sealed. As Victor Hugo aptly put it: 'Dynasties are founded by the bold, and brought to destruction by the rash'.

The charitable judgment of Philippe de Commines on Charles le Téméraire may stand:

I see no reason why he should have incurred the anger of God, except that he attributed all the honours and graces he received in this world to his own intelligence and virtue, rather than to God, as he should have done. For in truth there was much virtue and goodness in him . . . No prince gave audience more freely to his subjects and servants. He was not cruel at the time I knew him, but he became so before his death. He was magnificent in his dress, as in everything else – a little too much so – and very ambitious for glory. This was more responsible than anything else for leading him into war. He would have liked to resemble those princes of former days, who left a great name behind them, and he was as bold as any man of his time.

Also in the Salle des Gardes are two altar *retables* in gilded wood, of astonishing richness. They were ordered in 1390 by Philippe le Hardi for the Chartreuse de Champnol and were carved by Jacques de Baerze, gilded and painted by Melchior Broederlam. A third *retable* of the Antwerp school (fifteenth century) hangs between them, and on the wall above is a Flemish tapestry dedicated to Notre-Dame-de-Bon-Espoir, which came from the nearby church of Notre-Dame.

In the adjoining Galerie Bellegarde are paintings by Veronese, Frans Hals, Rubens and Guido Reni. Beyond that again are rooms devoted to sculpture, in particular the Salle Rude. François Rude (1784-1855) was born in Dijon, where his father was a saddler and blacksmith. He studied sculpture at the École des Beaux Arts, and afterwards in Paris, admitting later that he had wasted seven years of his life in academic studies. He continued to work for a time in his father's forge, followed his master, Premiet, into exile at the Restoration, and married his daughter in Brussels. Though he was a classicist by training, his favourite maxims derive from the Romantic revival: 'Everything is in Nature, everything comes from Nature, and everything returns to Nature; to observe is virtually to create'. The pick of his work here is a composition entitled 'Hebe and the Eagle', and a statue of a little Neapolitan fisher boy.

Another gallery has some charming examples of the Flemish school, including a Nativity by the Maître de Flemalle (circa 1425) with a cow peering through the broken slats of the stable. Elsewhere you will find a portrait of the ever seductive Diane de Poitiers (École de Fontainebleau) at her toilette. Naked to the waist and fingering her jewel box, she looks like a woman who knew when she was on to a good thing. The contrast with Jean Tassel's Cathérine de Monthelon – the long hands clasped in prayer, as Dürer might have painted them, and the rugged face brooding over the white collar and below the black veil – is very striking. On the second floor is a collection of French Impressionists, with works by Manet, Monet, Boudin and Vuillard, and on the third there are more rooms displaying a catholic mixture of pottery, faience, modern painting and sculpture, and art collections from China and Japan. The Palais des Ducs is still good value for money.

To the north of the great ducal complex is an interesting quarter with the **Church of Notre-Dame** as its centre. This was built substantially between 1220 and 1245, but not finally consecrated till 1334. We have already seen several examples of the way Gothic design developed in Burgundy, but this is one where the master's plan was unchanged by later events -- at least as far as the interior is concerned. The nave, choir and hexagonal apse all have a three-storey elevation similar to that of St-Etienne at Auxerre. Again the triforium passage runs behind slender columns which divide the arcades, but the clerestory passage is more daring, recessed back to the outer skin of the walls and actually piercing the side walls of the bays. In the choir and transept there is a third passage above the dado and below the main windows, while even the columns which support the arcades are detached from their wall. It is this breaking up of all the main wall surfaces which in a miraculous way combines strength with lightness, and the eye registers a series of screens through which the light of the windows enters the church. In some cases, notably in the north transept, the arcaded openings do not match the window spaces behind, but so delicate are the supporting columns that one is hardly conscious of the fact.

The whole effect is as sophisticated today as it was challenging to contemporary designers. Other outstanding features are the rosette windows behind the triforium passage in the apse, and the big rose window in the north transept which there replaces the triforium – notice the highly original tracery with its geometrically inscribed circles. To come to Notre-Dame after the sober magnificence of St Bénigne is almost like passing from darkness into light.

The apsidal chapel to the right of the choir contains a Black Virgin in wood, one of the most ancient of its kind in France. She was especially venerated for her part in saving Dijon from a desperate situation when attacked by an imperial army in 1513; she has Swiss bullets in her apron. To mark the same event the tapestry was woven which we saw in the Salle des Gardes of the Palais des

Ducs, but by some accounts there was a great deal more to the story than divine intervention. On 7 December that year, la Trémoille, Governor of Burgundy, was faced by a besieging army numbering about 30,000 men – Swiss, Germans, and a contingent from the Franche-Comté. To hold the town he could muster only about 6,000, and his appeals for negotiation was rejected. The enemy artillery had already made several breaches in the walls when la Trémoille sent out another deputation at the head of a convoy of carts loaded with barrels of wine. The wine of Burgundy had the final say, and the Governor was able to negotiate not only for the raising of the siege but for an end to hostilities in return for a payment of 400,000 crowns. Louis XII was not pleased and refused to ratify the treaty, but Dijon at least was saved. After a second liberation – from the Germans in September 1944 – a modern tapestry was commissioned from the Gobelins factory to commemorate both events; it hangs in the south transept.

The west end of the nave is approached through a three-aisled porch, with two magnificent multiple piers on either side of the central archway. Its sensational façade is crowned by sixteen arches, with three rows of false gargoyles (they have no practical function); one of them is a head with three faces at different angles, anticipating Picasso by several hundred years. Above to the right is the famous *horloge à jacquemart*, a mechanical Flemish clock brought back from Courtrai as a trophy of war by Philippe le Hardi in 1382. The device by which a male figure, or 'Jacques', strikes the hour on a bell with a hammer is not uncommon – there is a good example at Blythburgh in Suffolk which must also have originated in Flanders – but the family-minded dijonnais have given it some characteristic variations. In 1610 they decided that Jacques had been celibate too long and gave him a wife, Jacqueline; in 1714 their union was blessed by a son, Jacquelinet, who was given a smaller bell to strike, and finally in 1881 they added a daughter, Jacquelinette, to strike the quarters.

On the far side of the rue de la Chouette, opposite the *chevet* of Notre Dame, is the Hôtel de Vogüé, which recalls the family who settled for a time at Châteauneuf-en-Auxois and are the present owners of Commarin. It dates from the early seventeenth century, and was one of the first houses to be set aside for occupation by dignitaries of the Parliament. It has a richly decorated Renaissance portico which opens on to an interior courtyard. In the rue des Forges, which runs parallel to the rue de la Liberté, are a number of old houses of which the Hôtel Chambellan (nos 34 and 36) is especially notable. It was built in the fifteenth century and is now the office of the Syndicat d'Initiatives. The Maison Milsand (no. 38) has a fine Renaissance façade, and the Musée Perrin de Puycousin at no. 40 houses an exhibition of popular Burgundian art. It was the birthplace of Hugues Aubriot, Provost of Paris under Charles V, who built the Bastille and a number of bridges over the Seine.

St Michel, which stands at the eastern end of the rue de la Liberté beyond the Palais des États, was begun at the end of the fifteenth century in an expansive gesture of flamboyant Gothic. Work on it was held up for lack of money, but eventually it was completed by a Renaissance façade. The two western towers, heavily buttressed and rising in four storeys, were not built until the seventeenth century. The Last Judgement of the west door tympanum is the work of a Flemish artist, Nicolas de la Court.

If you now retrace your steps to the Place Royale and turn down the rue Vauban from its southern end, you will come to the **Palais de Justice**, where the Parliament of Burgundy used to meet. The door is a copy of the original by Hugues Sambin (now in the museum) and you will notice the panelled vault in the handsome Salle des Pas Perdus, and a ceiling in the Salle des Assises transported from the former Cour des Comptes.

About half a mile from the centre of the city, below and to the south of the N5 as it leaves Dijon for the west, are the grounds of a psychiatric centre which contain what is left of Philippe le Hardi's **Chartreuse de Champnol**. During normal daylight hours the visitor may enter at will and walk round the beautifully kept gardens. Patients are housed in separate well laid out blocks of one storey, each with its own medical staff and attendants. It is hard to imagine a more soothing ambiance for the mentally disturbed, or one more comforting for their families to visit. Among some bewildering medical signposting it is not difficult to pick out directions which guide you back to the fourteenth century and the real object of your visit.

The first stone of the Chartreuse, designed by Drouet de Dammartin, was laid by Philippe's wife Marguerite de Flandre in 1383;

the buildings were consecrated five years later by the bishop of Troyes. They were destroyed at the Revolution and, although a chapel was later rebuilt behind it, only the *grand portail* of Claus Sluter survives from the original church. Above the doorway are five statues by Sluter, the great Flemish artist who was called to Dijon in 1385 to succeed Jean de Marville as official sculptor to the duke. The Virgin and Child above the central *trumeau* have stone portraits of Philippe and Marguerite on either side, each paired with their guardian saint – St John the Baptist and St Catherine. A fragment of tower stands detached to one side.

There are more signs to guide you round the boundary wall to the **Puits de Moïse**, which was never a well, but the base of a Calvary which stood in the centre of the cloister. We have seen the head of the crucified Christ in the Dortoir des Moines next to St Bénigne. The base itself is a hexagonal pillar, surrounded by the more than life-size statues of six Old Testament prophets by Sluter, and an elevated walkway makes it possible to study these remarkable works at the closest of quarters. The most impressive and patriarchal is Moses, as you would expect, but the others have both dignity and individual character: Jeremiah appears a little sour, Zachariah bowed but benevolent, Daniel bewildered, Isaiah with the years heavy on him. Sluter's nephew, Claus de Werve, carved the charming little *pleurant* angels under the cornice, with their cleverly varied attitudes of sorrow.

Of the many sons of Dijon so far unmentioned there are two or three with differing claims to attention. Bernard de la Monnaye (1641-1728) may stand as well as any for the typical Burgundian. He lived here for more than sixty years and worked as a councillor in the Chambre des Comptes, but was more widely known as a poet. Eventually his Noëls – popular songs which had little to do with Christmas – upset the clergy, and he had to move to Paris. He was a devoted husband:

> Nous fûmes moins épous qu'amants;
> Dix lustres avec toi m'ont paru dix moments.

When his wife died, he wrote 'Je haïs la clarté du soleil'. He won the prize awarded by the Académie française so regularly that he was asked not to compete any more. His verses were written, he boasted, in Latin, Greek, French and Burgundian and, although Paris was his *séjour*, his *patrie* was Dijon.

The most famous president of the Académie de Dijon was Charles de Brosses (1709-77). In spite of his tiny stature – so small that when he spoke in public he had to stand on a stool – his personality was not one to overlook. Diderot's description was affectionate: 'It makes me die of laughter to see him in his official uniform, with his merry little head, mocking and ironical, lost in the immense forest of hair which all but obscures the rest of his tiny face'. Sainte Beuve on the other hand hailed him more seriously, declaring that he stood in the first rank of those independent, witty and enlightened men whose careers were still provincial. At a time when the provinces were becoming increasingly neglected, when eminent people were obliged to bow to Parisian customs and to the general code of behaviour in France, he remained sturdily faithful to Burgundy. He is the last and the most considerable of the great provincial men of letters, who preserved even in their new ideas something of the charm inherited from former times. A *bon vivant*, a traveller and a linguist, his books were widely read, but they were not enough to secure him membership of the Académie française – probably because he had quarrelled with Voltaire.

Gustave Eiffel (1832-1923), also born in Dijon, was an example of the engineering talent which has distinguished Burgundy in general and Dijon in particular. After working on the railway bridge at Bordeaux, the Douro viaduct and the Panama Canal, he constructed the Eiffel Tower for the Exhibition of 1889, and was given the right to exploit it for twenty years. He installed a meteorological laboratory inside it, and at the age of eighty he turned to a new interest – aviation.

One of the most popular of recent Dijonnais was the Chanoine Kir, for many years Maire of the city, and a member of the Chambre des Députés after the last war. His name crops up unexpectedly in many contexts, but most widely to describe a now universal Burgundian *apéritif*. Elsewhere it may be known as a *vin blanc cassis*, but in Burgundy it will always be a *Kir*. It can be refreshing and delicious, but for best results you should be sparing with the cassis.

Many who have never been to Dijon know about its mustard. This has been made since the fourth century to a recipe of Palladius, son of Exuperantius, Prefect of Gaul. A single hogshead containing three hundred quarts of mustard was consumed at a banquet given by the duke of Burgundy to Philip de Valois in 1336. It was favoured by Pope John XXII, who called his worthless nephew 'Premier Moutardier du Pape'. The rhyme went:

> De trois choses Dieu nous garde:
> De bœuf salé sans moutarde,
> D'un valet qui se regarde,
> D'une femme qui se farde.

Lastly, it should not be overlooked that Dijon celebrates several annual festivals. For bellringers there is the Festival du Carillon in the second week of August, for winelovers the Fête de la Vigne on the first or second weekend in September (which is also an international display of popular songs and dances), and for gourmets the *Foire Gastronomique* during the first fortnight in November is a must.

CHAPTER ELEVEN

The Pays-Bas and
the Valley of the Seine

Having come down into Dijon from the unexpected grandeur of the Montagne, with the riches of the Côte awaiting you to the south, you may not be immediately drawn to the flat country that stretches away to the east, traversed by the Canal de Bourgogne in one of its least interesting moods. Nevertheless within a radius of thirty kilometres or so from the city centre there is a lot to see – and Burgundy is never dull. The Côte and its glories can wait.

You can treat this section as a series of sorties to south, east and north of the capital, or by fetching a three-quarter circle round it from south to north-west. This follows at first the line of the Saône, the Vingeanne and the Marne-Saône canal; afterwards it leaves the plain to climb into the wooded hills above the Tille, finally coming down to find the source of the Seine and regain Dijon by way of St-Seine-l'Abbaye and the Val Suzon. At several points of the compass you will find pleasant places to stay for one or more nights.

Half an hour's drive south down the D996 will bring you to the **Abbaye de Cîteaux**, and all that remains of one of the principal sites of the Christian world. There is little to see there now, and nothing to evoke its past; the name alone draws us there. On low marshy ground, close to the little river Vouge (which as we shall see gave its name to the wine-lovers Mecca, the Clos Vougeot) a monastery was founded in 1098 by a powerful trio of churchmen. Their leader was Robert from Molesme, who had founded there some twenty years earlier a community which was intended to re-establish the rule of St Benedict in its pure and simple form – reacting against the growing laxity and artistic freedom of the Benedictines of Cluny. He had attracted to Molesme others of the same mind, including one who came all the way from Sherborne in the county of Dorset – Stephen Harding – and the future St

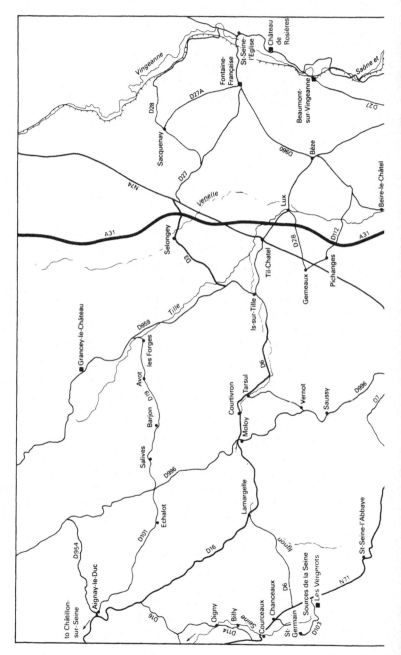

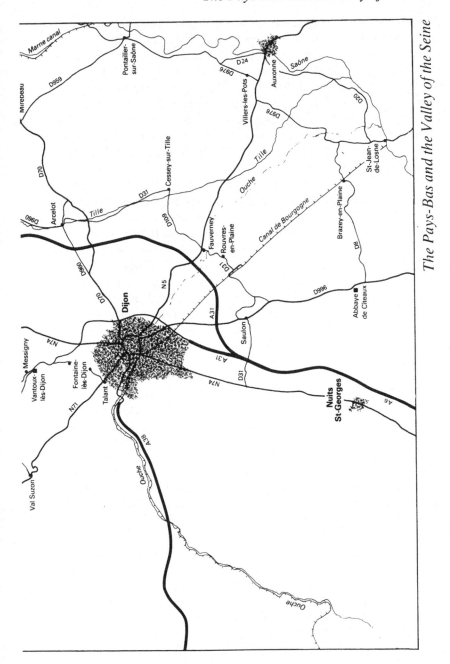

Albéric, of whose origins we know little. Still not satisfied that he had pared their life of poverty, prayer and labour down to essentials, he led a party of twenty-one monks to found a *novum monasterium* near the site of the Roman town of Cistercium. After a few years Robert returned to Molesme, leaving Albéric in charge as abbot until his death in 1109, when he was succeeded by Stephen Harding. It was the Englishman, later to be canonized as St Etienne, who in 1112 took the momentous step of admitting to the community a group of thirty well-born Burgundians led by a young man called Bernard.

We shall come closer to the origins of this remarkable man at the end of our circuit, just before we re-enter Dijon from the north. His restless energy allowed him to spend only three years at Cîteaux before he left it with a few followers to found yet another pure community at Clairvaux, just over the northern boundary of modern Burgundy in the department of Aube. Harding presided at Cîteaux until his death in 1134, by which time it and its original four daughters at La Ferté, Pontigny, Morimond and Clairvaux had multiplied their issue to the number of five hundred new abbeys founded in forty years. Within the next hundred years this number had doubled, and the Cistercian rule was established throughout Christendom, from Ireland in the west to Syria and Palestine in the east.

The abbey church at Cîteaux was built on the scale and on the impressively simple plan we have seen at Pontigny and Fontenay, but it was not so fortunately preserved. It and practically the whole of the monastic complex which grew up on the flat ground to the south was finally destroyed by the anticlerical fury of the Revolution. The monks were forced to scatter, and it was not until 1898 that their successors in the white habit returned to follow the rule which had been founded here 800 years before. The church of Notre-Dame alone is open to visitors – modern, dignified and functionally impressive. To one side are blocks of nineteenth-century buildings, to the other a range of farm-like dependencies; further south (with no access at present) is the only mediaeval survival, a two-storey brick building with an arcaded ground floor. This was the fifteenth-century *scriptorium* where the copyists still worked on the production and illumination of manuscripts – a tradition which had been enlivened by a fresh and inventive style which Stephen Harding had brought with him from England, and which was the only medium in which an artist could express himself under the strict Cistercian rule. Today the building stands half ruined, though there are plans to restore it.

If there are no palpable mementos of the regime we associate above all with St Bernard, the regime itself has not changed, and where better than at Cîteaux can we remind ourselves of it? The fifty monks of the modern community are committed as strictly as their fore-runners to a life of simplicity, work and prayer. In winter, for example, their day begins by waking for prayer at 0330, and again at 0615 for week-day Mass. They work in field, farm or library from 0730 to 1215. Their midday meal is accompanied by a reading from one of their number, but otherwise taken in silence. The afternoon is spent in work, prayer and meditation, with Vespers at 1730, an hour of relaxation, a simple supper, the last prayers of the day at 1930 and bed at 2000. As in most other communities they welcome *chercheurs de Dieu* to stay for a few days to share their silence and their prayers. As at la Pierre-qui-Vire in the Morvan, there is no Romanesque architecture to admire, but neither are there coach parties of tourists to disturb their peace.

Seventeen kilometres to the east of Cîteaux is the town of **St-Jean-de-Losne**, strategically placed at the point where the Canal de Bourgogne meets the already broad Saône, just below its confluence with the Ouche. A short way upstream the Rhine-Rhône canal takes off on its mission to join the Mediterranean with the Atlantic. Clusters of big barges assemble at a *gare d'eau* known as the Port-de-la-Hutte, which handles about 40,000 tonnes a year. The town, insignificant today, was an important stronghold in the fifteenth century; in 1636, during the Thirty Years' War, it withstood a siege by 60,000 Austrian troops. It is said that a mere 150 men with their wives and children held out for nine days until the flooding of the Saône and the approach of a relieving army compelled the enemy to withdraw. As a reward Louis XIII exempted the citizens from taxes, and when in 1814 St-Jean repelled an Allied advance Napoleon added the cross of the Légion d'Honneur to its arms. The middle span of the old eighteenth-century bridge across the Saône has been replaced by concrete, but this fine waterway can be viewed from simple hotels on either bank, and huge pleasure cruisers pass every week on their way down to Lyon.

The D20 will now take you north-east to **Auxonne**. This attractive town has earned – and deserves – the title of Station Verte de Vacances, and if you have a taste for boating, swimming and camping in pleasant surroundings you will hardly find a better stopping-place in the valley of the Saône. The Centre Nautique has cruising and water-skiing rights over 1,300 metres of the river.

In the principal square, opposite the fifteenth-century brick Hôtel-de-Ville, the statue of a young and pensive Bonaparte by Jouffroy reminds us that as a second lieutenant of eighteen he served in the garrison from 1 May 1788 to 1 September 1789. He then left for Corsica on compassionate leave because his widowed mother was in financial difficulties, but returned to Auxonne with his brother Louis on 1 June 1790. He left it for good in April the following year, having earned his promotion to first lieutenant.

The attraction for a young artillery officer was the Arsenal, with its eighteenth-century foundry and shop for cannon. Substantial relics from those days used to occupy the western side of an open yard, a particularly fine range with a roof carried by heavy oak beams. This has now been closed in to serve as a meeting place for *groupes scolaires*, presumably working on local and Napoleonic history projects. However the southern range, formerly used as the **Halles**, or roofed-in market place, is still recognizable as a fine building with square wooden pillars supporting a heavily beamed roof. The inner side is now bricked up, and a stairway leads to a chamber on the first floor which is used for receptions and local gatherings. A tour of the ramparts will give you an idea of the military importance of Auxonne (pronounced in Burgundian fashion as 'Aussonne'). To the north of the town is the Porte Royale, built by the comte d'Aprémont as part of his plan for the whole *enceinte*; the immense Tour de Signe close by, though it dates from the Middle Ages, was given a new coat of arms – and a salamander – by François I. The ramparts are seen at their most intact where they face the river and form the outer wall of what was the **Château de Prost**; this was begun in the reign of Louis XI and completed under Louis XII and François I – one of the first strongholds to be adapted to the use (and the threat) of artillery. Originally it commanded the river crossing, but all the central buildings have been demolished, leaving a huge empty courtyard surrounded by deserted red brick terraces – an area ripe for development, or at least restoration, on a grand scale. The building on the left as you enter the courtyard is used to good effect as the **Bonaparte Museum**.

The **Church of Notre-Dame** is of more than passing interest, with a twelfth-century Romanesque tower over the south transept. Building began about 1190, but the *chevet* and nave were reconstructed a century later. Among some unusual features of Burgundian Gothic – a style nothing if not adaptable – are the triplet windows in the eastern bays of the nave, with a continuous passage below, and the rare quatrefoil *oculi* behind the triforium of the hexagonal apse. There are traces of a fresco of Christ in Majesty on the vaulting of the choir, and of original colouring on the nave pillars. Some of the statuary is distinguished, especially the fifteenth-century Virgin with a skittish Child reaching for a bunch of grapes (surprisingly attributed to Claus Sluter), a sixteenth-century Christ de Pitié in the first chapel of the north aisle, and a striking St Hubert on a pillar to the right of the nave. Outside there is a long sequence of gables and gargoyles on the chapels which project from both side aisles, linked to the nave by flying buttresses.

Proceeding north along the D976 you come first to Pontailler-sur-Saône, enclosed by two branches of the river, and thence by the D959 to **Mirebeau**. Here the church of St-Pierre was built between the late twelfth and early thirteenth centuries, and much of it survives intact. The apse is unusually narrow, and attractively lit by a pair of lancet windows with a rosette above. The dignified interior makes it a suitable last resting place for the Dominican father V-P. Faitot, whose memorial tablet tells us that he was Doctor of Theology, Canon of Soissons, Prior of Angers, Dijon and St-Jacques in Paris; last Superior of the last community of Dominicans in France before it was suppressed in 1795. 'Intrepid defender of the Order and of his Faith', he was born in Mirebeau on 19 March 1736 and died at Paris on 22 July 1806.

The town suffered badly in the invasion by imperial troops of this corner of Burgundy in 1636, during the Thirty Years' War. After a siege of three days it was taken and pillaged, more than a hundred houses being totally destroyed. Today it would be a pleasant base from which to explore the country east and north of Dijon, and for this you will do no better than to stay at Les Marronniers, whose family connections seem to embrace the whole town. The rooms have been attractively modernised, and there is a smart new restaurant next door. However the little bar (where breakfast is served in person by Mme Perrin) still keeps in touch with local life.

The D959 leads on then to **Bèze**, and the first appearance of the river from which it takes its name. Its actual source is an underground stream which can be traced through a series of grottos in the hillside behind. An enterprising family has the franchise for taking parties by boat to explore them, but they have to watch the level of the water carefully before setting out. It is finally forced out through what is known as the 'trou du Diable', and gushes to the surface of a basin surrounded by plane trees at the phenomenal rate of 1,200 litres per second. You reach the spot by a path along the river bank above the town – a river which seems suddenly to have arrived from nowhere.

We shall presently see how the vineyards of Chambertin were indebted to the monks of Bèze, and in the town two towers remain of their priory. A long section of wall between them, traditionally occupied by the *sapeurs pompiers* of Beze, is now home to the Groupe Scolaire Claude Monet, an interesting substitution. Whoever works there, the place du Champ de Foire is one of the most charming spots in the town. Below it the swift-flowing Bèze washes the feet of one of the towers, where a little semi-circular platform with a classical portico makes an ideal stance for fishermen. The other tower is to your right, in the garden of a private house whose owner may allow you to climb an internal ladder up to the elaborate *charpente*; it also gives access to the ramparts, which shelter an attractive residential château.

The church has little of interest inside, but the lofty transept, with a second storey above both arms, remains from what was once a fortified building – as churches needed to be in these parts, not far from the frontier between Burgundy and the Franche-Comté. The heart of the town is the Place de Verdun, which contains a thirteenth-century façade worthy of the Veneto, and beside the little bridge you will find a mediaevally timbered *hostellerie* where it is no surprise to see a sucking pig being served (*sur commande)* at Sunday lunch. The Place du Chanoine Kir commemorates the *curé* of Bèze (and mayor of Dijon) who invented Burgundy's favourite *apéritif.*

North of Mirebeau the little river Vingeanne teams up with the Marne-Saône canal, running south through quiet farmland to join the Seine above Pontailler. Here is the chance for a detour for connoisseurs of serendipity. You can begin sedately by following the D960 from Bèze to **Fontaine-Française**, a comfortable small town whose name indicates that it and the forest beyond once formed part of a royal enclave within the duchy of Burgundy. Its chief historical interest lies just outside the town, at a place called the Pré Moreau, where on 5 June 1595 Henri IV gained his decisive victory over the forces of the Ligue under the command of the duc de Mayenne and the Constable of Castille. This effectively ended the wars of religion and established the king's authority throughout France. It was an astonishing feat of arms, for Henri had only 510 cavalry-men facing an army of 15,000. A monument on the road leading to St-Seine-sur-Vingeanne records the event.

The walls of the mediaeval fortress which gave him hospitality after the battle have been preserved, and form part of the distinguished château which was built here in 1750. It stands to the left of the road as you enter the town from the west, at the head of a large *étang* well populated with wildfowl, and it is well worth a visit if you can time it right. You will be following many famous guests, including Voltaire and Mme de Staël, who liked to frequent the literary salon of Mme de Saint-Julien. Regency furniture and Flemish tapestries embellish the *salon rose*, the *salon vert* and the *salle des gardes*. Your difficulty may be that the château is at present open only on some summer afternoons, so if you have begun your journey early in the day (or on the wrong day) you may have to return later.

On high ground to the north, by way of the D27A from Fontaine-Française, you come to **Sacquenay**, where there is a church with some interesting Romanesque features. First built in the twelfth century, altered in the thirteenth, it was partly destroyed by lightning in 1654 and had to be rebuilt. It has a strong Romanesque tower over a dignified western façade, and as at Bèze both arms of the transept have second-floor chambers above, reached by a *tour d'escalier* in the eastern angle of the transept.

At this point you can turn east and descend the valley which is so delightfully threaded by the Vingeanne and its attendant canal; it now forms the boundary of the Côte d'Or department, and as the Franche-Comté beyond it was a fief of the Empire in the early Middle Ages it was also the frontier of Burgundy. This explains the importance of some of the châteaux built here, and the presence of a number of well fortified churches. Nowadays nothing could be more peaceful. The little villages on the far bank — St-Maurice, Montigny-Mornay, Pouilly-sur-Vingeanne — all have charm and interest, and at **St-Seine-l'Église** you will find a sturdy grey Burgundian church with an outstanding three-storeyed Romanesque tower.

Then the winding country road passes the remarkable remains of the château of **Rosières**. You will see on your left a farm gateway beside a round tower, but this is dwarfed by the gigantic and heavily machicolated *donjon* — all that is left of the castle built in 1321 under Duke Eudes IV to guard the ancient frontier between Burgundy and the Franche-Comté. The farm which has swallowed up the rest was bought in 1980 by a historically minded farmer. Then it seemed to be in the last stages of decay. Ceilings and floors were caving in, the turret stairways were perilous, there were holes in the roof and rotten rafters; only the massive walls stood firm. Now M. Bergerot and his son (a builder by trade) have just completed the laborious work of re-roofing and restoring the fabric of this extraordinary building, work which included reconstituting the whole of a magnificent oak *charpente*. The rooms are of splendid proportions, with huge *cheminées* and mullioned windows, and you can follow the complete *chemin de ronde* of the battlements. On two floors they have managed to fit in what must be the most original *chambres d'hôte* in France, with all modern conveniences in a mediaeval framework — baths and a well equipped kitchen cunningly introduced into turrets and wall recesses. A different architectural note is struck when you enter the fortress by a seventeenth-century stairway leading to the Chambre des Ducs, a room panelled in wood with a decorated ceiling. This was contributed in 1680 by one Claude Bernard Maillard, parliamentary counsellor in the time of Louis XIII. A modest contribution of 10 francs to ongoing expenses is suggested, and if young M. Bergerot is available he will take you on a memorable tour of this unique place. You might even be tempted to take one of the *chambres d'hôte*.

Next comes a little group of villages with the enticing names of Attricourt, Licey-sur-Vingeanne, and Dampierre-et-Flée, a twin with a foot on each side of the river. If you keep to the right bank through Dampierre you come to **Beaumont-sur-Vingeanne**. Fork left in the village for Champagne-sur-Vingeanne, and look out for a farm lane on your right which brings you directly in front of the wrought-iron gates of a miniature eighteenth-century château. Behind you are the farm buildings which have taken over the mediaeval castle – witness the surviving towers – but in front of you is an entrancing oddity. It was built 'à la folie' in 1724 by the Abbé Claude Jolyot, chaplain to Louis XV, and the king himself came here for relaxation and perhaps for *la chasse* in the royal preserves of the Forêt de Fontaine-Française.

The façade of only two storeys is in pure classical style, with pediment and balustrade, suitably decorated with allegorical figures. The ground falls away on the far side, leaving room for a three-storeyed elevation overlooking a grassy slope which runs down to a swimming pool and groups of trees planted *à l'anglais*, with wild cyclamen showing beneath. The main doorway in front opens into a panelled hall with two gib doors for access to matching staircases leading to the upper floor. The *salon* is panelled too, in soft grey, with a comfortable study and tiny library beyond. The afternoon is visiting time, but only from mid-June to the end of July, and during the whole of September. Unique in Burgundy, and such a contrast to its solid contemporaries, it makes a perfect small family home.

The D27 brings you back on course to Mirebeau, and from there, if you are ready to continue the circuit, through Bèze again to the valley of the Tille. At **Lux** you will pass the late sixteenth-century château which was the scene of a mysterious event in the eighteenth century. A comtesse de Saulx-Tavannes shut herself up in a room of one of the towers, leaving her niece to sleep in the passage. One morning the door of the room did not open, and the niece was found lying outside, unconscious and demented. When the door was forced, the room was found empty except for a single slipper discarded on the floor. There was no way out except through the door, and the walls, floor and ceiling were thoroughly explored. The mystery has never been explained. Edgar Allan Poe could have resolved it in one way, Henry James in another. There is no admission to the château, but you can see it from the road, and perhaps the polygonal chapel in the park as well.

The road goes up to **Til-Chatel**, which was an important military station on the *Via Agrippa*, the highway between Saarbrücken and Chalon-sur-Saône. The late Romanesque church of St-Florent is one of the most interesting in Côte d'Or. The nave has no triforium, and its round pilasters rise to Corinthian capitals, connected by a delicate frieze at the point where the vaulting departs. This is a slightly pointed *berceau*, which has been ingeniously broken into by slanted openings to let in the light from fully rounded window embrasures. The intermediate pilasters of the nave bays have more lively capitals carved in the later Gothic spirit: the first to the right has four pairs of peacocks drinking from the fountain of life; opposite on the left are two winged sphinxes. The cupola over the crossing is an unusual lozenge shape, but it has the usual corner squinches.

Mounted on the wall of the south side aisle of the choir is a very remarkable mutilated twelfth-century wooden figure of Christ *en liens*, probably contemporary with the church, which was built about 1150. Below the high altar is preserved the stone on which the church's patron, St Florent, is supposed to have been beheaded in martyrdom. With a clear space outside the east end you have a good view of the beautifully balanced *chevet*, beyond which the roof of the choir rises in three stages to the base of the short tower.

When we reach Is-sur-Tille, five kilometres west of Til-Chatel past the Étang de Marcilly, we are due north of Dijon. Already the land level has risen well above the plains of the Pays-Bas, and a sortie further north up the valley of the Tille will take us into high forest land of much beauty, a region promoted locally as **Le Pays des Trois Rivières**. The three rivers are the Ignon, the Tille and the Venelle, of which the last two descend in parallel valleys from the northern boundary of Côte d'Or. The Ignon, on which Is-sur-Tille illogically stands, marks the southern limit of the Pays.

Taking first the valley of the Venelle we come to **Selongey**, where the church as it stands dates largely from the sixteenth and seventeenth centuries, but has been entirely restored between 1965 and 1984. This should not deter you from a visit, because the restoration has been faithful and the result is dignified. The key (should you find the church locked) is kept by the *curé*, who lives in the rue de Patenée next to a wine store. There is much pride and spirit in these parts, and a plaque on the wall to the left of the choir records the heroic resistance of the people of Selongey, who took refuge here on Ascension Day 1638 (the Thirty Years' War again) when the town's defences had fallen and their houses had been burnt. With the help of God, it says, and their own courage they preserved the church and themselves. Records like this show the value of defensive churches, and here as at Sacquenay and Bèze the strength lay in the transept, thrown out high and wide to north and south.

Crossing now to the valley of the Tille, we can take an exceptionally beautiful road (the D959 again) to **Grancey-le-Château**, almost on the boundary of Côte d'Or. No more than a village, its houses climb steeply up beside the main road to where a thirteenth-century fortified gateway commands the entry from the north. Substantial curtain walls, based on the rock, overhang the valley below, but the place is dominated by a four square eighteenth-century château, the property of the de Mandat-Grancey family, descended from the baron de Mandat of that time. The earliest castle would have been built on the site before 1100, as we know that an insubordinate seigneur de Grancey was besieged here by his overlord the duke of Burgundy in 1112. This siege had an important issue, for during a visit to his brothers who were involved in the siege the young St Bernard is said to have had the revelation which he interpreted as a call to religious life, and brought him to join the abbey of Cîteaux later that year.

Having been partly destroyed in the siege it was rebuilt at the end of the century by Ponce de Grancey, but falling foul of the dukes again in the fifteenth century it was destroyed in 1434 by Jean de Til-Chatel on the orders of Philippe le Bon and at the request of the people of Dijon. The present château occupies the most superb site of all the châteaux of Burgundy which are still inhabited. Ever since the last war – when the German occupiers vandalized it – the villagers and their visitors have been frustrated by the refusal of the Mandat family to allow access to the property. Now, however, guided tours are organized which take in the exterior of the château and the grounds, which incorporate the fourteenth-century collegial chapel of St John the Baptist, whose spire stands out among the trees. To make sure of a visit and its timing you are advised to call on or telephone the agent, M. de Bazelaire, at 54 rue des Forges in Dijon; the number is 80302831.

You should not leave Grancey without looking at the **Church of St-Germain** which lies below the castle hill at the end of a half-mile track along the river Tille. The key can be had from the two sisters La Tour who live in a large house in the lower part of the village. There was probably a Carolingian church on the site, but the present building is entirely Romanesque, dating from the eleventh century and beautifully restored between 1934 and 1939. The five low round-arched bays of the long nave spring directly from the plain rectangular pillars; its barrel vaulting is now covered with wooden slats and reinforced by tie-beams, and it has no light except from a rose window at the west end. In a church of such antiquity it is surprising to find that the most beautiful of its contents is a modern stone *pietà* in the chapel which closes the north aisle; on a simple raised slab the Mother is bending over the supine body of Christ and kissing his limp hand. From the east end of the north aisle there rises a lovely slim tower in golden sandstone, with twin-arched openings on all four sides.

If you have time for more exploration by the minor roads of the Pays des Trois Rivières, I suggest you return down the D959 as far as the junction of two branches of the Tille at a place called Les Forges, between the Forêt de Cussey and the Bois de Grandmont. From there follow the western arm of the river along a lovely stretch between Avot and Salives, cross the D996 to Echalot, and then take the D101 to **Aignay-le-Duc**. This is a fine little town with a handsome early Gothic church. The *chevet* is particularly impressive from the outside, with a lofty pentagonal apse buttressed on the corners. You see here a good example of the *corniche bourgignonne*, a decorative feature common in this part of Burgundy, which runs all the way round under the eaves of the tower, the transept and the *chevet*. Inside there is an extraordinary polychrome *retable* in stone, with scenes of the Passion and statues of St Claude and St Germain.

From Aignay you can cross into the valley of the Seine by more minor roads. If you take the D16 south, fork first right on to the D16E, then left on to the D114A, you come to **Oigny**, where are the remains of an abbey which first harnessed the waters to drive a mill. The mill house is at the lowest point in the road, past the church (there is no village called Oigny) and it hides from view the farm buildings which have all but taken over from the abbey. One long building remains, on the far side of a flowery courtyard with a fountain, and a range of cloister arcading to the left.

You will be close now to the sources of the Seine, but to reach them you will have to abandon the quiet countryside and join the N71 just north of **Chanceaux**, a roadside town which offers an eccentric amalgam of styles. On the right a neo-classical portico leads into a single-naved church, restored, but with sound Romanesque origins. On the opposite side of the road is the house which once belonged to Captain Brigaudet, killed at the side of Jean-sans-Peur on the bridge of Montereau in 1419.

As for the **Sources**, you reach them by a left turn some three kilometres further south which passes the farm called les Vergerots. There is no concealment, for apart from notices put up by the city of Paris (to which the site strangely if understandably belongs) you will find a line of cars pulled up on the opposite verge. In a park-like setting visitors follow paths beside several rivulets to a point where the principal spring trickles out into a hollow planted with fir trees. Here there is a grotto decorated – some would say disfigured – by the statue of a nymph which is a copy of one executed by Jouffroy in 1865. An absurd inscription describes the newly born river: 'Qui donne son nom au Département de la Seine'. Beyond this artificial enclosure a second spring emerges among the debris of a Gallo-Roman temple, where there was evidence that Jupiter and Juno shared it with the nymph Sequana. It goes underground near the hamlet of Courceaux, reappears a little further on at Billy-lès-Chanceaux, and so on to Oigny to drive the waterwheel for the abbey mill.

The main road now passes the source of the Ignon, beginning its journey to Til-Châtel, but our next stop must be at **St-Seine-**

l'Abbaye. Pause for a moment, though, just two kilometres out, at a point where the road rises to nearly 550 metres, for that marks the watershed between rivers bound for the Atlantic and those due to join the Saône and Rhône on their way to the Mediterranean. From here you look down on the red roofs which gather among the trees encircling the single tower of the abbey church of Ste-Marie-des-Cestres — which is the proper and original name of one of the oldest monastic foundations in Burgundy.

There is some doubt about the identity of St Seine, but it seems certain that he had nothing to do with the river. Legend says that a sixth-century contemporary of Bishop Gregory of Tours, whose family lived in the nearby town of Mesmont, was given the Burgundian by-name of Sigo. He first entered the monastery of Moutiers-St-Jean and afterwards founded a hermitage in the forest of Cestres (*silva sigestrensis*). This forest probably embraced not only the adjoining village of Cestre but also the hill on which the abbey was eventually built.

Architecture is a more reliable source than legend, and we do know that all earlier buildings were superseded by the one begun between 1205 and 1209 under the abbot Olivier — whose predecessor Nivard was a great-nephew of St Bernard. The original plan showed Cistercian influence in the squared-off *chevet* and the austere two-storey elevation of the nave, but it was not completed till 1235; twenty years later fire destroyed all but the choir and north transept. What we see now is therefore basically a late thirteenth-century reconstruction of this plan, in which the nave was shortened by two bays. Other modifications included a now familiar feature of Burgundian Gothic development, a well lit clerestory with an inner passage running all the way round nave, transept and choir. Additions in the flamboyant period included the three-arched sanctuary screen and the balustraded stone walls to north and south of the choir, against which the Louis XIV stalls were fixed.

The principal curiosity of the church is the series of paintings which decorate the back of these two walls. On the north side we have two rows of panels depicting events in the life of St Seine, the name which early chroniclers had derived from Sigo and was later related to Sequana, the Gallo-Roman nymph who was already identified with the river Seine. The paintings were commissioned in 1504 by the monk Parceval de Montarby, who is seen on the final panel being presented by the saint to the Virgin Mary. Behind the south wall there is a more complex sequence, of which the most important part is a Tree of Jesse which establishes the descent of the Virgin; it was contributed in 1521 by another monk, Claude de Durestal, who is himself presented by his own patron, St Claude.

The bases of the two towers were built in the early fifteenth century, but only the north one was finished. The porch was built at about the same time, and its decoration has pleasant Burgundian touches of vine leaves and *escargots*. Nothing is left of two earlier churches, St-Didier and St-Gilles, though some Romanesque capitals from the latter can be seen inside the first bay of the north aisle of the abbey church. The Hôtel-de-Ville was built on the site of the abbot's lodging, and the only monastic buildings to survive date from the eighteenth century and are in private hands.

Our planned circuit of Dijon is almost complete, but if you feel like a rest from travelling there is an attractive place to stay in **Val Suzon**. The Hostellerie Val Suzon is principally a *restaurant avec chambres*, with seven rooms in the main building, but there is a more secluded annexe with another nine. In either case there is good value for food and ambiance, and there is easy walking in both directions along the river.

Dijon itself now lies between us and our next move, which will be to follow the Côte and its vineyards all the way down to Beaune, but time should be set aside for three last visits before re-entering the city from the north. It would make a pleasant detour to follow the little road along the left bank of the Suzon to Messigny, and there take a loop in the D996 to the château at **Vantoux-lès-Dijon**. This could stand as a model for an early residential château, so perfect are its proportions and its symmetry. The most completely satisfying of its kind in Burgundy, it was built between 1700 and 1704 by the architect Mansard, who also worked on the Palais des Ducs in Dijon. Set amid sloping fields, with avenues of dark maples on either side, it looks more like a country house in England as painted by an eighteenth-century artist. A less formal range of buildings, on your right as you enter the grounds, dates from the reign of Louis XIII and provides a laundry, stabling for the family horses, and even spare accommodation for junior members of the family. Visitors in groups are admitted by appointment only during the summer, but well conducted individuals are invited to roam around the outside at any time.

The next stop is for a very different scene. A left fork off the D996 south of Vantoux leads by way of the village of Aluy to the suburb of **Fontaine-lès-Dijon**. Here on a hill above the neat rows of houses and gardens is the birthplace of St Bernard – a site which should attract anyone with a sense of history, though not perhaps those whose main interest is architecture. First the history. About 1080 Tescelin le Roux, seigneur of Châtillon, was entrusted by Duke Eudes II with a newly built château 'au sommet de la colline' at Fontaine. He was a friend of the duke, and his wife Aleth was the daughter of the comte de Montbard. They had six sons (who had no issue) and one daughter, Hombeline, who married Barthélémy de Sombernon, heir to a family of importance in Burgundy. Their son Bernard was born in 1090, so he was only twenty-two when he had the call at Grancey which took him to Cîteaux.

The château passed to the descendants of Hombeline, who held it until the fifteenth century, when it was bought by Nicolas Rolin, Philippe le Bon's great Chancellor. It changed hands again in the next century, and in 1613 it was bought by the 'Cistercians Feuillants', a branch of the order which came from Paris. With the support of Louis XIII and Anne of Austria they built a chapel to mark the actual room in which St Bernard was said to have been born, adding their monastic buildings beside it. At the Revolution the monks were dispersed, the monastery demolished, and a forge and a stable were set up in the Chapelle des Feuillants. In 1838 the ruins of the château (of which one tower remains) were bought by Pierre Renault, Vicar-General of Dijon, who lived there alone until his death. Pilgrims continued to visit the site of the chapel, and in 1893 a large basilica church was built for their use. Finally in 1980 the Cistercians returned. In association with the archbishop of Dijon the reformed order bought what was known as the 'maison natale', and restored it in the form we are visiting today.

What we see facing us across the pilgrim-worn patch of grass at the top of the hill is an incongruous range of nineteenth and twentieth-century buildings; central to it is a portentous façade which covers the entrance to a small, dignified, and beautifully kept modern oratory, where a simple placard reads:

Ici est né
St Bernard
Abbé de Clairvaux

To the right is the ugly neo-classical façade of the basilica; on a slightly lower level among trees to the left is the much altered fourteenth-century parish church.

If you leave here with mixed feelings, you should not find the same problem at **Talant**, where a magnificent early thirteenth-century church occupies a similar hilltop on the opposite side of the N71. The long nave (eight bays) is lit by high lancet windows set between the groins of the vaulting, which springs from a line of unusual five-sided pilasters – only the two nearest the choir are rounded. There is no transept, and the harmonious prospect to the east is spoilt only by a rather crude window which occupies the whole width of the choir. There is some interesting statuary, notably a bas-relief of St Hubert at the west end of the south aisle, and a fourteenth-century Virgin and Child in the north aisle which looks to have a touch of Champenois influence. There are two Sepulchres, of which the more dramatic is halfway down the south aisle; its figures are almost lifesize, and there are traces of colour to be seen. The superb view from the terrace takes in most of the city below; in the foreground is the Lac Kir, another reminder of the *curé* of Bèze and mayor of Dijon, where water sports of all kinds have plenty of room.

CHAPTER TWELVE

The Côte

Shakespeare's King Lear, in the opening scene of the play, tells his youngest daughter that she has an equal chance of marrying the vines of France or the milk of Burgundy in the persons of her two suitors; later the king of France disparages his rival the duke as 'waterish Burgundy'. Neither of these two sayings need be taken as a slur on burgundy as a wine, for then as now the cattle feeding on the lush pastures of the province produced milk in abundance, and the part of Burgundy most familiar to Shakespeare's England was the Low Countries, which have never been short of water. On the other hand, when Erasmus apostrophized Burgundy as 'heureuse mère d'hommes, que tes mamelles ont un bon lait!' he may have been allowing himself a sly metaphor. Burgundy has always been popular in the Low Countries, which were subject to the dukes in the fourteenth and fifteenth centuries.

As for England, burgundy was slow to find its way across the Channel to the tables of either the common drinker or the connoisseur. Claudius in *Hamlet* 'drained his draughts of Rhenish down', Falstaff's tipple was 'sherris sack', while Dr Johnson and Sir Walter Scott preferred claret. The long connection with Bordeaux was largely responsible for this, as it was easy for the great casks to come by sea to London and Edinburgh. George Meredith was the first writer to give burgundy its due, when Harry Richmond described it as the wine of princes, and many of us will sympathize with a character in the same novel who says 'Poor Jorian, I know no man I pity so much; he has but six hundred a year and a passion for burgundy'. Chesterton wrote of drinking the blood of kings for half-a-crown a bottle, and it was over a bottle of Moulin-à-Vent (strictly of course a Beaujolais) that he first met Belloc.

Neither the Burgundians themselves, nor those who visited or invaded their country, had any reservations. The dukes described themselves as 'seigneurs des meilleurs vins de la Chrétienté', and Petrarch had a simple explanation for the prolonged stay of the

Popes at Avignon: 'If the cardinals wish to stay on the other side of the mountains, it is because there is no Beaune wine in Italy, and they cannot imagine a happy life without their liquor'. For a time there was heavy competition from champagne, and it was Louis XIV who settled the matter, as he settled so much else. The king's digestion had suffered from over-eating, and his physician Fagon was sent on a tour of the country to discover the wine best suited for his royal patient. He picked on Romanée: 'Tonic and generous, Sire, it will agree with a robust temperament such as yours.' Yet, as André Lachet testifies, the average hardworking native does not need a Romanée to stimulate his appreciation:

Watch this old Burgundian take a wide glass, warm it paternally in his two hands, pour into it a little wine, shake it, look at it closely, turn it round, place it in the light to make sure it's clear, piously and lovingly inhale its bouquet, and finally drink it very little at a time, sipping it in a series of repeated motions like a bird.

The vineyards which produce true burgundy are confined to a narrow strip from Dijon south to Chagny and Santenay, the **Côte d'Or**. The Côte has been compared to a long and talkative street warming itself in the light of the rising sun, for indeed most of it faces almost due east. However, now and then the slopes have a habit of turning a little more to the south, and this together with gradations of height and variety of soil accounts for the subtle distinctions of *climat* which affect the quality of the wines. The plateau above is composed of sandy limestone, and the effects of erosion and cultivation have broken this down into soil and rubble which fall down the slope to nourish and drain the vines. Some little way up the slope of the Côte de Nuits there runs a narrow outcrop of marlstone, which creates a limy clay soil perfectly suited to producing wines of the highest quality when it becomes blended with the silt and scree. The vines were planted in rows to allow horses to pass between them, and latterly the tall narrow tractors, though once you would have seen cherry and pear trees dotted about among the plants. In late autumn, before they have been pruned, the vines have the colour of dark pink or delicate violet; in winter they look skeletal and almost dead – brown as the soil, which, as they say, would have been the poorest in France if it were not also the richest.

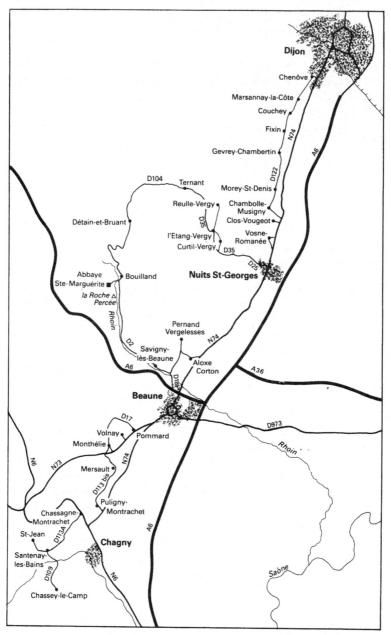

The Côte

In reality the Côte is too busy to be talkative, and intensive work goes on through all four seasons. In spring the vines are cut back in their final pruning, the ground has to be weeded, and a patient war waged against insects and other enemies − oidium, greyrot and downy mildew. The summer is an anxious vigil, with eyes and mind upon the weather, for a sudden hailstorm, excessive rain or a prolonged drought may ruin the vintage. Nature is mistress here, whatever man may do to help or fight her. The preparation, silent, skilful, industrious, never stops till the end of September. When the grapes have been picked there is the first pruning, the dressing of the vines, and the light manuring of the soil. Nor does work end here. Throughout the winter there are constant demands to meet. Stakes and supporting wires will need renewing, and most importantly the soil must be restored to its natural vigour and fruitfulness. This calls not only for judicious use of fertilizers, but for the laborious task of carrying back to the top of the slopes the precious topsoil which has been washed down by the year's rains.

The Côte stretches for fifty-six kilometres from Dijon to Santenay, with an important gap in the hills at Beaune, and to drive along it is like running your eyes down the wine list of a great restaurant. For the first fifteen kilometres you have a choice of two roads, and nobody in their senses would choose to drive down the N74 when there is the alternative of the D122 which runs parallel to it on the west side. Not only is it rightly called the 'route des grands crus', but it runs through unspoilt villages from which the names of great wines are derived. If you can pick this right-hand fork soon after crossing the canal to the south of Dijon city, it will take you when hardly clear of the suburbs to **Chenôve**, where the **Pressoir des Ducs** was set up by Alix de Vergy, widow of Duke Eudes III, in 1228. The great building has been described by Stephen Gwynn in his classic book *Burgundy*, written in 1934, as 'filled with scaffolding of fourteen-inch beams clamped together, and wooden screws of the same diameter which raised and lowered a block of stone weighing twelve tons and a half, whose descent could crush out the residue from sixty casks of wine. There it is still, a Gargantuan relic − still in perfect working order, and up to the end of the last century still used'.

Keeping to the D122 you pass Marsannay-la-Côte, from where a side road leads up to the Montagne and your earlier viewpoint at

Corcelles-les-Monts, and at **Couchey** you will find a good plain fourteenth-century Burgundian church. Near it in the village is the sixteenth-century château, a peacefully secluded dwelling in mellow stone. At **Fixey** there is a Romanesque church with narrow lancet windows, its plain walls supported by strong timberwork — the effect only slightly spoilt on the outside by the black and yellow tiles on the tower. The Renaissance château at **Brochon** was built by the poet Etienne Liègeard, and the pavilion in the park was a favourite of Crebillon. On a house in the village is the charming inscription:

> Qui a la paix chez soi
> Vit comme un petit roi.

On the hillside above **Fixin** we again meet Napoleon and the rhetorical sculptor François Rude. The **Parc Noisot** belonged to an officer of the first empire, who was a friend of Rude and commissioned from him the statue in bronze of Napoleon 'awakening to Immortality'. The custodian's house contains a little museum of Bonapartist souvenirs, and the statue bears the following inscription: *à Napoléon, Noisot, grenadier de l'île d'Elbe, et Rude, statuaire,* 1846. The bronze bust of Rude by Cabet stands nearby, and from it a path leads to the tomb of Noisot, where the old campaigner had wished to be buried upright, and facing his Emperor.

This is the northern section of the Côte, known as the Côte de Nuits after the large town of Nuits-St-Georges, halfway towards Beaune. From now on you will probably have no eyes for anything but the names of the *grands crus* as they unroll in sequence beside the road. The first, and among the most illustrious, belongs to the gentle slopes to the south of **Gevrey-Chambertin**, where the road actually passes through eight vineyards whose wines are so classified. The two regarded as *hors ligne,* Chambertin and Chambertin Clos de Bèze, occupy a long strip to the right of the road, where the higher slopes are generally more favoured than the lower ground to the left. Even so, you have on your left four other *grand cru* vineyards entitled to add Chambertin to their name, including the almost equally famous Charmes-Chambertin. Apart from an occasional signpost to a château, or the centre of a *commune,* there is little to show you are on such holy ground. In this part of the Côte there are no huge road signs advertising 'degustation libre' or 'vente en détail'; dignity and discretion mark a business where only serious customers are welcome.

Two-thirds of the production at Gevrey-Chambertin comes from the presses of a co-operative association of 139 small proprietors holding about 150 acres. Where the economic basis of Bordeaux is capitalist, in Burgundy it is cooperative, and that much closer to the mediaeval guilds. Everything sold from the *commune* of Gevrey is legally entitled to call itself Gevrey-Chambertin, and it is all made from the *pinot noir* grape, but it must be distinguished from Le Chambertin, which comes from that famous slope of 70 acres just south of the village. It has been called 'le roi des vins de Bourgogne', and it was Napoleon's favourite wine. He preferred it at five or six years old, never drinking more than half a bottle at a meal, and he complained bitterly that he was compelled to drink claret on St Helena, since claret was more easily brought there by sea. Chambertin has been compared, on the one hand, to 'the good Lord gliding down your gullet in a pair of velvet trousers', and on the other to the fifth, seventh and ninth symphonies of Beethoven (notice the odd numbers). Hilaire Belloc concluded his speech before the Saintsbury Club at the Vintners' Hall in London with the following words: 'When that this too too solid flesh shall melt, and I am called before my Heavenly Father, I shall say to him Sir, I don't remember the name of the village, and I don't remember the name of the girl, but the wine was Chambertin.'

The culture of the vine, like so many other arts, owes much to monasticism. In 630 the abbey of Bèze was granted a tract of land at Gevrey, part of which was already planted with vines. The monks quickly planted the rest of it and enclosed it with a drystone wall, and this became known as the Clos de Bèze. Then, as the story goes, a certain Bertin, who owned the adjoining land, emulated the monks, so that the Champ de Bertin came to rival the Clos de Bèze. The monks, not to be outdone, bought out the descendants of Bertin and joined the two properties together. In 1219 they sold it to the Chapter of Langres, who in turn made it over to a wine merchant called Jobert. He added Chambertin to his name, and by his management of the vineyard he established its reputation. Today the 70 acres of Chambertin and Clos de Bèze are the property of 25 different owners, and they produce a yearly average of about 108,000 bottles of robust, aristocratic wine.

The greater part of **Morey-St-Denis**, which lies next down the road, was planted by Cistercians from Cîteaux; the most precious *clos* was bought by a community of nuns, the Bernardines of Tart. It came to be known as the Clos de Dames de Tart (just over 17 acres) and subsequently Clos des Tart. Immediately to the south is the village of **Chambolle-Musigny** and the vineyards called after it. Here again you must not confuse the excellent wines produced in the *commune* of Chambolle with Les Musigny, which is a prince of the blood, if not the heir to the throne. As in the case of Gevrey-Chambertin, the village has annexed the name of its most famous *cru*. The 24 acres of Musigny stretch right up to the scrub of the slopes above, and the difference between the soil on either side of the dividing line is such that the vine growers are said to wipe it off their boots before they leave the vineyard, lest a particle of it should be wasted. In the *communes* of Morey-St-Denis and Chambolle-Musigny all the *grand cru* vineyards lie to the right of the road, including Bonnes Mares, which is shared between them; this is evidently a corruption of Bonnes Mères, for like the Clos des Tart it was acquired by the nuns of St Bernard.

At Chambolle-Musigny the *route des grands crus* unfortunately comes to an end, for the sequence of slopes is broken by the Combe Ambin slanting in from the north-west; the road follows it to join the N74, a nightmare of commercial traffic hurtling south from Dijon or north from Beaune. Escape is at hand, though, for in a moment you will see the noble Renaissance château of **Clos Vougeot** standing proudly above its vineyards away to your right, and you can turn up with relief to visit it.

St Bernard's monks, needing material for their new abbey at Clairvaux, found a useful quarry in the *commune* they called Vougeot (in memory of the river Vouge which flows near Cîteaux) and nearby slopes suitable for the cultivation of the vine. By the middle of the twelfth century they had built themselves a cellar, and a hundred years later the four gigantic presses of the *cuverie* were in place. They were made of oak from the forests round Cîteaux, and ten men on each arm were needed to work them. In 1162 Duke Eudes II renounced his rights over the Cistercian vineyards, and in 1164 Pope Alexander III placed the abbey of Cîteaux and the Clos Vougeot under papal protection. He is said to have been encouraged to do so by judicious gifts of its produce.

Gregory XI rewarded a later abbot with a cardinal's hat, soon – though not indecently soon – after receiving a present of thirty hogsheads. The château as we now see it was built in 1551 by Dom Poisier, forty-eighth abbot of Cîteaux; his successors ruled there until 1790.

At the Revolution the property was bought by a timber merchant from Paris, who defaulted on his agreed instalments, and the last cellarer of Cîteaux, who had the appropriate name of Dom Goblet, administered it for the nation. In 1791 he retired with a private cellar so renowned that Napoleon sent for some of its contents to celebrate the victory of Marengo. The monk's reply has passed into history: 'I have some Clos Vougeot forty years old. If he wants to drink it, let him come here. It is not for sale.' In 1818 the property passed into the hands of a war profiteer, and in 1889 it was sold to a consortium of wine merchants. By the 1980s, as the result of more sales, family deals and legacies, there were over a hundred separate plots on the Clos and a total of seventy-five different owners. Some of the plots measure little more than half an acre, from which the grower can expect to make just three barrels of wine a year. This is where the big *negociant* merchants come in, buying the grapes from individual owners and making and bottling the wine on their own premises – a genuine *grand cru* on which they are entitled to put their own labels.

The château, as distinct from the Clos, belongs now to the Confrèrie des Chevaliers du Tastevin, founded in 1934 after three disappointing vintages to promote the appreciation (and of course the purchase) of burgundy. Fifteen *disnées* are held annually in the cellar of the château, which easily accommodates four hundred people. Each *disnée* (sometimes called a *chapitre*) is preceded by the *intronisation* of new members, whether as *chevaliers*, *commandeurs* or *grands officiers*. The bizarre ritual for this ceremony was inspired by Molière's *Divertissement du Malade Imaginaire*. A scarlet and orange ribbon, with a silver *soucoupe* attached, is hung round the neck of the new member, who is expected to wear it for the rest of the evening and at any subsequent gathering of the kind. The officers of the Confrèrie, in academic robes of scarlet and gold, enter the cellar in procession, preceded by trumpeters and halberdiers, and the more important initiations take place on a stage from which the Cadets de Bourgoyne – an empurpled choir of *vignerons* – have been enlivening the evening with old Burgundian songs. Each *chapitre* has its appropriate name, and a *tenue de soir* is prescribed for all of them except for the St Vincent Tournant in January, which is held at noon though it finishes when the evening is well advanced. These are great occasions, of course, but a more jaundiced view is worth quoting: 'One laughs for an hour, smiles for the next, sweats for the last three. It's too much!'

Visits to the château are well organized, especially in that individual visitors are separated from the herds that come all day by coach-load, and they are given what is a very civilized and informative tour of the premises. The principal feature is the **Grand Cellier** itself, with its low-pitched roof, its stone pillars and oak rafters; it even boasts an eighteenth-century Gobelins tapestry on one wall. Yet more people may be intrigued by the sight of the magnificent oak *pressoirs* and the enormous vats which stand around on the floor of the *cuverie*, just as they did in the thirteenth century. The visit ends in the **Dortoir des Moines**, another room of the same period, covered by one of the most splendid oak *charpentes* you have ever seen. A film show rounds things off, depicting various scenes and functions connected with the Confrèrie. Famous figures can be seen being decked with the scarlet and gold insignia; an unexpected one is Rostropovich. Processions pass in jolly if uncoordinated mood, and the lusty Cadets are seen delivering their Noëls from the stage.

The next *commune* beside the N74 is **Flagey-Echézaux**, where just over the wall from the Clos Vougeot are two more vineyards with *grand cru* rating – Echézaux and Grands Echézaux. Together they are of about the same acreage as Vougeot, but are divided between fewer owners. Then comes **Vosne-Romanée**, a village which might as well have called itself Vosne-Richebourg or Vosne-La Tâche, for both these prestigious vineyards are included in the *commune*. Romanée, however, deserves the distinction by its name, its history and its quality. The name suggests with reason that vines were cultivated here in Roman times. Its history as a vineyard probably goes back like Chambertin to the seventh century, with a grant of land to the monks of Bèze, but in the thirteenth century it is recorded as belonging to Alix de Vergy, who built the *pressoir des ducs* at Chenôve. Part of it she made over to the abbey of St-Vivant in the adjacent *commune* of Nuits, and part of it – La Tâche – to the chapter of Nuits. A third part remained in lay hands and was sold in 1760 to the Prince de Conti (a title assumed by another branch of the Condé dynasty) against the bidding of Mme de Pompadour, and this is how the most exclusive of all the Burgundy vineyards acquired its name.

The four-and-a-half acres of Romanée-Conti are unique among French vineyards in having preserved the original stock, *malgré* phylloxera, until 1946. It was only the lack of carbon sulphide during the last war which exposed it to a fatal attack of the disease. Another unusual feature it shares with neighbouring La Tâche is in belonging to a single proprietor. Between them they produce only about 25,000 bottles in a good year; they are the most expensive wines in the world. It was a Revolutionary authority who declared it was the best wine in the Côte d'Or, indeed of all the vineyards of the French Republic, and could give back life to the dying. However, no wine can claim divine status by right, and it would be surprising if a blind tasting did not sometimes prefer the Richebourg, the La Tâche, or even the Echézaux.

Now comes **Nuits-St-Georges**, an important town which marks the end of the Côte de Nuits, of which it is nevertheless the commercial centre. The vineyards of its *communes* cover about 950 acres, and the wines they produce anticipate the gentler and shorter-lived *crus* of the Côte de Beaune. There are no *grands crus* among them, and you must distinguish between the officially classified *premiers crus*, entitled to call themselves Les Saint-Georges, Les Vaucrains and Les Cailles, and the ordinary wines of the *communes* which will be labelled Côtes-de-Nuits or Côtes-de-Nuits-Villages. The label which proclaims a Nuits-St-Georges, even if an *appellation controlée*, has been much abused; it could come from anywhere in the area of the *communes*, and if you see it on any but a most respectable wine list you cannot be sure what you are buying.

As a break from such intensive vineyard-crawling, and to escape for a time from the N74, you can take the D25 westward from Nuits St-Georges into the largely unexplored country beyond and above the slopes of the Côte. If perhaps you have decided to spend a peaceful night or two at the Hostellerie Gentilhommière, a mile out of town to the left of the road, that could be a useful starting point for such a project. This is Vergy country, which recalls Alix the strong-minded widow of Eudes III, for after Villars-Fontaine the road turns north and passes near the three villages of Curtil-Vergy, l'Étang-Vergy and finally Reulle-Vergy. Above Curtil are the scattered ruins of the abbey of St-Vivant, beneficiary of Alix's gift of part of the Romanée vineyard, but to find them you may have to take a walk along the stretch of the walkers' highway, the Grande Randonnée 7, which weaves its way through this attractive piece of country. You can, however, drive to **Reulle-Vergy,** and that is an opportunity not to miss.

The village itself is fun, with a comprehensive little museum of country life. It has an evocative assembly of tools and machinery for the old Burgundian ways of viniculture and farming, and an upper floor for specimens of local fauna, flora and lepidoptera. If you visit the mayor in his pleasant modern house (the old Mairie is a charming oddity, built above the village wash-house) he will gladly lend you the key to the **Church of St-Saturnin,** to be found high on the hillside to the south. The church is all (or nearly all) that remains of the early mediaeval *forteresse* of the seigneurs de Vergy, which until 1609 (when it was destroyed by the Huguenots under Henri IV) occupied the long spine of the hill. Within it is displayed a model showing a walled *enceinte* with a total of fourteen towers, a *donjon, a manoir,* and a large bastion occupied by the present church.

It was built in the second half of the twelfth century on the site of a sixth-century sanctuary of St Saturnin, martyr of Toulouse, and the cemetery around it goes back to the Merovingian period – witness a sarcophagus beside the entrance decorated with the herringbone motif. The east end is the oldest part, where the half-dome of the apse with its lancet Romanesque windows is clearly of the twelfth century. The slightly pointed barrel vaulting of the nave choir must be of roughly the same date, but there are interesting features from several different periods thereafter – right up to the pews in the nave, which were all numbered and marked with names in 1772. A short square tower with a tiled hat rises over the crossing, which is lower than the later nave, and there is a wonderful view over a wide sweep of country to north and west. South of the church a path through the woods passes a few traces of fortification, and joins the GR7 leading to the ruins of St-Vivant.

You are now only five or six miles from the Côte, but in a different world where no vineyards can be seen. There is an easy way back to Nuits, but if you are minded to explore further – at the risk of losing your way quite pleasantly in this forgotten part of Burgundy – you can stick to the D35 as far as Ternant, then make your way up hill and down dale by way of Détainet-Bruant to **Bouilland**, where the Hostellerie du Vieux Moulin offers lodging and food (at a price) as satisfying as anywhere on the Côte, and far more peacefully.

From Bouilland there is an easy drive down the delectable valley of the Rhoin to Savigny-lès-Beaune, and so on to rejoin the Côte at Beaune itself, but there could be one more discovery to distract you. In the hamlet of la Forge just south of Bouilland, look for a narrow road on your right which leads to the ruined **Abbey of Ste-Marguerite** and the **Roche Percée** where the saint (who was Marguerite de Vergy) escaped from her wicked pursuer by taking refuge in the supernaturally cleft rock. Of the abbey, which has escaped the notice of all guide books except Georges Pillement's invaluable *France inconnue*, a great deal has survived. It was an eleventh-century foundation, developed by the seigneurs of Vergy in the sixteenth century, and you pass first through a gatehouse which does double duty as a *colombier*. An approach path goes round to the east end of the church, from where you have a view through the transept and down the length of the roofless nave to the west portal, which has a window above it with delicate quatrefoil tracery. The apse has gone, but each transept has an apsidal chapel – the northern one pure Romanesque, the southern pierced by a window with Gothic tracery. The nave has a classic look about it, with fluted pilasters and some Romanesque capitals, but there was no triforium and the overall date looks to be somewhere in the twelfth century. Behind the blank south wall of the nave was the cloister, but the door to it is now half blocked, and only one pillar base of its arcading remains. The scene as a whole would have delighted a romantic visitor of Byron's day, but its tranquil elegance speaks for all time. Wild bees have a nest in one of the nave arcades, and flowers are sprouting from the capitals, but there are already signs of a slow and patient programme of restoration, beginning with the walls of some outer abbey buildings, and a grotto has been built round the re-discovered well. We hope a balance will be struck between romance and historical correctness.

The valley of the Rhoin runs deep between the wooded ridge on your right (still followed by the GR7) and the limestone cliffs of the Forêt du Grand Hâ, flattening out as it approaches the little mediaeval town of **Savigny-lès-Beaune**. This makes another very eligible base, with the excellent and reasonably priced hotel of L'Ouvrée on your left as you come in from Bouilland. Though there are more glamorous hotels and eating places in Beaune, a base outside the city is not a bad idea, and daytime parking in Beaune is not as difficult as it is in Dijon. Meanwhile there are things to be seen in Savigny, and only the vineyards of Beaune and Pommard produce more red wine at this end of the Côte.

There are several pleasant-looking *manoirs* in the town, and a number of rather sententious inscriptions on walls and gateways, dating apparently from the eighteenth century; the most relevant of them reads: 'Les vins de Savigny sont des vins nourrissants, theologiques, et morbifuges.' Who in these parts would wish to argue with that? Certainly not M. Yves Doudet, head of the long-established firm of Doudet-Naudin, who fiercely maintains his family's pride in producing the finest burgundies by traditional methods. Their headquarters are at the opposite end of the town from L'Ouvrée, on one of the exit roads to Beaune.

The best view of the **Château de Savigny** is from the west, through the formal gates at the head of a tree-lined avenue. The entrance however is in a side road round to the north of the château, where you will find the reception office for visitors. This is not just a ticket office, for the eighteenth-century stable block has been converted to a *musée des vins*, with a series of pleasant reception rooms leading off it and there are wine cellars underneath.

It was built as a *château fort* about 1340 for Eudes IV, last but one of the Capetian dukes, but in 1478 it was dismantled by Louis XI as a punishment for its then owner, who had taken the side of Marie de Bourgogne in the final struggle between the kingdom and the duchy. Two of the earlier towers survive with their machicolations, but early in the seventeenth century the body of the château was restored and 'agrémenté' by Etienne Bouhier, member of a distinguished Burgundian family which further embellished the property over the following decades. A nineteenth-century owner was the academician Joseph de Pesquidoux, who

Montréal: the brothers Rigolley

Château de Bussy-Rabutin: the garden front

Church of St-Père-sous-Vézelay

was President of the Board of Viniculture for the Côte d'Or from 1854 to 1879 , and in 1979 it was bought by M. Michel Pont for use by an international wine-producing company.

Some of the cellars under the château date from as early as the fourteenth century, and together with the smaller rooms on the ground floor they have been stylishly equipped as anterooms for what lies above. The first floor is given over to a series of grand banqueting suites for big occasions and company entertaining. The surprise comes on the second floor, when we find there is a unique museum of motorcycling – a collection of models dating from 1903 to 1960, representing practically every country of manufacture. Britain is represented, nostalgically, by Norton, BSA and Triumph, and there is a French *moto* once ridden by the ubiquitous Canon Kir of Bèze and Dijon. There is a collection of various aeroplane types in the park, but some visitors may be more attracted by a family of roe deer which crop the grass of the now dry moat under the patriarchal eye of a buck with a splendid head.

2

Before moving on into Beaune there is a chance to look at the important group of vineyards which mark the beginning of the Côte de Beaune. It begins in the territory of **Aloxe**, with which is associated the great name of **Corton**. We know that in 858 Modoin, bishop of Autun, gave his holding of vines in Aloxe to the cathedral, but even before that Charlemagne is credited with an interest here. When the Saracens ravaged Saulieu and sacked the church of St-Andoche, he gave these vineyards to the clergy in compensation for their losses. This gift is remembered in the name of one of the most distinguished white wines in France, the *grand cru* Corton-Charlemagne. Camille Rodier is quoted in Pierre Poupon's *The Wines of Burgundy* as hailing 'a seductive wine high in alcohol content, golden in colour and spreading in the mouth'. It has a perfume of cinnamon and a hint of gunflint in its taste. Corton itself produces both red and white wines, and is the largest *grand cru* in Burgundy. Corton *rouge* was the favourite wine of Voltaire and de Maupassant – though the former is said to have offered only Beaujolais to his guests. Aloxe-Corton, as a *premier cru,* is associated with the names of several vineyards in the immediate neighbourhood. The Comte de Grancey had a château here, now known as the **Château de Corton-Grancey**, and it is the headquarters of the renowned firm of Louis Latour.

On slightly higher ground inland, as it were, from the Côte, are the almost equally venerable vineyards of **Pernand-Vergelesses**, first mentioned in 1375, which produce some well regarded *premiers crus* of red wine which keep well. The village is also known as the home of Jacques Copeau (1879-1949) who founded the *Nouvelle Revue française* in association with André Gide and Jacques Rivière. He later turned to theatrical production, and had some successful seasons at the Vieux Colombier in Paris, including a staging of *Twelfth Night* which Granville-Barker declared the best he had seen. In 1924 he left Paris for Pernand-Vergelesses, where he gathered round him a company of young actors – to whom the village postman gave the name of Les Copiaux. They rehearsed in a disused *cuverie* lower down the hill on the road to Aloxe-Corton, and gave performances in the surrounding countryside. They travelled in a bus with their costumes and properties, announcing by a drum when the play was about to begin – sometimes in a garden or a park, sometimes in a square or a dance hall.

Beaune always seems easier to get into than out of, perhaps because the N74 from the north leads straight through the Porte-St-Nicolas into the rue de Lorraine, which delivers you into the heart of this surprisingly human capital city – for it counts as the commercial capital of the whole Côte. Compared with Dijon you will find it smaller and gentler, with more open space and greenery, with quiet corners and pedestrian precincts. There are even accessible car parks and spaces for on-street parking. On the other hand there is no obvious exit except to the north, and the ring road you must reach to escape in any direction lacks clear signs.

Beaune takes its name from the god Belenus -- thought by some to be a Gallic variant of Apollo, though the ambience of the town is more Dionysiac than Apollonian. 'Vinum Belense super omnia vina recense' was a mediaeval jingle, and Erasmus longed to live in France not to have the command of armies, but to drink the wine of Beaune. In 1328 Reims paid it the compliment of consuming 150 barrels to celebrate the coronation of Philip VI of Valois;

in 1377 du Guesclin received a pipe of Beaune wine from the citizens of Bayeux as a reward for his exploits against the English; in 1512 Louis XII sent thirty puncheons to James IV of Scotland to cement the 'auld alliance': and in 1701, we are informed, the wine of the Côte de Beaune was an annual item in the Pope's personal expenditure.

The *commune* of Beaune has 1,345 acres under the vine, but of these fewer than 200 produce a wine of outstanding quality. They include, among the *premier crus* owned by the firm of Bouchard Père et Fils, the one known as Les Grèves Vigne de l'Enfant Jésus – a name as gentle as the wine is smooth. M. Claude Bouchard says the vineyard was named by the Carmelite monastery which owned it in the time of Louis XIII, and that it was not unconnected with the late conception of Louis XIV by Anne of Austria. The name of Beaune, like that of Nuits-St-Georges, is too often taken in vain; you need to be as sure of the name at the head of your invoice as of that on the label of your bottle.

When you see the words 'Hospices de Beaune' on a label you are rightly impressed; this wine was served to King George VI and Queen Elizabeth at the luncheon given in their honour at Versailles in 1937, and as Queen Mother the latter's affection for France (which is mutual) is as genuine as her taste for its wines. Twenty-four red and eight white vineyards of the first importance have in the course of time been bequeathed to the Hospices, all of them in the Côte de Beaune, though not all in its *commune*. The **Hospices de Beaune**, or Hôtel-Dieu, was founded in 1443 as a hospital for the poor by Nicolas Rolin, Chancellor of Burgundy under Philippe le Bon. You may see his portrait in the Louvre, kneeling before the Virgin and Child. Louis XI, not himself a charitable man, observed that having made so many people poor and homeless, he could well afford to make his peace with the Almighty by providing for some of them. You may visit the long ward with its curtained cubicles and an altar at one end so that the bed-ridden can at least hear Mass – a grandly proportioned room where space creates serenity. Viollet-le-Duc thought it so beautiful that he longed to be ill there.

The roof, as in the Hôpital des Fontenilles in Tonnerre, is a full barrel vault, strengthened by oak tie beams, with its under surface covered by insect-resistant chestnut slats. It has never needed repair since it was put up. Notice on the right of the entrance the superb fifteenth-century life-size figure of Christ de Pitié. Two rooms adjacent to the main hall (the Salle de St Hugues and the Salle de St Nicholas) have been fitted out in a life-like recreation of the treatment of invalids, with sisters in their grey and white habits attending to those who must have been their wealthier patients. Beyond is the pharmacy, with the blue and white vessels which could have contained ancient remedies, but are in fact replacements acquired elsewhere. In another room there is an animated tableau with a spoken commentary, in which you can follow the daily regime in the kitchens – from early rising and lighting the fires to tidying before prayers at night. But none of this would have been possible if Rolin and his wife Guigone de Salins (who has a memorial brass plate in the floor before the altar of the chapel) had not endowed the Hospices with some of the finest vineyards on the Côte. Two of them bear the names of its benefactors.

The glare of publicity falls upon the Hospices on the third Sunday in November, when the wines of the current year are auctioned . The tradition goes back to 1851, and for a long time the sale – which is also a ceremony – took place in the courtyard of the Hospices, decorated with tapestries hung there for the occasion. Now it has been transferred to the closed market of the town, where there is more room for happy spectators and hopeful buyers. Tasting takes place on the previous day, and tickets for this and for the auction are hard to get. The wines, sold in lots of 304 bottles, are auctioned 'à la chandelle': the last bidder before the candle goes out gets the lot, and the precise moment of extinction can lead to controversy.

Candlelight is also prescribed for the dinner held the same evening in a bastion of the city walls called the Bastion de l'Hôtel-Dieu. This is the second of the events called 'Les Trois Glorieuses', the first having been celebrated the evening before by the Chevaliers du Tastevin at Clos-Vougeot. The menu imitates, on a reduced scale, the virtuosity of a ducal feast: hot pâté of thrush, fillets of pike cooked with grapes, guineafowl cooked in wine of the *commune*, roast ham *forestière*, and a triumphal procession of the great vintages from the Côte.

The exterior of the Hospices is a superb example of late Gothic architecture. The façade of four storeys is crowned by a sloping roof of polychrome Burgundian tiles, a thin spire thirty metres high, dormer windows, pinnacles and weather vanes. The *cour d'honneur* has been described as 'a lodging for a prince rather than a hospital for the poor'. On two of its sides, turrets and a double row of dormers stand out from the patterned tiling of the roof. A wooden gallery, supported by slender columns, runs round the first storey, giving it the same effect as a cloister at ground level. In the centre stands a well-head on a stone base behind a wrought-iron railing.

Two rooms behind the Salle St Louis, at the right-hand end of the *cour d'honneur*, have been converted to a **Museum** – though they are primarily a setting for one great painting and some unusual tapestries. The painting is Rogier van de Weyden's masterpiece, a polyptych of the Last Judgment commissioned by Nicolas Rolin for the chapel of the Hospices, and it is the finest to be seen anywhere in Burgundy. It is also superbly displayed, in necessarily subdued lighting, and an ingenious movable lens has been set up in front of it so that you can see in detail any part of this rich and wonderfully executed picture, which occupies almost the whole of one wall of the principal room.

In the centre panel Christ sits enthroned on a rainbow among the clouds. St Michael weighs the worth of souls while the angels sound their trumpets on either side, and the Virgin and the Baptist implore the divine compassion. The apostles and various other personages add their supplications, among them the supposed likenesses of Pope Eugène IV, Nicolas Rolin and his son the Cardinal. Below, the dead emerge from their tombs, and either make their way towards a Paradise of gold or are seen already suffering the contortions of the damned. The polyptych used originally to be open only on Sundays and the greater feasts; on the wall to the right you can see what it looked like when closed, in a modern reproduction, with portraits of Nicolas Rolin and his wife, and *grisaille* paintings of St Sebastian and St Anthony, patrons of the Hospices. To the left of the room is hung a lovely Flemish tapestry of the early sixteenth century, which tells the story of St Eloi in a setting of *mille fleurs*. Opposite the polyptych are two of a set of thirty red-ground tapestries which used to be hung in the Hospices for wine sales and other great occasions. Adorned liberally with turtledoves, they carry the arms and the interlaced initials of the founders, Nicolas and Guigone.

The **Collegial Church of Notre-Dame** was a daughter of Cluny. Begun about 1120, the choir, ambulatory and apses are good examples of Burgundian Romanesque. In the next century three bays were added to the nave, reproducing the style of the original elevation. It all therefore remains in the Cluniac tradition, with frequent use of fluted pilasters in the arcading and in the mostly blind triforium. The porch, added in the late thirteenth or early fourteenth century, is a light and elegant contribution to the overall design. The fine square tower has a Romanesque first stage of five blind arcades, is Gothic above, and not incongruously capped by an Italianate dome and *lanternon*. The *corniche bourgignonne* is used to decorate both stages of the tower and appears under the eaves of nave and transept.

The chief treasures of the church are the richly coloured tapestries woven in wool and silk which hang in the choir behind the high altar. They were commissioned by Cardinal Rolin, woven from designs by Pierre Spicre, a Burgundian artist, and presented to the church by Canon Hugues le Coq in 1500. They are a sequence of scenes in the life of the Virgin, from birth to assumption, and they catch the eye at once by the remarkable range of facial expression they achieve, and the very human situations they present. Who, for instance, would have imagined a competition among suitors for the earthly hand of the Virgin Mary, in which each competitor was given a bare staff of wood to see which would flower? The winner was Joseph, and here we see a disappointed suitor breaking his staff in disgust. At the time of writing the original panels had been removed for treatment at an arts centre in Mayenne, and replaced by photographic copies. Spicre was also responsible for the frescoes of the raising of Lazarus and the stoning of Stephen in the second chapel of the north aisle. The thirteenth-century cloister has been well restored, and the Chapter House converted to a sacristy.

Just to the right of the western façade is the entrance to the **Musée de Vin**, once the Hôtel and secondary residence of the dukes. From the half-timbered courtyard you enter the *cuverie*, where you can see types of *pressoirs* which have been in use for over three centuries. Here and on the two upper floors you can follow the whole process of traditional viniculture from beginning to end in a vast collection of machinery, tools, and vessels connected with the trade. One pressoir, with a stone framework, dates from the sixteenth century, another was still in use till 1968. Another room has a very instructive relief model of the Côte de Beaune, showing the varying contours of all the notable vineyards. Upstairs there are bottles and glasses of all shapes and periods, and a little room presents a mock-up of a working couple's living room. This floor ends in a *salle d'honneur* with a huge dining table and an extravagant tapestry created in 1946 by the well-known contemporary designer Lurcat. The room is dedicated to 'Les Ambassadeurs de Vin', with the triumphant slogan 'Le Vin, source de la vie et vainceur de la mort'.

To stroll about the streets of Beaune is a rewarding and surprisingly peaceful occupation. Of the fine timbered houses near the centre, you will find the Hôtel de la Rochepot near the corner of the rue de Lorraine and the rue des Tonneliers, the Maison du Colombier in the rue Fraysse, and in the Place Fleury the Hôtel de Saulx with its turret and inner courtyard. The Hôtel-de-Ville was formerly the Ursuline convent, and contains the Musée des Beaux Arts and the Musée des Métiers bourgignons. The **Couvent des Cordeliers** is in the rue Hôtel-Dieu; it has an arcaded courtyard and a balustraded gallery at the level of the first floor.

To find the thirteenth-century **Church of St-Nicolas** you will have to go out through the Porte-St-Nicolas. It stands a few hundred yards up on the right-hand side of the main road, in the *quartier des vignerons*. It has a Romanesque tower and a twelfth-century doorway with a tympanum which shows St Nicolas saving the three young girls from their father's evil designs. Inside you will find an unusually short nave with a wide transept and choir, and a strange *montage* where a fragment of the Rock of the Apparition from Lourdes is displayed in a grotto.

In theory there is a walkway, or *chemin de ronde*, round the ramparts of Beaune, sections of which survive fairly intact in all but the north-western sector. In practice they are difficult to follow, as they are frequently interrupted by private property and public gardens, but you can at least get a view of some of the chief bastions on the east side. The best approach is down the rue des Tonneliers, still mainly mediaeval in character, which leads to the rue du Château. This passes between the corner towers of the Bastion St-Jean, the major fortification of the town, to meet the ring road at its most easterly point. To the north are the gardens and greenery at the feet of the Tour Blondeau and the Bastion Notre-Dame; to the south are the Bastion St-Anne and the Grosse Tour.

Of the vineyards immediately south of Beaune the best known are Pommard and Volnay. **Pommard** was named after a temple dedicated to Pomona, goddess of fruits and gardens; it was a favourite wine of Victor Hugo. **Volnay** earned the Latin tag which runs, '*Et sine Volneo gaudia nulla mero*', and history has paid it many compliments. Philippe de Valois found it much to his taste, and Duke Eudes IV sent six dozen casks of it to the French court. Louis XI ordered the entire vintage of 1477 to be sent to his château at Plessis-lès-Tours. Cardinal de Bonsi despatched a heavy consignment to Warsaw for the coronation of John Sobieski, and the fame of the wine spread to northern Europe when a group of Protestants from Volnay left the country in 1687 after the revocation of the Edict of Nantes. It has always been popular in England, though Pommard and its *premiers crus* run it close. Just a little further along the road from Volnay you come to **Monthélie**, said to be the sunniest village on the Côte, and **Auxey-Duresses** – both reputable communes, but overshadowed by the great white burgundies whose territory lies close at hand.

Mersault is a pleasant little town with a gaily roofed Hôtel-de-Ville and its own Hospices, modelled on the Hospices de Beaune. Here too are the vast Cistercian cellars of the comte de Moucheron, which can hold 400 hogsheads and contain his collection of 300,000 different bottles. The *commune* can boast of nearly sixty *crus*, of which twenty are ranked as *premiers*; as in neighbouring Montrachet, all these are made from the Chardonnay grape. A Mersault-Charmes may appeal for the sound of its name, and a Mersault-Sous-le-Dos-d'Âne for its odd implications. A compliment to the Mersault vintages is their widespread use as the first offering in a winetasting. They also produce an excellent red wine, Santenots, although you will rarely meet it on the English side of the Channel.

The third of the 'Trois Glorieuses' of Burgundy is held at Mersault on the Monday after the auction at Beaune. The function is known as the Paulée, a word which signifies the midday break to which the vinegrowers, like everyone else, are naturally entitled.

This is a popular festivity organized by the owners of the vine-yards, who offer wines from their private cellars in a spirit of hospitable emulation. The menu is simpler than at Beaune or Clos Vougeot, but the robust fare is suited to robust appetites.

Just south again from Mersault we find the eighteen priceless acres of **Le Montrachet**. Courtépée, the eighteenth-century histo-rian of Burgundy, called it 'the most excellent white wine in the whole of Europe' and, although he might have met some contra-diction from the banks of the Rhine, many have agreed with him. Alexandre Dumas, ever the romantic, declared that it should be drunk kneeling, with one's head bared. Belloc wrote to a corre-spondent that he proposed to drink a bottle of Montrachet to the confusion of his enemies; perhaps we should prefer to drink one to the comfort of our friends. The vineyards of Le Montrachet and Bâtard-Montrachet are shared between the *communes* of Puligny and Chassagne, who have each attached it to their names. Even Romanée Conti, not content with its own pre-eminence, has bought a plot in Montrachet.

Nevertheless red burgundy has the last word on the Côte, and one of the best. If you continue for about four kilometres down the D113A from Chassagne, you reach **Santenay-les-Bains**. Here the Roman baths have been converted to a modern spa, much recom-mended for digestive troubles, gout and rheumatism – the springs are among the richest in the world for helium and lithium. The vineyards cover well over 300 acres, a hundred of which produce wines of exceptional quality. To drink a bottle of Santenay, grown from the heart of the Roman amphitheatre in the hollow of the hill, and close to the small thirteenth-century **Church of St-Jean**, is to enjoy the essence of an honest Burgundian vineyard. To reach the church take the narrow road out of Santenay to the north-west; you will find it under the cliff face of the Mont de Sène, and it is worth a visit. It has a distinctive high-gabled tower, with Romanesque lancets to north and south, and a wooden porch. The key is kept at a nearby café.

If you are now looking for rest and recreation of the spirit, as well as for a base for further expeditions, you may like to put up at the delightful Auberge du Camp Romain at Chassey-le-Camp, beside the D109 as it runs south from Santenay and Chagny. You will find no Roman remains or camp site, and the food and accommodation may not be quite as *recherché* as at the Lameloise in Chagny (a major hotel with *three* Michelin rosettes for cuisine), but it will not make such a hole in your purse. There are family *appartements*, as well as quiet and comfortable rooms at accessible prices. The terrace is a blissful place for drinks or summer meals, though breakfast in late summer can be a battle with wasps.

CHAPTER THIRTEEN

From Chalon to Autun

Although we have left the *grands crus* behind us, the vineyard slopes continue to the south until at the farthest boundary of Burgundy they merge with the hills of the Beaujolais. What is still quite properly called a 'route des vins' brings us first into the Côte Chalonnaise, where the communes of Rully, Mercurey, Givry and Montagny produce fine wines at prices a good deal lower than those of their illustrious neighbours to the north.

First, though, if you should be staying at Chassey-le-Camp, take time to look at its twelfth-century church, and a little farther down the road at its counterpart in **Chamilly**, which has a little dunce's cap spire in stone, and at the *château-ferme* with its round tower, to the right of the road as you approach the village. At the next village, Aluze, a left turn will take you down the parallel valley of the Talie to **Rully**, where the combination of a notable thirteenth-century château and a distinguished white wine has a special appeal to connoisseurs of either. The inside of the château can be seen only by appointment, but the opportunity of seeing the outside at weekends between April and October should be taken when possible. It stands on a rocky spur beyond the village, and has been inhabited by the same family – the comtes d'Avian de Ternay – for 700 years, though both title and property have passed in the female line.

Its first recognition as a fief of Montégu (or Montaigu) is recorded in 1268, and the original *château-fort* certainly goes back to the thirteenth century, when it had a square keep and four towers linked by a *chemin de ronde*. The whole building was crenellated and surrounded by a dry moat; the only entrance was over a drawbridge leading to a gateway with portcullis. The keep was lowered in the fifteenth century, and as you enter the courtyard today what you see ahead and to the right all dates from that time, though built inside the earlier walls. The left-hand range was rebuilt in the last century by the present owner's grandfather. It

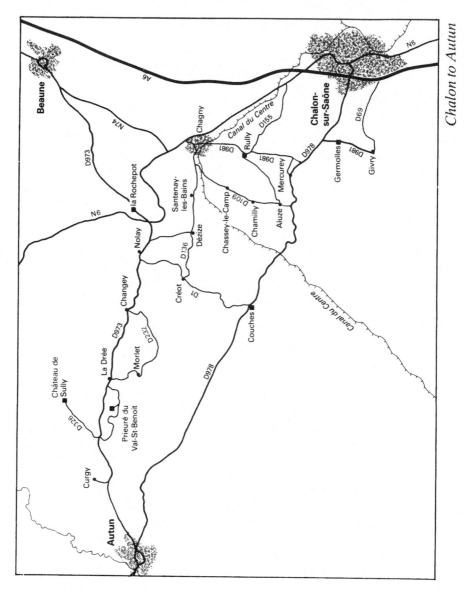

Chalon to Autun

was he who filled in the moat in front of the entrance after falling into it on a dark night – a misadventure which did not amuse him. High up in the wall of the left-hand flanking tower is a large opening which converted it to a *pigeonnier* with accommodation for 1,200 birds. The outbuildings date from the fifteenth and eighteenth centuries and are roofed with the heavy tiles known as *laves* – a word supposedly derived from the Burgundian pronunciation *laver* for *lever*, meaning to lift or heave up, for these wide flat stones are not easy to lift, and need strong underpinning.

If you can arrange a visit to the interior you will be well rewarded, especially if the comtesse can be detached from her family preoccupations. The truncated keep contains a *salle des gardes* on the first floor, and is roofed by a magnificent oak *charpente*. Several sections are left of the *chemin de ronde* and the thirteenth-century walls, and the view from the ramparts takes in the whole of the Val d'Or and even (on a clear day, as they say) the Jura and Mont Blanc. The vaulted mediaeval kitchen is still in use, though not the spit of the great fireplace, which used to be turned by a dog.

The comte de Ternay owns and cultivates three hectares of the surrounding vineyards, two of which produce the red and one the white wine sold as Château de Rully. He has inherited a sixteenth-century wine glass which can hold three litres; this would be drained in one go, it is maintained, by his ancestor Charles de Saint-Ligier, though one imagines a lot would have been spilt in the process.

If you have not already visited Chalon-sur-Saône (the Roman Cabillonum) now is the opportunity, for you can reach it quickly by way of the D981 and the D978. The industrial outskirts are forbidding, but the older quarters of the town have considerable charm. It has always been a major crossroads; Julius Caesar chose it as a depot for his stores during the Gallic wars, and King Gontran lived here from choice in the sixth century. In the Middle Ages hunting and fishing were the main occupations of the Chalonnais – they were allowed to fish in the Saône and hunt in the countryside around. They still do this with or without permission, and the midsummer *Foire aux Sauvagines* (25 June) is a market for wildfowl and miscellaneous game which goes back to those times. They also have a week's carnival in March.

At the end of the eighteenth century the building of the Canal du Centre, the Canal de Bourgogne and the Rhône-Rhine link brought commerce to Chalon, and in 1839 the Schneider factories at le Creusot founded a petit Creusot here, which now specializes in metallurgical and pharmaceutical industries. For a base in the city you will appreciate the accommodation and food at the Hotel Saint-Georges in the avenue Jean-Jaurès, which has a convenient lock-up garage close by.

Chalon's favourite son is Nicéphore Niepce (1765-1833). His statue stands in a small square opening on the Quai Gambetta, and the **Museum** which bears his name faces the river just east of the point where the rue Général Leclerc debouches on to the Quai. It displays a unique collection of photographic apparatus from 1811 to the present day, as fascinating to the layman as it is to the specialist. Niepce served as a second lieutenant with the armies of the Revolution, but was obliged to resign his commission for moral misconduct. He was a friend of Daguerre, and he discovered the principle of photography by using a simple box and the lens from a pair of spectacles.

In a series of beautifully laid out rooms in the eighteenth century Hôtel des Messageries Royals – surely the most splendid Post Office ever built – you can see not only a mockup of the first camera projection in the world (1816), but rarities ranging from the first Kodak camera of 1888 to a machine carried by the Apollo spacecraft to the moon in 1968 – necessarily a copy, as the original is still on the moon. There is a section devoted to underwater and aerial photography, there are panoramic cameras from Lumière's *Periphote* of 1901 to the *Globuscope* of 1981, and in the Bernard Lefebvre room you can see a collection of miniature cameras used in criminal investigation. The *Photocravate* of 1890 could be hidden under a tie, the *Invisible* of about the same date under the shirt front, and the *Invisible Walter Talbot* behind an outer coat. There is Lumière's *Cinematograph* and the Duboscq lantern used to project micro-documents from the Franco-Prussian war. Lest you think Niepce's talents were confined to the dark room, here is a bicycle he built in 1818 with handlebars and a brake, and evidence that he was at least a competent painter in oils.

A more conventional place is the **Musée Denon**, on your right off the broader end of the Place de l'Hôtel-de-Ville. This handsome

Renaissance building was (as so often happened in the new order) taken over from the Ursulines. It is named after an engraver of the *ancien regime* who organized the museums of France under the Empire. On the first floor is a varied collection of paintings from the seventeenth to the nineteenth centuries, but the most interesting exhibits are on the ground floor, where there is a collection of flint tools from southern Burgundy, some Gallo-Roman bronzes, and objects from the Merovingian period.

If you now cross the rue General Leclerc and follow the rue Chatelet which runs parallel to the river, you will come to the **Quartier Saint-Vincent**, which though now a little seedy contains a few mediaeval houses. It takes its name from the church of St-Vincent, which was a cathedral from the fourth century until the Revolution. Its neo-Gothic façade conceals an interior of much interest. At first sight it may seem austere, lacking obvious charm, and an uneasy mixture of styles and materials. The original Romanesque nave, though not completed till the early fourteenth century, has retained some earlier features, notably the capitals. Among the historiated ones you can pick out various country scenes: figures (perhaps Adam and Eve) picking fruit from a tree; two eagles which have caught a hare, with a young eagle eating it; a more puzzling one of a figure holding a piece of meat on a spike in front of two griffins, who make as if to carry the meat up to heaven.

The triple elevation and the use of flat fluted pilasters point to Cluniac influence, though there is an unusual balustraded passage below the clerestory which is continued round the choir and apse. Behind the altar is a sixteenth-century triptych of the Crucifixion, full of expression and movement, and in the south apsidal chapel there is a fine Renaissance tapestry in which various scenes involving the Eucharist are peopled with figures in contemporary costume; this gives a curious atmosphere to the Last Supper. The matching chapel to the north has a modern bronze tabernacle of imaginative design by R. Rigot, dated 1984, which won the Prix de Rome in the following year.

The fifteenth-century cloister has been restored, and in it have been placed four wooden statues of Ste Claire, St Pascal of Baylon, Ste Reine and St Jean de Capistran, an oddly unfamiliar quartet of saints. Other *objets trouvés* include a dramatic Crucifixion of

St Peter, taken from the church of St-Pierre elsewhere in the town, and a sixteenth-century reproduction of Michaelangelo's Christ Resurrected, where Christ treads on a snake, with what look like *escargots* at his feet. The entrance to the Chapter House from the cloister has been blocked off, and a new one made from the south aisle.

You can save yourself a fruitless journey across the Pont-St-Laurent in search of the chapel and refectory of the sixteenth-century Hôpital, which features in most guide books. Almost the whole area of this island site is taken up by a modern medical complex, where nobody has heard of any older building. A flight of steps off one courtyard does lead to the blocked entrance to the deserted chapel, but that is all. You will sight the fifteenth-century **Tour du Doyenne**, which was moved here from a site near the cathedral in 1928, but that in itself is not worth the crossing.

From the rue St-Cosme leading south from the town centre it is not difficult to find the beginning of the D69, which ducks under the autoroute to reach **Givry**. This is a pocket *cité* of individual character, where a monumental gateway dated 1771 incorporates an unusual Mairie; the town walls continue on either side. The church is an extraordinary nineteenth-century extravaganza by Gauthey, a nest of cupolas and elevated neo-classical porticos. In the centre of the town an eighteenth-century rotunda is used for municipal functions.

The red wines of Givry, though they include no *premiers crus*, are among the most respected *appellations* of Burgundy. In the Middle Ages they ranked level with those of Beaune, and in 1390 Marguerite de Flandre ordered for her cellars at Germolles forty-five *queues* of Givry as against ten of Beaune. The **Château of Germolles** is only three kilometres away to the north, so delivery of her wine would have been no problem. She had married Philippe le Hardi in 1369, five years after he succeeded to the dukedom, and the old thirteenth-century castle was converted for her use as a 'maison de plaisance ducale'. It still makes a pleasant dwelling for its owners, with some attractive fourteenth-century farm buildings attached. The two original towers guard the entrance to a long courtyard, with living quarters to the left and gardens beyond. Guided visits are allowed only during July and August; at other times one can circulate discreetly round the outside.

Beyond the village a left-hand fork puts us on the D978 for Autun, but that is a 25-kilometre journey. For the present we pass along the straight main street of **Mercurey**, another flourishing centre for the red wines of the Chalonnais — five vineyards here are classified as *premiers crus*. Their reputation was established as early as the sixth century, and it was a Roman temple to Mercury, later replaced by a windmill, which gave rise to the name of the *commune*.

The main road crosses the Canal du Centre and continues to **Couches**, where the impressive château which towers over the village figures a good deal in the history not only of Burgundy but also of the royal houses of France. A small *château-fort* was created here at the end of the Carolingian era, but it was in the eleventh century that the oldest parts of the present château were built by one Gaudrey, the first recorded *seigneur* of Couches.

It is a surprise to find as you enter the precincts how little of the early and mediaeval structure has survived. From the earliest fortifications there is only the square *donjon* on your right, the foundations of a tower halfway along the western battlements, and parts of the ramparts which face you to the north. Parts of the earliest chapel also survive, but they are incorporated in to the later fifteenth-century building, while the two towers at either end of the northern rampart are the only significant relics of the thirteenth century. This leaves a good deal of empty space, a situation deliberately created when repairs to the whole fabric were begun in 1947. It was decided to concentrate on making good only the older parts of the château (where this was possible) and to clear away the ruins of later periods without any attempt at reconstruction, and this seems to have been a wise decision.

The two best known inhabitants both had royal or ducal connections. Marguerite de Bourgogne was the daughter of Duke Robert II and granddaughter of Saint Louis of France. At the age of fifteen she was married to Louis le Hutin of Navarre, who in 1314 became Louis X of France and promptly moved to get rid of his young wife. She took refuge at Couches, where she had spent the happier years of her childhood and enjoyed the protection of her cousin, Marie de Beaufremont; she died here in 1333. The most prosperous time in its history was during the fifteenth century, when Claude de Montaigu, descendant of Robert the Pious

and last of a long line of *seigneurs* of Couches, was made a
Chevalier de la Toison d'Or by Charles le Téméraire, and undertook major additions to the château. They included a new chapel,
consecrated in 1469 by Cardinal Rolin of Autun. Although he
fought and died for Burgundy in its struggle for independence
against Louis XI, his cousin-german Claude de Blaizy who succeeded him took sides with the king, and had to defend himself
against an assault by the formidable Marie de Bourgogne, daughter and heiress of Charles le Téméraire. Her success here and her
marriage in 1477 to Maximilian of Austria delayed the union of
Burgundy and France till her death in 1482.

An intelligent guide will show you round the impressive remains. On the ground floor of the *donjon* is the guard room, with a
collection of weaponry including a tremendous two-handed sword.
The first floor contains the *salon de seigneur*, where the family
repaired when under siege – now decorated with Aubusson tapestries. At the far right-hand corner of the *enceinte* is the Tour du
Prison, where the prison itself was on the ground floor underneath
the *salle de justice*. A sinister oubliette received those condemned
to death, and a subterranean passage allowed the bodies to be
recovered. Next door is the fifteenth-century chapel, reached
through the vestiges of its predecessor. In a typically flamboyant
chamber you will find fourteenth-century wooden statues of St
George and St Sebastian, and a striking modern head of Christ by
George Roualt. These visits are possible only in the afternoon
during the summer months.

Rather than proceeding directly along the D978 to Autun, there
is profit to be had by turning northward by the D1 to **Nolay** – or
more pleasantly by the little winding roads which pass through
Dracy-les-Couches, Mazenay and Epertuilly. The goal is the same,
and here we must reflect that Burgundy produced two of the greatest soldiers in the military annals of France, Vauban and Lazare
Carnot. Carnot was born at Nolay in 1753, and his genius was
quick to declare itself. At the age of nine, watching a play in the
theatre at Dijon, he called out to the actors: 'Get on the north side
of that bastion!' Inspired by an admiration for Vauban he joined
the engineering corps in 1789, and won the *éloge de Vauban* at the
Académie de Dijon. He was a friend of its President, but there is no
doubt that he won the award on merit. When the brother of the

King of Prussia offered him promotion he refused, and accepted an appointment with the Republican army.

Carnot had tasted the insolence of the *ancien régime*, for on sending a memorandum to the Secretary of State he had received no acknowledgment. He thereupon addressed a personal complaint to Louis XVI, but the reply – no doubt from an official – asked merely, 'Since when has a poor plebeian not been satisfied to be a captain and a cavalier?' As a member of the Convention he voted for the death of the King, but admitted that no duty ever weighed more heavily on him. The Brunswick manifesto tipped the scales in his divided mind. Louis XVI would have been saved if the Convention had not deliberated with daggers at their throats. In his relations with Bonaparte, he approved neither the consulate for life nor the imperial regime, although Bonaparte offered him 'everything you want, when you want it, and how you want it'. Later he rallied to Napoleon, he was appointed governor of Antwerp, and acted as the Minister of the Interior during the Hundred Days. He was then 60 years old. Yet Carnot had little taste for politics; and his recipe for those who practise it has not been generally followed:

The true friend of the people is the man whom you have to spend a long time in persuading to assume a political responsibility; who retires from it as soon as he can, and is poorer than when he took it on; who gives himself to it from a sense of duty; acts more readily than he talks; returns with eagerness to his family; and resumes the exercise of the private virtues.

Carnot returned whenever he could to his family at Nolay, teaching them Latin and mathematics and, when they were little, wheeling them about in a wicker pram. He was also a great walker. A man of warm humanity both in the council chamber and on the battlefield, he defended Danton and closed the curtains and windows of his house on the day when the great tribune was executed; just as he had obtained the reprieve of a young soldier condemned to death for failing to rejoin the regiment. 'I thought you were a Brutus', the lad remarked. 'Yes', replied Carnot, 'when I have to be'. When Napoleon offered to make him a count, he objected that he neither wished to wrap up his name in a soubriquet, nor to bring fresh enemies against Napoleon with a noisy refusal. He went into exile at the Restoration and died at Magdeburg in 1823 – the Cincinnatus of the Revolution, as he has been called. His statue stands in front of the house where he was born, which still belongs to the family. The big fifteenth-century church, largely restored in the seventeenth, has an odd-looking bell tower from which a wooden jack-of-the-clock strikes the hours. The square fourteenth-century **Halles** have a fine timber roof covered by heavy *laves*, and all around you can see houses which would have been familiar to Carnot.

From Nolay a brief sortie eastward along the D973, passing under the N6 trunk road, brings you to **la Rochepot**, where there is another château important for its connections with Burgundian notables. As at Couches the primitive twelfth-century fortress was made into a more comfortable residence during the fifteenth. It saw the birth in 1428 of Philippe Pot, who became the principal chamberlain to Charles le Téméraire and Burgundian ambassador to London, and it was in his honour that the name of the château was changed from la Roche-Nolay to la Roche-Pot. It suffered rather more heavily than Couches during the Revolution, but was later bought and restored by M. Sadi Carnot, son of the nineteenth-century President of France, and descendant of the Carnots of Nolay.

There is a good deal for the visitor to see and take in, with illustrations of the life lived here over many centuries. Of the twelfth-century fortress little is left; the keep was irretrievably destroyed in the Revolution and replaced by a terrace which commands the village below. From the *chemin de ronde* you look down on the *cour d'honneur* and its mainly fifteenth-century surroundings – though the well-head with its wrought-iron crown is dated 1228. It was bored into the rock, 72 metres deep, and gave access to underground passages which could be escape routes in times of crisis. The *salle des gardes*, big enough to hold the popula tion of the village, has the usual display of mediaeval weaponry, but the bedroom of the Captain of the Guard above it contains a polychrome statue of the Trinity which is unique in France (there are two other examples in the museum at Munich). It shows God the Father encircling the crucified Christ while the dove representing the Holy Spirit perches above – 'who proceedeth from the Father and the Son', as the Nicene Creed has it. This remarkable object was unearthed in the grounds, where it had been hidden during the Revolution.

The kitchens, bread oven and *colombier* illustrate the domestic life of the château, while the early Gothic chapel served its spiritual side. Among the other curiosities you can see a fifteenth-century wall safe with a combination lock and an alarm bell, and a bed-warmer known as a *moine* because it replaced the monkish practice of introducing a boy acolyte into the bed to warm it for his superior. The kitchens were restored by the Carnots and represent the *tout confort* of the last century, with an iron *gauffrier* and a coffee machine of the Cona principle made of hand-blown glass. The dining room has Renaissance features, a Gobelins tapestry, a seventeenth-century Dutch clock showing the phases of the moon, a portrait of Charles le Téméraire and a Louis XIII baby chair, while the dining table is unmistakably Charles Dix.

The most surprising room in the north tower is furnished entirely with Chinese works of art, brought here by President Carnot after his term as French ambassador to China. There are dragon tapestries, Chinese beds and a statue of Buddha – even the tiles in the fireplace are oriental. The patterns of coloured tiles which cover much of the roof space of the château are not to everybody's taste, but they are a feature of many Burgundian buildings, sacred and secular; here they are part of the restoration work done by the Carnot family.

The church in the village is basically Romanesque on the Cluniac plan, but the original stone vaulting proved too heavy for the widely spaced pillars of the nave; it was replaced, after a collapse, by a wooden roof. Some twelfth-century capitals survive, including the venerable Balaam confronted by a sweet-looking angel, and an Annunciation where the Virgin seems to be protesting at the news so confidentially imparted by the archangel.

To reach Autun, our eventual destination, we must go back to Nolay and continue westwards along the D973. However, soon after the crossroads at la Drée, look for a little turning on the left which runs deep into the woodlands of the Forêt des Battées. From this a track on the right leads to a spot where you must leave your car if you want to visit the **Prieuré du Val-St-Benoit**, one of the most romantic sites in Burgundy. It was built in the thirteenth century by Gauthier de Sully in honour of the Virgin Mary, and later fell into ruin and obscurity; only in the past decade has a slow process of restoration begun. The work has been done by voluntary teams of local and visiting enthusiasts, and after a few changes of use it received in 1982 a community of the 'Sœurs moniales de Bethléem', who live a life of solitude and communion with Our Lady, awaiting the glorious return of Our Lord. Its new title of Notre-Dame-de-l'Adoration proclaims their purpose and their convictions. There are fifteen sisters, most of them young, and you will have a cheerful welcome if you are not disturbing their habitual privacy.

Entering by the west door of the church you will be immediately struck by the elegant stripped oak woodwork of the choir stalls, the simple modern lectern and the imaginative touch of the dove hovering over the altar to preserve the Host. On any Sunday quite a few visitors will drive in to attend Mass. To the left of the choir is the transept used by the sisters for their private worship, while to the right is the more worldly sight of the *flamboyant* entrance to the Chapelle des Loges – a sixteenth-century contribution by an aristocratic local family, now beautifully restored.

Recently the space once occupied by the cloister has been developed to provide the sisters with their own individual lodgings, or *hermitages*, where they can carry out their self-imposed regime of meditation in absolute privacy and silence. Needless to say no visitor can expect to get even a glimpse of these arrangements. This is one of the loveliest places in the world for worship, such is the peace and beauty, and above all the silence.

From the west one enters the nave, with a view up to the simple altar; in 1987 the choir was still walled off for restoration. The same was true of the lovely Chapelle des Loges with its flamboyant doorway, to the south of the altar. Apart from this chapel the church is almost Cistercian in its simplicity, particularly the *bras nord* (in effect an elongated north transept) which is used by the sisters for their devotions. There are plans to make a new entrance into the Chapelle des Loges beneath the rose window of its western façade. The family of Loges were the *seigneurs* of the neighbouring château of Morlet, and their tombs and armorial bearings can be seen in the chapel. Considering the ruinous state of the priory in the late 1970s, its restoration has been a success which would have delighted St Benedict. The peace within its enfolding woods is almost complete – only disturbed now by the TGVs hurtling down the nearby main line, so alien that they can be ignored.

The winding road through the woods will bring you back to the D973, which you should cross and then immediately bear right for the famous **Château de Sully**, seat of the duc de Magenta and of his forebears since the beginning of the eighteenth century. It was, as we have seen, one Gauthier de Sully who was guided (miraculously, it appears) to build the chapel in the woods which became the Prieuré du Val-St-Benoit. He died in 1240, and it is believed that the oldest surviving tower of the château was built in his day. The *seigneurs* of Sully and Couches were allied by marriage at an early date, though there were constant bickerings between the families, chiefly on the subject of hunting rights. The monks of St-Benoît, 'braconniers à l'occasion', took every opportunity to poach game in the forest.

The time came when both proprietors were Montaigus, the last of whom was killed at the siege of Buxy in 1470. He left a natural daughter whom Louis XI legitimized as Jeanne de Montaigu. This was a momentous act, for Jeanne then married Hugues de Rabutin from nearby Épiry, from whom was descended not only Bussy-Rabutin but both the father-in-law and the husband of Ste Jeanne de Chantal, and hence Madame de Sévigné. It was Madame de Sévigné who described Sully as the 'Fontainebleau de la Bourgoyne', and the interior court as 'la plus belle cour de château de France', and she had every opportunity to know.

In 1515 Christophe de Rabutin sold Sully to Jean de Saulx, husband of Marguerite de Tavannes. The characters and adventures of their immediate descendants are well told in the entertaining brochure by Denis Grivot which is on sale at the reception point for visitors to the château. It was Gaspard de Saulx-Tavannes, Lieutenant-General of Burgundy during the wars of religion (which split the family in two) and Marshal of France after the victory of Jarnac, who first laid plans to build a new château at Sully. His widow commissioned the architect Ribonnier, but it was not until 1553 that their son Jehan was able to complete the design – after several periods when he was imprisoned by Henry IV, as much for his obstreperous behaviour as for his leadership of the Catholic Ligue.

The layout of Sully is simple, handsome and authoritative. You approach it down a long avenue of low flat-topped yews, with symmetrical rows of stabling on either side. The moat, now filled again with water from the Drée, is crossed by a bridge of five graceful arches which starts from a terrace with a curious stone balustrade. The interior is not open for visits, but the view of its four differing façades and beautifully kept surroundings is worth the modest entry fee. Of Jehan de Saulx's château only the Renaissance west front remains. The south and east ranges have been restored in different styles at different periods, but the most splendid construction of all is to be found on the north side. In front of a severely classical façade, broken only by a simple pediment, a majestic flight of steps descends to a semi-circular balustraded terrace which projects into the moat – deliberately widened at this point.

This ensemble was achieved in the eighteenth century by the family of Morey, who bought the château in 1714. They began the connection with the present owners, the MacMahons, whose most famous ancestor was Maurice, comte de MacMahon and duc de Magenta, Marshal of France and President of the Republic from 1872 to 1879. Though he never owned the château or lived there after his infancy, his statue in formal military uniform stands on a grassy sward to the south of it. To understand how the unlikely name of MacMahon and the strange title of Magenta fit into the story of Sully we must go back to 1742, when a young Irish doctor set up his practice in Autun. Dr MacMahon's skill was rewarded when after successfully treating the aged Jean-Baptiste Morey (who nevertheless died a few years later) he married Charlotte, the young widow of his second marriage, and became master of Sully. Charlotte survived her second husband, and played her part in a bizarre drama which ensured that the château went more or less unscathed during the Revolutionary period. She was arrested, but having undertaken to provide pay and equipment for two volunteers in the army she was allowed to return to Sully with the understanding that the château would not be confiscated in her lifetime. As she was a very old lady this was perhaps a cynical concession, but when she did die in 1798 her family and retainers kept up the pretence that she was alive by preserving her body in alcohol, putting it back in bed whenever a commission of enquiry arrived. One wonders how close the commissioners were allowed to approach the pickled châtelaine.

Maurice MacMahon, grandson of the doctor but only third in line of his own generation, was born at Sully in 1808. After a brilliant military career, which included service in Algeria and the Crimea (where he captured the Malakoff redoubt) he commanded Napoleon III's army which in 1859 invaded northern Italy with the aim of dislodging the Austrians. After the rather shaky victory at Magenta and the bloodier one at Solferino he was created duc de Magenta (the name we associate with the colour was given to a newly discovered aniline dye simply because it was first used at that time). Defeated at Wörth by the Prussians, and wounded at Sedan in 1870, he helped Thiers to stamp out the Commune and recapture Paris; in 1872 he became President of the new Republic of France.

Meanwhile the MacMahons of Sully (a marquisate since 1752) had prospered. They undertook the restoration of the south front in its original Renaissance style, and dug out and refilled the moat. The curious ornamentation of the parapet by the bridge, a series of cannon balls, pyramids and sunbursts, dates from 1890 and represents the emblems to be seen on a marquis's coronet. It was the grandson of the President, another Maurice de MacMahon, duc de Magenta, who was the first of that line to inherit Sully. Born in 1903, he served in the French Air Force, and after 1940 he led the Resistance forces of the north, evading the Gestapo thanks to the coolness and resource of his wife. He died in an accident in 1954 and was succeeded by his son Philippe, the present owner.

It seems appropriate to dwell on the personalities connected with Sully, for apart from Bussy-Rabutin no other estate has so much to tell us about the character and history of the often closely connected aristocratic families of Burgundy. Nowhere else in France, or perhaps anywhere in Europe, have the owners of great properties held on so tenaciously to their inheritance despite centuries of war, revolution and foreign occupation. Not by any means all wealthy people by modern standards, they have preserved, tended and restored their homes and their lands, and are still determined to leave them undiminished to their successors.

Do not leave Sully without looking in at the *nouvelle église* in the village. It replaced the now abandoned chapel in the park, where the great Marshal was christened, and it contains several works of art removed from there. These include a naïve fifteenth-century *retable* with rustic scenes from the Nativity and the Assumption. Of the same period but in a totally different mood is the statue of Ste Agathe, represented as a lovely girl in a deliciously natural pose – one would like to have known the model used by the sculptor. Ste Agathe was a third-century martyr, put to death in Sicily after having her breasts cut off, but this statue (which shows them unharmed) was considered so provocative in the nineteenth century that she had to be disguised for a time as the Virgin Mary.

There is one more call to make on the road to Autun. This is at **Curgy**, just north of the main road about seven kilometres out, where there is one of the purest of early Romanesque churches. It was founded in the eleventh century on the site of a Carolingian chapel, and it preserves most of that period's simple character. Although the apse was panelled in wood in the eighteenth century (the window embrasures show the thickness of the original walls) its half-dome retains a twelfth-century fresco of Christ in Majesty with the symbolic figures which represent the four evangelists.

You are now almost under the walls of Autun, and to see all that is to be seen within them you will need to spend two whole days there. For lodging in comfort and a traditional atmosphere you will not find better value than at the old Hôtel St-Louis et Poste in the town centre, though if your main requirement is gastronomic you may prefer the quiet Hostellerie du Vieux Moulin, just beyond the Porte d'Arroux beside a little tributary of the river.

CHAPTER FOURTEEN

Nevers and the Nivernais

The Nivernais is among the least known and least frequented regions of France. Not a single autoroute passes through it, and except for the city which gives it its name it must be doubtful whether the most travelled British francophile could identify a town or monument (apart from Nevers) which lies within its borders. Waterways are a different matter. Of the only four towns here with a claim to sophistication, three stand beside the Loire, that enigmatic and surely feminine river which glides its way unpredictably from the heart of the Massif Central to the Atlantic coast of Brittany. The reason they are there is obvious. for the river brought trade direct to their waterfronts and so to their streets. Nevers, La Charité and Cosne-sur-Loire all once had ports on which the towns and their hinterland depended.

Just as important to the region as a whole was the Canal du Nivernais, one of the key waterways of central France, which connects the Yonne near Joigny to the Loire and its attendant canal at Decize. A motorist driving through the centre of the Nivernais may be bewildered by the number of times his road crosses and recrosses it, and by the number of still working locks he sights. Today it and the rivers it serves are no longer industrial highways, and the traffic you see negotiating its locks are almost all pleasure craft. The Nièvre itself, from which the *département*, the region and the principal town derive their names, is a comparatively insignificant river which makes its way down from two sources in the Bazois hills to join the Loire at Nevers.

The character of the Nivernais is hard to define. In effect it fills a gap between the rolling valley country typical of the Loire basin and the thickly wooded heights of the Morvan to the east. Much of the land to the west is arable farming country, with the inevitable crops of maize and sunflowers dictating the seasonal patterns of the countryside, but even here your road is liable to plunge into heavily planted *fôrets domeniales*, which will remind you that the timber trade, with access by river to customers as far away as Paris, has been a money-maker for the region. It still is, as

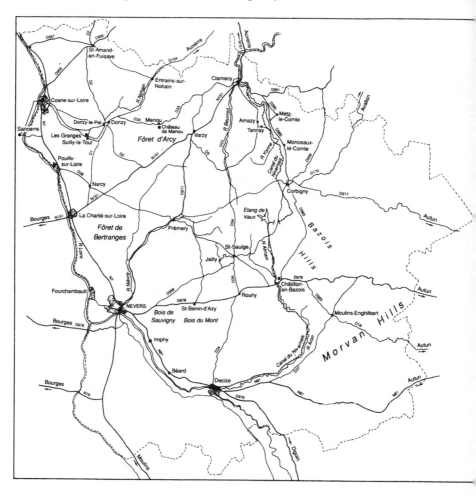

you will realise when your car is held up for miles behind a *camion* loaded with vast trunks of oak or pine.

Timber is still king when you cross the upland plateau of the Bazois into the foothills of the Morvan, where a network of small rivers runs through steep green valleys – steep enough to give welcome shade in high summer, but a little melancholy in the mists of winter. Where the country opens out you will see the white shapes of Charollais cattle dotting the green slopes in their typical family groups.

256

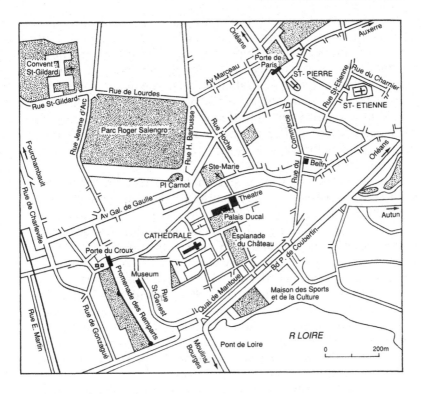

Generalizations must be suspect, but the people of the Nivernais seem mostly reserved and occupied with their own business, though always friendly. There is little sign of the commercialism or robust cynicism you find in more populated and popular parts of Burgundy. You will hardly ever find a church in town or village locked against the casual visitor.

The plan of this chapter is to suggest a few suitable bases from which to explore the region at leisure, with an account of interesting places at a convenient distances from each. The distances are not great, however, so it would be easy to make eclectic sorties from whichever base is chosen – or you can treat it as a convenient side entrance to Burgundy from the west, and pick your route accordingly.

The obvious starting place is **Nevers**, the administrative capital of the *département* of Nièvre. Little is known of it until the sixteenth century, when Luigi di Gonzaga of Mantua inherited the duchy of Nevers in 1565. Like most Italian rulers he was a patron of the arts, and he brought in designers and artisans from Italy to produce the glass and earthenware which brought fame and profit to the city. Products were shipped down river to the big cities of the middle Loire, where wealthy nobles already ensconced in their splendid châteaux were natural customers. The duchy, founded by François I, was acquired in 1659 by Cardinal Mazarin and it stayed in his family until the Revolution. With little demand for such fancy goods in Republican houses, the industry collapsed. though three major workshops survive today and produce *faience* to the modern French taste.

The town rises by way of steep narrow streets from the river, where the waterfront is mostly industrial. The main entrance from the south is across a big red sandstone bridge which leads to the remains of one of the original gates into the walled mediaeval city. Better preserved is the **Porte du Croux** at the northern end of the still traceable western ramparts, where the roadway runs through a noble square machicolated tower. From here it is a short walk to the west end of the **Cathedral of St-Cyr and Ste-Julitte**, but there are no public car parks in this area, and a more convenient and rewarding approach would be from the large *parking* to the east of the tree-lined Esplanade du Château, which stretches all the way up from the Quai du Mantoue to the **Palais Ducal**, itself one of the most impressive buildings in the town.

If you walk westward from the car park you will see first on your right a charming porticoed building which is the town's eighteenth-century **Theatre**. Next in line is the ducal palace, which will remind anyone who has seen it of the François I wing of the château at Blois. Ahead, across the pleasant green spaces of the Esplanade, appear the flamboyant tower and high-standing Gothic *chevet* of the Cathedral.

Once inside – and one hopes that recent repair work will have cleared the main west doorway – you will look east to see a very fine fourteenth-century Gothic nave leading into a graceful Gothic choir and ambulatory. The open triforium runs without interruption round it all, and if you look carefully you will find that at the base of every short pillar is carved a caricature of some local type, each one different. If they are too difficult to make out from ground level, you can buy postcards of some of them from a stall at the west end.

Turning now to the west, where you may have entered without noticing anything unusual, you will see that what seem to be the last two bays of the nave are purely Romanesque, and that they lead into another choir and apse in the same style. All this part of the building is built in a light pinkish stone, quite different from that used further east. What you are looking at is a rare example of what is sometimes called 'westwork', where an early Romanesque church may have semicircular apses at both ends – a practice dating from Carolingian times. In this case the west end is all that remains of a church built in 1028 and dedicated to Ste Julitte, an otherwise little-known saint who shared the martyrdom of St Cyr in Asia Minor during the fourth century. It was destroyed by fire in 1211.

The two Romanesque bays in fact span the crossing of a double western transept, the north arm leading into a survival from a much earlier church, a sixth-century baptismal chapel encased within the thick outer walls. This was discovered in 1948 during repairs to make good the damage caused by an Allied bombardment at the end of the war, but during the recent programme of restoration it has been closed to visitors. In the *cul-de-four* of the western apse a twelfth-century fresco has survived in quite good condition, showing Christ in Majesty supported by the four evangelists. Beneath the Romanesque choir is a contemporary crypt which contains a fifteenth-century polychrome *Mise au Tombeau*.

Apart from a few additions in the fifteenth and sixteenth centuries, everything farther east belongs to the new church built after the fire and consecrated in 1331. There is no transept, and you will notice that from the choir eastward the centre line of the building shifts slightly to the right. This was no careless lapse by the architect, but a deliberate move to reproduce the usually depicted tilt to the right of Christ's head on the Cross.

A pleasing sixteenth-century secular addition to the cathedral is a tall free-standing clock in a rectangular wooden base, to be found in one of the bays of the south aisle. It has a striking mechanism which activates a 'Jack-of-the-Clock', and its face is a delightful concoction of spidery tracery picked out in gold. Of much the same date is the little flamboyant doorway off the southern half of the Romanesque transept, leading to a protruding openwork stairway which on a much smaller scale recalls the façade of the Palais Ducal. A feature throughout the Cathedral is the beautifully designed modern glass, which contributes even more delicacy to the Gothic windows and is used to great effect in the western apse.

Before moving on to the last of the great monuments in Nevers, you may be looking for refreshment in the narrow streets of the old town – many of them now *rues pietonnées* in the modern vein. There are plenty of restaurants, but local folk in their lunch hours know they can eat well, cheaply and quickly at one of the many *brasseries* to be found there, with a choice of tables set either inside or outside on the broad pavements where you can watch the human scene at close quarters.

Thereafter you can reclaim your car and proceed by way of the rue du Commerce to a large parking place next to the seventeenth-century church of St-Pierre (which need not detain you) some way to the north-east of the Cathedral. Frequent road signs will point you the way, and close by is the **Church of St-Etienne**, an imposing Romanesque church of great character.

St-Etienne once formed part of a priory controlled by Cluny, and it was built between 1063 and 1097 at the instigation of Count William I of Nevers. Although all its three towers were destroyed in the Revolution, leaving only a stumpy remnant over the crossing, there has been little change in the body of the church since the eleventh century, and its Romanesque credentials are unchallenged. On the other hand it seems to have suffered a long period of neglect, which a good deal of restoration has not altogether put right.

Architecturally it is magnificent. The six bays of the nave, with its pure barrel vaulting, twin-arcaded blind triforium, high ambulatory arches, and above all the complex structure of the *chevet* as seen from the rue du Charnier – all this adds up to one of the most complete Romanesque churches in Burgundy. As in other great examples – notably St-Philibert in Tournus – the soaring half-columns of the nave go straight up from floor to vaulting, with exhilarating effect. There are original features too; the height and span of the crossing arches are extraordinary, and there are inner arches to support each arm of the transept at the halfway mark.

Yet the whole effect manages to be sombre, a verdict perhaps prompted by the texture of the stonework, especially where it has been too obviously restored. One successful piece of restoration is the undoubtedly Carolingian high altar of biscuit-coloured stone

Dijon:
crypt of St-Benigne

Dijon:
Puits de Moïse

Charles le Téméraire, school of Rogier van der Weyden

with a simple cross carved on its central slab. You leave St-Etienne impressed by its power and originality, yet it remains a building difficult to love.

The city of Nevers, however, is one which grows on visitors the more they see of it. Some of the suggestions in this chapter assume that they will be coming in from a base outside the city centre, and it must be said that the two strongest candidates for a few days' stay are not within easy walking distance of the chief monuments described.

To explore the country east of Nevers, leave the town by the exit marked (3) on the Michelin maps, taking first the D978 for Autun, and after a few kilometres forking right on the N81 for Decize. This road keeps the Loire close on your right hand as it passes through Imphy and reaches **Béard**. Here the sturdy little church of St-Laurent is a good example of the small-town Romanesque inheritance of the Nivernais. Yet it might never have survived to tell its tale. In 1359 the lawless and philistine Engish troops of the Hundred Years' War burnt it almost to the ground. When peace returned a sensitive programme of restoration began, and the church was as good as recreated in the original style and proportions. The new philistines of the Revolution undid it all again, robbing the church of all its valuables. and then selling it in 1806 for use as a barn. Finally in 1919 it was on the point of being pulled down as a dangerous structure, to be rescued only by strong local feeling. The turning point came in 1926, when the tower was classified as historic monument.

Life really only returned in 1972, when the whole church was classified, and an inevitably slow process of full restoration could begin. Without the resources available in the more prosperous departments of Burgundy it was only in the 1990s that the effects began to show. While the short four-square tower, with its two double arches in both upper storeys, is complete in its Romanesque confidence, the inside has only laid bare its fine bones. Most of the sacriligeous depredations have been made good, but there is a long way still to go before Mass can be heard here again. In spite of everything St-Laurent is a lovely little church.

Four and a half kilometres further on is **Decize**, a much bigger town with a bigger church – still Romanesque in character. To reach it you have to leave the main road, turning right to cross the wide green trough which used to be the principal channel of the Loire. The real waterways here are confusing, with the Canal du Nivernais and a network of small rivers converging on the town. Decize, like Nevers and La Charité, had its own port beside the old river channel, and prospered as a result. This is why the church of St-Are is more impressive than any outside the main towns of the region.

St Are was Bishop of Nevers around 550, and there was a church here by the beginning of the seventh century. Traditionally it began as a hermitage for Saints Euphrastor and Auxilius, both friends of St Are, but the only trace of the early foundation is the barrel-vaulted crypt, a rare Merovingian survival which also has a monolithic altar from the time of Charlemagne. There is no admission to the crypt, but by a sensible arrangement you can look down into it from an opening at its west end.

There is a good deal of interest above too, where the church built in the eleventh century has a big nave with five Romanesque bays and authentic barrel vaulting. There is little decoration – no carved capitals and no triforium – but the fabric has been well and sympathetically restored. Not so in the choir, which is still waiting for attention, but it has one eye-catching feature. Round the semi-circle of the choir stalls is a brightly coloured sequence of tapestry panels, framed by pilasters, which illustrate the life of the Virgin from her presentation in the temple by her mother Ste Anne to the final scenes of her Assumption and Coronation. It began life as a sixteenth-century *retable* designed for the crypt, and was discovered under its floor during restoration in 1841. On view recently have been photographic copies mounted there when the originals were sent away for treatment at an arts centre in Mayenne. A final look eastward from the nave will reveal that, as in the Cathedral of Nevers, the choir and sanctuary have been offset slightly to the right, and for the same reason.

To make this a comfortable round trip, follow the N81 on to the east, diverging from the D979 a few miles out of town, and then turning left on the D37 for **Moulins-Enghilbert**. For the first part of the journey you will be in close company with the Canal du Nivernais and the river Aron, another tributary of the Loire. The town when you reach it turns out to be an amalgam of old and new. The old is represented by the remains of a mediaeval château, some attractive old houses, and a Gothic church of no great interest; the new element comes to bustling life every Tuesday in the cattle market, where auctions of Charollais cattle are conducted electronically. Each animal is identified on a large screen with its weight and lot number, while the punters are all seated with a number to press to register their interest and the amount of their bid. It must be a lively scene, for this is the principal market town on the edge of the cattle-rearing foothills of the Morvan.

A left-hand turn here on to the D985 joins the D978 on its way back to Nevers. You soon reach **Châtillon-en-Bazois**, whose importance today comes chiefly from its position astride the river Almain at its confluence with the Aron and the ubiquitous Canal du Nivernais. This has attracted enthusiasts for inland waterway cruising, though the boatyards seem to have little business these days.

The most impressive feature of the town is the château, built mostly in the sixteenth and seventeenth centuries and privately occupied. You will probably miss it on your left as you drive in from the east, though the entrance gate above the road has a notice telling you the opening times – afternoons only in July and August at present. If this is unhelpful, there is a good view of the château from the towpath of the canal behind, which in any case would make a pleasant walk to stretch your legs. Prominent in this view is the thirteenth-century round tower, all that remains of the mediaeval *enceinte*.

The last call on this tour could be the village of **Rouhy**, ten kilometres beyond Chatillon, where there is an upstanding little church of mixed origins. The solid tower looks Romanesque in its lower parts, with some impressive blind arcading, but the windows above are Gothic, and it has a short unconvincing spire. There is a good Romanesque south doorway, but the interior has been much restored. If the church is shut, the key can be found at a house on the left of the road leading down to a garage, and nearly opposite it.

The road back to Nevers runs through two big stretches of forest, the Bois du Mont west of St-Benin-d'Azy, and the Bois de Sauvigny, which crowns the last bit of high ground before you dip down to the Loire valley again.

2

Another riverside base worth considering is **La Charité-sur-Loire**, a less busy and more immediately accessible town than Nevers. The long waterfront of the former river port has kept its old houses — mostly now shops and cafés — which blend easily with the roofs of the mediaeval town which rise in tiers behind them. The two quays, the quai Maréchal Foch to the north and the quai Clemenceau to the south, are in fact just a straight stretch of the N7 which follows the river bank through the town, so there is an easy entry from either direction.

From whichever direction you come, you will have a good view of the magnificent eighteenth-century bridge which describes a long gentle arc across the Loire in its now shallow bed. Best of all, before following the line of the bridge up into the town centre, drive across it and look back at a Canaletto-like view of the skyline, dominated by the two towers associated with the **Church of Notre-Dame** and the walls of the mediaeval château away to the left of the picture.

If you should be coming in by the N151 from Bourges, that will take you straight across the bridge up into the town, and (*sens unique* permitting) near the west door of the church — or at least into the *place des Pecheurs* from which you can approach it. At this point there are different possibilities. If you have decided to make your base in La Charité, there is one outstanding candidate in the shape of the Grand Monarque, a *restaurant avec chambres* on the quai Clemenceau, which has a wonderful view across the Loire and up to the bridge; most of its rooms are set some way back from the busy road, and behind a well kept garden area. Rooms and menus in an excellent restaurant are reasonably priced, and if you have checked in there the night before it will be an easy walk up into the town. The same is true if you choose to leave your car at a convenient car park at the end of the quay where the road turns inland.

If however you stick to your car as far as the place des Pêcheurs, you may still find an opportunity to park in the Cour du Prieuré, a large open space at the heart of the former Benedictine priory to the north of Notre-Dame. (This is being developed to house an exhibition centre, and may eventually be closed to traffic). To reach it you turn left past the tall Romanesque tower which dominates the skyline, through a passage-way in the former Porter's Lodge, and right at the top end of the Cour du Château. This will give you a chance of walking back through this interesting group of surviving priory buildings. You pass a little doorway in the Cour du Château marked 'Cellier des Moines '(the old wine press was directly opposite), and in the bottom left-hand angle of the Cour is a flamboyant doorway into the stairway turret of the Prior's Lodging.

Regaining the place des Pêcheurs – a name which reminds you of one of the main occupations of a riverside town – you can now have a good look at the church buildings themselves, and it takes some time to puzzle them out. To begin with the **Tour de Ste-Croix**, with its magnificent elevation of Romanesque arched windows and elegant slate spire, it turns out to be the survivor of two such towers which framed the main western entrance to the eleventh-century priory church, dedicated first to Ste-Croix and later to Notre-Dame. It now stands detached from any other building after a fire in 1559 which destroyed its fellow and gutted the western half of the nave. Through the remains of the entrance doorway, replaced in the Gothic style after the fire, you reach an open space called the *place* Ste-Croix, where high up on the north side you can still see traces of the original triforium.

A new western entrance leads into the surviving parts of the Romanesque church. There are now only four bays of the nave (poorly restored in the seventeenth century), with corresponding side aisles, and the noble transept has two eleventh-century apsidal chapels in either arm. The crossing has an authentic dome on squinches supporting a short octagonal tower, and the choir leads into a fourteenth-century Lady Chapel. The scale of what has been preserved is a reminder that the original priory church was the second largest in France after its mother church of Cluny, and could hold a congregation of five thousand. A little history may help to explain its importance. It springs from an eighth-century foundation, which in spite of some ferocious Saracen invasions flourished well enough to inspire later generations to build this splendid church. The hospitable monks cared for all classes, dispensing 'la Charité de Dieu' to pilgrims and the poor, thus inventing a new name for the town, until then known as Seyr. During the

Hundred Years' War it was besieged by Joan of Arc in an attempt to recover it for the newly crowned Charles VII from the Anglo-Burgundian alliance. The siege failed, with the mediaeval walls intact, but in 1436 the Treaty of Arras saw it returned to the king.

To conclude a tour of the present church, you can get a good view of the partly restored cloister through a glass-fronted opening in the north aisle. Beside the south transept doorway is mounted the tympanum removed from one of the doorways of the Ste-Croix tower. Its subject is the Transfiguration, with the usual Romanesque decorations. The transfigured Christ is accompanied by the four evangelists, while the lower register presents a lively pageant of the three Magi and the Presentation in the Temple. Over the west doorway is an ornate seventeenth-century wooden gallery, and above that a window with good modern glass.

Although the streets around the church are narrow and crowded, they are kept as clean and orderly as at Nevers, and there are some intriguing old houses to be seen round about. A break for lunch would be no problem – there are plenty of *brasseries* here too. Later in the day you may like to visit the **Museum**, which is behind the northern end of the *quai* Maréchal Foch before you come to the old city ramparts. The collections are in two distinct categories: the rooms on the lower floor are devoted to mediaeval discoveries made during recent excavations around Notre-Dame, while the rest of the building is given over to a fascinating collection (unusual in this context) of *art nouveau* and *art déco* work by twentieth-century artists.

East of La Charité there are three places of interest to visit – one of them a remarkable discovery. All three could quite easily be reached from Nevers too, but they are obvious attractions for those staying further down the Loire. The road to take out of La Charité is the N151 in the direction of Varzy and Clamecy. After a dead straight stretch of nine kilometres, there is a right-hand turn on to the D38. This takes you out of a low-lying area of arable land up into the outskirts of the extensive Forêt des Bertranges, through which it carves another straight path to **Prémery**, a town of unusually diverse interest. Built in a loop of the Nièvre, in a sheltered dip between wooded hills, you would expect it to be first of all a market town for cattle and farm produce. It is that, yet its most important practical employment comes from a big factory which produces a variety of industrial chemicals. Add to this a history which contributed a mediaeval château for the bishops of Nevers, of which a fine fourteenth-century gateway survives, an early Gothic church, and some venerable houses. The church in particular is worth a visit both for the purity of its architecture and for a notable *Pietà*. The lasting memory, though, is of a self-contained and dignified small town in a delightful setting.

The next two visits could be made in either order, though it is tempting to suggest keeping the more intriguing one to the last. In that case, follow the D38 out of Prémery to **St-Saulge**, where you will find another elegant Gothic church in the middle of the town. Later than the one in Prémery, its nave is not so high, as the vaulting springs directly from a line of short pillars on either side. The east end may have had a Romanesque origin, but later alterations have had an incongruous effect.

The great feature of the church is a range of beautiful stained glass windows all down both side aisles. They date from the sixteenth century and illustrate biblical subjects in glowing colours. The best one of all is the Tree of Jesse in the south aisle, a natural composition with very fresh-looking green leaves; on the outside of each nave pillar is a placard telling you the subject of the window opposite. You may be lucky enough to hear the two mellow and sonorous bells being rung to announce one of the church offices, always well attended by the townsfolk.

The next objective is the tiny village of **Jailly**, deep in the country about three kilometres west of St-Saulge. Have a good look at the map before you set out, and perhaps ask a passer-by to put you on the right road. It has no number, is very narrow, and it takes a winding path through the woods, but it gets there in the end. As you pass through the few houses which make up the village, look over to your left across a small valley, where you will see the tower of Jailly's Romanesque church, almost smothered in trees. An even narrower track will lead you to it, and land you in some surprise outside a majestic Romanesque gateway, standing on its own about thirty yards from the west door of the church.

The reason for this is that it began life as a priory, dependent like so many local ones on the abbey of Cluny. Like others too it lost its own dependencies during the Revolution, and the nave (which looks as if it once extended as far as the gateway) was curtailed to its present length. The effect when you enter is of a large church compressed into a very small compass. A broad flight of modern steps leads up into the nave (the church is set into a sloping hillside) which like its wide side aisles and its pilastered apse is is of the purest Romanesque vintage. The crossing has its proper dome on squinches to support an octagonal belfry, from which two bell ropes hang down and are nonchalantly gathered in the front of the nave. There are carved capitals of twelfth-century character, but confined to natural foliage or simple sculptural patterns, there is a probably Carolingian holy water stoup, the pews are old and well worn, and apart from some dull stained glass and a few religious statues there have been no later intrusions.

For an unbriefed visitor this must be a surprising discovery. What emerges is that the church is well looked after (apart from perhaps inevitable bird droppings in the nave and chancel) but seldom used. One more intriguing thing about it is its dedication, which is to St Silvestre. A natural one in its woodland setting, could it also suggest a pagan origin for the site in honour of Silvanus or even Pan? The church is normally open during the summer, but should it be locked you can fetch the key not from the cottage next door but from the last in a row of farm cottages down the road and off to the right. It needs a double turn to unlock the door.

3

A little further down river is **Pouilly-sur-Loire**, not a town to compare with Nevers or La Charité – in fact little more than a big village. It does however have two great assets. The name itself suggests vineyards, but here we need to be clear about which Pouilly we are talking about. The most famous Pouilly vineyards are in the Mâconnais away to the south, which produce the white wines of Pouilly-Fuissé. Here we are concerned with three other areas producing white wines, of which the most prestigious is Sancerre, where the hill-top town on the west bank of the Loire is surrounded by acres and acres of the Sauvignon Blanc vines. Across the river to the north are the vineyards of Pouilly-Fumé, which produce a wine which some (mistakenly) compare favourably with Sancerre. It is the neighbouring patch to the south, which relies more on the less favoured Chasselas grape, that carries the *appellation* of Pouilly-sur-Loire.

This brings us to the second great asset to the town, the hotel known as Le Relais Fleuri, with its accomplice the restaurant Le Coq Hardi. Here Madame Astruc runs – as she has done for many years – a very tight ship. She oversees everything herself, even the sometimes clumsy parking of her visitors, and everything is done in the tradition of the best French provincial hotels. The attractive low building, with its mature garden and terraces overlooking the Loire, has been well modernized. So has its elegant restaurant, whose emblem is a life-size stuffed cock which has lorded it over the foyer for more than fifty years and seen out three generations of *patron*. A sure test of a restaurant is the support it gets from the neighbourhood, and you cannot make light of a hotel which is taken over entirely – its restaurant and all its rooms – for a Saturday night's wedding festivities. To eat its *soufflé de brochet* or its *goujons frites du Loire* with a bottle of Pouilly-sur-Loire is to appreciate cuisine at its simplest and best.

The Relais Fleuri is not actually in Pouilly itself, but in the long straight avenue which runs parallel to the main road linking Cosne-sur-Loire with La Charité. This allows a quick exit in either direction as well as easy access to the countryside east of the river. Again, a suggested tour could almost as easily be undertaken from La Charité, though perhaps not from Nevers.

You can if you like begin by driving the short distance north to **Cosne-sur-Loire**. This is the second largest town in Nièvre after Nevers, though there was a time when Cosne was good deal more important commercially than the present departmental capital. For one thing it is significantly further down the Loire, which gave it an advantage in trade. Coal had been mined in the Nivernais for centuries, and by the eighteenth century it not only could be shipped profitably down river but also fed the furnaces for its principal heavy industry. The Cosne forges produced military hardware as well as essential parts for shipping – capstans, anchors and the like – and in 1781 they were bought up by Louis XIV. Unfortunately for the seller, the king was a late payer, and he never received his money. By the end of the century the forges were in decline, and the trade passed to Guérigny, a town on the

Nièvre a few miles above Nevers, which was still supplying the French navy in 1970.

The church of **St-Agnan**, not unusually in these parts, was originally part of a Cluniac priory, but all that is left of its Romanesque past is the apse and the western doorway – though the latter is an example of the style at its richest. The most rewarding visit here is to the **Museum**, which you will find close to the river Nohain just before it flows into the Loire. Among the exhibits are relics of the trade which brought wealth to the Loire towns, while as at La Charité an upper floor has a distinguished collection of the work of modern artists. Traffic congestion has not been greatly eased by moving the N7 to bypass the town centre, and again one has to negotiate narrow streets and a complicated one-way system. However there is always a breath of fresh air along the quays, and there is a pleasant retreat at hand in the Auberge à la Ferme on the road to Cours, three kilometres away to the north-east, on the far side of the N7.

Whether you start from here or from Pouilly, there is an interesting expedition you can make in a fairly straight line to the east, with variations possible on the way back. When you duck under the N7 and emerge into field after field of maize or sunflowers, it would be easy to forget that two or three hundred years ago the woods which now appear only fitfully along your route would have stretched almost without a break from the edge of the Loire basin to the banks of the Yonne. Forest clearing by commercial timber extraction is one of today's environmental problems, yet it went on all over Europe until quite recently, and still goes on unchecked in less developed countries of the world.

Back in the present, the first objective would be **Donzy**, an attractive small town with its older part cut in two by the river Nohain. The big château on the hill above cannot be visited, and the Gothic church is hardly worth it, but what you should look for is not in the town itself but in a suburb marked on the map as **Donzy-le-Pré.** This can be difficult to approach from within Donzy itself, as the river always seems to get in the way, but as it lies just to the south of the D33 from Cosne-sur-Loire you can either take it in as you approach Donzy proper or turn back that way from the town centre. The suffix 'Le Pré' turns out to be an abbreviation of 'Le Prieuré', and there on the left of the main road you will see a long stone wall in which is set a Romanesque gateway. Most of the building behind is ruinous, but the gateway itself and its tympanum of the Virgin and Child enthroned in a pillared enclosure has been cleaned and well restored. Work is still going on to restore what would have been the priory church, of which a few pillars with Romanesque capitals are still standing. It will be interesting to see what emerges from this work.

The next stop on your way along the D33 must certainly be the **Château de Menou**. The road has now left the land of maize, and though sunflower crops still fill any open spaces, the woods of the Forêt de Donzy close in on both sides, until you are driving up and down hill through a green tunnel. When you reach the little town of Menou, take the second turning on your right, which leaves the church on your right. There is a formal approach to the château along a tree-lined avenue with a badly laid surface, which lands you in front of an iron gateway with a coat of arms above it. This impresses on you that it was the residence of the dukes of Menou, a title going back to the seventeenth century, but the usual way in to the grounds is through a little gateway on the west side of the château as you come up past the church. It is still a residential château, dating from the seventeenth and eighteenth centuries, still lived in and cared for. It passed to other branches in the female line, the last of which was the Blacas family, who also settled in England at the end of the last century; one of its members married the châtelaine of Lantilly, which we have visited in an earlier chapter. The Blacas sold it in 1987 to the present owners, who have already left their mark on the place. You can visit it only from mid-August to the end of September, in the afternoon, with guided visits which seem to be at irregular times. Each visit lasts thirty to forty minutes, and is well worth waiting for. With this in mind, as you may have arrived much too early, it could be left for the return journey.

The principal rooms range in their *decor* from Louis XIV to Louis XVI, with furniture chosen to suit each period. The most impressive is the 'Chambre du Roi' on the first floor, which Louis XIV occupied on a visit to the château. No attempt has been made to furnish it, but its intricately patterned parquet floor, painted ceiling – and a magnificent *cheminée* – are decorations enough.

The Louis XV dining room is surprisingly intimate, and there is a Victorian *salon* stuffed with objects and portraits of the time. The outbuildings are just as interesting, and their origin as part of a mediaeval *château-fort* are clear. The moat has been concentrated to make an ornamental lake, a thirteenth-century round tower is still a dovecote, there is a beautifully laid-out vegetable garden. and the brick-floored stables are still in use.

The D33 proper now diverges from the main road to Clamecy, and climbs into and through the Forêt d'Arcy to join the N151 five kilometres out of **Varzy**. This was once a fortified town where the bishops of Nevers had a holiday home, and the early Gothic church of St-Pierre has a strikingly elegant triforium. The Treasury to the right of the choir (if you can find someone to open it) contains an odd mixture of reliquaries and one beautiful sixteenth-century Crucifixion in wood. The nearby museum is another apparently random collection which even contains Egyptian sarcophagi and musical instruments from the seventeenth to the nineteenth centuries; the Aubusson tapestry of Queen Zenobia is one of the best things here. The town itself would be a pleasant place to stop for a rest and refreshment.

The road now leads on to Clamecy, but that splendid town will be the centrepiece of our next section. Whether you are returning to Pouilly or to Cosne, it would be easy to call in at Menou on the way, and after Donzy it would also be possible to turn south along the D1 which follows the valley of the Nohain for a final visit to **Suilly-la-Tour**, where there is a spectacular church, and just out of the town to the north a late Renaissance château called Les Granges — presumably because it was later brought into use as farm buildings. The huge church, with its impossibly bulky tower, is a strange mixture of a supposedly Romanesque west doorway, a lofty nave with an exaggerated neo-Gothic east end, and neo-classical Corinthian pillars framing both the doorway and the windows of the bell chamber. The north transept ends in a square fortified tower which rises as high as the roof of the nave. It remains a curiosity rather than a thing of beauty, but that is not true of Les Granges. Not visitable at present, it has an elegant facade with dormer windows, and the turreted *enceinte* which encloses it and its outbuildings must belong to a much earlier date.

4

Now to **Clamecy**, which many people rate the finest town in the Nivernais. For its position it too has to thank the confluence of two important rivers, the Yonne and the Beuvron, perched as it is between the two, with the attendant Canal du Nivernais joining in from the north. Again its streets are narrow and winding, but the *sens unique* works, there is no litter, public services are well conducted, and there seems to be a cheerful spirit abroad.

In the thirteenth century Clamecy made a contribution to history unique in France. The Counts of Nevers had been prominent Crusaders since 1101, when Count William I was involved in some unsuccessful skirmishes after the First Crusade. His son William II joined the Second Crusade after its dramatic send-off by St Bernard at Vézelay, and in 1167 Count William IV led a contingent from the Nivernais to Palestine, only to die of the plague at Acre in 1168. In his will he left one of his properties in Clamecy to the bishops of Bethlehem in perpetuity, a legacy which proved a godsend when the kingdom of Jerusalem fell to Saladin in 1187, for the then Bishop of Bethlehem escaped to Clamecy and continued to style himself as before.

This curious anomaly held good until the Revolution, by which time fifty bishops had been so consecrated, adding to the bishoprics already existing at Autun, Auxerre and Nevers. Although in practice their see extended only over the Hôpital de Panthenor, part of the property bequeathed by William IV, the name of Bethlehem survives in the Pont de Bethléem which crosses the Yonne from the east, and in Notre-Dame-de-Bethléem, a modern church built in 1927. This is not a beautiful building, and it hides the remains of the twelfth-century chapel of the bishop's palace.

Commercially the town began to flourish when in 1547 one of its patrons developed the practice of 'flottage', or the floating of huge rafts of timber down the Yonne to Paris by way of the Seine, which it joins at Montereau. This avoided the slow and costly return of barges up stream, though the method would not have been practicable on the Loire, with its endless sandbanks and constantly changing channels. It continued on the Yonne for more than three hundred years, until transport by barge in both directions on the canals proved more economic. Another use for timber in the Nivernais involved converting it to charcoal, and a factory which did that at Clamecy was still working until 1983.

Clamecy may no longer be a cathedral town, but the **Church of St-Martin**, which stands high above the surrounding roofs, could well be taken for one. You would normally enter the town either by the D977 from the west, crossing the Pont du Beuvron, or on the N151 from the south. In either case if you follow the signs for 'Centre Ville' you should end up in the car-park near the west end of the church.

Inside, its character is overwhelmingly Gothic, and early Gothic at that, though its purity was in part debased by Viollet-le-Duc, who erected a huge stone rood loft to correct the inward bowing of the eastern nave pillars. Sadly this obscures the view of the elegant vaulting beyond, but the chapel at the head of the south aisle displays its lovely Gothic arches and some good early stained glass. It is dedicated to St Roch, who appears in a statue with the wound in his thigh showing – though there is no sign of his dog.

Behind the modern altar here are two carved stone tablets, taken from a sixteenth-century rood screen destroyed in 1773. One is a lively and original view of the Last Supper, where the disciples are contemplating with obvious pleasure a sucking pig on a dish in the middle of the table. St John has keeled over with his head in Jesus's lap. The other panel is an equally vivid Entombment. Above the organ at the west end is a beautiful rose window with some very imaginative designs in modern glass.

The contrast of style outside could not be greater, where the whole tone of the west end is blatantly but magnificently flamboyant. The façade is richly ornamented, even if the statues have disappeared from their niches, and especially in its upper storeys, where elaborate flying buttresses join two absurdly conceived square pinnacles to the main structure round the rose window. Nothing in this vein matches the great tower which rises over the south-west corner of the nave. Of its three main storeys each one is more elaborate than the last, and you may be immediately reminded of the tower of St-Père-sous-Vézelay – though this is on a far bigger scale. Gargoyles stretch their long necks from every corner of the last stage, and the final touch is added by the French *tricouleur* floating triumphantly above it all.

If you like wavy old roofs and half-timbered walls, you will find plenty in the streets round St-Martin. The Syndicat d'Initiative occupies the most heavily timbered of them all, and like the others it must be a genuine mediaeval survival. Yet if you follow the narrow streets eastward from the church, one of which needs a flight of steps to bring it to a lower level, you will come to the welcoming open space of the *place* E. Zola. This is where you will find everyone's first choice for a stay in Clamecy, the Hostellerie de la Poste, a well appointed (though modestly priced) hotel, where the *accueil* and the service can hardly be bettered.

If you choose to stay here for a few days, it will give you the chance of seeing two or three places of interest in the neighbourhood, to reach which would take a long time from a base on the Loire. Before leaving the town, though, you ought to take time off to visit the town's **Museum**, or to give it its full title the 'Romain Rolland Museum of Art and History'. That and the rue Romain Rolland which leads to it remember the name of the man of letters born here in 1866, who wrote so evocatively about the Burgundian countryside.

The museum proper is housed in a *hôtel* once owned by the duc de Bellegarde, a short walk either from St-Martin or from the place Zola. The exhibits are a familiar mixture of finds by local archaeologists, objects connected with the town's history, and a haphazard collection of paintings. The most interesting room is taken up with fascinating illustrations of the process of 'flottage' on the Yonne, while an underground passage leads to others containing the personal belongings of Romain Rolland and editions of his writings.

South of Clamecy there is a cluster of small towns and villages on either side of the Yonne, of which three deserve attention, principally for their churches. Not far down the D34 is **Amazy**, where the Gothic church of Ste-Croix is surprisingly big for such a tiny village. A few original details stand out, in particular at the west end, where a wooden crucifix stands on a long horizontal beam fixed to the wall over the door. All along the beam are carved spears and other instruments of the Passion, and a little angel confronts a death's head under the Cross. Notice there are no capitals, and as you often find locally the vaulting springs directly from pillars decorated only with an impression of palm leaves.

Close by is **Tannay**, a small town set among vineyards which produce a popular white wine. The collegiate church of St-Leger is even bigger; its nave is actually taller than St-Martin's in Clamecy. Again there are no capitals, but the Gothic arches of the nave are exceptionally high. A break in style comes at the crossing, beyond which is a fine Romanesque east end. This is squared off and lit by three windows with a rose window above; the effect of some graceful tracery is spoilt by unworthy nineteenth-century glass. There is no transept, and the two side aisles lead only to chapels at their head. The view westward down the Gothic nave is reassuringly harmonious; Tannay is right to be as proud of its church as it is of its wines.

From Tannay the D165 runs north to meet the busier D985, where a quick right-left turn puts it on course for **Metz-le-Comte**. The church here stands on a low hill to the west of the village, and is a rarity among the minor Romanesque churches of the Nivernais. There is a plain tower offset to the north, with a pitched roof and gable ends, not unlike the one on the village church of St Roch at Uchon, the 'pearl of the Morvan', which we have still to visit. We must suppose that this village, like another further south called Monceau-le-Comte, was built on property owned by the crusading Counts of Nevers.

Here the church is Romanesque throughout in style, though there were a few alterations in the fifteenth century. What strikes you at once, in contrast to the two at Amazy and Tannay, is its unusually low profile; its very low roof is hung with heavy rough tiles reaching almost to the ground on the south side, and there are pigmy buttresses on both sides whose only function is to hold up long wooden gutters. Not surprisingly in such a secluded position the church is normally kept shut, but the key is kept at the Mairie in the village; out of hours you can try the Presbytery in Tannay, but a sensible concession means that you can look eastward through a wire grill at the west end. What you see is a miniature Romanesque gem, with just three bays to the nave and narrow side aisles. The only light which enters the nave (except from where you are standing) is through tiny square windows at the outside ground level. The three windows of the squared-off east end are of a later date.

The other wonderful thing about this place is its position. To the west the ground falls away through extensive vineyards, which unlike those at Tannay grow a black grape – one hopes with as good results in the way of red wine, which you seldom find produced in the Nivernais. The view northward from the graveyard takes in the valley of the Yonne on its way to Auxerre. To the east and south rise the Morvan hills, all the way from Avallon to Autun, where the next chapter begins.

CHAPTER FIFTEEN

From Autun to Paray-le-Monial

Autun is to the south of Burgundy what Auxerre is to the north – both a natural centre and the seat of a powerful bishopric from very early times. The Romans dignified it with the name of their first-century emperor, calling it Augustodunum ('hill-fort of Augustus'); the five syllables were reduced to two by the same telescoping process which reduced Mediolanum to Milan. The map shows main roads radiating from Autun like the legs of a spider; only due west and south are the gradients too steep for them. Westward are the hills of the Morvan; to the south the ground rises abruptly to a wooded spur where in 1945 the first stone was laid of a huge granite cross which overlooks the town – the **Croix de la Libération**, set up to mark the end of German occupation. This emotional ceremony was performed on the ninth of September by Mgr Piguet, bishop of Clermont-Ferrand, on his return from the prison camp of Dachau. Two years later it was consecrated by the Cardinal archbishop of Lyon.

There is no better introduction to Autun than to stand beside the cross and look down from a height of more than 500 metres on the town below. The oldest part (the Gallic *dunum*) was built on a ridge which slopes down gradually northwards to the green water-meadows beside the river Arroux. Through a belt of trees rises the central tower of the cathedral, which you will never see so clearly once you are down among the crowded mediaeval buildings below. To either side you can trace the ramparts, which converge at their most southerly point on the **Tour des Ursulines**, a tall thin tower which is all that is left of the old convent. The road which runs beneath the western ramparts has been renamed the Boulevard des Resistants Fusillés, which tells its own story – more clearly when you realize that it overlooks the approaches to the Morvan, where so much of the Resistance was based. That is a secret country, if ever there was one.

Away beyond the northern limits runs the Arroux, and beyond that you can make out the weird outlines of the so-called **Temple** of **Janus**, a hollow three-sided mass of masonry, twenty-three metres high, now isolated in a green meadow. This misnomer (probably given because its two main walls appear to 'face both ways') dates only from the sixteenth century; it may not be Roman and it was certainly not a temple – more probably a watch-tower, part of the fortifications covering the **Porte d'Arroux** by which the main road from the north enters the town. The gateway is unmistakably Roman, though slighter and less well preserved than the **Porte St-André** to the north-east. That is a lordly monument, built in the classical style, with two high semicircular arches for wheeled traffic flanked by two lower ones for pedestrians. Above the archways an arcaded gallery completes a symmetrical design whose grandeur suits a city named after Augustus. The other legacy of Rome is the **Roman Theatre**, though not much remains of the seating for an enclosure which could hold 15,000 spectators, said to have been the biggest in Gaul. Not easy to locate, it is tucked away in a public open space beyond the army barracks at the end of the Avenue du 2ème Dragons – which is the beginning of the road to Beaune and Dijon.

No matter where you have chosen to spend your nights, your first daytime objective is likely to be the **Cathedral of St-Lazare**, not only for its beauty and architectural importance but because it contains the undisputed work of a major sculptor, perhaps the finest of his age. Its history is well documented. We know from inscriptions preserved in the museum that by the end of the third century Christianity was established at Autun, and in 314 the first bishop, who was called Reticius, took part in the Council of Arles. At the end of the tenth century, in circumstances which remain mysterious, the body of St Lazarus was brought to the city by Bishop Gérard. Yet it was not until the first years of the twelfth century that Bishop Etienne de Bagé, the friend and disciple of Cluny, undertook to enshrine the relic in a building worthy of the veneration it inspired. The ground for this was given to the Chapter by Hugues II, duke of Burgundy and nephew of Pope Calixtus II, who had spent the Christmas of 1119 at Autun.

The new church was dedicated by Pope Innocent II on 28 December 1130. It could hardly have been completed by then; when the records speak of an *ingressus*, the reference is probably to the first bays of the nave and the sculptured portal. In 1195 the

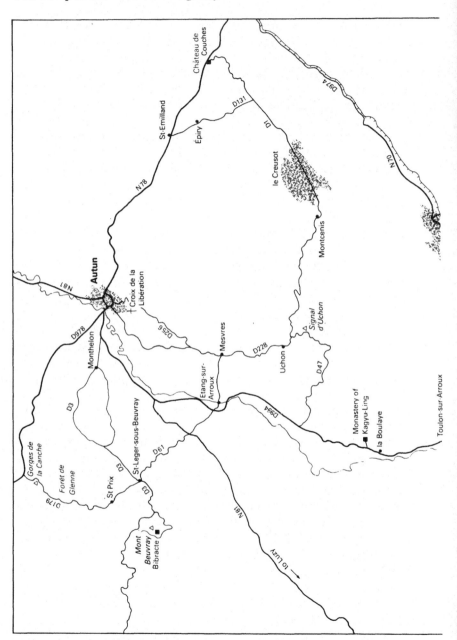

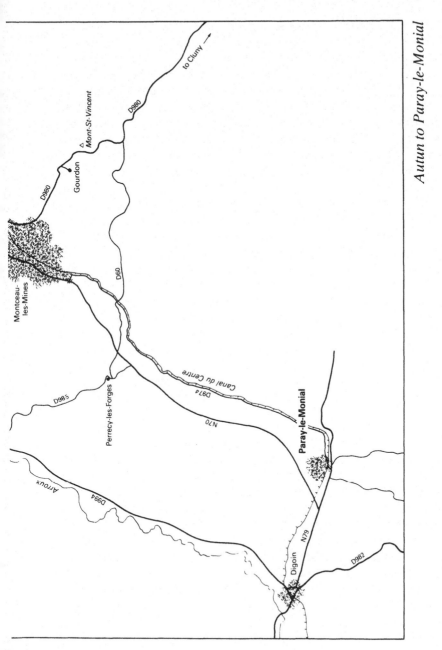

new church supplanted the old basilica of Saint-Nazaire as the cathedral of Autun. In 1469, after the Romanesque tower had been struck by lightning, Cardinal Jean Rolin, the son of the Chancellor and a native of Autun, replaced it with a much bigger structure crowned by an octagonal steeple. At the same time he raised the height of the central apse, substituting an ogival vault for the original half-dome, and the flamboyant chapels were added beside the north aisle. The eighteenth century brought more ruinous alterations, when the tomb of St Lazarus in the sanctuary was dismantled, and the matchless western tympanum of the Last Judgment was – incredibly – plastered over. This did save it from even worse sacrilege at the hands of the revolutionaries, who merely re-dedicated the cathedral first to the Goddess of Reason, then to an anonymous Supreme Being.

In the nineteenth and early twentieth centuries much was done to redeem the damage. The tympanum was cleared of its plaster, and in 1939 the rococo marble columns and panels which had masked the lower courses of the apse were stripped away. Not until 1948 was the head of Christ restored to its proper place in the tympanum, having been severed in the process of plastering, and later relegated to the museum. In 1954 the capitals which had been removed during the restorations were put on display in the Chapter House, where you can study them more carefully than *in situ*; skilful copies now occupy their original positions inside the church.

The immediate effect as you enter the nave, though striking, is not as overwhelming as at Vézelay; rather it grows on you as the harmony of the design and the richness of its detail sink in. The cathedral was planned in 1120 under the influence of Cluny, but whereas the abbatial church of Cluny (which in any case dwarfed it for size) had an ambulatory with radiating chapels the architect of St-Lazare was content with a central apse and a smaller one on either side. The seven bays of the nave are spanned by slightly pointed arches; the barrel vaulting is also slightly pointed, and the pillars are faced with fluted pilasters, rising in four stages to the vaulting. It is easy to see how Cluniac architects could be influenced by Roman buildings close to hand; here we immediately recognize in the lower part of the central apse the pilasters and the semicircular arcading of the Porte St-André.

While the classical influence lends richness to St-Lazare, what will always bring you back to Autun is the work of one supreme artist. To appreciate this, first stand in front of the west portal, under its protective porch, and study the **Tympanum**. This is made up of twenty-nine pieces of hard, whitish limestone, not from any local quarry but similar to what is found near Chalon; it is the treatment rather than the material which rivets the attention. To compare it with the tympanum over the entrance to the nave at Vézelay is unnecessary – both are masterpieces, but differ profoundly in scope and feeling. Whereas at Vézelay you are caught up in the rhythm of the figure of Christ, at Autun the stillness of the pose and the mingling of majesty and mercy in the expression make you catch your breath. The composition of this extraordinary work can be studied at leisure in many fine photographic reproductions, notably in the superb volume *Gislebertus, Sculptor of Autun*, published in 1961 by the late Arnold Fawcus of the Trianon Press in Paris, but some of the details repay study on the spot.

First, the inscription running round the edge of Christ's mandorla reads:

OMNIA DISPONO SOLUS MERITOSQUE CORONO
QUOS SCELUS EXERCET ME IUDICE POENA COERCET

or, in translation:

I alone dispose of all things and crown the just;
those who follow crime I judge and punish

The mandorla is supported by the fluid figures of two angels who face away from it. To the left the Virgin enthroned in heaven looks down on the brilliantly composed group of apostles. St Peter is prominent with an enormous key as he assists a child on its way to heaven, while on the extreme left of the upper register an angel sounds the trump which announces the Last Judgment. To the right two other seated figures, probably Enoch and Elijah (who took the short cut to heaven while still alive) look down on a vivid scene where St Michael is weighing souls in a balance – one is already floating heavenwards. Facing the archangel is the Devil, a gruesome figure supported by all the horrible bestiary and symbolic menace he commands, while undeterred in the lower corner another angel sounds his trump.

Below the feet of Christ, stretching right across the semicircle, is a narrow band of stone which carries the most significant of the inscriptions. It is divided into two parts, of which the left-hand sequence reads:

> QUISQUE RESURGIT ITA QUEM NON TRAHIT IMPIA VITA
> ET LUCEBIT EI SINE FINE LUCERNA DIEI

or:

> Thus shall rise again everyone who does not lead an impious life, and endless light of day shall shine for him

Beneath this section are grouped the figures of the elect, among them a trio of ecclesiastics, two pilgrims with staff and scrip, and three children escorted by an angel. To the right the inscription continues:

> TERREAT HIC TERROR QUOS TERREUS ALLIGAT ERROR
> NAM FORE SIC VERUM NOTAT HIC HORROR SPECIERUM

or:

> Here let fear strike those whom earthly error binds, for their fate is shown by the horror of these figures

and beneath it an angel has kept apart the bodies of the damned – all naked, among them a miser with his bag of money, a drunkard with his barrel of wine, an adulteress with a pair of snakes biting her breasts, and a head gripped by a pair of diabolic pincers.

Most significant of all for us today are the three words carved immediately beneath the feet of Christ and above the sentinel angel, separating the two parts of the inscription:

> GISLEBERTUS HOC FECIT

This is the only occasion where the sculptor of a major mediaeval religious work has been allowed to proclaim his identity, which in itself says much for the reputation he enjoyed in his own day.

In the vernacular he would have been known as Gislebert (as in Dagobert and Ethelbert, both men of royal status), and today he would be called Gilbert, yet but for his name we know nothing of

THE CATHEDRAL OF
ST LAZARE AT AUTUN

1 & 2. Simon Magnus falls, head foremost
3. The stoning of St Stephen
4. Samson pulls down the temple
5. Noah prepares to load the ark
6. C16th doorway to the sacristy
7. Entrance to the salle capitulaire
8. The relics of St Lazare are preserved under
   the High Altar
9. Jesus appears to St Mary Magdalen
10. The second temptation of Jesus
11. C16th window of the Tree of Jesse
12. Painting by Ingres representing the
   martyrdom of St Symphorien at the Porte
   St André
13. The Nativity
14. Tympanum

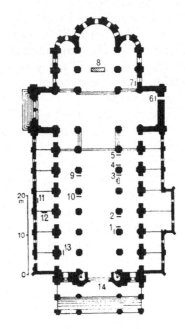

him directly. Only by detecting and comparing work of a similar quality, whether in other parts of St-Lazare, or in St-Andoche at Saulieu, or even in the Madeleine at Vézelay, can we trace his influence on the art of the twelfth century. The surprise is that whereas in the other cases there is clear evidence of different hands at work – some of them likely to have been pupils of Gislebert – here at St-Lazare it is accepted that one man was responsible for nearly all its decorative carving; this is true not only of the tympanum but of most of the historiated capitals of the nave, choir and apse. The whole task is estimated to have taken him ten years to complete – most probably from 1125 to 1135 – and whoever commissioned him has earned the gratitude of the civilized world.

The technique which produces such mastery of style and form is matched by the imagination which can instil such drama into the composition. Observe the emotion of the figure which emerges from the sarcophagus, high to the left; the compassion on the face of St Peter, and the Devil's intensity of malice. Central to all is the serene and majestic figure of Christ, 'Disposer supreme and Judge of the earth'. The tympanum of St-Lazare is not only a masterpiece of sculpture; it will tell you a great deal of how the men of the Middle Ages behaved in this world, and of what they believed about the next.

The two semicircular bands which surround the tympanum to complete the arch are more conventional in design, though still faultless in execution. The outer ring, like the inner one at Vézelay, carries medallions which alternate the labours of the months with the signs of the Zodiac, while the inner one has an undulating motif of foliage and fruit.

Next it is best to look at the **Capitals** which have been removed to the Chapter House area south of the choir, and are among the finest carved by Gislebert. They were placed originally near the high altar, on the north side of the choir. Four of them describe the infancy of Christ, and two of these are outstanding even in this company. The best known is the one showing *The Magi asleep and the Angel awakening them*. Three crowned heads share the same pillow and the same rich counterpane. One of them has his eyes open and his arm resting on the coverlet; the angel has touched his little finger, while the other two – one is bearded – are sleeping peacefully. The angel's left hand points to the star shining above their heads. *The Flight into Egypt* is no less remarkable. The Virgin, staring into space, is contemplating a mystery greater than this hurried exodus, and the Child with his hand on an orb looks out over the world he is presently to redeem. St Joseph trudges forward, the bridle of the donkey in one hand, a stick over his other shoulder.

Also in this collection is a capital which celebrates *The Presentation of the Church*, probably by Duke Hugues II to Etienne de Bagé, and the highly dramatic *Death of Cain*. Taking his cue from the text 'and the Lord set a mark upon Cain, lest any finding him should kill him', the sculptor has put horns upon the head of the first murderer. Lamech, mistaking him for a wild animal, launches an arrow while his son Tubalcain guides his left arm. Observe the contrast between the hunter's smile of satisfaction and the anguish on the face of Cain. Here too is the original of the frightening

Hanging of Judas, of which there is a copy in its former position in the choir.

As for the capitals, or their copies, which remain in the apse, the choir and the nave, you will find a key to them in the antechamber off the south aisle of the choir, below the stairs which lead to the *salle capitulaire*. They can all be sought out and studied, though some are difficult to make out in a dark corner, and many are hard to interpret. Two of them illustrate the dramatic feeling which Gislebert could evoke. One is the tender *Appearance of Christ to Mary Magdalene*, which has its parallel in St-Andoche at Saulieu; the other is *The Fall of Simon Magus*, in which two apostles on the left watch with awe as the magician dives headlong to the ground, horror in his face, a protruding tongue and a sagging lower jaw. On the right a horned devil squats and gloats.

What we can no longer see, even in a reconstruction, is the sculpture of the north doorway, once the principal entry to the church through the north transept. Only the columns at either side, with their capitals, and one thin arch carved with foliage remain *in situ*. Four fragments from the tympanum and one from the lintel are preserved in the **Musée Rolin**, which faces the road on a corner site only a few yards from the west end of the cathedral. It occupies a wing of the house built for Chancellor Rolin in the fifteenth century, and the whole of the nineteenth-century Hôtel Lacomme which replaced the rest of it.

The two parts of the museum are entered separately from the courtyard. On the ground floor of the Hôtel Lacomme are seven rooms given up to Gallo-Roman antiquities; notably a little three-horned bull on a stone altar; a bronze Roman parade helmet; a third-century sarcophagus with a carving of a boar hunt; wrestlers, gladiators and acrobats; jewels and brooches which illustrate the fashions of the time.

Nothing here compares with what you see on the ground floor of the Hôtel Rolin, for here is the one fragment rescued fortuitously from the lintel of the north doorway of St-Lazare, and the greatest of all the individual works of Gislebertus. Originally it seems that the whole lintel was taken up by a scene of the temptation in the Garden of Eden, Adam to the left, Eve to the right, with the serpent lurking behind her. It is **Eve** who has survived, discovered during demolitions in 1856, built into the wall of an eighteenth-century house and broken into two parts. She lies on her side, naked, her lower body masked only by foliage. Propped on her right elbow she whispers behind her to her left, while her left hand slyly plucks an apple from the tree. The head, arms, breasts and legs are carved virtually in the round, and the expression of tremulous sensuality leaves no doubt of the kind of temptation to which she has succumbed – or which she is attempting. So wonderful is this fragment that one forgets it is just part of a work whose sublety and beauty we can only glimpse, quite outside the experience of the twelfth-century beholder and unique in mediaeval sculpture.

Other fragments and capitals from the north doorway include a remarkable *Assumption*, where Mary is being helped from a well furnished tomb by two angels, and some graphic scenes involving Lazarus and Dives. There are also the surviving figures from the tomb of St Lazare, removed from the sanctuary and broken up by eighteenth-century 'improvers' – as iconoclastic in their way as the revolutionaries.

Paintings on the first floor of the museum include the famous *Nativity* by the Maître de Moulins, where Cardinal Rolin figures as donor, and the equally fine polychrome statue known as the *Vierge d'Autun*. There is a lovely painting on wood, dated 1505, where the risen Christ is with Mary Magdalene in the centre, the empty tomb to the left, and on the right Christ is seen with the disciples on the way to Emmaus. Representative of later periods are a fascinating portrait of the Abbé Lamennais by Paulin Guérin, where the eyes of this disturbing man seem to follow you as you move round the room, and some good examples of the impressionist work of Louis Charlot (1878-1951). You should be warned that from October to March the museum closes at 1600, and does not open on Tuesdays.

2

If you are prepared to stay in Autun a little longer (and who would dissuade you?) you can spend a less demanding day out in the Morvan, a part of Burgundy we last saw in the neighbourhood of

Avallon. You should in any case not miss an opportunity to go in that direction from Autun, and if you leave town by the N73, forking right at la Guingette, you will quickly come to the village of **Monthelon**. There a lane skirts a low-lying meadow by the river Selle to reach the 'château' where Jeanne de Chantal lived with her unpleasing father-in-law from 1602 to 1609, and often received St François de Sales. The inverted commas indicate the homely nature of a building distinguished only by a single pepper-pot turret from the farm of which it is now a part.

A short flight of steps leads to a double doorway over which a stone plaque carries the Chantal coat of arms and the motto VIRE-SCIT VULNERE VIRTUS ('Courage is renewed by suffering'). The great charm of the place is enhanced by a wooden-pillared balcony just beneath the eaves. There has been no attempt to smarten it up, and there is no organization for visits. The little stream behind is alive with ducks, and the farm buildings to the left complete a delightfully natural scene.

However pleasant, this would not be your main objective of the day. If you follow the D296 westward you will soon come to the boundary of the Parc Régional du Morvan. Carry on past the ruins of the château de Vauteau, and then by the D3 to St-Léger-sous-Beuvray. Still on the now upgraded D3, after three-and-a-half kilometres you can embark on a long loop to the left which climbs to the summit of Mont-Beuvray. This was in fact the Gallic *oppidum* of **Bibracte**, the capital of the Aedui which Julius Caesar captured in 52BC. Although the site has been known for a long time – it was an archaeologist of Autun called Bulliot who suspected in 1859 that remains might be found there – methodical excavations started only in 1985.

There has not been much progress yet, but the ramparts which enclose a huge area of pine woods can be traced for most of their five-kilometre circuit. More use has been made of the woodland glades by the naturalists, who have put up informative boards to illustrate the range of fauna, flora and lepidoptera which have taken over from the Gauls. It makes a lovely place to walk in, and except perhaps at weekends you can enjoy a great deal of peace – and even make a few archaeological discoveries yourself. One curiosity in a far corner near the road is the little chapel of St-Martin, a saint who visited the place in the year 376. It was built only in 1876, but it is on the site of a Gallo-Roman temple to the nature goddess of Bibracte.

You are now on the boundary between Saône-et-Loire and Nièvre, and in the heart of the Morvan. If you decide to return to Autun there is a choice of routes from St-Leger. The one most scenically rewarding follows the D179 through country typical of the region. After passing St Prix you enter the Forêt de Glenne; then by way of the Gorges de la Canche you will strike the main D978 about eighteen kilometres from Autun. Almost as attractive a way is by the D61 to Étang-sur-Arroux and Mesvres, and home by the winding tree-lined D256. This will give you another chance to turn aside and stand by the Croix de la Libération to contemplate the town below.

Whichever way you have returned to Autun, when you finally leave it you should take the southerly exit by the D256 to Mesvres, and then an outstandingly lovely road which climbs to the tiny village of Uchon, just below the Signal d'Uchon, at 680 metres an eastern outpost of the Morvan. The slopes around are full of curious rock formations, with names like 'le crapaud', 'l'escargot', 'la griffe du diable' and 'la pierre qui croule'. *Crouler* means to totter, but this huge granite boulder has been stable since 1872. Neither these oddities nor the superb view over the valley of the Arroux complete the attractions of Uchon, sometimes not unjustifiably called 'la perle du Morvan'. Just on the outskirts, to the right of the final climb to the village, is a little sixteenth-century oratory. Firmly perched on a rock base, with a stone-tiled cap, it has empty niches for saints, though the figure of the Virgin is modern . Then without delay you should make for the **Church of St-Roch** (formerly St-Sebastien) which stands as it was built in 1347 by Jeanne de Navarre, the daughter of Louis le Hutin and Marguerite de Bourgogne. Its simple tower, which has a little pitched roof with gables to north and south, disguises the importance of the church — especially when it was a centre of pilgrimage to St Roch after the plagues of 1502 and 1652. Built on to an earlier one of the twelfth century, it preserves a Romanesque nave and one or two other legacies of the period, such as the cross above the main altar and the font which serves as a *porte-cièrges*, and if you poke around this fascinating little building you will find all sorts of treasures from later times.

In its twelfth-century state (as St-Sebastien) this was the chapel of the feudal château of the seigneurs of Uchon, who came at different times from the houses of Châteauvillain, la Trémoille and the comtes de Chalon. The remains of the château are still there among the trees on the opposite side of the road. The ground plan of the keep has been excavated, and there are ruins of a tower on the west side, but the most interesting development is that the ground to the north has been levelled to make a stage, and a flight of ceremonial steps adapted to form an auditorium. This was the work of M. Truchot, who lives in a nice old house below the church – just past a more elegant one which used to belong to Louis Charlot, the painter whose work we saw in the Musée Rolin. If you need any more information, or have difficulty in getting into the church, apply to M. Truchot.

You may be tempted to linger in this delectable country, and one would be loath to recommend such an immediate contrast as a visit to **le Creusot**. It would be wrong, however, to ignore it altogether while you are in the neighbourhood. It lies about thirty kilometres south of Autun, at the head of a 'bassin industriel' whose development was due first to its natural resources; coal was discovered in the early sixteenth century and was used to fire the steel furnaces bought in 1836 by the Schneider brothers for two million francs. After the Canal du Centre, which links the Saône to the Loire, was opened for navigation their trade expanded, and they began to build steam locomotives and engines for ships. In 1841 one of their engineers invented the steam hammer, which enabled the foundry to expand still more. In spite of damaging bombardments by the Allies in 1942, and by the Germans in 1944, the Schneider factories were employing over 10,000 people by the 1970s – though world recession in the steel market since then has reduced the number considerably. If you decide to brave this industrial scene, your reward could be a visit to the **Château des Verrières**, which takes its name from the glass factory transferred from Sèvres in 1787 to manufacture crystal for Marie Antoinette. The two conical furnaces stand in front of the château, one converted to a theatre in the eighteenth-century style, the other used occasionally for exhibitions.

You will probably prefer for the present to stay in the country for your journey south from Uchon, for which you need to make your way across to the D994 by way of la Tagnière, itself a still beautiful drive. Just north of la Boulaye on the main road a track to your left leads to the château of **Plaige**, as it is marked on the map. What the map does not tell us is that this unremarkable eighteenth-century building is the headquarters of the Tibetan Buddhist monastery of **Kagyu-Ling**. It was founded in 1974 and attracts large numbers of bemused Burgundian visitors on Thursdays and at weekends during most of the summer. For them the central attraction is a garish multi-coloured temple which contains an enormous enthroned Buddha. Prayer flags flutter on poles beside the paths, and you should not overlook the real purpose of this foundation – indoctrination, meditation and prayer.

After only a few minutes drive further on you will be back in the early Romanesque world at **Toulon-sur-Arroux**, where the late eleventh-century church of St John the Baptist has been beautifully restored after a century of neglect. A local association of 'les amis du Dardon' negotiated to buy it for one franc from a variety of owners who had inherited the property. For sixty years, from 1884 to 1924, it had been used as a warehouse by a wine merchant, then almost abandoned and allowed to decay. What has now been revealed is a church which is not only an exceptional example of early Romanesque but one of two in Burgundy which combine principles of architecture associated with both Cluny and Vézelay.

Once inside you will register a nave elevation of three storeys, each purely Romanesque, with a false triforium of two blind arches surmounted by a single deep embrasure for a lancet window. Then if you look upwards you will see that the vaulting of both nave and side aisles is groined, whereas in the usual three-storey elevation derived from Cluny the nave has a barrel vault, and only the side aisles are groined. Another touch which follows the Cistercian rather than the Cluniac practice is that the rounded pilasters which support the transverse arches end several feet above the ground. Details like these will fascinate the *cognoscenti*, but the ordinary visitor will treasure the chance to see such a lovely example of a Romanesque interior, uncluttered and almost unaltered . Only the original *cul-de-four* of the apse has gone, replaced by a flat end wall with two tall narrow lancets. Outside, things have changed, for the west front was too far gone to restore, and the big entrance doorway is a modern replacement.

The enthusiasm with which 'les amis' have pursued the restoration was shown on Sunday 20 September 1987, when a new cock was hoisted to the top of the old fortified watch-tower above the choir during a cheerful inauguration party. The old bird was found to be riddled with bullet holes.

To find the church whose architecture is most closely associated with this one, we need to go to Gourdon, but as that is some distance away on the far side of Montceau-les-Mines we can delay a visit there and go further south in the direction of Paray-le-Monial. At **Perrecy-les-Forges** the church of St-Pierre and St-Benoît has elements which remind us of the great abbey churches of the north, yet look forward to the smaller priories and parish churches of the Brionnais which we shall be coming to presently. It is all that remains of the priory founded in 840 by the heirs of Childebrand, brother of Charles Martel, with the blessing of Louis le Débonnaire. It was important both as a dependency of the abbey of St-Benoît-sur-Loire and by virtue of its position on one of the main north-south routes connecting Lyon with Autun and on through Auxerre to Paris and Boulogne.

The church we see now was built between 1020 and 1030; the north transept was rebuilt and strengthened in 1095, and about 1125 the great western porch was added to accommodate the increasing numbers of visiting pilgrims. Six prosperous centuries and fifty-nine priors followed each other, until in the eighteenth century a Jansenist aberration by Prior Louis Berrier led to its decay and eventual suppression in 1776 by Louis XVI. The forges of Perrecy were set up by the monks in 1634, using water power from the Oudrache, and produced special ammunition for the French navy.

The almost Cistercian plainness of the façade and outer walls disguises an original and intriguing interior. First though there is this splendid porch, which extends across the three doorways of the western façade, and for two unequal bays at right-angles to north and south. It has two storeys, but unlike the narthex at Vézelay it has an empty space behind it, surrounded by a tribune on four sides. The vaulting over the three front bays is supported by pillars with decorated capitals. Most of them carry only foliage, but one to the right of the northern bay shows a pair of elephants with hooves like a deer's and tusks like those of a boar. Clearly the artist had never seen such an animal outside the pages of a mediaeval manuscript; those who have been in the church of St-Peter at Aulnay in Aquitaine may remember that the sculptor of a similar work thought it necessary to add the information below: HI SUNT ELEPHANTI. More typical of southern Burgundy are the two symbolic representations of lust – a woman with her breasts attacked by snakes, and a mermaid, or *sirène-poisson*, with her twin tails held apart.

The space above the actual portal allows a good view of its tympanum, which may be our first sight of the small-scale decorative carving which distinguishes so many of the little churches of the Brionnais. There are no large groups of symbolic figures, no sculptured dramas involving heaven and hell. Christ sits alone in his mandorla, his right hand raised in blessing, while just two angels of the higher order of Seraphim – notice their three pairs of elegant pointed wings – support the mandorla. The lintel, a favourite opportunity for native Brionnais sculpture, has a closely packed sequence of figures who enact scenes from the Passion. Offstage, as it were, to the left of the lintel proper, the disciples sleep in the Garden of Gethsemane. Then as the newly awakened group advances from the left, naïvely carved with overlarge heads and a row of bare toes beneath their loosely draped garments, Judas greets his master with a kiss. In the centre Jesus is arrested, to the right Peter raises his sword in futile resistance, and Jesus appears before the High Priest.

The nave (which has no vaulting, only a wooden roof shaped like a half barrel) surprises the eye by its lightness and subtlety of design. The light comes first, as is natural, from the high windows over the south aisle, but more streams in from the unusual lantern-like crossing, enclosed by four Romanesque arches which carry pairs of smaller arches above them. The lantern is so tall that there is room for three more windows below the cupola, so that light converges from all directions upon the choir. More still comes in from the tall Gothic windows of the apse, where the glass is modern, with light blue tones predominating. The north aisle has gone, dismantled in the fifteenth century, leaving a blank wall on that side below a line of Gothic windows.

The bell tower over the northern bay of the porch is a forerunner of towers we shall see in the Brionnais. Here there are two storeys above roof level, with three richly mounted Romanesque arches on each side, three levels of *corniche bourgignonne*, and blind arcading below. An imaginative recent touch has been to plant the area once occupied by the cloister with flower beds, low bushes and grass.

Now is your chance to pass south of Monceau-les-Mines to look at the church of the Assumption at **Gourdon**, and that is a chance not to miss. Unlike its sister church at Toulon-sur-Arroux, it is the only one in a tiny village, perched on a granite spur above the D980. For many years it suffered from the same neglect, but a programme begun in 1988 and completed in 1992 has transformed the interior, and the church now revealed is in many respects even finer.

Its origins were more distinguished, for we know that Gregory of Tours visited a monastery here in 570, and in 1845 a farmer working a few hundred yards from the church unearthed a gold chalice encrusted with garnets and turquoises, and a lovely little rectangular paten, or communion dish, with a central cross also glowing with garnets. These relics, known as the **Trésor de Gourdon**, are now in the Bibliothèque Nationale in Paris, but there are treasures of another kind to relish here.

The post-monastic history of Gourdon is obscure, but the present church dates from the early twelfth century, when it was part of a Cluniac priory. The stone is of a warmer tone of granite than that at Toulon, and it shows off to great advantage the same rare combination of groined vaulting and a three-storey elevation in the nave. The blind triforium continues here round the west end above the entrance, and the central apse with its two absidioles have all been restored in their original Romanesque form.

The joy here is that you can now see clearly a lovely fresco of Christ in Majesty, supported by winged creatures representing the four evangelists. Other fascinating frescos have been brought to light in the choir, most of them executed in the same reddish-brown ochre. An exception is to be found at the base of a wall to the left of the altar, where the head and forelegs of an elephant in grey-blue tones can be made out – one of a group of now indistinct sketches of wild life, including a stag and a whale. Some of the pillar capitals show a lively Burgundian treatment of sin and its punishment. In an unusual architectural arrangement there are diagonal 'squint' holes which give a view of the altar from the side chapels.

The interest at Gourdon is not confined to the church. Do not leave the village without seeking out Marc Lachaize, an artist extraordinary both in the field of modern sculpture and in one he has made his own – and he has even invented a word to describe it. He calls it 'Luminoxygraphie', an elaborate process whereby intricate designs are etched on to steel and then polished to brilliant effect. He will show you examples of his work in his *atelier*, a hundred yards from the west end of the church, while round about stand blocks of light-coloured stone carved with allegories from the natural world. 'C'est un original', as his countrymen acknowledge as far away as Paris, where he is a member of the Maison des Artistes. Finally if you need refreshments, or even a bed for the night, there is a cosy little *auberge* at hand, with a garden and terrace looking south towards Cluny and the Maconnais.

A few kilometres down the road you will see on your left the wooded heights of **Mont-St-Vincent**. There are two approach roads, so if you miss one you can take the next, and both of them climb steeply to a plateau which conceals a surprisingly large and populous village. Two structures compete for attention, a modern meteorogical station and the twelfth-century priory church of St-Vincent. Its unusually long nave ends in a western 'pilgrimage' porch with two big rooms above. Much-needed cleaning and restoration is in progress, and should reveal another fine Romanesque interior. The four pillars of the crossing are massive, and ought surely to have been enough to support the tower, which nevertheless collapsed early on and has never been rebuilt; only the regulation dome on squinches remains. Here too there are wonderful views, this time eastward from a grassy terrace below the apse – just the place for a picnic.

3

To reach **Paray-le-Monial** from here the most interesting way is to return by the D60 past the little airfield south of Montceau to the banks of the Canal du Centre. Having crossed that you can follow its west bank all the way down to the point where it joins the N79 from Charolles. It is important to take this main road into Paray, because only then will you have the chance of catching the first wonderful view of the **Basilique du Sacré-Cœur** from the bridge over the Bourbince, perhaps lit by the evening sun and reflected in the still water.

The domain on which it stands was offered towards the end of the tenth century to St Mayeul, abbot of Cluny, by the comte de Chalon on the advice of his son Hugues, bishop of Auxerre – the great-uncle of St Hugues de Semur who ruled Cluny as abbot for sixty years. The first church built on the site was consecrated in 1004. Nearly a century later a very much larger one was begun on plans inspired by St Hugues himself, and with the *abbatiale* at Cluny already under construction it was natural that it should follow closely the Cluniac model. Its design and elevation are very similar, the chief difference being the shortness of the nave – only three bays at Paray – though this happily enhances the height. The church was in fact a good deal too big for its original community of twenty-five monks, but St Hugues would always build for size as well as for splendour. Its survival has proved crucial to architectural studies after the ruin of Cluny.

The narthex was probably built before the main edifice, though not as early as was once believed, and it has been rather clumsily restored. Two square towers of different design rise directly over its wings, of which the one to the south is simpler and more directly appealing, though the richness of the northern one fits in better with the big two-storeyed octagon over the crossing. Once inside the nave you will see at once that architects from Cluny have been at work, or at least practitioners from the same school. There is more variety, and so a greater lightness, in the way the three stages of the elevation have been built up than we find in what remains of Cluny; great variety too in the decoration to be seen round the inner surfaces of the arches of nave, ambulatory and apse. Although exactly the same three storeys continue all round the nave and both arms of the transept, the effect is never tedious. The ambulatory, with its semicircle of tall slender columns (it has been called the angels' lobby), adds to the lightness – the architectural lightness, that is.

The literal lightness, the pervasive 'lumière' of the basilica, is achieved by the masterly arrangement of the light-inducing windows themselves. The upper windows of the nave, transept and choir form an unbroken chain, while from behind the ambulatory two more rows flood the sanctuary with yet more light. You can study the fenestration just as well from the outside, where it forms part of an architectural rhythm mounting from the apsidal chapels to the central octagonal tower (which was restored in 1860). It is good to report that a recent programme of cleaning has not only brought more daylight still from all these sources but has restored a true golden colour to the outer stonework. There is some good modern glass – brilliant in design and colour – in the high windows of the south transept, but some banal earlier examples at the west end. The fifteenth-century fresco of Christ in Majesty was discovered and renewed in 1935.

There are only two or three capitals inside the church carved with anything but formal designs, and they are unexceptional. On the other hand the theme of decorative bands round the archivolts is taken up even more richly in the doorways leading to the two transepts. In particular the south doorway, with its exotically carved pillars and archivolts, suggests an eastern or Moorish influence; we are reminded that St Hugues paid two visits to Spain, in 1072 and 1080, at the time he may have been planning the basilica at Paray. He was evidently inspired by the Moslem virtuosity in design, allied to pure form; the human shape is ignored in the decoration of both these doorways.

The pilgrims who in the Middle Ages would have congregated in the narthex of the basilica now converge in greater numbers on the **Chapel of the Visitation**, which next to Lourdes is the most popular centre of pilgrimage in France. It celebrates the life of Ste Marguerite-Marie Alacoque (1647-90) who was born in the diocese of Autun and educated in a convent at Charolles. Paralysed at ten, and unable to walk for four years, she entered the convent of the Visitation at Paray in 1671. Expressing a wish to be a candle burning itself out before God, she was at once energetic and visionary. She had a series of revelations in which Christ appeared to her in person, and this convinced even Louis XIV of her mission to establish a new cult of the Sacré-Cœur. In the quarrel between orthodox Catholicism (as expounded by the Jesuits) and the new Jansenist movement, its emotional revelations proved more popular than the moral and intellectual scruples of Pascal, and helped to decide many an issue. The convent was confiscated at the Revolution, but the sisters refused to give up the body of Marguerite-Marie; her coffin was sealed on orders from the mayor of Paray, and they were allowed to return. She was beatified in 1864 and canonized in 1930. The crowded chapel, whose services are held almost continuously for pilgrims, is bright but not beautiful. The saint's body is preserved in a gilt and silver shrine within the *Sanctuaire des Apparitions*, an extension of the chapel – where silence is strictly enjoined on all visitors.

The shrine and the conventual quarters can be found in the rue Visitation, which runs northward from near the east end of the basilica. On the feast of the Sacré-Cœur and the anniversary of the saint's death (17 October) the sisters open their gardens to the public. At other times the **Parc des Chapelains** (entrance is near the south-east corner of the *chevet*) has plenty of space for the crowds, accommodation for pilgrims, and even a diorama to illustrate the life of Marguerite-Marie Alacoque.

In the northern part of the town, at the western end of the rue de la Paix, stands the square sixteenth-century **Tower of St Nicholas**. The church to which it belonged is disaffected, and the tower is used for conferences and exhibitions. Close by is the Hôtel-de-Ville, with a gorgeous Renaissance façade, built in 1525 by a rich draper called Pierre Jaillet.

At the very far, or eastern, end of the rue de la Paix, conveniently placed for exit or entry by the D248, is the **Musée du Hieron**, which is open at the usual hours between the middle of May and the end of September – unless, as often seems to happen, it is closed for alterations or repairs. It shows paintings of the Italian, French and Flemish schools from the sixteenth to the eighteenth centuries, with a few Florentine primitives, but the chief Burgundian attraction is a marvellous twelfth-century **Tympanum**. This was carved for one of the priory gateways at Anzy-le-Duc in the Brionnais, and saved from destruction during the Revolution. If, as seems certain, there was an original school of sculpture at Anzy-le-Duc, this is an example of its work at its most exciting and refined.

There remains the question of where to stay in Paray-le-Monial, for you will need to spend at least two nights here – more if you use it as a base for further exploration. While there are no large or prestigious hotels, you will find both comfort and good food at Les Trois Pigeons, near the Place Lamartine and the Tour St-Nicolas, especially if the son of the house continues as its chef and is not tempted elsewhere. Do not attempt to stay anywhere in Paray during its two principal festivals – 17 October and the third Sunday in June.

CHAPTER SIXTEEN

Through the Brionnais to Charlieu

The Brionnais will always be a favourite with those who have penetrated this quiet green land. The smallest of the *régions* of France, it is sandwiched between the middle reaches of the Loire and the richer pastures of the Charollais, and through it wander little streams on their way to join the Loire. The roads meander too, connecting the old farms which still pursue the only industry the Brionnais knows – the rearing and tending of the white Charollais cattle.

This is a different world from the plateaux and alluvial valleys of the north, with their acres and acres of arable land, sown in season with maize, sunflowers and the bright yellow patchwork of rape; different too from the regimented vineyards of the Mâconnais and the Beaujolais away to the east. Nor will you find big herds of cattle grazing on horizonless pastures – just family parties of clean white cows and their offspring, grazing or ruminating in sloping meadows above streams too small to be named on the map.

The people here have found their own word for the newly-born calves which in spring lie on the bright new grass to rest their wobbly legs. They call them *marguerites*, and in a land of flowers they assort well with the cowslips, orchids and milkmaids under the hedgerows – which are themselves sprouting blackthorn and wild cherries. Each farm is independent, a family inheritance, and few have more than two dozen cattle in their herds. If this is the inefficient French farming scorned by the wheat barons of East Anglia, then long may it survive with the help of government subsidies. As it is, a few months' old Charollais calf will fetch a good price in Marcigny, Charlieu or la Clayette – when the soft-hearted farmer's wife can bear to separate him from his mother.

There are few regular villages, but in any of them you are likely to find a Romanesque church built perhaps eight centuries ago by local craftsmen in the local warm-coloured stone, preserved as

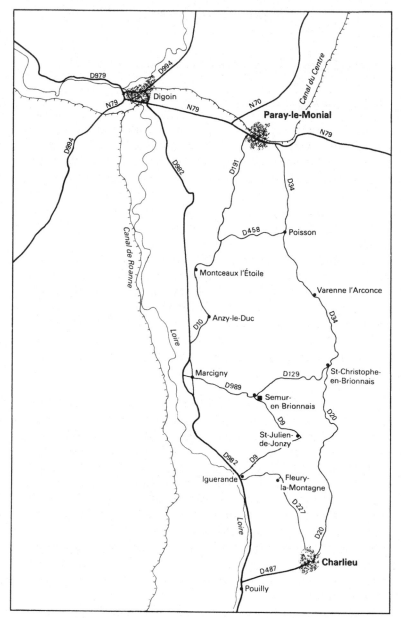

Brionnais to Charlieu

faithfully as possible and in many cases restored to beauty by local initiative and labour. The tourist authorities of Saône-et-Loire have mapped out and signposted a route they call the *Circuit des Églises Romanes*, but it would be a pity to try to cover them all in a day; this guide at least was content to wander round them at will.

From Paray-le-Monial the main road south is the D34 to Charlieu, and if you turn right at the improbably named village of Poisson (a case of *poisson d'avril*, perhaps) you will soon get the flavour of the Brionnais. Eventually, after about eight kilometres and much wandering, you reach **Montceaux-l'Étoile**, where you will appreciate what we said about the tympanum at Perrecy-les-Forges. This one is Brionnais sculpture at its most charming. Two angels support a mandorla in which a triumphant Christ stands erect; their graceful attitudes recall the tympanum from Anzy-le-Duc which is preserved in the museum at Paray. Christ is holding high the Cross which marks both his suffering and his victory over death, saluted from below by the two groups of apostles who surround the Virgin Mary. (St Peter's key is almost exactly the same size as himself.) Only one of the softly moulded archivolts carries any decoration, and the economy of the whole design is a wonderful example of *multum in parvo*. The interior is equally simple, just a single barrel-vaulted nave, with one bay carrying the support for a cupola, and a cul-de-four in the apse.

Neither the flowering of an architectural style nor the impulse to build churches can happen without motivation from some common source. The drive which produced in the early eleventh century the white harvest of Romanesque churches throughout Burgundy came initially from Cluny. Thereafter it was the bishops and abbots of the local cathedrals and monasteries – most of them cultivated and travelled men – who set aside land and money for building smaller priories and parish churches. Often an abbot was appointed from an old seigneurial family, which introduced another source of land for building. Where the technique and the artistic feeling came from to produce such simple masterpieces among village churches, that is harder to say. They did have the perfect material to hand in the soft yet durable gold-tinged sandstone which lies under their green fields, and there was certainly a school of sculptural artists who learned and applied the technique, but the spirit behind their creations seems to have been indigenous to the land.

In practical terms it was the priory of **Anzy-le-Duc**, a few miles south of Montceaux-l'Étoile, which provided both the impulse and the training. It had itself been founded at the end of the tenth century by the now vanished abbey of St-Martin at Autun, on ground given by the Chevalier Liébaud of Anzy. The first prior was a Poitevin named Hugues, not to be confused with St Hugues of Cluny, though he too achieved sanctity at his death. This Hugues was a friend of Abbot Bernon of Gigny, the very founder of Cluny, so from its beginnings Anzy-le-Duc was at the heart of the Benedictine tradition.

Prior Hugues died in 930, and his tomb attracted such numbers of pilgrims that it was decided to build a church worthy of so popular a cult. The present building, which has many features which recall the original ground plan (all that remains) of the Benedictine abbey of Charlieu – which predated the Cluny of St Hugues – is a small masterpiece of the Romanesque. It was erected in three stages: first the choir was built over the crypt which had served as the priory church until then, and a transept was added; then came the nave and side aisles. A stone set in the high altar tells us that the completed work was dedicated to The Most High and Indivisible Trinity, to the Venerable Cross, and to the Holy Mother of God, the Virgin Mary.

The priory suffered at the hands of the English under the Black Prince, and of the Huguenots under Prince Casimir; in 1562 a thunderbolt destroyed the spire on the church tower; on 8 August 1594 it was burnt by the forces of the Ligue, and in 1791 it was sold to the highest bidder. Abandoned to any and every use – principally as a distillery – it was bought in 1808 by four inhabitants of the village, and ten years later the *commune* acquired it as their parish church. Such a history is typical of so many churches in southern France; the wonder is that so much has survived or has been restored for us to treasure today.

To go back to the eleventh century, it would seem that the choir was begun soon after the solemn interment of its founder's bones in 1001, and the nave during the second half of the century. We find that the nave had hardly been finished when a native of the Brionnais, Renaud de Semur, became abbot of Vézelay. On the one hand he was a great-nephew of St Hugues the builder of Cluny; on the other he had spent his childhood in the château of Semur-en-Brionnais, only a few miles south of the new priory at Anzy-le-Duc, which he had very probably watched being built. Was it only a coincidence that the basilica of la Madeleine at Vézelay, rebuilt after the fire of 1120, followed closely the plan of Anzy and Charlieu rather than that of Cluny? To build Vézelay its architect must have been in close contact with those who had worked at Anzy, if indeed he was not among them.

In both churches we find the two-storey elevation, the fully rounded arches, and above all the groined vaulting and the great cross-arches of the nave – all features which run against the current fashion set by Cluny, which favoured broken arches, barrel vaulting and a triforium. At Anzy we find more than that. The three-storeyed octagonal tower is the finest in the Brionnais, as handsome as it is strong. Although the west portal was badly damaged at the Revolution, when the author of the sacrilege offered three *sous* for each angelic or saintly head struck off, the **Tympanum** survived and is of great beauty. The Christ of the Ascension has a book in his hand, seated in a mandorla supported by two angels with their faces turned towards it. On the lintel the Virgin and the Apostles appear, their tunics lightly ruffled by the breeze. Round the first archivolt revolve the twenty-four elders of the Apocalypse, much mutilated, but each holding a cithern and a golden cup. The supports for the cornice on the exterior walls are carved with a kind of truculent fantasy – masks, grimaces and mustachios galore, the full gamut of mediaeval caricature.

The **Capitals** on the pillars of choir and nave may not have the inspired quality of the work of Gislebertus at Autun, but like it they illuminate the architecture of which they are an important part. Moreover they have a more coherent sequence which alternates foliage with human and animal figures, and considering their early date (*circa* 1050, it is reckoned) they are cleverly executed and well preserved. They also illustrate two principles of this form of Burgundian art. According to one, the capitals in the nave which face the altar are mostly of foliage, while those which face west (and therefore the congregation) present more lively and sometimes indecorous scenes. In the other scheme those on the left side of the nave, the *côté du diable*, are more concerned with conflict than those on the right, the *côté de Dieu*, which tend to be more *paisible*. Examples of the former are Samson blinding the lion, a man doubled up on his back being attacked by snakes, St Michael with shield and sword despatching a devil, and (nearest the choir) two men pulling each other's beard in furious unarmed combat. To the right, in the second bay up from the west door, an odd group involving musicians and acrobatic dancers may be to do with a wedding celebration.

In the north transept there are steps leading down to the **Crypt**, a very complete one with four short pillars in the nave, groined vaulting and two side aisles – perhaps an older model for the church above. There is a light switch (a *minuterie*) at the head of the steps, which gives you three minutes for one franc.

The enclosure to the south of the church is attractively laid out with grass lawns and gravel paths, and the eastern range of buildings ends in a big square tower which guards the southern approaches. The tympanum over the western entrance to the enclosure was the one we saw removed to the Musée Hieron in Paray, but the one above the southern gateway is still in place. To see it you have to go back outside and pass behind the remaining priory buildings, for the gateway itself is closed by an iron grille. The composition is vigorous, though clumsily grouped and probably later than the other two belonging to Anzy. It has also been worn by the weather, but you can make out clearly the Virgin seated in profile, the Child on her lap and her feet resting on a footstool as she receives the gifts of the Magi. Adam and Eve appear incongruously close to the right; underneath, the elect are rising from their graves while the damned are chained to a serpent's tail.

There is no doubt that from early in the eleventh century there was an important school of sculpture here, with a busy workshop, and that most of the distinctive carving we find in the Brionnais churches was influenced if not actually carried out by its masters or their pupils. We also find that in its long history there was a time when it flourished artistically and a time when it declined. Perhaps it is a pity that we cannot visit the churches in the order in which they were built and decorated, but that would need a lot of research and some difficult navigation.

The substantial church of St-Pierre-en-Liens at **Varenne l'Arconce** is built on quite different lines from those of Anzy-le-Duc.

The sadly neglected nave has a pointed barrel vault and high side aisles, a combination which allows it no direct lighting. The best features are to be found outside – a square Brionnais tower and a carefully composed west façade. The tympanum there is blank, but the magnet for the visitor is the little one over the south entrance. Unlike any other in the region, it nevertheless accords perfectly with the spirit of the local craftsmen we encounter elsewhere. Nothing could be simpler or appear more artless than the Paschal Lamb at the centre of the semicircle, doing a graceful u-turn with its neck to honour the Cross above and behind it. A half ring of five rosettes surrounds the Lamb, and round it all runs a thin moulded dripstone ending in two modest curlicues. This is the kind of art which conceals itself, and it is strangely moving.

It is only a step from here to **Semur-en-Brionnais**, which as a town is as important as Anzy-le-Duc. It has many advantages, not least its position at the head of a lovely valley running westward towards the Loire. Although the most complete historic building there today is the church of St-Hilaire, in the eleventh century the most important one was the *château-fort* of the seigneurs of Semur where St Hugues, the builder of Cluny, was born. There is enough left of the massive keep and two of its round towers to make an interesting visit. You are invited to be your own guide with the help of an easily read pamphlet – in French or English – and clearly marked numbers at the points it describes. There is a panoramic view from the battlements, and it is easier to imagine young Hugues de Semur surveying the country from here than its role as a prison in the eighteenth century. By its position it has always been closely involved with the town, and below the walls a big open space makes a natural arena for games of *boules*, and that always generates a cheerful and friendly atmosphere. The Mairie occupies an eighteenth-century law court opposite the east end of the church, and there is a group of mediaeval houses round its west end. To the north is a substantial range of buildings connected with the former priory.

As for the church, though it superficially follows the Brionnais model, nothing seems quite right. The upper storey of its squat octagonal tower has deeply recessed windows which are already quite sharply pointed in the Gothic manner. The *chevet* too has a low profile which seems out of proportion with the highstanding pediments of the choir and transept. Transepts, choir and apse were completed by about 1125, the nave and side aisles not until nearly the end of the century – both stages a hundred years later than at Anzy-le-Duc. Inside, the three-storey elevation shows that the architect was loyal to Cluny, though the triforium is unusually deep and elaborate. It continues all round the west end, where a curved tribune is supported by an extraordinary inverted cone looking very much like an icecream cornet – perhaps intended to imitate a similar tribune in the chapel of St Michael in the abbey church at Cluny. The earlier parts to the east are more orthodoxly Romanesque, though some of the decoration there is odd. Notice the squat figure at the base of one of the crossing arches: he has a particularly knowing grin as he takes the weight on one hand, while round on the other side a companion is making heavy weather with two.

This tendency towards caricature, a sign of the lateness and even decadence of Brionnais work here, is more obvious in the tympanum over the west doorway. The fluid Seraphim of Perrecy have been replaced by a cock and a clumsy bird with a human head. The body of Christ is foreshortened and lumpish, and the creatures representing the evangelists are awkwardly grotesque. The scene on the lintel below is puzzling. Who are these characters sitting in threes like stuffed owls on a pair of uncomfortable seats? Why is another sitting on the floor, and why is an angel helping him to rise? We are told the scene is the Council of Seleucia in the year 359, and the figure sitting on the floor is St Hilaire, the patron saint of the church. He is being given divine aid to rescue him from the malice of Léon, the Arian anti-Pope, and his fellow prelates. It makes an amusing caricature, but the contrast of the whole tympanum with the ethereal compositions of Anzy and Perrecy could not be greater. It seems that after more than a century of marvels the Brionnais genius for sculpture has at last exhausted its talent.

Rather than leave Semur on a sour note, go round to the south side of the church, where there is a simple and perfectly proportioned doorway, framed by two slim columns, with a plain cross on the tympanum. Above and to the right is a small window whose more lavish decoration is not at all out of place.

The village of **St-Julien-de-Jonzy**, at nearly five hundred metres, is one of the high points of the eastern escarpment of the

Les Hospices de Beaune

Clos de Vougeot: inner courtyard

Château de Couches

Autun:
Eve in the Musée
Rolin by
Giselbertus

Anzy-le-Duc:
southern gateway to
Priory

Alphonse de Lamartine, by Decaisne in the Musée Municipale, Monceau

Brionnais, looking across the valley of the Sornin to the now not so distant mountains of the Beaujolais. The church we see today was not built until the twelfth century, but the tower at the west end proves to be mounted over the crossing and cupola of an earlier one, which now constitute the narthex. The tower itself is handsome, though it betrays a sequence of styles: the lower storey has authentic blind arcading and short fluted pilasters, while the one above smacks strongly of restoration, and the whole is crowned by the kind of spire one associates with Viollet-le-Duc. The interior, however, is a genuine, well proportioned and properly restored example of Brionnais Romanesque.

As usual the tympanum over the west door attracts most attention. Although we have not yet visited the remains of the abbey church at Charlieu, it will be interesting when the time comes to compare this one with its close parallel over the north portal of the narthex there. It has been suggested that the same artist carved both of them, and though the subjects are different the style is remarkably similar. They both mark a high stage of technical skill, but have lost the freshness and grace of the earlier eleventh-century examples we have seen. At St Julien both Christ and the supporting angels are strong and vigorous, even aggressive in their poses . The lintel is a *tour de force* of realism, showing the table laid for the Last Supper with plates and dishes, and the cloth falling in neat folds above twelve pairs of apostolic feet. The surrounding embellishments – especially the outer archivolt and the pillar capitals – are formal and elaborate.

The church of St-André at **Iguerande**, just off the D982 and overlooking the Loire and the Roanne canal, will be a surprise. This dumpy building in yellow sandstone, with its short, sturdy, foursquare tower, will surely never fall down, but one is not prepared for the beauty of its perfectly restored interior. The purest Romanesque forms have been preserved, and the clean golden stone is blissfully well lit by the windows of nave and choir. There is no liturgical clutter, just architectural form at its simplest. No tympanum has survived from the west door, but the entrance has been sympathetically cleaned and tidied up. Its two slim columns are decorated with pinecones and scallops, motifs repeated on some of the capitals in the nave. Other capitals have imaginative carvings of human figures and mythical beasts, and there is a charming pair of owls on the base of the left-hand pillar of the arch leading to the choir.

We have now reached the southern limits of Saône-et-Loire, and so strictly speaking of Burgundy itself. The last outpost of the Brionnais is **Fleury-la-Montagne**, where in spite of its pretty name it is sad to find that decadence has set in. This is obviously so of the interior, which has been wretchedly treated by recent generations, but it is also true of the tympanum – though it does have some idiosyncratic interest. The upper part is dull, where Christ is a perfunctory symbol and the figures beside him characterless and static. The lintel is an amusing but contrived version of the Adoration of the Magi. The Virgin and Child shelter in a convenient rosette, into which a kneeling Magus peers to proffer his gift. Behind him the next wise man is still riding his horse, and the third is also mounted, but an unexplained figure in the rosette on the left (which is meant to balance the one occupied by the Virgin and Child) is perched on the back of an elephant.

Charlieu is just over the border into the department of Loire, but its connections with Cluny were so close that it deserves to be included in any account of Burgundy. As a town it was a busy trading centre in Gallo-Roman times, on the road which connected the valleys of the Saône and Loire. Today it keeps up a modest silk industry, relying on private workshops as well as factories. The **Benedictine Abbey** was founded in 871, and so predates Cluny, though it became a dependency sixty years later; in 1050 it was down-graded to a priory. The conventual buildings were put up early in the eleventh century by Odilon, abbot of Cluny, who was also responsible for the new church at Anzy-le-Duc; the main church here was finished by the end of that century, and the narthex added in the twelfth. In all the work the influence of Cluny is clear, though of the church itself nothing remains after wholesale demolition in the Revolution. The narthex has survived, but east of the first bay of the nave there is only a rectangular site covered with vestigial masonry. Nevertheless by sifting through the ruins the archaeologists have been able to sort out the plans of several earlier churches, including the primitive sanctuary.

Of the narthex, the authors of Zodiaque's *Bourgogne Romane* have this to say:

A solitary genius, impossible to place in any established category of time or school, seems to have been abruptly projected from the darkness into the blinding light of his own creation, for he has devoted to the sacrament of the altar the most prodigious association of themes. He may have formerly sculpted the highly expressive diabolic figures which support the pilasters of the choir at Semur-en-Brionnais. His chisel, which miraculously relieves the stone of all its heaviness, his ardent visual imagination nourished on the Bible, and the religious frenzy of an epic temperament, all triumph at Charlieu.

The **Narthex** has two storeys, of which the upper one served as a muniment room. The capitals below – a head with horns and hands over its eyes (which illustrates the shame of cuckoldry), and another with cow's ears and fanged teeth – are in the robust vein of fantasy we have seen in the Brionnais. It is the north façade of the narthex, conveniently facing the road, which catches the attention of all visitors. The main portal is the one whose tympanum will remind you strongly of St-Julien-de-Jonzy, though the carving – especially of the tetramorph, or symbols of the four evangelists – is if anything more exuberant, and the Lamb brooding overhead is an original touch. The scene is the Ascension, with the Virgin, the apostles and a pair of angels sedately seated below; they seem to have accepted a *fait accompli* rather than to be witnessing a tremendous event. Notice the figure of Lust on the left of the doorway (a favourite object lesson in southern Burgundy) conceived as a naked woman in the coils of a serpent and gnawed at by an enormous toad. One supposes that a woman depicted as an object of lust is equally aimed at the man who gives way to it – otherwise it seems a one-sided lesson. The side columns and the archivolts are elaborately decorated, and the whole effect is sumptuous to the point of over-indulgence.

The smaller portal to the right is more unusual in its subject and treatment. The outer arch is carved in high relief with the *dramatis personae* of the Transfiguration – St Peter, St James, St John, Moses and Elijah – all of whom were beheaded in the Revolution; Christ transfigured occupies the crown of the arch. The iconography was probably influenced by Peter the Venerable, who introduced the Feast of the Transfiguration into the Cluniac calendar in 1132, and that would help to date the work. The tympanum proper is therefore free for a more general subject, in this case the Wedding Feast at Cana (not, if you look closely, the Last Supper). However, you will recognize the furnishings of the table and the folds of the cloth from the lintel at St-Julien-de-Jonzy. The lintel here carries the most original part of the composition, a crowded and disorderly scene of pagan sacrifice which contrasts with the dignified one above.

The **Cloister** is still there. It dates from the end of the fifteenth century, though the entrance to the Chapter House is flanked by a double row of squat Carolingian pillars recovered from the oldest of the earlier churches, or possibly from the eleventh century cloister. Projecting from the cloister is the private chapel of the Prior, of which the oldest part is tenth-century work. It contains a lovely wooden statue of the Virgin, with the Child holding a dove, which came from the church at Aiguilly.

The chapel backs on to the courtyard of the **Hôtel du Prieur**, surrounded by a delightful group of buildings with steep tiled roofs, turrets with jaunty spires, and a well-head in the middle. The entrance to this is on your left as you enter the abbey grounds, near the imposing **Tour Philippe Auguste**, a reminder that in the twelfth century the king asserted his authority over Cluny by fortifying the abbey.

To the west of the town, outside the line of the old walls and beside the D4 exit from Charlieu, is the **Couvent des Cordeliers**. The name of these establishments, frequently found in Burgundy, does not as you might imagine connect them with a mediaeval guild, but with the Franciscan order, whose habit was always worn with a rope round the waist. In the early days there was friction between them and the Benedictine establishment, and they were only allowed to build outside the limits of Benedictine property.

The fortunes of this community and its buildings fluctuated strangely. Founded at the end of the thirteenth century, demolished in the 1360s and rebuilt at the turn of the fourteenth to fifteenth centuries, it was finally closed down in 1792 after the last three monks had been turned out. The main buildings to survive were the church, which is an interesting hotchpotch of irregular construction, and the extremely beautiful Gothic cloister, built by the family of Chateaumorand between 1370 and 1410. They could not have foreseen that in 1910 it would be bought by a Paris antiquarian for a wealthy American who planned to re-erect it round his tennis court. It had been partially dismantled when in October that year it was saved by the intervention of the State, who bought it back for the nation.

The garth is grassed over and planted with cypresses, and on a hot day it is a place to linger in gratitude. The capitals of the graceful arches are intriguingly carved with small animal figures — you will find a corner one where the head of a sad-looking dog is enveloped in a monk's cowl. Off the cloister is almost the only remaining part of the conventual buildings, the monks' library. The ground floor is now used as a display point for books and leaflets, but the floor above is a beautiful arched and vaulted chamber, the original library, with large windows on three sides which flood it with light.

If you find it convenient to spend the night in Charlieu, you can do so comfortably and quietly at the modern Relais de l'Abbaye, which is not at all near the abbey, but built imaginatively on the wide green spaces south of the river Sornin. It has a good view of the mediaeval town without being involved in its traffic.

CHAPTER SEVENTEEN

From Charlieu to Cluny

We begin by skirting the Brionnais to the east, but before long we shall be entering the lusher pastures of the Chalonnais, then climbing eastwards into the hills which look down on Cluny, cradle of the monastic world. Shortly after leaving Charlieu on the D987 we come to **Châteauneuf-sur-Sornin**, to be distinguished from Châteauneuf-en-Auxois, which we have already visited in Côte d'Or. The château here was a comparatively humble affair, and is now only partly occupied, but it has an inviting position with a terrace overlooking the Sornin and embellished by an ancient and rampant wisteria. The church of St-Paul, built on the same level, has retained its importance and is a good example of late Brionnais architecture. Unusually tall, it was much restored in the fifteenth century, but remains basically Romanesque, with high windows in the nave, an octagon-based cupola and a rounded apse with two abs idioles. Notice especially the decorative columns in the central apse. The west doorway is devoid of carving, but the main entrance is now from the south, where the tympanum is blank but the twelve apostles appear in a tidy row on the lintel.

The main road continues along the wooded river valley in the direction of la Clayette, but, for a last look at the happy little region we are leaving, turn left after a few kilometres for **St-Laurent-en-Brionnais**. Do not be put off by the heavy-looking outside and the nineteenth-century spire, for the Romanesque interior is harmonious and well restored. The long groin-vaulted nave is lit by high windows above each of its five bays, and the capitals on the nave and crossing pillars reproduce many now familiar fantasies: animals devouring men, others with human heads, scenes of armed conflict between humans, and the same view of Samson mastering the lion which we saw at Anzy-le-Duc. The appearance of carving at the bases of the last two columns before the choir is unusual, and so are the subjects – to the right, two crowned figures are brandishing hammers; to the left, one face has

314

a tangle of snakes and on the other a hare is gently nibbling flowers.

Up a short lane to the north-west of the church is an imposing classical gateway, once the entrance to a château, now only a farm. To the west is a long building, identified as a 'Canonnerie', which had a private Gothic chapel and an enclosed courtyard; it all makes up a distinguished group of buildings of various dates, including a few good seventeenth-century houses, watched over by some ancient limes and chestnut trees.

You have still not quite done with the Brionnais, for if you carry on from St-Laurent to meet the D989 just east of la Clayette, a left turn there will bring you to **Vareilles**, where the church has one of the finest towers of all – second perhaps only to Anzy-le-Duc. Its three stages are logically connected by rounded pilasters rising from one to the other, and there are neat dormers in the short spire. Inside, just the crossing and apse remain of the original church, though only the seventeenth century could have produced the boxed-in pews on either side of the altar, and the semicircle of seating round the apse.

At **la Clayette** (pronounced 'Clayte') we enter the more sophisticated life of the Charollais. The racecourse two kilometres up the road to Charolles is the setting for *concours hippiques* as well as for the renowned annual race meetings. The town's most important natural feature is its lake, which provided water power for manufacturing, and assured the town's prosperity long before the château was built in 1380. Situated on the frontier between the comté of Mâcon, which depended on the king of France, and the Charollais, which was a fief of the dukes of Burgundy, la Clayette was directly involved in the quarrels of the Hundred Years' War. The local seigneur, who had been page to the duchess, was faithful to his allegiance, and by the Treaty of Arras in 1435 la Clayette, with the rest of the Mâconnais, remained a Burgundian possession. During the wars of religion the lake apparently protected the château from the depredations of either party; it owed much also to the volatility with which the châtelain, Claude de Chantemerle, changed sides in the conflict. The Revolution spared it material damage, though it was requisitioned and the Feast of the Supreme Being was celebrated in the park. It is not open to the public, but you can see the large round tower, with its onion-shaped lantern,

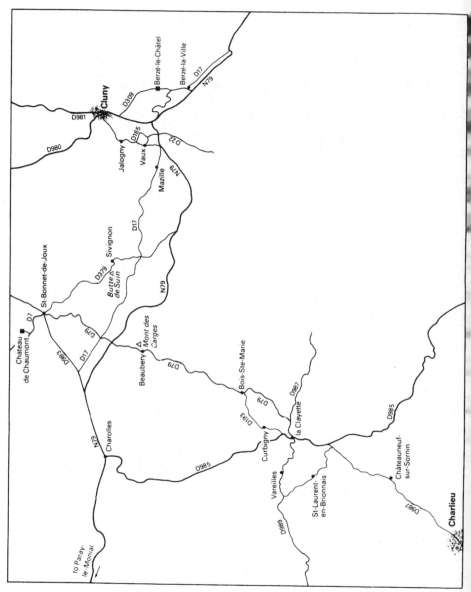

Charlieu to Cluny

rising out of the wide moat – where carp proliferate. The west façade looks on to the road, with slender machicolated towers on each side of the entrance.

We can continue now on the D79 to **Bois-Ste-Marie**, whose church is the most important we have seen since Anzy-le-Duc. Though radically restored in the last century it has many of the features we associate with the Brionnais tradition – which was strong enough to influence building well beyond its proper borders – and on a grand scale. Set on a terrace in the highest part of the town it has a double flight of steps leading up to a majestic façade with tiers of Romanesque arcading. The oldest part is the choir with its ambulatory, which goes back to about the year 1000. Each of the six narrow bays of the ambulatory has two large pillars with two smaller ones behind to support them, an arrangement unique in France. The transept and nave were not begun till a century later, and it can be seen how the profiles of the nave bays gradually change from Brionnais to Cluniac models as you go west. The capitals in the nave are typical Brionnais subjects, involving dogs, lions, fighting men, peacocks, eagles, a *sirène-poisson* (or sexually inviting mermaid), wrestlers and a wild boar. The most horrifying shows a man being tortured by a pair of devils, one clasping his head, the other pulling out his tongue (or soul) with pincers. You can imagine the sculptor, chisel in hand, standing before a virgin block of stone and asking himself 'what next'?

The view eastward from the nave is a wonderful vista of soaring arches ending in the half-dome of the apse, pierced by three lancet windows. Through the final bay of the ambulatory, level with the top of the altar, appears the central window of the outer hemicycle – a magical effect of lighting. The little tympanum over the south door, though a charming vignette of the Flight into Egypt, was bought in Paris and put there by the nineteenth-century restorers. There is a good view of this handsome church from the road below.

The district of the Charollais is not a loosely defined *région*, but a feudal entity, a *comté* which has changed hands often over the centuries. In 1237 it belonged to Hugues IV, duke of Burgundy, who gave it to his grand-daughter Beatrice in 1272. Beatrice married Robert de Clermont, the son of St Louis, and their granddaughter brought it as her dowry to Jean, the first comte d'Armagnac. In 1390 it was sold back to Philippe le Hardi, who made it over to his eldest son, and it passed in succession to the later dukes. After the death of Charles le Téméraire it was taken over by Louis XI and given to Philip, archduke of Austria. In 1529 it passed to the emperor Charles V, and in 1556 to Philip II of Spain. It returned to the crown under Louis XV. No company quoted on the Stock Exchange has had so many take-overs, and there must have been something special about the Charollais even then.

Today the something special is more than two million head of white cattle bred on the rich pastures of the Arconce and its tributaries. Thousands of cattle come to the market every week from May to December, and in October there is a special sale of young bulls at **Charolles**. The Brionnais contributes its share, and there is another big weekly market at St-Christophe-en-Brionnais. An *entrecôte grillée Charollaise marchand de vin* can be enjoyed at any time of year, and you have only to look out of the window to see where it comes from. You can sample it either at the Hôtel Moderne or in the restaurant de la Poste, but otherwise there is nothing particular to see in Charolles.

For a breather, and perhaps a little exercise, take the D79 from la Clayette to Beaubery and turn up to your right for the summit of the Mont des Carges. This was a centre of resistance during the German occupation; a monument to the maquisards of Beaubery and the Charollais battalion stands at the top. The view is magnificent in every direction. Turning north again you can follow the D79 to another market town at St-Bonnet-de-Joux. From here the D7 leads after a couple of kilometres to the **Château de Chaumont**. This has remained in the same family – the la Guiche – since 1416, but it was not until 1502 that Pierre de la Guiche – who had negotiated the marriage between Henri II and Catherine de'Medici, and had been ambassador in England, Germany, Italy and Spain – undertook the building of the present château. Unfortunately most of it was demolished in 1801 and rebuilt during the last century in neo-Gothic style. There are two approaches to the château, the first a roundabout way through the woods, the other a little further on which is a straight track through an avenue aimed at the entrance gates.

The whole property is beautiful, and the eastern front of 1510 has survived, but the most remarkable part of it are the unique stables, 65 metres long, built on two floors between 1648 and 1652 by Henriette de la Guiche, duchess of Angoulême. Over the central doorway is the equestrian statue of Philibert de la Guiche, Grand Master of Artillery under Henri III and Henri IV. Philibert had accompanied Mary Stuart when she returned to Scotland as queen, and as Governor of Mâcon he had prevented the massacre of St Bartholomew taking place in the town. There was room on the ground floor for at least a hundred horses, but only the king had the right to that number, so stalls were provided for just ninety-nine; the statue made up the number to a hundred, but being in stone it avoided the charge of *lèse majesté*. Four superb stone staircases with balustrades mount to the first storey, where the men-at-arms (and later the grooms) were lodged. An entire forest was said to have been felled to make the roof, which was restored, possibly for the first time – in 1987. The vaulting is supported inside by its original twenty-eight columns, and stabling is still provided for eighteen horses. There is an exhibition of various types of horse-drawn vehicle, and armorial bearings and personal monograms from the past vie with plaques recording prizes won at the Concours Hippique de Paris before the last war. There is a busy and flourishing farm at the back of the stables, and you can see a curious contraption in wood for securing cattle during milking – or possibly surgical operations.

Unless you are in a great hurry to reach Cluny it would be a pity to go by the main roads from St-Bonnet. Instead the little D379 climbs to nearly 600 metres below the Butte de Suin, and for the Charollais it is a spectacular drive. You join the cross-country D17 soon after Sivignon, and it carries on up and down hill for another ten kilometres before it meets the N79 and your approach road to Cluny. Just before that, turn off to **Mazille** to look at the church, which has a tall and striking Romanesque tower. Although not in the village itself, but down in the fields to the north-east, it would be sensible to enquire there whether it is open, and if not to locate the key. If you fail, it is still worth going down for a closer look at the first of several you will find in the Mâconnais (where you now are) with this elegant breed of tower. Its two upper storeys with double window openings rise high above the gabled façade and the single polygonal apse. The hillside opposite is disfigured by an ugly modern convent for Carmelite nuns, though no doubt they live a healthy and rewarding life there.

Having stopped at Mazille, do not on any account miss the nearby village of **Vaux**, which is not easy to find. The best way is to join the N79 for two kilometres, turn left as for Cluny on the D22 and look for a sign on your left for Vaux and Jalogny. One more left fork, and you pass under a tunnel of young beeches to reach the little Romanesque church, devotedly restored between 1971 and 1972 by the scouts of Cluny and the villagers of Vaux. You enter it under a semicircular archway, through a wooden-beamed porch, and up a *perrot* (a flight of semicircular steps) which all date from the seventeenth century. There are more fine oak beams in the nave, which goes back another five hundred years, while the choir looks and is a hundred years earlier still. Thanks to the good taste of the restorers the altar is now a plain slab of rustic stone, which looks well against the seventeenth-century *retable* brought from the former convent at Mazille. The stained glass in the lancet windows was designed and made by the scouts, and one can excuse the enthusiasm which covered the whitewashed walls of the nave with texts from St Paul and St John in coloured scripts – it is after all a live Christian building as well as an architectural gem.

2

The influence of **Cluny** has been so much with us in the latter part of our journey that the place, when you come to it, is liable to disappoint. What it stood for, whether in the building of churches, the carving of stone, or the cultivation of vines, can more easily be invoked and studied elsewhere. Nevertheless it would be impious to pass it by. There is still a good deal to see, and even more to remember; here we can quote from words spoken at the millenary celebrations in 1910:

Between the two great intellectual cultures, the Classical and the Christian, which divided the world, its desire was to create an understanding.

Like the great minds of the fourth century, its teachers reconciled wisdom with the Gospel; when they affirmed the Faith, it was neither to curse nor to condemn the imperishable works bequeathed to us by the reason and imagination of pagan antiquity. A man like Peter the Venerable could be the chief theologian and chief man of letters of his time, combat the heretics and stretch out the hand of friendship to Abélard, comment on the scriptures and talk like Plato. This great monk is something more than a name – he is the symbol both of his Order and of his country.

The abbey was founded by William the Pious, duke of Aquitaine, on 11 September 910. Its first abbot was Bernon, later known as St Berno, who brought a small party of monks from Gigny in the Franche-Comté and from his monastery at Baume-les-Messieurs in the Jura to answer the call of the duke – and, we must presume, of God. The gift included a great deal of fertile land, and it was soon exempted from episcopal jurisdiction and independent of any temporal power. Popes came to the abbots for advice, and kings bowed to their arbitration. It was to count 1450 foundations in different parts of Europe from Poland to Spain, and more than ten thousand monks lived by its Benedictine rule. Addressing St Hugues in 1098 Pope Urban II described them as 'la lumière du monde', and the saying ran in Burgundy:

> Partout où le vent vente
> L'Abbaye de Cluny a rente

St Bernard, however, was soon denouncing abbots vowed to poverty who could not go twelve miles without a train of sixty horses. Later they acquired the habit of commuting as they chose between Cluny and Paris, and being frequently appointed from wealthy and landed families they found it difficult to renounce their privileges. Decadence set in, and by the sixteenth century the abbey was an easy prey to the Huguenots, who pillaged the library and robbed the church of much treasure. The Revolution completed its decline. Closed in 1790, it was put up for sale on the pretext that labour required for its upkeep could be better employed elsewhere; it was bought by a merchant from Mâcon. Further mutilation followed, and by 1823 nothing remained of the greatest church in Christendom but the fragment you see today. The mind reels at the thought of such iconoclasm, yet, as far as we know, not a voice was heard in protest.

There had in fact been three churches at Cluny. The foundation stone of the third and by far the largest, dedicated to St Peter and St Paul, was laid in 1088. Urban II consecrated the high altar on 25 October 1095, and exactly thirty-five years later Innocent II set his seal on the completed church. It was conceived by Hugues of Semur, who ruled for sixty years, and his plan was brought to final fruition by his successors. Of the seven great abbots who gave Cluny its prestige, only St Hugues was a Burgundian by birth. The interior of his church was 177 metres long, only nine metres short of St-Peter's at Rome. It comprised a narthex, five aisles, two transepts, four large towers over the choir and apse, and two smaller ones at the west end. There were 301 windows and 225 stalls for the monks. The vault over the sanctuary was painted, and supported by a marble colonnade. The nave of ten bays was over thirty metres high, and its arches were borne on columns faced with fluted pilasters at triforium level, rising to a barrel vault. There were five bays to the narthex, and a tympanum over the

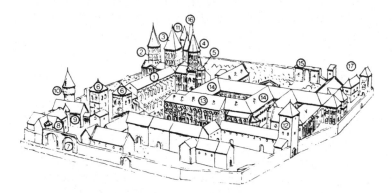

**THE ABBEY CHURCH OF CLUNY
AT THE END OF THE 18TH CENTURY**

1 The abbey church of St Peter and
  Paul
2 The Tower des Bisans
3 The Tower of the Choir
4 The Tower de l'Eau Bénite
5 The Belfry
6 The Barabans
7 Principal entrance
8 Palace of Jean de Bourbon

9 Palace of Jacques d'Amboise
10 Fairy Tower
11 Round Tower
12 Tower des Fromages
13 Façade of Pope Gelasius
14 Claustral buildings
15 Gate into the gardens
16 Lamp tower
17 Granary

west portal. The hierarchy of forms and levels, whether seen from the outside or the inside, was imitated a little later at Paray-le-Monial. Throughout this immense building the classical note predominated, both in proportion and detail – St Hugues would have seen to that. It is easy to appreciate what Albert Thibaudet meant in describing Cluny as a Benedictine Versailles.

Your best approach is by the rue d'Avril through the centre of the town, where a number of mediaeval houses with balconies over their lower storeys are not much younger than the abbey, and it brings you to the monumental gateway of the vast monastic enclosure. Through it you see the octagonal **Tour de l'Eau Bénite**, flanked by its square turreted staircase, the **Tour de l'Horloge**. To your left are the two abbatial palaces. The first, built by Abbot Jean de Bourbon in the fifteenth century, is now the **Musée Ochier**; the second was built by his successors between 1485 and 1518 and is now the Hôtel-de-Ville, surrounded by a pleasant public garden. Beyond this was the northern gateway, protected by the **Tour Fabry**, of which the lower section was built around 1350 by Abbot Hugues de Fabry, and the out-corbelled upper part added in the fifteenth century.

The rue Kenneth Conant, named after the American scholar who did so much to reveal the greatness of Cluny, will bring you to what remains of the façade of the narthex, in particular the bases of its two western towers, called the Barabans. From here you can judge the colossal dimensions of the church which once stood in that tragic gap. The southern arm of the main transept, alone left standing, marks a point at about two-thirds of its total length, and the tall trees to the east are the site of the chevet.

The abbey is now maintained by the École Nationale des Arts et Métiers, and a competent guide will show you round when your turn comes. A little preliminary homework may help. You enter by a small door in the Place de l'Abbaye, from where two flights of steps take you into the crossing of the Romanesque transept – which is all we possess of the original third church of Cluny. Two bays with their vaulting frame the octagonal cupola which supports the Tour de l'Eau Bénite, and rises to a height of more than thirty-two metres – as audacious a feat in its day as that of the builders of Amiens and Beauvais. Two chapels open to the east of the main transept. From the second, dedicated to St Martial, a little turreted staircase leads to the Romanesque chapel of St Michael above it. An inscription recording its dedication by the bishop of Pamplona, who died in 1115, is a clue to the date of the transept, and shows how far the church had progressed by the beginning of the twelfth century. Of the smaller transept beyond, very little remains but the flamboyant **Chapelle de Bourbon**, a lovely example of late Gothic, and its Romanesque apse.

Leaving behind you the monastic buildings reconstructed in the eighteenth century, you now cross the formal gardens. Sad to say, the ancient lime tree which was given the name Abélard has died. Abélard took refuge here at Cluny towards the end of his life, and Peter the Venerable welcomed him, absolving him on his deathbed at St-Marcel-lès-Chalon. On your right is the **Granary**, with the Tour du Moulin at its southern end, built by Abbot Yves I between 1257 and 1275. The ground floor, a beautiful vaulted chamber, contains sculptures from the abbey and other sites in the town. The upper storey has a fine barrel roof of oak and chestnut, and here you can see not only models of the abbey church as Professor Conant reconstructed it, but also the reproduction on a smaller scale of the sanctuary, with the capitals rescued from the choir. There are ten of them, arranged in a semi-circle and centring on the altar of Pyrennean marble which could well be the one dedicated by Urban II in 1095. There is a strong tradition that the master sculptor of Cluny went on to carve the tympanum at the entrance to the nave at Vézelay. However that may be, his successors at Autun and Saulieu would have been inspired by what he did here; indeed, Gislebertus is thought to have been trained at Cluny.

The two outer capitals, to left and right, were probably attached to the pillars which marked the entry to the choir – picturing respectively the fall of Adam and Eve and the sacrifice of Abraham. The other eight come from the free-standing columns which held up the arches of the colonnade. The first of these has no distinguishable theme, apart from Corinthian-inspired foliage. Then from left to right we can make out, sometimes with difficulty, the following: three athletes, of whom two have been identified as a discobolus and a wrestler; a bee-keeper cleaning out his hive; the three theological virtues of Charity, Humility and Hope, and the cardinal one of Justice; Prudence surrounded by spring flowers (a difficult interpretation to follow); the four rivers and the four trees of Paradise; finally, on the last two capitals and occupying all four faces of each, graceful figures enclosed in recessed oval medallions and playing on musical instruments. They represent, as is clear from the inscriptions round the medallions, the eight tones of plainchant. Whatever the symbolism of the others, these last illustrate better than any the marriage of pure art with religion in the consciousness of the time – at any rate in the world of St Hugues of Cluny.

Other capitals can be seen in the **Musée Ochier**; also a carved head which was the keystone of the fifth bay in the narthex, and a charming twelfth-century carving of the Agnus Dei with the inscription: HIC PARVUS SCULPOR AGNUS – IN CELO MAGNUS, or 'Here am I carved as a little lamb – in heaven [I shall be] great.' The Lamb balances the Cross jauntily on his upturned right forefoot. Also in the museum is a series of water colours by Conant and his pupils which portray the abbey as it was in the twelfth century, and allow you to compare it with other buildings of the same or an earlier date. The museum is shut on Tuesdays.

Still within the abbey precincts is the **Tour des Fromages** (its mediaeval function was just that) from which you have a marvellous view of the town if you can face a climb of 120 wooden stairs; entrance can be arranged through the Syndicat d'Initiatives. Immediately opposite the tower is the **Church of Notre-Dame**, one of the first Cluniac churches to be enlarged and transformed when the Gothic fashion came in, and it remains a good example of thirteenth-century Burgundian Gothic. The Roman tiles and ochre-coloured walls lend to the town a southern look, and from the Promenade de Fouettin, replacing the former ramparts, you get an enchanting view of Cluny itself and the valley of the Grosne.

In Cluny, despite its popularity with tourists (who mostly come and go in coachloads) there is no great choice of hotels. The most fashionable is the Bourgogne, which has a starred restaurant and is conveniently placed between the Hôtel-de-Ville and the abbey. Outside the walls to the south you have a more modest choice between the Moderne, a sensible place near the bridge which carries the D980 over the Grosne, and the Abbaye, of more attractive appearance near the railway station. Both these are good value, and either could be a useful base for another short but important expedition.

It is vital here to have an up-to-date map of the road system between Cluny and Mâcon, as the old N79 highway has been replaced by a *Route de Vitesse*, a dual carriageway which ignores the side roads leading just where you want to go. Fortunately there is a very minor road which crosses the railway to your left, soon after leaving Cluny on the D980, and leads to **Berzé-le-Chatel**. The very fine feudal château here protected the southern approaches to Cluny, and belonged to the oldest barony in the Mâconnais, raised to a *comté* by Henri IV. The seigneurial family included the thirteenth-century poet Hugues de Berzé, but its military importance was shown by several sieges in the fourteenth and fifteenth centuries. It was captured in 1421 by the Dauphin (the future Charles VII) and surrendered in 1591 to the duc de Nemours.

The castle stands on a high slope among vineyards – the first we have seen for some time -- and you enter it through a gateway equipped for portcullis and drawbridge, and between two bulky towers. From there an avenue of *parterres* set off by topiary leads to a second gateway, beyond which the domestic buildings are private. You can, however, walk round the outside and enjoy an uninterrupted view of the Mâconnais countryside to the north. More open than the Brionnais, its wider green pastures support not only cattle but sheep and goats too. In spring every turn brings the joy of uncut verges and flowering fruit trees.

The peace of the valley behind you, though, has been permanently broken not only by the Route de Vitesse but by the rushing mighty wind of the TGVs as they hurtle down to Lyon. Mercifully the old line of the N79 has been preserved as a *route touristique*, which you can join just south of Berzé-le-Chatel. This means that you can arrive in peace at **Berzé-la-Ville**, for its size one of the most important sites in Burgundy. At the end of the eleventh century the little *obédience* of Berzé (too small to rate as a priory) was taken over by Cluny from the priory of Marcigny in exchange for the similar *obédience* at Iguerande. This gave particular pleasure to St Hugues, who in his old age enjoyed coming here – a journey of only five leagues – for peace and rest from his overwhelming responsibilities. Berzé was one of the three foundations mentioned by name in his last will and testament.

He had good reason to remember it, for on one of his visits the place was struck by lightning and a great part of it went up in flames. The monks were astonished to see their abbot emerging safely from the ruins, and naturally attributed his escape to divine protection. He entrusted the restoration of the chapel to one Séguin, the chamberlain of Cluny, but the magnificent frescos which bring us here today are probably of a slightly later date. Berzé was sold at the Revolution and passed through various hands. Then in 1887 the Abbé Jolivet, curé of Berzé (whose name deserves to be recorded), discovered the head of Christ beneath the whitewash which had providentially preserved it, and gradually the whole painting was uncovered. Shortly after the last war the chapel was bought by Joan Evans, daughter of Sir Arthur but an archaeologist in her own right. In 1947 she presented it to the *Académie de Mâcon*, and she is remembered here on the anniversary of her death in 1977.

The **Chapelle des Moines**, as it is now called, is all that is left of the eleventh-century foundation, for the priory buildings that adjoin it were rebuilt in the eighteenth century. Together they occupy a triangular spur of rock above the village, overlooking vineyards and farmland. Like other small monastic establishments in the Mâconnais it was as much concerned with the life of the soil as with the life of the cloister, and the dun-coloured stone of which the chapel is built is clearly derived from the surrounding hills.

The lower storey may have served as a crypt, but it was soon reduced to the status of a cellar for the season's new wine. The chapel above has a claim to attention apart from the glory of its frescos. Its single nave, barrel vault, and the slightly bulging arch which leads into the sanctuary and apse, are all of authentic Romanesque pedigree. Enough light comes in from the three central windows of the apse, and the five in the nave, to illuminate vividly the decoration of the apse and its surroundings. All is subservient to the figure of Christ in Majesty, seated in his mandorla more luxuriously than usual, on an oriental cushion with tassels. Indeed, the handsome oval face, framed by dark hair and a short beard, eyebrows arched over piercing dark eyes, looks more Byzantine than Romanesque. Admittedly one is comparing different media, but there is no resemblance here to the regal, nordic, square-bearded Christ of the tympanum at Autun. If the sculptors of Burgundy were the best, its painters may have had to learn from Byzantine models. The deep blue of the mandorla is studded with round holes, which must have held pieces of metal or glass to represent stars. Christ's right hand is raised in blessing; with his left he hands his testament on a phylactery, or strip of parchment, to St Peter, and they are surrounded by the other apostles.

The two outer bays of the apse are filled in and painted (which supports the theory that the painting was done some time after the chapel was built), the subjects being the martyrdom of St Blaise on the left and of St Vincent on the right. The legend goes that St Blaise had persuaded a wolf to bring a piglet to a poor woman, who turned some of it into brawn and brought it to him in prison. The upper picture shows the dish being brought, garnished with the animal's head; underneath, the saint's head falls to the ground as he is decapitated by a soldier. On the opposite side the Roman prefect Dacianus watches as St Vincent is pinned down by long forks to the red-hot surface on which (like St Laurence) he is being grilled.

In between the curves of the arcatures there appear the busts of six saintly women, holding up vessels which perhaps contain oint-ment. Only three of them have been identified, as Saints Agatha, Laurentia and Consortia (a Lyonnaise who was venerated at Cluny), but their jewels and headwear have been compared with the adornment of the Empress Theodora in the mosaic of San Vitale in Ravenna. Certainly the impression of this riot of colour approaches that of a mosaic, as it overflows the triumphal arch and spreads on to the surface of the wall between choir and apse, where the Paschal Lamb appears under the *oculus* between two flying angels. No description can convey the delicacy and bril-liance of colour – purple and green, ochre and azure – nor the virtuosity of design. Somehow the static art of Byzantine mosaics and wall paintings has come to life, for here is the Byzantine serenity but little of the Byzantine stiffness.

As for the technique, superior to any we have met so far in Burgundy, a fascinating description is offered (with other helpful material) inside the chapel, which is worth repeating here. The stages were:

1. Milk of lime, tinted with ochre, is washed over the stone.
2. A layer of coarse mortar with chopped straw (the mediaeval plastering process) is applied.
3. The surface is washed with thicker milk of lime.

4. A blue-tinted colour wash is applied.
5. A layer of very fine mortar (4-5mm thick) is pasted on,
    mixed with lard to make it smoother.
    A draft drawing is now made in red ochre, followed by
    painting in a simple palette of eight colours.

Down in the village below, and mostly unregarded by the visitor, is the little parish church with its seductive square twelfth-century tower. The inside is in poor shape and is usually kept locked, but the key can be traced nearby.

It would be a mistake now to go any farther down the road to Mâcon, or stray on the other side of the railway tracks, for that would bring you face to face with the leading figure of nineteenth-century French romanticism, and involve you in scenes and reflections utterly different from those we have just left and those you will soon be experiencing. We have already found the scent of Alphonse de Lamartine briefly at Montculot in Côte d'Or, and we shall come across his traces again on our way north to Tournus in the next chapter, but he was born in Mâcon and looked on the Mâconnais as his *terre natale*. We can afford to wait till we reach Mâcon on the last leg of our journey through Burgundy to appreciate the full impact of his remarkable life and personality.

CHAPTER EIGHTEEN

From Cluny to Tournus

This is a journey through the heart of the northern Mâconnais, the most beautiful part of a beautiful region, and for many people the ideal Burgundy countryside. There are no towns of any size until you reach Tournus, no fashionable hotels or restaurants, and no historic or cultural sites which attract large numbers of tourists. Yet not far away to the east the scorching traffic on the A6 autoroute passes by without time for a glance at some of the most interesting and evocative places to be found in Burgundy. Mercifully the traffic on the N6 highway also spares the little roads which wind along the valleys and between the green hills – a background for the spring and summer wild flowers and the golden tints of autumn.

To the west the boundary is the modest D981 road which follows the valley of the Grosne, a much pleasanter way to reach Beaune and the Côte from the south. On or beside it lie several sites no intelligent traveller should miss. First, though, try plunging into the green world of the Bois de Bourcier and the Forêt de Goulaine, a route followed by one of the best stretches of the Grande Randonnée 76A between Cluny and Chalon. Walkers stick mostly to the line of the hills, but the D15 through the valley arrives first at **Donzy-le-Pertuis**, a small friendly farming village where the Romanesque church has (like many Mâconnais churches) a characteristic outside stairway to the belfry. A figure of St John the Baptist with a lamb is unusually placed on the outer wall of the apse. For a change, if you enjoy grottos, there is a good example near **Azé**, about five kilometres south-east of Donzy, with a subterranean river running through it. It was a prehistoric site, and some Neolithic as well as Gallo-Roman remains can be seen in the village museum. Notices by the road will direct you to the grotto and tell you the opening times.

Closer to Donzy, and on your most likely route north, is **Blanot**. This is a more primitive village, but it has the remains of an eleventh-century priory, one of the oldest possessions of Cluny. It is now a farm, and like many farms in the neighbourhood the tower of the priory church has a curious overhanging tiled roof; there are traces of early Lombardic arcading on its rough stone surface. It was a fortified priory, and a later more military-looking tower guards the entry to the farm, though an *insouciant* wooden balcony over the archway seems more appropriate than a portcullis. About twenty Merovingian tombs have been discovered inside and outside the little courtyard (there is a plan of them outside) and you can see one of them beside the road to the right of the gateway.

The D146 now runs close under the summit of the Mont-St-Romain (where there is another extensive system of grottos) and it will take you to **Chissey-lès-Mâcon**. The church is what people come to see, for it has a fine example of the Mâconnais tower, tall, square and finely proportioned, with the Italian influence showing in its arcades and window openings which we saw at Mazille. It also has a well preserved Romanesque interior, and some interesting capitals on the north side of the nave – subjects we rarely see presented like this. Here for instance is David with Saul, David and Goliath, and David by himself, playing on his harp . By contrast there is a modern altar-front of the Nativity, beautifully carved, with the Infant in the tightest of swaddling clothes perched high up in a cradle behind his earthly parents – who seem for once more interested in their own loving relationship. On the memorial for parishioners 'morts pour la France' in the 1914-1918 war, one name stands out: the simple entry says 'Philibert, Duc, Septembre 1914'.

Four kilometres west of Chissey, on the D981, is the château of **Cormatin**, which has recently been rehabilitated as a centre for the arts as well as for tourism. This impressive Renaissance building was put up on the site of a thirteenth-century fortress by Antoine du Blé, baron of Huxelles and Governor of Chalon. His son Jacques, well known in Paris as a patron of the arts, was made a marquis by Louis XIII, who visited the château with Richelieu in 1629. Two generations later Nicholas du Blé, a Marshal of France under Louis XIV, negotiated the Treaty of Utrecht which ended the War of the Spanish Succession, and was described by Voltaire as one of the wisest and most far-seeing men of his time.

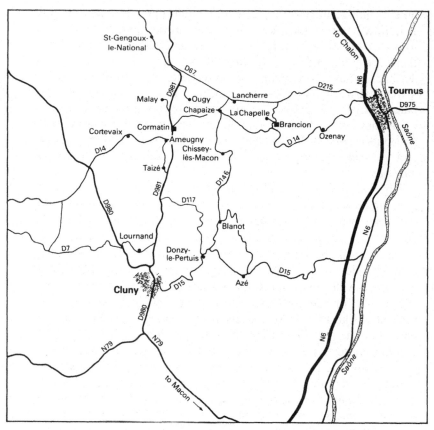

Cluny to Tournus

Five years before the Revolution broke out, Cormatin passed by marriage to one Pierre Dezoteux, who had just returned from fighting the armies of George III in the American War of Independence. A man of the world, he was able to pacify the rebellious peasants by supplying them with good Burgundy wine, and personally obliterating all the crowns from the elaborate gilt *décor* of the rooms furnished by Jacques de Blé. His daughter Nina married Guillaume de Pierreclos, and this brings into view for the second time the incorrigibly romantic figure of Alphonse de Lamartine, an old friend and neighbour of the Pierreclos family. Nina seems to have spent little time with her husband, instead playing the part of an accomplished hostess at her father's house, and welcoming there many artists and men of letters. Lamartine was a frequent guest – he had a special room reserved for his visits – and the inevitable affair resulted in the birth of his only son, Léon de Pierreclos.

The literary connections of Cormatin continued when it passed – again by marriage – to the poet Henri de Lacretelle, who was also a friend of Lamartine. His grandson Jacques, who died not long ago, was a distinguished novelist and an *Académicien*. During the *belle époque* it was bought by Raoul Gunsbourg, director for fifty years of the Monte Carlo opera. He left the gilded rooms untouched, but turned other parts of the château into apartments in various styles – Louis Quatorze, Byzantine, even Roman – and entertained musical celebrities of the day. They included Caruso, Chaliapin, Fauré, Massenet and Saint-Saëns, with actresses Sarah Bernhardt and Cécile Sorel in supporting roles!

After the first world war there was a long period of neglect, and it was only in 1981 that Cormatin was bought by four friends who planned to restore it and open it to the public. This has come to pass, and so has another part of their scheme – to organize exhibitions and artistic events there – in which they are being helped by the Ministry of Culture and the *département* of Saône-et-Loire.

The highlights of a well-guided tour are the famous state apartments, or gilded rooms, decorated for Jacques du Blé in about 1625 by Parisian artists, the marquise's bedroom with its original magnificent ceiling and painted panelling, and St Cecilia's Study, devoted to the patroness of music; this is a quiet but sumptuous room on the north side, with allegorical figures on the panelling. The main staircase is exceptional – an *escalier vide à la moderne*.

The word *vide* indicates a rectangular space enclosed by flights of balustraded stone steps, supported all the way up by four corner pillars which frame arches between them at every level. Do not miss the wood-panelled kitchen and its nineteenth-century equipment, nor the contemporarily furnished bathroom with its freestanding painted metal bath, towel rail and *bidet*, and a built-in wash-basin with a gas-heated hot tap. The cellars are approached separately, from the courtyard, and were used as a prison and a cobbler's workshop as well as for the storage of wine.

The severe late Renaissance front at the rear of the château looks across the moat to a leafy avenue, four hundred metres long, which tradition says was the favourite walk of Lamartine. It would have suited his autumnal moods, one feels.

At this point we have to turn south on the main road, stopping briefly at **Ameugny**, where the purposeful little twelfth-century church is built of golden limestone from the local quarries. The tower is shorter than at Chissey, even squat, but it too has characteristic blind arcading on all four faces. Our main objective, though, is a little further on, at **Taizé** – both villages being set back a short way from the road. You will experience the spirit of this extraordinary place immediately after you cross the railway and turn right for the village church. This is one of the most perfect and moving little buildings – just a simple Romanesque nave below a serenely elegant tower. Inside you will find silence and near darkness, relieved only by golden light filtered through the modern glass in the narrow windows. There are no pews or chairs, nothing but the altar and a few wooden kneelers scattered on the floor of the nave. After the bright sunshine outside it may be a few minutes before you can take it in, and perhaps see that a dark shape on the floor is a young man lying prone on a mat, totally relaxed in prayer.

The atmosphere it creates is indescribable, and to discover what lies behind it you should climb the fairly steep hill through the village until you come out on a level ridge looking west over flat fields. This is where the international community of Taizé was first conceived by a young Swiss pastor called Frère Roger, who took up his duties as *curé* here in 1940. The village was just south of the demarcation line between occupied and unoccupied France, and for two years Frère Roger's house was a refuge for members of the Resistance and for those fleeing from Nazi persecution – many of them Jews. A visit from the Gestapo luckily missed him when he was on a visit to Geneva, where he was joined by his first companions. After the Liberation they returned to Taizé, and made contact with a camp for German prisoners of war nearby. The prisoners were allowed to visit them and share in their community prayer.

In 1962 they built a new church on the hill, and called it the **Church of the Reconciliation**, as a reminder that those who had been enemies had been reconciled in that place. Its design is roomy and airy, more like a huge tent than a church, and save for the altar it has none of the trappings of the Catholic or Anglican rituals. There is banked seating which overlooks the altar area, and it can be used for meetings, discussions, lectures or concerts. Yet at all times it is instinct with religious feeling. Lighting is normally kept dim, the daylight filtered through stained glass designed and made in the Taizé workshops; the artificial lighting is discreet and subdued, the atmosphere hushed until some community event brings it to vibrating life.

The seventy or so brothers who form the religious side of the community commit themselves to it for their lives, in a form of the traditional monasteric vows. They are drawn from all the main Christian denominations, and if you are present at one of their daily offices you will have no way of telling which brothers are Anglican, Lutheran, Roman Catholic or Orthodox. A vital moment in their history was the invitation from Pope John XXIII to be present at every session of the second Vatican Council. When John-Paul II was lying near to death after the attempt on his life, the attendants outside his room were puzzled by an inconspicuous figure in canonical dress who repeatedly asked for the latest news, and to be remembered to His Holiness. For a time they ignored him, but in the end they told the Pope, and hearing that it was Brother Roger out there he immediately ordered them to admit him. They talked and prayed together for a long time, and against medical expectation the Pope recovered.

That a foundation like this – evangelical in the truest sense – should have grown up so close to Cluny may or may not be a coincidence, but Taizé has no intention of founding other communities in the same mould, like the network of abbeys which spread out from Cluny across all Europe. Yet you will never find all the brothers here at the same time. Small groups go and live for a time in other continents – in Brazil, Calcutta or parts of Africa for example – and the brothers themselves come from America, Africa and Asia, as well as from almost every European nation.

This aspect of Taizé may not be the best known, for since 1966 it has been famous as a gathering point for young people, mainly between 18 and 30. Even if you are not within those ages you would be welcome to come and assimilate what Taizé is about. This involves spending several days in the community, sharing in opportunities for common prayer and attending whatever gatherings interest you. Conditions are not as spartan as they once were, for permanent cabins have been put up as well as tents for the tens of thousands who come here every year, and catering is well organized within the separate groups. The first sound you may hear as you walk round is that of hundreds of hands washing up plates, cups and cutlery in their own messes – a cheerful din which contrasts with the silence of devotion at other times.

While pilgrims of all ages come here, and from farther afield than they did to Canterbury and Compostela, the reverse process happens too, for every year in some world capital or city a gathering is organized to draw in those who have never been able to go to Taizé, or may not even have heard of it. The theme is always peace and reconciliation, than which nothing is more desperately needed in the world today. Whether in the Church of the Reconciliation or back in the village church (which has been put at the disposal of the community), you will feel almost palpably the silence and the peace. It is hard to imagine a place more dense with prayer, and you will stand or kneel there with the consciousness that your deepest thoughts are shared by others.

Before turning east for Tournus – though it means retracing your steps northwards through Cormatin – it would be a pity to miss the two villages of Malay and Ougy on either side of the D981. Both have Romanesque churches of great charm and purity of style. To the left is **Malay**, where the short sturdy tower is more like Ameugny in its proportions. It has two double-arched openings on each face, and a strongly marked cornice below a low-pitched roof. The *chevet* is complex, with a central apse and two

absidioles, a projecting sacristy and a flat-ended choir and transept, all with different roof levels. Seen across the green meadow
to the east, cropped by sheep with young lambs in spring, it is an
irresistible sight. The inside – and the whole of the east end dates
from the end of the eleventh century – has been faithfully restored
by 'les amis de Malay'.

The sister church at **Ougy** on the other side of the road has an
outstandingly fine tower. Tall, with a four-sided stone spire, it
looks remarkably like the one at Chissey-lès-Mâcon, and in the
same tradition as those at Mazille and Taizé. The church itself is
less sophisticated than Malay, with just one wide semicircular apse
and is slightly later in date.

If you continue north on the D981 and take the first fork to the
left on the D67, you will come to **St-Gengoux-le-National**. Gen-
goux is the French form of Gengulphus, a Burgundian nobleman
said to have been murdered by his wife's paramour in 760. Until
1789 the town had been called St-Gengoux-le-Royal ever since
Louis VII acquired it from the abbey of Cluny. The Revolution
believed in nationalization, and where it affected the status of
towns the policy has never been reversed; succeeding governments might privatize, but have never dared to royalize again.
Apart from its resounding name, this is an interesting and dignified mediaeval town with many old houses and turreted corners.
The church has one remarkable oddity. Its octagonal tower is in
the Brionnais tradition (though handicapped by an outsize slate
spire) but close by it rises a slender finger of stone which is a
separate twelfth-century *clocher*, joined to the tower by an iron
walkway. This too has been given an incongruous slate hat,
crowned by a *lanternon*.

The nave inside is serenely Romanesque, though the choir was
altered in the fifteenth century. The resulting big eastern window
is filled with some surprisingly good nineteenth-century glass, and
so is the rose window to the west. The pillars of the main crossing
have historiated capitals, and on the pillar at the entrance to the
south apse you can see an early carving of the Virgin and Child
being serenaded by a mixed orchestra of saints and angels, playing
on what would now be called authentic instruments. Wandering
round the town you will find other pleasures and curiosities. On
the north side of the Avenue de la Promenade there is a

distinguished row of seventeenth-century houses with grey shutters, behind a line of ancient plane trees.

From St-Gengoux you will have to turn back and take the D67, which (after a brief spell on the D981) runs very straight through the woods to the south-east. After nine kilometres turn right for **Chapaize**, and you will soon see ahead of you the finest of all the Lombardic towers of the Mâconnais. The church of St-Martin formed part of a priory built about the year 1000 by the Benedictines of St-Pierre in Chalon, but the church is all that remains. From closer to you will appreciate the lovely proportions of its tower, pierced by perfectly spaced double window arches above tall blind arcading. Inside, it is exciting to find a virtually Carolingian nave with side aisles. The thick and unadorned pillars in rough natural stone and the low rounded arcades are unlike anything we have yet seen in Burgundy – above ground, that is, for we have seen crypts of the same or earlier date. The thickness of the walls can be judged at points where fairly large windows have later been inserted in the side aisles. As for the tower, elegant rather than obviously robust, it has stood unharmed for almost a thousand years. Its builders knew what they were about.

Just to the north of Chapaize, on the D215, are the ruins of the priory at **Lancherre**. A convent of canonesses, all of noble birth, it was founded in the eleventh century. Each of them lived in her own little house with her personal servant. In the twelfth century they embraced the rule of St Benedict and so were dependent on Cluny, but they were protected by the seigneurs of Brancion nearby. The church was built in 1300, and parts of the nave and the apse are still standing. Knights were buried there by permission, and you may see their tombstones set up against the walls of the crossing. The status of the priory was raised to that of an abbey in 1636, when it moved to Chalon, and thereafter the abbesses were appointed by the kings of France. The Revolution put an end to a highly aristocratic way of contemplation.

From Chapaize you can take your last journey through the Mâconnais hills before reaching Tournus, and it will be one to remember. For a time the D14 runs straight, as it crosses the Forêt de Chapaize, but then with many *virages* it begins to climb to a point where you have your first view of the château of **Brancion**, just before you reach the col. Rising through the trees you can see its two main landmarks, the keep and the Tour de Beaufort, and you will soon find that this is no ordinary ruin. If you follow the side road up from the col, you will be civilly received at the reception point for visitors, where the owner's family is in charge. A helpful leaflet, with both French and English versions, tells you something of its history and provides a key to the various numbered sites.

The fortress dates back to the tenth century, and for the next three hundred years it was the bastion of the family which bore its name. Their nickname was 'le Gros', but they lived up to their motto: 'Au plus fort de la mêlée'. Joinville tells us that Jocerand de Brancion met his death by the side of St Louis in the battle of Mansourah in 1250, but his son was ruined by equipping an army for the next crusade, and had to sell his estates to the duke of Burgundy in 1259. It passed to the French crown in 1477. Since 1860 the family of the comte de Musard has undertaken to preserve one of the most intriguing of *monuments historiques*.

The Tour de Beaufort was built by Eudes IV of Burgundy early in the fourteenth century. It contains the *salle de justice*, which has a fireplace emblazoned with the arms of the later Valois dukes, and an exhibition of life as it was lived here in the Middle Ages. Next to it is the Tour de la Chaul, a classic mediaeval flanking tower with slit openings or *meurtrières* from which the archers could shoot in three directions. Just before you reach the keep are the foundations of the tenth-century castle, distinguished by courses of *arêtes de poisson*, or stones laid in herringbone pattern, which are a feature of Carolingian and earlier building.

In the principal room of the keep the account by Joinville of the death of Jocerand de Brancion in Egypt is inscribed above the fireplace. Next to it is the huge space, which occupied two storeys, once occupied by the *salle des gardes* and sometimes called the Grande Salle de Beaujeu. To the right are the Tour des Archives, where all the records of Brancion were burnt during the wars of religion, and the Tour du Guet, or watch-tower, where you can appreciate the sanitary arrangements of the fifteenth century. Rather less well defined, above the steep slope which marks the line of the *enceinte*, are remains of the chapel of St Catherine, and cut into the slope itself is a food store with an air vent – not, as was once believed, an underground prison. There are few places where it is easier to reconstruct the feudal way of life.

Coming down to the village below you will find that it has also kept much of its mediaeval character, with a fifteenth-century inn and covered wooden **Halles** of the same date. The **Church of St Peter** stands almost alone on the edge of a cliff which has a lordly view over the valleys of the Grison and the Grosne to the north-west. It has been carefully restored without and within, and it is a surprise to find that it dates only from the end of the twelfth century, for the interior will remind you of Chapaize. A remarkable series of fourteenth-century frescos has been preserved (in some cases only partially) in different parts of the church. You will find a key to them in the leaflet you were given at the château. The most striking, and in the best condition, is a view of pilgrims arriving in Jerusalem, to be found in the chapel to the right of the choir, but for simple charm you may pick the Nativity in the left-hand chapel. The Infant, in very tight swaddling clothes (as reproduced in Chissey-lès-Macon) has been put on a shelf inside a curtained alcove, while his Mother is comfortably propped on a couch below. The colours are in much the same range as we saw in the Chapelle des Moines at Berzé-la-Ville. In the last bay of the north aisle is the tomb of Jocerand de Brancion, hero of the Crusades.

The grassy terrace outside the church is the scene of curious happenings at midsummer (the Sunday night nearest to June 24). The *Feux celtiques de St Jean* involve a bonfire and other jollifications, and both the church and castle are floodlit. Traditionally the villagers turn out in religious costumes, though this custom seems to be on the wane.

As a last stop before reaching the end of this particular journey, the village of **Ozenay** is worth a look. There was a château here in the thirteenth century, altered and added to in the seventeenth; though it is now a farm and in private hands you may be able to glimpse its impressive south front from the field behind. The church is more accessible. Built about 1180 by the canons of Chalon, it has a timbered porch with a tiled roof, and a simple tower with a pitched roof and gables north and south. The restoration of 1751 was by no means mistaken, and the big eighteenth-century *retable* has its points.

If you would like to break your journey at Brancion you can do so in peace and comfort at the modernized hotel called Montagne de Brancion, set well back on the left of the road leading up to the castle. It has no restaurant, but you can eat in the village. If you decide to wait till you reach Tournus you can both stay and dine in splendour at the Hôtel de Greuze, just outside the abbey gateway, though both your room and a meal at Jean Ducloux's restaurant will cost you a great deal more. Le Sauvage, in the Place Champ-de-Mars, is a more modest alternative.

2

The D14 winds over the last ridge of the Mâconnais and brings you down into **Tournus**. The ground begins to slope gently through the town towards the Saône — which the Romans called the Arar. It has widened a good deal since we last saw it at Chalon, and it will be wider still when we leave it at Mâcon. This was never one of its important crossings, for the country to the west was secret and impenetrable; in Roman and mediaeval times it was more a staging post on the trade and pilgrimage route which came up through Mâcon from Lyon and Marseille and ran north to the inland port of Chalon.

It was here that St Valerian was martyred towards the end of the second century, and the pilgrimage to his tomb inspired Charles the Bald to found a monastery in 875, which was to contain not only the bones of St Valerian but also those of St Philibert, which a party of monks had brought with them from their primitive foundation at St-Philibert-de-Grand-Lieu on the Normandy coast. They had been expelled and relentlessly pursued across France by invading Norsemen until they found safety behind the walls of Tournus. In 937 the monastery was destroyed by the Hungarian invasion, to be replaced eventually by the present building. Enough progress had been made for a dedication ceremony to be held in 1019, but the final consecration of the abbey was not possible until 1120, by which time St Philibert had ousted St Valerian from the place of honour. Today **St-Philibert-de-Tournus** stands as a transcendent example of Romanesque architecture; there is nothing comparable to it in France or anywhere else.

The west front faces you like a fortress, great cliffs of pinkish stone rising on three sides for a hundred feet or more, with no windows other than narrow slits in the masonry until the topmost stage of the flanking towers is reached. Towards the end of the eleventh century the northern tower was extended to form a *clocher*, but starting at that height it seems irrelevant to the overall design. The surfaces below roof level, which would otherwise have been monotonously bare, are decorated with inset patterns of Lombardic arcading, very much like what we have just seen at Chapaize, though over a much larger area.

The likeness to a fortress is even more apparent when you enter the **Narthex**, for its two storeys remind one more of a *donjon* than of an *abbatiale*. There is no adornment except for a patch of chequer-board painting and the shadowy remains of a fresco on the vaulting of the lower chamber. The massive round pillars and severe arches which carry the whole weight of the building are repeated in the upper storey, which is twice the height of the lower one – almost a church in itself. It is in fact known as the **Chapel of St-Michel**, and if you look up at the west end from outside you will see a cross-shaped window opening just below a crenellated parapet. That is the high window in the west wall of the chapel, and gives an idea of the immense height of the narthex. Note that the spiral stairway leading to the upper storey is a 'military' one – it turns clockwise on the way up, so as to give a right-handed defender the advantage for his sword arm.

Until 1629 the central archway at the east end of the chapel opened on to the nave, but then it was blocked in to allow the organ to be built in the usual seventeenth-century position. This arch has been the subject of much speculation, if not mystery, which has an important bearing on the dates we ascribe to different parts of the church. The mystery concerns an inscription on one of the stones built into the right-hand section of the arch, which reads:

> GERLANNUS
> ABATE ISTO MO
> NETERIUM E
> ILE

However shaky the Latin, and whatever the last few letters mean, it indicates that an abbot named Gerlannus (Guerlain?) had some part in the building of the narthex, though we know nothing more about him.

The impost of the arch on this side is formed by two projecting stones, with a block between them on which is carved a figure in profile who holds a hammer in his left hand while he gives a blessing with his right. Is this meant to be Gerlannus? Or is it a self-portrait of the master mason? It is no help to turn to the corresponding block on the left of the arch, which shows a low-browed, fat-cheeked, bearded character with protruding ears – an unidentifiable caricature, one would say. These are among the earliest examples of figure sculpture in Burgundy, matched only by those in the crypt of St-Bénigne at Dijon. This and other correspondences have suggested that work done on the narthex of St-Philibert was at least influenced by that done for William of Volpiano at St-Bénigne, and its date has been put at about 1000, with the upper narthex understandably later than the ground floor, though not by much . As a whole it was a necessary adjunct to the crypt-church which contained the bones of the saints – until then the only place where pilgrims could gather.

What, then, did the first pilgrims see when they looked through the *arc de Gerlannus*? Perhaps only a building site, for it seems unlikely that the nave of a new church could have been built by then – though the intention was probably there, even before a terrible fire in 1006 destroyed all of the earlier sanctuary except the actual shrines of the saints. After that there would be two aims: first to repair the original structure in the form of a crypt; then – and it was the kind of opportunity which the eleventh century rarely missed – to build an entirely new church above it and abutting on to the narthex, which was already in position. The dedication in 1019 shows that all was going well, but between 1030 and 1033 an extraordinary famine hit Burgundy, leading (if we are to believe one account) to acts of cannibalism in the neighbourhood of Tournus. Progress was delayed for so long that the building was not finally consecrated by Calixtus II until 1120.

It is better in any case to have your first view of the nave of St-Philibert from ground level. Visitors to Burgundy will always be debating whether that moment is more breath-taking here or at Vézelay. A lot depends on the light, and on your own mood, but the truth is that the two experiences are incomparable – in both the particular and the general sense. In St-Philibert the effect of the triple avenue of rose-coloured columns, rising without a break and without capitals almost to the main archivolts, is unique in church architecture. Somehow a Gothic sense of soaring weightlessness has been achieved by strictly Romanesque methods. In the central nave there was a need for short half-columns to carry the arches to their full height, but in the side aisles there is no break at all, and this is what makes the view along them in either direction surpassingly beautiful.

This is one of the rare churches where the nave outshines the choir and sanctuary. There are two theories, not necessarily conflicting, to explain the discrepancy between the two parts in both style and materials. One says that from the crossing eastward a separate team of masons was at work; if so, it would be understandable at a time when there was so much talent available from different sources. The other supposes that the choir was reserved for the monks, the nave being used by the pilgrims, who had access to the shrines below by way of the north transept. In this case there is the problem of where to include the crossing, for the cupola is much more elaborately constructed than you would expect by comparison with the nave. Notice how the four squinches are cleverly absorbed into the composition by the intervening arches, and by the rows of short columns which enclose the angles — not a fussy design, but somehow out of character with the direct message of the nave.

All, however, is purely Romanesque except in the north aisle and the north transept, where Gothic windows appear. Much use is made throughout of modern glass, and its subtle colouring tones particularly well with the stonework of the nave and side aisles. Not for the first time one appreciates the French taste and technique in modern stained glass, which always seems appropriate to the building in which it is set. There can be two opinions of the continuous rendering of Gregorian chants on tape; some (including the writer) find it distracts from an ensemble which is noble and moving enough by itself.

Descending to the **Crypt** by the stairway from the north transept, we find ourselves within the walls of the primitive abbey of St Valerian. His sarcophagus, empty since it was robbed during the wars of religion, is still there at the end of the central colonnade.

He was a converted Roman citizen who escaped with a few disciples from persecution at Lyon, only to be arrested here by the Roman governor in 177 and beheaded two years later. His remains were preserved, and long after Christianity had been accepted within the empire they were incorporated in what is described as a *petit monastère*. This was the building which in 875 received the bones of St Philibert (now in a gold casket at the far end of the main apse) and was destroyed first by the Hungarians in 937, then by fire in 1006. What we see today is probably the result of the first rebuilding campaign, and in both its plan and its materials it matches the chevet of the church above. The central aisle is an avenue of slender columns with delicate capitals of pierced foliage, very different from the sturdy grandeur of the rotunda of St-Bénigne, and carved from blocks of whitish limestone.

The **Cloister** is entered from the south side of the narthex, just by the staircase leading to its upper storey. Only the north range remains from the eleventh-century plan, with solid arches and a wide groined vault; the eastern arm includes some handsome arcading beside the entrance to the Chapter House, which was rebuilt by Abbé Bérard in 1239 after a fire. It now houses an exhibition of sculpture, which includes two battered full-length mediaeval figures, probably uprights from the sides of a doorway. The south side is occupied now by the Bibliothèque Municipale.

Of the other monastic buildings, you will be lucky if you find the **Refectory** open after a long period under repair, but it is a superb twelfth-century hall – known in Tournus as 'le Ballon'. New excavations, which prevent access for the time being, have already turned up some valuable finds. Between it and the narthex is a range of buildings on two floors, now used for exhibitions; the basement was the abbey cellars. The atmosphere within the whole monastic enclosure is still peaceful and dignified. To the south the line is marked by the Tour du Portier, opposite the refectory, and further on by the much bigger Tour de Quincampoix, whose foundations go back to the tenth century. Continuing east, on the far side of the Place des Arts you will see the late fifteenth-century abbot's lodging. In the north-east corner is the seventeenth-century house of the municipal treasurer, bequeathed to the town by the literary critic Albert Thibaudet (1874-1936) which now houses the **Musée Perrin-de-Puycousin**. It is devoted to folklore, with wax models in regional costume – populating a farm in the Bresse or a kitchen in Tournus, busy at their looms or setting their still-room in order.

The **Musée Greuze** in the rue du Collège, like the famous restaurant of M. Ducloux, does honour to a native of Tournus. Jean-Baptiste Greuze (1725-1805) was born here of an artisan family, and studied painting under Grandin at Lyon, and later in Paris. He was much admired by Diderot, and the Goncourts wrote of 'ces têtes blondes qu'un rayon éveille, que le soleil caresse et frise'. Greuze went to Italy and fell in love with the daughter of a duke; it may be her likeness that we meet in *L'Accordée du Village* and *La Laitière*. With his tendency to sugar the portrait, he was much sought after, although he refused to paint the Dauphine because she was too made-up; he was eclipsed by David when neoclassicism became fashionable. Greuze married unhappily and separated from his wife. 'I hope you'll come to my funeral', he remarked to a friend, 'you'll be there all alone, like a poor man's dog'. He is most characteristically represented here by his sentimental engravings of family life, but there are more professional portrait engravings of Rameau, Gluck, Diderot and Robespierre, and pastels of himself in youth and old age.

Do not leave Tournus without going down to look at the broad river on its slow, placid course between the old town and the newer buildings of the *rive gauche*. These are now joined by a new bridge completed in the summer of 1988. The view, whether from the bridge or from the farther bank, does justice for the first time to the two Romanesque towers of St-Philibert, clear of the surrounding or intervening roofs.

CHAPTER NINETEEN

La Bresse and Mâcon

If you leave Tournus by the N6 going south, take time to pass under the autoroute to your right and visit the church at **Farges-lès-Mâcon**. You will find it reproduces on a small scale some of the features of St-Philibert — especially the round columns built of rose-coloured stone. There are frescos in the apse, and in the nave there is a tombstone which covers the remains of Dame Marie-Anne Poulain, 'veuve en premières noces' of Jean Magnon, poet and royal historian, companion and friend of Molière. Stay this side of the autoroute, and at **Uchizy** you will see another of the remarkable church towers of the Mâconnais. This one has no fewer than five stages, each with a different arrangement of window openings, and the almost flat tiled roof which suits this kind of architecture so much better than the slate spire.

A curiosity here is that the inhabitants are said to be the descendants of a Saracen colony established after the victories of Charles Martel. Others maintain, more probably, that they are of Illyrian or Hungarian descent. Former generations were reputed to have had dark eyes, brown hair, thick eyebrows, burnished skin and white teeth. The girls wore their hair short and went about in knee-length skirts; the older women wore turbans. After careful scrutiny one must sadly say that nothing of the kind is to be seen here now.

Our goal now is **Bourg-en-Bresse**, which means leaving Saône-et-Loire for the department of Ain, a journey strictly speaking outside the boundaries of Burgundy, but one we are not going to refuse. The best route is to continue on the D210 as far as Viré, then cross the autoroute, the N6 and the Saône in quick succession to reach Pont-de-Vaux. From there it is easy going on the D26 to join the main road into Bourg with only 17 kilometres to go. Having crossed to the east bank of the Saône, we find that the Bresse has a good deal in common with the Pays-Bas east of

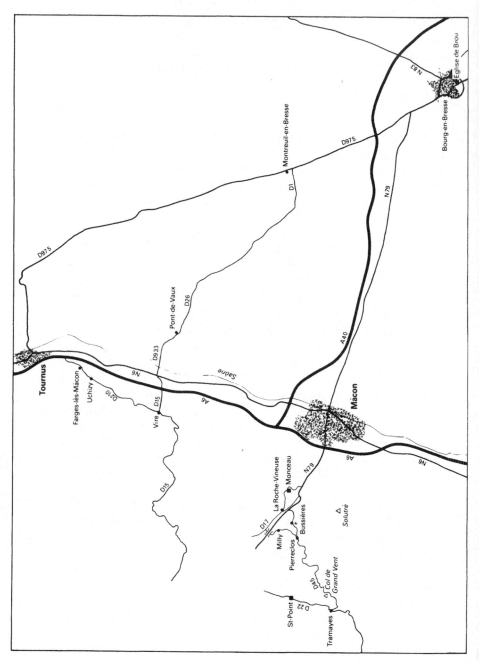

La Bresse and Mâcon

Dijon, though beneath its placid and fertile exterior it hides a character of its own.

The clayey subsoil is carpeted with lime and produces a rich harvest of maize. Maize was introduced here in the sixteenth century, long before it became the staple crop of huge areas of France. The isolated farms are built of red brick and tiles round a large yard, with a lofty shed for machines, a smaller yard opposite, and one big room in the house where most of its life goes on. Further south, beyond Bourg itself, is the area known as **la Dombes**, where the *étangs* are thicker on the ground than anywhere in France.

What brought fame and good living to Bresse is its poultry, a breed which was started 350 years ago. The chickens are fed on the maize and left at liberty until they are rounded up for the market at Louhans, and for the great Foire de la Baume near St-Germain-des-Bois on 26 August. For her *poularde demideuil* the celebrated Mère Fillioux from Lyon ordered 20,000 fattened pullets a year from Louhans, all of them plucked at seven or eight months old. A metal band in one of three colours was strapped to the leg of every authentic Bressan bird -- black if it came from Louhans, grey from Bony, and white from Besy. While in Bresse, you need not confine yourself solely to chicken; Barbey d'Aurevilly, the great nineteenth-century dandy, was of the opinion that a *gigot* from the Bresse was as tender as a woman's buttocks.

In the tenth century Bourg was nothing more than a collection of huts surrounding a *château-fort*, but the line of feudal overlords died out, and in the thirteenth century it passed to the dukes of Savoy, under whom it grew and prospered as the capital of the region. In 1536 François I seized it after the duke had refused passage to his troops on their way to attack Milan, but Henri II restored it in 1559. In 1600 the Bresse was invaded by Henri IV, who attached it permanently to the French crown. Today Bourg is a flourishing market town, and the centre of a trade in furniture, made from ash, wild cherry and pear wood in the style known as 'rustique Bressan'. However, its most famous activity is still the breeding, rearing and marketing of the *poulets de Bresse* which feature on menus for miles around.

If you would like to stay in Bourg there is a choice of several good hotels, most of them without restaurants – for this is a town where eating is an occupation that calls for undivided attention from both restaurateurs and their clients. Those who know it would probably choose the Terminus, a delightfully old-fashioned hotel (with one of those open-work clanking lifts) which has been in the family for several generations. The father of a recent *patronne* was said to have eaten a record number of escargots at a sitting – a hundred dozen of them, but his daughter did explain that he ate nothing else at that meal. There is convenient parking in a quiet garden area at the rear. The two largest hotels are not in the town proper, but in the suburb of Brou, close to the flamboyant **Église de Brou**, its most popular attraction.

It stands on the far side of the main N75 through road, about a mile from the town centre. In 1480 Philippe, comte de Bresse and duc de Savoie, was seriously hurt in a hunting accident, and his wife Marguerite de Bourbon vowed that if he recovered she would transform the modest Benedictine priory of Brou into an abbey. Philippe did recover, and lived for another seventeen years, but his wife died before she could keep her promise. The fulfilment of the vow was entrusted to their son, Philibert le Beau, who had other matters on his mind, including a brief but happy marriage to Marguerite dAutriche, daughter of Marie de Bourgogne and so the grand-daughter of Charles le Téméraire. Her father was the Emperor Maximilian of Austria, and she had been a pawn in the power game of Europe since her childhood.

At the age of two she lost her mother, and was affianced by her father to the Dauphin of France (later Charles VIII). After he came to the throne he began to look elsewhere for an alliance, and in 1491 he repudiated her (she was still only eleven) in favour of Anne de Bretagne. At seventeen she was married to Don Juan, *infante* of Spain, only to be left a widow after six months. Maximilian's next candidate for her hand was Philibert le Beau of Savoy, with whom she had played as a child at Amboise while waiting for her marriage to Charles. It was a happy union, but Philibert spent a good deal of his time hunting, leaving his wife to manage their affairs and nourish her own ambition to become a power in the land where her ancestors had ruled for four generations.

They had been married only three years when he died in 1504, probably from pneumonia while hunting in the Jura, and his widow in her bereavement suspected a sign of divine displeasure at the unfulfilled vow. To ensure the repose of her husband's soul she decided to build the new monastery round the cloisters of the old priory, and next year she moved to Bourg from Pont d'Ain to oversee the work. However, the following year saw the death of her brother, Philippe le Beau, the last male heir to the duchy of Burgundy, which radically altered Marguerite's life and changed her priorities. With her father's agreement she established herself in Malines as Regent of the Netherlands and of the Franche-Comté, in the name of her six-year-old nephew Charles, Maximilian's grandson. Having lost his father, and being effectively deprived of a mother by the madness of Jeanne de Castille, he was put in the care of his aunt for his early education.

Nevertheless the monastic buildings at Brou were completed by 1508, and she employed the French architect Jean Perréal (whom she had also known as a girl at Amboise) to draw up plans for the new abbey church, and called on an elderly master mason, Michel Colombe, to execute them. The ground plan had already been laid out on the site by 1511, when Marguerite decided that the Perréal designs failed to match the grandeur of her new position. Colombe had in any case died at the age of 83, and she now commissioned a distinguished Flemish master, Loys van Boghem, to take over the whole responsibility with *carte blanche* to employ whatever specialist artists he needed. For the major work of the princely tombs he brought in the German sculptor Conrad Meyt.

In 1519 Maximilian died, and his grandson was crowned as Charles V. Marguerite, whose visions of grandeur were partly at least influenced by jealousy of her sister-in-law, Louise de Savoie, widow of Charles de Valois and mother of the future François I, insisted on having a stone model of the imperial crown erected at the top of the *clocher* which was planned to go over the crossing of the new church. Van Boghem was alarmed at this extra weight being added to the central vault, and managed to have the tower transferred to the south side of the choir. His anxiety was justified, for in 1659 it collapsed and the crown had to be replaced by a wooden spire.

Meanwhile the rest of the work went ahead, but in 1530 Marguerite died from septicaemia after treading on some broken glass. A third tomb had to be provided to accompany the still unfinished ones of her husband and his mother, and the western façade had not been built, but under strong compulsion from the new emperor van Boghem was able to declare 'fin de chantier' early in 1532. To have accomplished so much in twenty years was a remarkable if not a record achievement.

As for the monastic quarters, Marguerite had installed an Augustinian community from Lombardy to relace the Benedictines. In the seventeenth century they gave way to their French *confrères*, but their peaceful tenure was ended by the Revolution. Horses were stabled in the nave, and the monastery became in turn a prison, a barracks, a home for down-and-outs, and a lunatic asylum. Rescued from further decay in the nineteenth century, it has been scrupulously restored and preserved by the State as a *monument historique*, though it is no longer used for worship.

Coming here so soon after Tournus, Paray-le-Monial and Autun it may be difficult to be objective when you find that late Gothic has so flamboyantly supplanted Romanesque. The very magnificence of the Église de Brou confirms the suspicion that it was not entirely inspired by love and *pietas*, but was also intended to display to the rest of France the wealth and prestige of the last heiress of the Burgundian dynasty – and especially to her sister-in-law Louise. There are, however, many symbols of more tender emotions. On the tympanum of the west portal Philibert and Marguerite, with their patron saints, are shown at the feet of Christ. The church is dedicated to St Nicholas of Tolentino, because it was on his feast day that Philibert died. The initials P and M, linked by *lacs d'amour*, appear again and again as part of the decoration inside, though so does Marguerite's personal and enigmatic motto: 'Fortune Infortune Fort Une', most simply rendered as 'Through good and bad fortune one woman remains strong'.

You will be struck as you enter the nave by the luminous whiteness of the stone, quarried from Revermont and untouched by time. The pillars, composed of clusters of thin columns, rise without capitals or imposts to the vaulting, and a passage with an elaborate stone balustrade separates the arcades from the windows above. The nave is closed off from the choir by an even more elaborate *jubé*, or rood screen. As well as hiding the exclusively monastic areas of the east end from the public view – which it does all too effectively – it formed a bridge by which Marguerite would have been able to cross unseen from her apartments in the cloister to her private oratory in the north transept.

From here you must wait for a guide to continue your visit. The seventy-four **Stalls** were designed and executed by a local carpenter, Pierre Berchod; they were carved out of huge single blocks of wood which had been softened and seasoned by prolonged dousing in the *étangs* of la Dombes. Behind the seating on both sides biblical figures are carved – Old Testament to the north, New Testament to the south – but a more mediaeval note is struck by the caricatures of the seven deadly sins below them. Among the *miséricordes* is the famous carving known as 'la correction maritale', though the birching pictured could just as well be of an apprentice by his master as of a husband by his wife.

Prominent beyond the stalls are the **Tombs** of the three noble patrons, Philibert, Marguerite, and Philibert's mother Marguerite de Bourbon. None of them had been completed by the time of the younger Marguerite's death, and it was Charles V who saw to it that her memorial matched the other two. The workmanship throughout is extraordinary. The ornamentation and lesser statuary were executed mainly in a Flemish workshop set up in Brou with French, German and Italian assistants. They used the soft marble of Saint-Lothian, working on it with only wooden tools. The effigies themselves were carved from blocks of marble imported at great expense from Carrara. Conrad Meyt, though a German by birth, was trained in Flanders and worked from designs by Jean de Bruxelles. The figures each lie on a black marble slab, Philibert in the centre facing the altar, with his mother to his right and Marguérite d'Autriche to his left. Their heads rest on finely embroidered cushions; at their feet the two women have greyhounds, symbols of fidelity, Philibert a lion signifying strength and nobility. Cherubs and angels escort all three to Paradise, while at the four corners and halfway down the long sides of Philibert's tomb is a set of lovely young female statues – once strangely identified as 'sybils', more plausibly now as 'virtues' but in either case beautiful studies of femininity. There are two representations of St Catherine – one on each of the two outer tombs – and it is not clear which of them Belloc described as 'of a beauty beyond this world', though both are charming. Philibert and his wife are both represented 'à la moderne', first as they appeared in life, below as *gisants* in their shrouds – a striking departure for the time.

On the left of the apse the chapel called after Marguerite d'Autriche contains a magnificent altar-piece of white marble, perhaps the finest sculptural group in the church. Known as the **Retable des Sept Joies**, it illustrates the happier events in the life of the Virgin, from the Annunciation to the Assumption. Next to it are the two personal oratories which Marguerite planned one above the other, with a connecting staircase. They are in effect a private suite of rooms with a fireplace, an opening through which she could have 'assisted' at Mass, and on the upper floor a door on the level of the *jubé*. It is poignant to see all these practical arrangements and realize that she died before she could use them, though in the church as a whole she would know that her family's debts had been paid to God, honour done to her husband, and her own place in history assured. The larger chapel to the west, really a part of the north transept, is named after Laurent de Gorrevod, Governor of Bresse and Marguerite's chief counsellor. A corresponding chapel in the south transept was similarly connected with the abbé de Montecuto, who was her confessor and almoner.

As you would expect, there is some outstanding stained glass in the windows, for which van Boghem commissioned the Flemish artist Nicolas Rombouts to design the cartoons, and entrusted their execution to the lyonnais *atelier* of Jean Brachon. The five windows of the apse show Philibert and Marguerite kneeling with their patron saints and framed by the armorial bearings of their families. The central window represents the two appearances of the resurrected Christ. Less conventional is the window in the Gorrevod chapel where the doubting Thomas is touching with his fingers the wound in Jesus's side. The corresponding chapel of Montecuto has an equally rich portrayal of Christ with the pilgrims of Emmaus, while the finest of all is the one in the south transept of the story of Susannah – accused by the elders above and acquitted by David below. It seems a miracle that all this sixteenth-century glass has survived war, revolution and time almost intact.

There are three **Cloisters**, reached in succession from the south transept. The first and smallest (and the last to be built) has a gallery connecting Marguerite's private apartments with the upper level of the *jubé*, and so with her oratory in the north transept. The

Great Cloister gave access to the main monastic premises – chapter house, refectory and dorter. They now contain the **Musée de l'Ain**, a series of rooms displaying sculpture, faïences and tapestries of various origins and dates, Bressan furniture of the sixteenth century, and paintings of Flemish, French and Italian schools from the sixteenth to the nineteenth. There is a portrait of Marguerite d'Autriche from about 1520 by van Orley.

The third cloister, known as the 'cloître des cuisines', has an Italian air about it, and is all that remains of the fourteenth-century Benedictine priory. The most attractive and interesting of the three, it has an old covered well in the centre, and a collection of bygone implements and machinery. There is also a reconstructed 'maison bressane' where you can see a kitchen with its fire in the middle of the room, a spinning-wheel, dresser, long-case clock, spoons, and loaves on a rack above the dining table. The bedroom has a four-poster bed with a cradle attached, and there are figures of peasants with clogs and tasselled caps, straw toppers and bagpipes.

2

It is no distance now to **Mâcon** and the Saône, and there is nothing much of interest to see on the way. The town is not immediately attractive, apart from the line of quays on the right bank of the river, and if you plan to explore the Mâconnais and the Lamartine country to the west you may prefer to stay outside. In fact the most luxurious hotel, the Mercure Bord de Saône, is outside the city limits to the north, but a good rule if in doubt is to go for a Logis de France; the Terminus in the rue Victor Hugo is one such with many advantages.

We owe a debt to Charles Brosse, that enormously tall – *septipède* – vine grower from Charnay-lès-Mâcon, who introduced the wines of the Mâconnais to Louis XIV. With two barrels of his *meilleurs crus* on a cart, drawn by a pair of oxen, he arrived after a journey of thirty-three days at Versailles, in time to assist at the King's Mass. Louis was struck by his unusual height, and called for him to be presented. Brosse quickly explained the nature of his errand, hoping to sell his wine to some noble of the court. The king tasted it on the spot and found it better than the vintages from the Loire currently served at court. Charles Brosse became a rich man, and spent much of his time travelling to and fro between Charnay and Versailles. It is not easy to imagine an enterprising wine-grower from our south coast arriving today at Buckingham Palace and being thus received — though once past security his mission might not prove hopeless. The *ancien régime* had its own notions of democracy, not always inferior to our own.

The Mâconnais vineyards extend from Tournus in the north to Romaneche-Thorins in the south, where they come up against those of the Beaujolais. They cover over 200,000 hectares, of which two-thirds produce a white wine from the Chardonnay grape. Until the nineteenth century the red predominated, but it never achieved the quality of the white. The five villages of the Pouilly district nestle among the limestone hills — so favourable to the Chardonnay — under the escarpment of the huge **Solutré Rock**. Here the prehistoric hunters would drive their quarry over the edge, so that the bones of slaughtered deer form a subsoil in the ground below. The place has given its name to a period of the Stone Age (15,000 to 12,000BC), and excavation began in 1866. A hundred thousand animal skeletons were found, and in 1922 three human skeletons of an even earlier period, with others more recent (Neolithic) and pottery from the Bronze Age. Examples can be seen in the Musée Municipal in Mâcon, and Solutré is an easy drive of eight kilometres to the west of the town.

Mâcon will not let you forget that Lamartine was born here, though you will not easily recognize the town he described:

The upper town is abandoned to silence and repose. You would think you were in a Spanish city. The grass grows in summer between the paving stones. The high walls of former convents darken the streets. A school, a hospital, churches — some restored, others dilapidated and now used as shops for the coopers of the district; a large square planted with lime trees at either end, where children play or old men sit in the sunshine on a fine day.

He was born at 18 rue des Ursulines, and in later life he stayed from time to time at the family Hôtel d'Ozenay, 15 rue Lamartine. The two halves of his life were in strong contrast. Until he was forty he was seen as a Byronic figure, writing poetry and constantly involved in affairs with younger women. In 1820 he married and took to politics. In 1833 he was elected to the Assembly as Deputy for Bergues (in the *Nord*) and shortly afterwards for Mâcon. During the revolutionary year of 1848 his liberal sympathies carried him to the head of the Provisional Government which proclaimed the Second Republic. His defence of the *tricouleur* as the national flag made him a popular hero, and only his liberal principles prevented him from becoming the sole 'ministre exécutif' of the newly elected Constituent Assembly. Eight months later he stood for the Presidency, but his supporters had drifted away and he received only 18,000 votes against 5,500,000 for Louis Napoleon. This was the end of his political career – indeed, he was always too much of a poet to be an effective politician. The city of Paris gave him a grace and favour chalet at Passy, but a severe stroke in 1867 led to his death two years later.

To follow Lamartine's earlier career as an impressionable boy, an uninhibited womanizer, and a poet who reflected the newly aroused romantic imagination of the time, we should follow the advice of the local tourist organization and undertake the 'Pèlerinage lamartien'. Our first visit should be to the little country village of **Milly**, twelve kilometres west of Mâcon. The reader may now appreciate that it will be less of a shock to move from the extravagances of Brou to the romantic world of the early nineteenth century than it would have been from the Romanesque world of the Chapelle des Moines and its Byzantine decoration. The two places are almost within a stone's throw of each other on opposite sides of the *route de vitesse*, but worlds apart in other respects.

Alphonse de Lamartine was born at Mâcon on 21 October 1790. He was four years old when Pierre Lamartine, released after a year's imprisonment as a suspected royalist, decided to move to the house in Milly which his wife had brought him as part of her *dot*. The village, which the poet always thought of as his 'terre natale', the church at which the family worshipped, and the house (which figured in his early work *La Vigne et La Maison*) have changed little since those days. The house, which has a plaque by the gate quoting two lines from his poetry, could be a rectory or a doctor's house in an English village, with its two-storeyed, deep-windowed, creeper-clad front. 'At Milly', he wrote, 'everything remembers me, everything knows me, and everything loves me'. He was to recall 'the sweet and melancholy voices of the little frogs that sing on summer evenings, as they do on the marshes'. Here was the wide light corridor with its spacious cupboards, the kitchen on the right and the dining room on the left, with the buffet and pinewood table; the ten bedrooms and the rough stone staircase. He liked to go back there to sleep from time to time, imagining that he heard 'the voice of my mother when I wake up, the footsteps of my father, and my sisters' happy cries, and all those sounds of youth, of life and of love, which for me alone echo beneath the old beams'.

Two kilometres to the south, in easy walking distance, is the village of **Bussières**, where Alphonse was sent for his first lessons in Latin and French literature. His tutor was the *curé*, Abbé Dumont, a strange man whose influence must have unconsciously directed the boy towards some of the adventures of his youth. A follower of Voltaire, he had marked an intermission in his priestly life by conducting an affair with the daughter of the neighbouring seigneur of Pierreclos. If not then, the *curé* must certainly have told Lamartine the story later, for it is the theme of one of his best known narrative poems, *Jocelyn*, which he wrote after Dumont's death in 1832. The château of Pierreclos is now the centre of a Mâconnais vineyard. Near the east end of the Bussières church is the so-called 'tombe de Jocelyn' on which appears the epitaph which the poet wrote for his old friend and tutor. There is also a memorial plaque on the wall of the former presbytery.

At the age of eleven the boy was sent off to boarding school in Lyon, but rebelled and ran away. Put in the care of the Jesuits at Belley, he found there his first literary enthusiasm — for the works of Chateaubriand — and felt an urge to become a writer himself in the romantic vein. When he returned at seventeen to live with the family, sometimes at Milly, sometimes in Mâcon, he soon became bored with local society. There was no question of him taking up a career in the army, government or civil service, for his family were profoundly royalist and would have nothing to do with the Bonaparte regime. He did enjoy holidays spent with his uncle the abbé Lamartine at Montculot -- the château which we visited in Côte d'Or — and its surroundings inspired some of his best poetry, but even lyric poetry and experiments with verse tragedies failed to occupy the energies of a young man who was nearly twenty-one. He seems to have had his first affair at the age of sixteen, but though (as was his habit) he made literary use of it later on in the episode of Lucy in *Confidences* we know nothing more about it. More serious was an affair with Henriette Pommier, daughter of a Justice of the Peace in Mâcon, which caused his parents to send him off to join some cousins in Italy.

The uninhibited life of Naples, with its gloriously romantic surroundings, was just the opportunity Alphonse wanted for his own romantic adventures. The first to fall – he was a very good-looking young man – was sixteen-year-old Antoniella, who worked in a tobacco factory run by one of his cousins. Genuinely in love – for four months – he had to leave her and Naples in April 1812 and return to France. Again, she figures as Graziella in two poems included in his *Harmonies*:

> Sur la plage sonore où la mer de Sorrente
> Déroule ses flots bleus au pied de l'oranger
> Il est, près du sentier, sous la haie odorante,
> Une pierre petite, étroite, indifférente
> Aux yeux distraits de l'étranger.

This was the tomb of Graziella, though she died not of love (according to the poet) but of tuberculosis, on 31 May 1816.

On the fall of the Empire the Lamartine family was only too glad to secure a commission for Alphonse in the army of Louis XVIII, but the return of Napoleon from Elba gave him an excuse to visit Switzerland to avoid being recruited for the imperial army during the Hundred Days. A happy stay by lac Leman included an affair with the daughter of a boatman with whom he was lodging, but after Waterloo he returned to the Mâconnais. There followed a period when he was a frequent visitor to the château of Cormatin, where, as we have seen, his hostess was Nina Dezoteux, wife of Guillaume de Pierreclos, by whom he had a son – his only male offspring.

By this time life seems to have caught up with him. His doctor diagnosed a liver complaint and recommended a stay at Aix-les-Bains in Savoy. Here began the most purely romantic chapter in his life, of which we read a great deal in his *Meditations*. Also at

Aix-les-Bains for her health was the young wife of an elderly doctor, Julie Charles. Within ten days of his arrival, Alphonse had rescued her from drowning on the lac du Bourget, and fallen deeply in love. But Julie was tuberculous, and physical love was soon ruled out by her worsening condition. They met again in Paris in January 1817, and when in May he had to return to Mâcon they made a rendezvous at Aix for the following summer. Lamartine kept it, unaware that Julie had died just before Christmas. The poem 'le Lac' is one of the most beautiful of his *Meditations*. It begins:

> O lac! l'année a peine finie sa carrière
> Et près des flots chéris qu'elle devait revoir
> Regarde, je viens seul m'asseoir sur cette pierre
> Où tu la vis s'asseoir.

and ends:

> Que tout ce qu'on entend, on voit, ou l'on respire.
> Tout dise: Ils ont aimé!

Three years later he decided to settle down. In 1820 he married a young Englishwoman, Marianne Birch, who was a recent convert to Catholicism, and they lived a happy life together till her death in 1863. Their first home was the château of **Saint-Point**, which Pierre Lamartine had bought in 1802 and now gave them as a wedding present. By then the publication of Meditations had established Alphonse as a major poet. It has been called 'le véritable début du Romantisme' in France, and perfectly expressed 'le mal du siècle, cette exquise mélancolie' which had settled on the country since the Revolution. His fame brought him brief employment as an attaché of the French embassy in Naples, but though he enjoyed being back among the scenes of his youth he soon tired of the job and returned to Saint-Point to pursue a purely literary career.

To reach the château from the neighbourhood of Milly is not easy. You can cross the main road to Berzé-la-Ville, rejoin the N79 just before its junction with the D980, turn left at the junction and left again on the D22 towards Tramayes. Or you can rely on the map to take you by an adventurous route from Pierreclos over the col de Grand Vent to Tramayes, then north on the D22. The house

– for it is more a *maison de plaisance* than a château – has great domestic charm, especially now that all the rooms in one wing have been refurbished and laid out just as they were in the days of Alphonse and Marianne. You will see how they lived, and there are souvenirs of different stages of their lives – including his premarital *amours*. Here is the bust of Graziella, his first Neapolitan conquest; an engraving by Aymond de Virieu, his friend since Jesuit days, of the boatman's daughter of lac Leman; the crucifix on which Julie Charles breathed her last in 1817, and Lamartine his in 1869; and a portrait painted by his wife of Julia, their daughter who died at the age of ten while the family were on a voyage to the Holy Land.

Personal mementoes include his travelling writing desk, his top hat, the bed on which he died, letters from Balzac, Victor Hugo, Chateaubriand and Alfred de Vigny. The walls of his study were padded to prevent disturbance from the world outside, though he was also happy to sit and write at a stone bench and table under a lime tree in the garden. Lamartine is buried beside his English wife – his partner for forty-three years – in a monumental *tombeau* outside the village church.

The last act of his life – in some ways the crowning part of it – was played in Paris, far from his beloved Mâconnais. His poetic inspiration had flagged, and while he was supporting the republican party in the 1840s he began to write *L'Histoire des Girondins*, as a contribution to the history of the Revolution. He wrote most of this at the château of **Monceau**, which he had inherited from an aunt in 1833. To find it you have to return once more to the far side of the railway and the N79, and take the *route touristique* along the north side of the valley. It is now an old people's home, but it looks a comfortable one, and its inmates can enjoy its terraces and well kept garden. To escape from his constant visitor and political discussions he built a liitle octagonal pavilion among his vines, where he could work on his *Histoire*. It is still there to be visited, the property of the Académie de Mâcon.

After the final revolutionary explosion of June 1848 he gave up politics, dismayed by the triumph of Louis Napoleon, and returned to Monceau. His finances were in poor shape, and even renewed literary efforts failed to pay off his debts. He sold Milly in 1860, his wife died three years later, and for the last years of his life he was looked after by his niece, Valentine de Cessiat.

At Monceau you are well on your way back to Mâcon, and you can say goodbye to Lamartine in the **Musée Municipal**, formerly the Ursuline convent – a seventeenth-century building in the rue de la Préfecture. Here among the relics and the erudite reconstruction of Solutré, elegant furniture and ceramics, paintings by Greuze, Courbet, Monet and Braque, you will find (if they have not all been put '*en reserve*' by the management) the superb portrait of Lamartine by Decaisne. It is a *locus classicus* of the period. Slim and serious, romantic and a little irresolute, seated on a grassy bank against an autumnal landscape, with one hand caressing a whippet, obviously as well bred as its master, and a book bound in Morocco leather just visible behind him, Lamartine looks out on the Mâconnais. We too may look upon it, and other landscapes we have seen, for the last time, and drink in with Hippolyte Taine:

the delicate and lively greens – delicate with a colour pale, distant and diluted; the resigned and pensive air of the poplars in their serried rows; and above all the thick and humid woods. This land has drunk its fill; it will always be green.

This is an autumnal picture which Lamartine would have recognised. That there is another Burgundy of blue skies, bright sunshine, radiant flowers, mellow stone and soaring towers, we have seen evidence in abundance. After all, if Burgundy has drunk its fill of water, Burgundians have turned the water into wine.

Wine-making in Burgundy

However small the area covered by the Burgundy vineyards – and, in contrast to the vast expanses covered by maize or other cereals, rape and sunflower crops, it is small indeed – they are part of one of the biggest industries in France. It is also the most varied, complicated and unpredictable in its output. So many bewildering factors go to produce a bottle of French wine, from a *grand cru* to a *vin de table*, that a single chapter can cover only a simplified outline of them. Soil, climate, grape varieties, methods traditional and modern, scientific measurement and human judgment – all these contribute to an end product whose variety delights and intrigues the connoisseur as much as its friendliness comforts the ordinary tippler.

The most crucial factor is the soil in which the vines are grown. Hardly detectable variations in the Bordeaux vineyards can make a wine great or mean; true champagne cannot be made except in the chalky uplands round Reims and Épernay, with their larding of fossilized crustaceans and their unique cellar-caves. In Burgundy more things combine to complicate wine-making than anywhere else, and the soil variations need a geologist to unravel. In general the basic rock is limestone, though in Chablis it combines with Kimmeridgian strata of clay and marl, mixed with the shell beds of *ostrea virgula*, to produce a unique white wine; in the Beaujolais it gives way to granite and porphyry. Other variations on a limestone base are the compact clays of the Auxerrois, the silica and iron oxide of the Chalonnais, and the light marlstone which feeds both the white and the red wines of the Mâconnais. Yet it is on the precious slopes of the Côte d'Or that the most famous wines of Burgundy are made.

Here various geological strata, including a narrow but crucial outcrop of marlstone, produce a calcareous flinty soil on which vegetable moulds accumulate as they wash down from the unproductive higher ground, and where pebbles and small broken stones help drainage. The subtle differences between the wines of the Côte de Nuits and the Côte de Beaune have been explained in these terms: the rich marls and crumbled rock full of potassium and phosphorus give weight to the former; a flinty clay and a lighter calcareous marl give more finesse to the latter, and are particularly suited to its great white wines.

Not only the soil, but the variations of contour and aspect affect the way vines behave. In Burgundy they are called *climats*, and as you travel down the Côte you can see how the generally south-facing slopes vary in steepness, sometimes looking more to the east or more to the south, while beyond Beaune their aspect turns more and more to the south. This can explain why every little parcel of land has something different to contribute to a vintage, though throughout the length of the Côte it is the moderate slopes before they begin to flatten out in the plain which produce the greatest wines.

Next in importance for regional differences are the vines to be planted – all varieties of the original *vitis vinifera* which the Romans knew, though since the phylloxera disaster of the late nineteenth century they have been grafted on to louse-resistant stocks of American origin. In the Bordeaux area the Cabernet Sauvignon, the Cabernet Franc and the Merlot combine in differing proportions to make clarets of differing quality. In the Champagne the white Chardonnay is used, blended sometimes with the Pinot Noir *au jus blanc*. Chablis uses only the Chardonnay, as do almost all Burgundy vineyards for their white wines, but in the Côte d'Or the Pinot Noir is king – indeed, it is the only permitted grape for the higher appellations of the region, and it was known in Burgundy as early as the fourteenth century. The joker in the pack is the Gamay, for in the Côte it is grown only on the less prestigious flat ground and used to make a *passe-tous-grains* which is far from being a true Burgundy. Yet on the granite-based slopes of the Beaujolais it comes into its own, and from it comes the qualities behind those delicious early-maturing wines. Of lesser importance are the Aligoté, which crops plentifully and makes a fresh white wine sometimes on the acid side, the fruitier Sauvignon which is used in the Auxerrois, and the interestingly named César. This too is found in the Auxerrois region, notably in the vineyards of Coulanges and Escolives. Near the latter has been found a bas-relief carving of the second or third century which shows a small naked harvester picking a bunch of grapes with deeply indented leaves – recognized by experts as belonging to the local César plants. Its alternative name 'Romain' reinforces the belief that it was imported by Roman colonists in the first place.

The Pinot Noir grows in tightly bunched cone-shaped clusters of small grapes. Generally speaking, wine-producing grapes are much smaller than the juicier dessert varieties, because they contain a higher proportion of sugar (and eventually alcohol) to liquid volume. In this connection the saying 'the older the vine the better the wine' holds good, for their fruit becomes smaller as they age, and specimens of up to forty or fifty years old can be found in the top vineyards. The vine has a remarkable ability to survive on soil unsuitable for other vegetation, sending its roots far down into the crevices of the rock in search of moisture. In one Beaune tasting cellar you can see them threading their way down through the limestone slabs from the vineyard above.

Young vines are planted, pruned and trained individually by hand, though tractors which straddle the rows are used to spray chemical disinfectants and remove surplus leaves after fruiting. Pruning is done according to established systems, and the resulting shoots are trained as appropriate for the different vines and terrain. For example the Chardonnay in Chablis are trained horizontally on wires running up and down the steep slopes, whereas the Pinot Noir in the Côte always run in straight lines across the contours. The Gamay in Beajolais is grown in pyramids with no wire support. An important task in the early months of the year is to replace the soil which has been washed down the slopes by the winter rains – traditionally by carrying it up again in hods to the top so as not to lose its essential qualities.

When the time comes for harvesting, two factors are uppermost in the grower's mind – the development of the grapes and the weather. An old tradition held that picking should start a hundred days after the flowering of the vines, but today science is called in to analyse grape specimens every day as the potential date approaches. A verdict is issued by the oenological station of the region, but the grower has to take the final responsibility for his vines. In Burgundy picking will begin ten days or so earlier than in the Médoc, and earlier still in the Beaujolais district to the south. Warm days of early autumn, even though they are getting

short, can make up for a disappointing summer, but heavy hail-
storms or constant rain can ruin a vintage which promised well
until the last moment. Picking is manual throughout Burgundy,
done by groups of workers hired for the purpose (often from other
countries) by the estate managers, who have to house and feed as
well as pay them.

We come now to the biggest difference (apart from soil and
grape varieties) between wine production in Burgundy and in the
rest of France – the question of ownership. The tidy and rational
arrangement in the Bordeaux area, whereby one great institution –
say Château Margaux – owns, plants, tends, harvests, vinifies,
matures, bottles and sells its own property in its own time, does
not happen in Burgundy. Let us take one of the most famous of
Burgundy vineyards, the Clos Vougeot, as an example (if an
extreme one). Although confiscated from its monastic owners by
the State in 1789 it remained a single property until 1889, when it
was sold off to six Burgundian merchants. Over the next hundred
years, by further partial sales and the divided inheritances characteristic of French rural society, the number of individually owned
plots has risen to well over a hundred. Out of a total of fifty
hectares under vines in the Clos, no one proprietor owns more
than five, some less than a quarter of a hectare (or little more than
half an acre). The same kind of situation arises in many other
vineyards, so that (looking at it from the other end) a major wine
merchant may own thirty or more parcels spread between the
grandest of the *grands crus* and the humbler *villages* growths. An
exception is the historic domaine of Romanée-Conti, which not
only owns the whole of the vineyard which bears its name, but the
almost comparable *grand cru* of La Tâche and half of Richebourg.

Under this system it is not surprising that many different systems of vinification are found, varying from the obstinately traditional to the aggressively modern. However, not all the
hundred-odd proprietors of hallowed patches in the Clos Vougeot
will make their own wines, let alone bottle or sell them. The
practice is growing whereby small proprietors throughout Burgundy sell their grapes to a merchant with greater facilities, or,
having made the wine in their own fashion, sell it in cask for
bottling and marketing. The complications of classification and
labelling which arise are too great to go into here. On the other

hand roadside invitations to 'dégustation libre' or 'vente directe' come on the whole from smaller growers who want to cut out the middlemen in the trade, and perhaps to circumvent some of the tortuous regulations imposed by the government.

Inevitably British wine merchants will deal mostly with the bigger *négociants* who can command more facilities for packing and shipping, not to mention public relations. So if we want to trace exactly what goes into your rare bottle of Chambertin Clos de Bèze, or your everyday purchase of Côte de Beaune or Mâcon Villages, it is easiest to follow procedures within the *cuveries* and *caves* of a big firm like Louis Latour in the Côte de Beaune. Founded in 1797, it has been in the same family ever since. Including as it does among its own properties one hectare (or about two-and-a-half acres) of Chambertin and seven hectares of Corton-Charlemagne, it is in a position to manufacture two of the most prestigious red and white wines in France, though by judicious purchase (but only from strictly comparable sources) it can increase its output of both considerably. From a range of properties with an only slightly lower reputation it can contribute to the market ten or twelve *premiers crus* of the highest quality. At the same time it buys wines of varying quality from other wine-producing areas of France for bottling and shipping to world markets. Its methods of vinification (the conversion of grape-juice into wine) combine the traditional and the modern in a way which makes it a useful study for our purpose.

Let us picture the first load of Pinot Noir grapes arriving from the Chambertin vineyard up the road in the Côte de Nuits. Waiting for it at the business entrance of the Château Corton-Grancey in the village of Aloxe-Corton is a machine called an *égrappoir* whose function is to separate the fruit from the stalks, at the same time gently breaking the skins of the grapes to release their juice. The resulting combination of liquids and solids is drawn off into large copper pans, which run on an overhead railway into the vatting cellar, or *cuverie*. Here are ranged (unusually for such a large firm) the traditional open-topped oak vats into which each copper pan funnels its contents as it passes overhead – but not before certain essential things have been added.

The fermentation which converts sugar to alcohol is caused by several forms of natural yeast latent in or adhering to the fruit. Not all of these yeasts are beneficial to the wine. To eliminate those which are harmful, and to kill off any bacteria which may have been introduced, a carefully measured dose of sulphur dioxide (SO_2) is introduced with each panful. With lesser wines, and in years of poor vintage quality, a strictly regulated quantity of sugar may be added at the same time to make up for natural deficiencies. This process is still called *chaptalisation* after Chaptal, Napoleon's Minister of Agriculture, who first authorized it. This licence is sometimes abused by less scrupulous firms, but in good years of the *grands crus* it should never be necessary.

The process of fermentation takes from five to six days, in the course of which the solid débris of skins and pips is lifted to the top of the vats by the action of the carbon dioxide gas released when it starts. This forms a *chapeau*, or hat, which has to be broken up to ensure a proper mixing of the elements which constitute the must. Here ancient and modern methods differ. Some large firms have installed huge enclosed stainless steel or fibreglass vats, with internal machinery which prevents a *chapeau* from forming, or gently breaks it up at intervals. Louis Latour sticks to human machinery, as being more flexible and thorough. Twice a day men wearing only the minimum (if that) climb to the top of each vat, trample or hack at the *chapeau*, mixing solids and liquids by treading and sloshing – while holding on to the rim of the vat to avoid total submersion. The claim is that they can reach pockets of unmixed matter more easily than a rotating mechanical mixer. The liquid must is also pumped over on to the top from time to time to keep things moving.

When fermentation is complete – and this is established by chemical analysis in the laboratory without which no modern firm can operate – the free wine (as it now is) is allowed to drain off by tap and transferred to another container. The lees (the solid residue of skins and pips) are then shovelled or pumped out and carried to modern *pressoirs* which extract further wine to add to the waiting 'vin libre'.

Without more delay the wine is drawn off into casks (of the many words in use for them in France the Burgundians prefer to call them *fûts*) which are stacked in the firm's extensive cellars at a temperature of 11.007 to 12.007 centigrade. Red wines are kept in cask for eighteen months, and as evaporation through the seams is inevitable (the English word is 'ullage') a constant check is kept on the levels within. This can be done by inspection with electric torch or candle, after withdrawing the upper bung, or by tapping on the outside for resonance (only for real experts). According to the rules the lost liquid can be replaced only by a wine of the same origin and quality, but it is admitted that the rules are often broken. There is a temptation to introduce powerful wines from the Midi, Italy or Corsica to achieve the rich colour and vinosity which can be the uninformed consumer's idea of a good burgundy; in the case of our *grand cru* Chambertin it would be neither necessary nor contemplated.

Two or three times during its life in cask the wine is racked off the remaining lees and transferred to new casks, always made of the oak which contributes so much to the nose and tannin content of the wine. This is the time of the second, or 'malolactic' fermentation, when malic acid is converted to lactic acid, removing all traces of unnatural sharpness and contributing to the smoothness which is properly looked for in a good burgundy.

Before it is bottled the wine is chemically analysed to make sure that the vinification has been successful in every respect, then gently filtered and refined by chemical agents. The bottling process is now a matter of mechanical ingenuity, and a big operator can handle thousands of bottles an hour in a continuous operation which fills, corks, seals, and can even label and package them appropriately.

For the *vins de garde*, however, as all reputable vintage wines are called, the bottles are transferred to other cellars and stacked until required to fill orders. Labels are no use here, as the damp moulds prevailing in the cellars would soon work them loose. Instead, each *cru* is stacked in a separate compartment, with a slate to show its name, year, and code figures corresponding to computer entries. It is just as moving an experience as a tour of the Côte d'Or vineyards to pass by these stacks of hundreds of anonymous mould-encrusted bottles containing 70 to 75 centilitres of a wine which may be selling at £20 to £25 a bottle in a few years' time, or auctioned after twenty years for anything up to or above £2,000 a case.

In one corner of these cool dark depths a space will be reserved for the rituals of tasting – whether this means serious investigation by potential bulk customers, professional tests or comparisons, or a gesture to members of the general public, native or foreign, which Burgundians so generously offer. What they enjoy, perhaps more than their equivalents in the Bordeaux trade, is to have their wine properly appreciated.

White wines need different treatment in the early stages, when everything has to be done quickly to produce a clear uncontaminated must. This is especially so when the Pinot Noir *au jus blanc* is used, to avoid colouring from the skins. The whole bunches are crushed and fed as quickly as possible into the vat without destalking. The *vin libre* is run off first, then the remainder solids are pressed, sometimes twice. The resulting liquids are blended in proportion and transferred to new oak casks, where the fermentation takes place. To allow for this – which can take as long as three weeks – several litres of ullage space are left to leave room for froth to be thrown up. The extra tannin derived from the stalks will help to clarify the wine, which is topped up as necessary, racked off the lees perhaps twice, carefully fined and filtered, and bottled after twelve months in cask.

Before we leave the Côte de Beaune there is a story to tell of a firm even more committed to tradition than Louis Latour. The house of Doudet-Naudin has its headquarters in Savigny-lès-Beaune (see p.228). It was founded in 1849, and in the 1930s it was run as a family partnership between Marcel Doudet and his father-in-law Victor Naudin, and they made a speciality of producing the finest burgundies for connoisseurs prepared to pay a proper price for them.

Progress on these lines was halted in 1939, and a year later Marcel Doudet decided to cease trading commercially and foil any threat from the occupying forces by walling up one whole cellar containing 35000 bottles of his best vintages. Their quality can be judged from the vineyards owned by the family, where a total of seven hectares produce two *grands crus* and five *premiers crus* of the finest red burgundies. He went on making wines from his vineyards, but kept them in reserve uintil the war should end. When that happened he made the shrewd decision to leave his rare vintages where they were, but sell off the wines he still had in store from the wartime years.

In 1955 the walls were broken down, to reveal an undisturbed hoard of great wines in prime condition, going back as far as forty years before the war; some of these bottles are still there. Marcel Doudet died in 1987, to be succeeded by his son Yves, who carries on a flourishing business with a personal touch, combining all the traditional methods of vinification with modern marketing skills.

Traditionalists may shudder at the idea of sparkling burgundy, but the *appellation* Crémant de Bourgogne has established a considerable market. Made almost entirely of white grapes – principally the Aligoté, the Gamay *au jus blanc* and the Yonne Sancy – it is produced in the same way as champagne. Those unfamiliar with the fascinating 'methode champenoise' may like to have a brief account. Champagne begins its life as a still, dry white wine made from a complicated blend of harvestings, which may include the produce of earlier years. Before bottling it is given a substantial extra boost of sugar and already fermenting yeasts, which the bottles are left to digest for anything up to two years in a horizontal position. Special clamps are fitted to the still ordinary wine corks to prevent blow-outs as the carbonic acid gas develops under fermentation. During this time a heavy sediment is deposited on the under side of the bottle.

At the end of their rest period the bottles are put in a special inclined rack which allows them to be tilted very gradually until they stand on their heads. Every other day they are also given an eighth of a turn by hand, so that the sediment is gradually dislodged from the sides, and will have been precipitated into the neck by the time it is fully inverted. The tricky moment comes when the bottle has to be decorked to expel the collected sediment under the pressure which has built up, and recorked without losing too much wine. The modern method of *dégorgement*, as it is aptly called, is to freeze the neck of the bottle so that all the sediment is collected in an ice pellet, which can then be popped out rapidly and economically.

It remains to replace what liquid has been lost with the acid content of another bottle, plus a measured amount of sweetened liquor – measured, that is, to meet the demands of different markets. The vocabulary is again apt. The refilling is called *dosage*, the sweetener is the *liqueur d'expédition*. In the case of champagne the degrees of sweetening are given a scale from *brut* (literally stark) through *extra sec, sec, goût Americain* (!) to *demi-doux* and *doux*. One wonders who enjoys the last-named.

The special mushroom cork is now inserted, the wire muzzle fixed over it. After a further short period of digestion the bottle can be sealed, labelled, sold – and drunk. Vintage champagnes are made only when the years quality justifies it, and these are allowed to mature in bottle for as long as the market will stand.

There is one further illustration of the diversity in the Burgundy wine trade. The solids still remaining in the vats after perhaps two pressings, whether from red or white grapes, are further crushed and their liquor later distilled to make an *eau-de-vie* known here as *marc de Bourgogne* (the 'c' is silent). While maturing as long as possible in oak casks the tannin in them turns it a light caramel colour, and it grows in strength and roundness through gradual evaporation. There are strict controls on its production, bottling, labelling and sale, but though little known outside Burgundy it makes one of the most justifiedly popular *digestifs* on the French market.

Genealogical Tables

1. The Merovingian kings
Descendants of Clovis

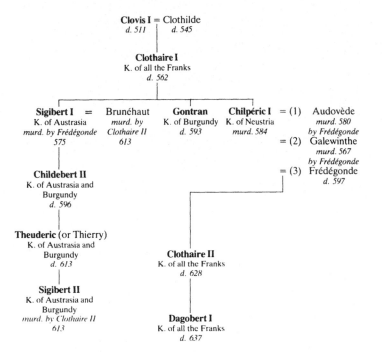

2. Kings of France

(a) The early Carolingians

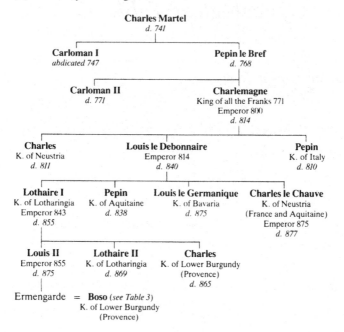

(b) The Capetian inheritance

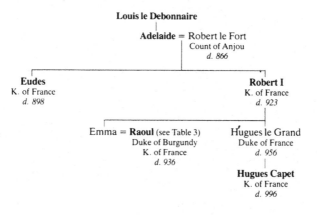

3. Dukes of Burgundy

(a) The early dukes

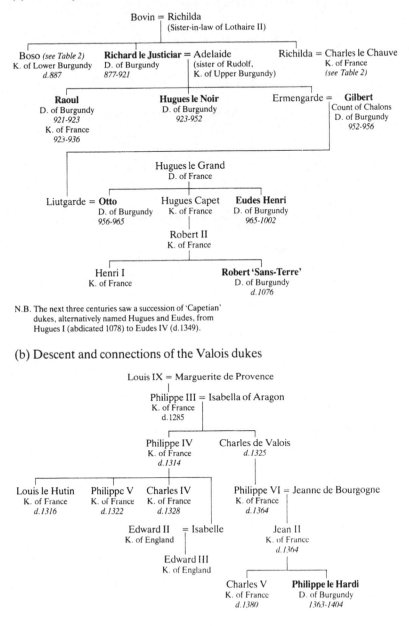

Bovin = Richilda
(Sister-in-law of Lothaire II)

Boso *(see Table 2)*
K. of Lower Burgundy
d.887

Richard le Justiciar = Adelaide
D. of Burgundy   (sister of Rudolf,
877-921   K. of Upper Burgundy)

Richilda = Charles le Chauve
           K. of France
           (see Table 2)

Raoul
D. of Burgundy
921-923
K. of France
923-936

Hugues le Noir
D. of Burgundy
923-952

Ermengarde = **Gilbert**
             Count of Chalons
             D. of Burgundy
             952-956

Hugues le Grand
D. of France

Liutgarde = **Otto**
            D. of Burgundy
            956-965

Hugues Capet
K. of France

Eudes Henri
D. of Burgundy
965-1002

Robert II
K. of France

Henri I
K. of France

Robert 'Sans-Terre'
D. of Burgundy
d.1076

N.B. The next three centuries saw a succession of 'Capetian'
dukes, alternatively named Hugues and Eudes, from
Hugues I (abdicated 1078) to Eudes IV (d.1349).

(b) Descent and connections of the Valois dukes

Louis IX = Marguerite de Provence

Philippe III = Isabella of Aragon
K. of France
d.1285

Philippe IV
K. of France
d.1314

Charles de Valois
d.1325

Louis le Hutin
K. of France
d.1316

Philippe V
K. of France
d.1322

Charles IV
K. of France
d.1328

Philippe VI = Jeanne de Bourgogne
K. of France
d.1364

Edward II = Isabelle
K. of England

Jean II
K. of France
d.1364

Edward III
K. of England

Charles V
K. of France
d.1380

Philippe le Hardi
D. of Burgundy
1363-1404

(c) The Valois dukes and their successors

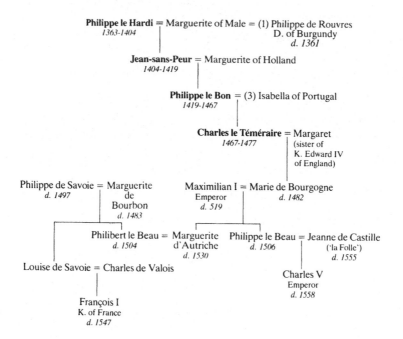

Philippe le Hardi = Marguerite of Male = (1) Philippe de Rouvres
1363-1404   D. of Burgundy
                                                   d. 1361

Jean-sans-Peur = Marguerite of Holland
1404-1419

Philippe le Bon = (3) Isabella of Portugal
1419-1467

Charles le Téméraire = Margaret
1467-1477   (sister of
                              K. Edward IV
                              of England)

Philippe de Savoie = Marguerite   Maximilian I = Marie de Bourgogne
d. 1497   de   Emperor   *d. 1482*
                    Bourbon   *d. 519*
                    d. 1483

Philibert le Beau = Marguerite   Philippe le Beau = Jeanne de Castille
d. 1504   d'Autriche   *d. 1506*   ('la Folle')
                    d. 1530   *d. 1555*

Louise de Savoie = Charles de Valois

                                                   Charles V
                                                   Emperor
                                                   d. 1558

François I
K. of France
d. 1547

4. The House of Condé

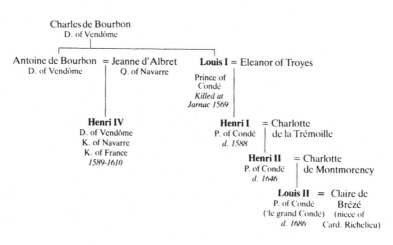

Charles de Bourbon
D. of Vendôme

Antoine de Bourbon = Jeanne d'Albret   **Louis I** = Eleanor of Troyes
D. of Vendôme   Q. of Navarre   Prince of
                                        Condé
                                        Killed at
                                        Jarnac 1569

Henri IV   **Henri I** = Charlotte
D. of Vendôme   P. of Condé de la Trémoille
K. of Navarre   *d. 1588*
K. of France
1589-1610   **Henri II** = Charlotte
                                        P. of Condé   de Montmorency
                                        d. 1646

                                        Louis II = Claire de
                                        P. of Condé   Brézé
                                        ('le grand Condé') (niece of
                                        d. 1686   Card. Richelieu)

Select Bibliography

Aubert and Goubet, *Romanesque Cathedrals and Abbeys of France*, 1966

R. Branner, *Burgundian Gothic Architecture*, 1960

J. Carcopino, *Alésia et les ruses de César*, 1959

Yves Cazaux, *Marie de Bourgogne*, 1968

M. Clement, *Les Grands Hommes de Bourgogne*, 1966

K.J. Conant, *Carolingian and Romanesque Architecture*, 800-1200

Christopher Cope, *Phoenix Frustrated: the lost kingdom of Burgundy,* 1986

H. Drouot and J. Calmette, *Histoire de Bourgogne*, 1928

H.A.L. Fisher, *History of Europe*, 1936

Arthur Gardner, *Mediaeval Sculpture in France*, 1931

Denis Grivot and G. Zarnecki, *Gislebertus, Sculptor of Autun*, 1961

Stephen Gwynn, *Burgundy* (wines), 1934

Anthony Hanson, *Burgundy* (wines), 1982

Violet Markham, *Romanesque France*, 1929

G.H. Neel, *European Genealogy*, (unpub.)

Charles Oursel, *l'Art de Bourgogne*, 1924

Odet Perrin, *Les Borgondes*, 1968

Georges Pillement, *France inconnue*, 1963 (also in English)

P. Poupon and P. Forgeot, *The Wines of Burgundy* (trans. E. & M. Ott), 1983

Steven Runciman, *A History of the Crusades*, 1953-4

V. Sackville-West, *Daughter of France*, 1959

William R. Tyler, *Dijon and the Valois Dukes of Burgundy*, 1971

Richard Vaughan, *Philip the Bold*, 1962
> *John the Fearless*, 1966
> *Philip the Good*, 1970
> *Charles the Bold*, 1973

Jean Virey, *l'Abbaye de Cluny*, 1950

Zodiaque Press, *La Nuit des Temps: l'Art Cistercien*, 1962
> *La Nuit des Temps: Bourgogne Romane*, 1979

(Both volumes produced by the Abbey of la Pierre-qui-Vire)

Index

The Companion Guide to Burgundy

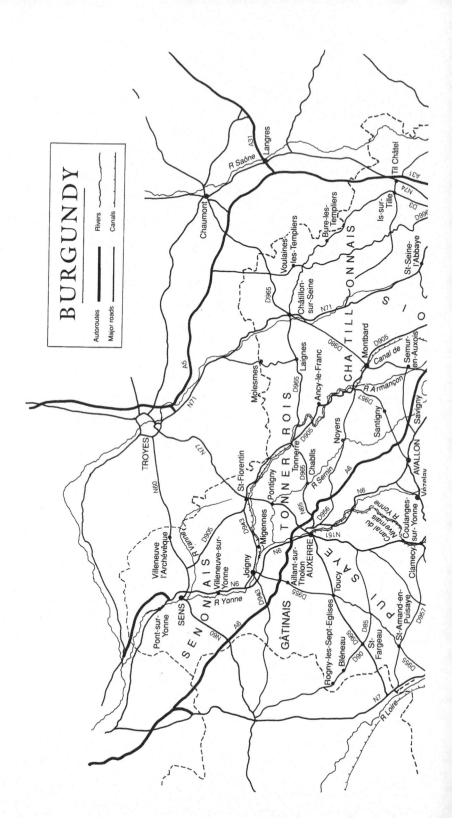

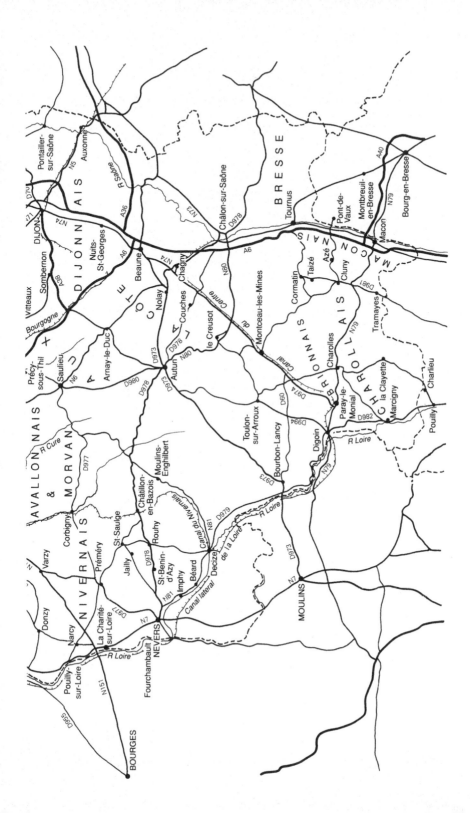

CPSIA information can be obtained
at www.ICGtesting.com
Printed in the USA
LVOW13s0553230218
567474LV00015B/125/P